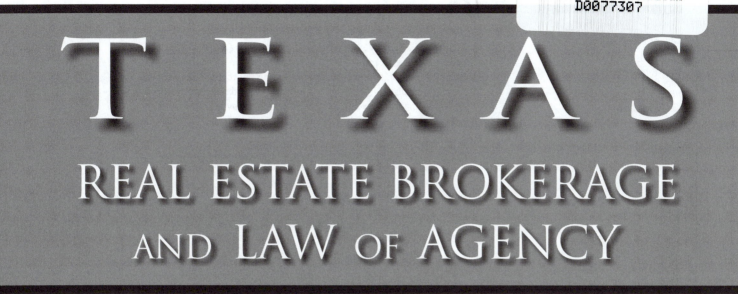

TEXAS
REAL ESTATE BROKERAGE
AND LAW OF AGENCY

CHARLES J. JACOBUS
DREI, CREI

★

GEORGE C. STEPHENS
CRB

CENGAGE
Learning™

Australia • Brazil • Japan • Korea • Mexico • Singapore • Spain • United Kingdom • United States

CENGAGE Learning™

Texas Real Estate Brokerage and Law of Agency, 5E
Charles J. Jacobus
George C. Stephens

Vice President/Editor-in-Chief:
Dave Shaut

Executive Editor: Scott Person

Acquisitions Editor: Sara Glassmeyer

Senior Marketing Manager: Mark Linton

Frontlist Buyer, Manufacturing:
Kevin Kluck

Senior Art Director: Bethany Casey

Content Project Manager:
Corey Geissler

Production Service: ICC Macmillan Inc.

Internal Designer: Chris Miller,
Cmiller Design

Cover Designer: Chris Miller,
Cmiller Design

Cover Image: iStockphoto.com/
Brandon Seidel

Library of Congress Control Number: 2008925877

ISBN-13: 978-0-324-59250-4

ISBN-10: 0-324-59250-7

Cengage Learning
5191 Natorp Boulevard
Mason, OH 45040
USA

Cengage Learning products are represented in Canada by Nelson Education, Ltd.

For your course and learning solutions, visit **academic.cengage.com**

Purchase any of our products at your local college store or at our preferred online store **www.ichapters.com**

Printed in Canada
1 2 3 4 5 6 7 12 11 10 09 08

CHARLES J. JACOBUS

Charles J. Jacobus is an attorney with law offices in Bellaire, Texas, and Executive Vice-President of Charter Title Company in Houston, Texas. He is board certified by the State Bar of Texas Board of Legal Specialization in both Residential and Commercial Real Estate Law.

He is a member of the Houston Real Estate Lawyers Council, and he has served as chairman of the Real Estate Section of the Houston Bar Association, president of the Real Estate Educators Association, and Course Director for the Advanced Real Estate Law course for the State Bar of Texas. He has served as chairman of the American Bar Association committee on Real Estate Brokers and Brokerage, and served on the board of trustees for the Appraisal Foundation. He is listed in Woodward/White's "The Best Lawyers in America," Martindale-Hubbell's "Bar Registry of Preeminent Lawyers," and Marquis's "Who's Who in the World." He was a member of the Council of the Real Estate, Probate, and Trust Law Section of the State Bar of Texas, and is currently a member of the Texas Real Estate Commission's Broker-Lawyer Committee and the Texas Real Estate Center's MCE Advisory Committee.

He is the author of *Texas Real Estate,* now in its 10th edition; *Texas Real Estate Law,* ninth edition; *Real Estate: An Introduction to the Profession,* and *Real Estate Principles*, both in their tenth edition; and *Texas Title Insurance*. He is the editor-in-chief of the *Texas Forms Manual for Real Estate and Title Documentation* and coauthor of *Texas Real Estate Brokerage and Law of Agency* and *Keeping Current with Texas Real Estate, an MCE Publication.*

He is an adjunct professor of law at the University of Houston Law Center, and a frequent speaker at State Bar of Texas real estate courses, Texas Land Title Association courses, Real Estate Educators Association annual conferences, and the ARELLO National Conferences. He has served as Mayor of Bellaire, Texas, Secretary/Treasurer of the Harris County Mayors and Councils Association, and was a Scoutmaster at the 1999 Boy Scout World Jamboree in Chile.

GEORGE C. STEPHENS

Stephens is licensed as a real estate broker in Texas, Georgia, and Massachusetts, and holds a mortgage broker license in Texas, where he is the mortgage broker for www.CelebrationLending.com. He served, from 1979 through the present, as the President and Broker of Record of deRaat Stephens, Inc. The firm acquired an ERA® franchise in 1995, and is now doing business as ERA® Stephens Properties (www.erasp.com).

He was appointed by the Texas Real Estate Commission for a six-year term to the Texas Real Estate Broker-Lawyer Committee in 1993, and for a three-year term to the Texas Department of Savings and Mortgage Lending's Mortgage Brokerage Advisory Committee in 2005 followed by a reappointment for a three-year term in 2008. George's REALTOR® activities include serving on numerous committees at the local, state, and national levels. He served as Chairman of the 25,902-member (as of 10/31/2007) Houston Association of REALTORS® ("H.A.R.") in 1998 and Chairman of the 90,000-member (as of 10/31/07) Texas Association of REALTORS® ("T.A.R.") in 2003.

The consumer and licensee resource column, "Ask George & Chuck" (coauthored with Charles J. Jacobus, J.D.), appears in the Houston Chronicle, TexasRealEstate.com, and has appeared in RealtyTimes.com and Inman.com. Its Web address is www.AskGeorge.net. The column has been published online by Inman News Features, RealtyTimes.com, TexasRealEstate.com, AustinHomeSearch.com, and eRealty.com. In 1997, Stephens received the TAR Educator of the Year award for his years teaching CORE real estate (including Contracts) and mandatory continuing education courses. In 1998, H.A.R. recognized George's teaching and technological contributions to the industry by naming its computer-equipped training facility the "George C. Stephens Technology Training Center."

CONTENTS

Agency Learning Objectives and Competencies

It is important to have a historical perspective of the law of agency to understand current events, ideas, and changes in the way we perceive agency. Having successfully completed this text, the reader should:

- Have a basic understanding of the relationship between this history and the present interest in agency.

- Be familiar with the ways to establish agency and be able to name and explain the types of agency.

- Understand who is the broker, and who is exempt from licensure in Texas.

- Be able to explain the fiduciary relationship between the principal and the agent, including the duties and obligations owed the principal by the agent and vice versa.

- Understand the complexities of the various types of agency.

- Be familiar with the parts of the Texas Real Estate License Act and the Deceptive Trade Practices-Consumer Protection Act that affect agency.

- Be able to demonstrate when and how to use disclosure forms and understand the importance of disclosure.

- Know and be able to discuss ways to terminate agency.

- Have an insight into real estate brokerage, attorneys, and the practice of law.

- Understand the complexion of various types of agency.

- Be familiar with alternative relationships to the traditional principal/agent, seller agency, and be able to address the advantages and disadvantages of each alternative.

- Be aware of other federal and state legislation affecting real estate licensees.

- Understand the listing agreements, employee vs. independent contractor, and other employment issues.

INTRODUCTION

PURPOSE

After carefully reading Chapter 1, the student will be able to:

- Recount the history of agency.

- List the reasons for renewed emphasis and focus on real estate agency.

- Better understand the expectations of clients and customers, agents, principals, and third parties and use this knowledge in the real estate business.

- Apply the Canons of Professional Ethics and Conduct for Brokers and Salespeople.

- Identify and define: *agent, principal, fiduciary, TREC, TRELA, "caveat emptor,"* and *subagent.*

Key Words to look for in this chapter:
1. Broker/Brokerage
2. Texas Real Estate License Act (TRELA)
3. Fiduciary relationship
4. Fidelity
5. Integrity
6. Competency
7. Subagent
8. Dual Agent
9. Client
10. Customer

The law is constantly growing and changing. One often looks at the law as though it is carved in stone, but it is more like water that ebbs and flows in response to societal needs. The change is not only in the statutes and judicial interpretation, but also in the way that society looks at, perceives, and interprets the law.

Let's look at a particular part of the law, called the law of agency, and how that law affects the real estate business. It is important to understand the historical background of and recent interest in the law of agency.

THE HISTORY OF AGENCY

To understand the law of agency today, one needs to consider its history. The concept of agency began when people agreed to act on behalf of one another. The person acting for another becomes that person's **agent**. The person for whom the agent is acting is the **principal**. Their relationship is a **fiduciary** relationship—one of trust and confidence.

Agency exists when one person is given the authority to act for or in place of another person. The term "broker/brokerage" came to us from the French word for wine broker. A broker has a special knowledge of the supply, demand, marketing, and types of goods available in a particular field of endeavor. In many cases, "broker" is a middleman who buys or sells on behalf of his client. The first agents were probably family or friends. Later came the representatives of these people, who had little time to deal with some issues and delegated their authority to others.

Agency is not new to the real estate business. There is some question, however, as to just when real estate licensees took on the cloak of agency. In real estate, a broker/agent (with certain exceptions) is a person who represents one who buys, sells, exchanges, sells at auction, and/or leases for another for compensation or the expectation of compensation. It was in the early 1900s when we began to look at real estate representatives as agents.

In 1919, California was the first state to offer a real estate license. Texas passed its first real estate act, the Texas Real Estate Dealers Act, in 1939. Until the late 1940s, Texas offered a "dealer's" license in real estate, not a "broker's" or "salesperson's" license. The **Texas Real Estate Commission (TREC)** was created by the **Texas Real Estate License Act (TRELA)** of 1949. It was the TRELA that introduced the broker and salesperson's license to Texas law. Early versions of TRELA make few references to the terms "agent" and "agency." Most of these reference someone other than the dealer/licensee/broker. It is in later amendments that we see the term "agent" more often applied to licensees.

In 2003, the Texas Real Estate License Act was incorporated into the new Occupations Code (Chapter 1101). It can be reprinted from the Texas Real Estate Commission Web site at http:\\www.trec.state.tx.us. It was not intended to be a substantive revision of the statute, but a reorganization of a chart showing the old provisions and how those provisions are incorporated into the new statute (see Appendix A).

The **Canons of Professional Ethics and Conduct for Brokers and Salespeople**, now Chapter 531 of the Rules of the Texas Real Estate Commission, emphasizes the agency/principal relationship as established by the Texas Real Estate Commission, and is a mandatory topic for MCE updates. Pay close attention to the bold provisions:

Canons of Professional Ethics and Conduct for Real Estate Licensees

ARTICLE 1

FIDELITY

A real estate broker or salesperson, while **acting as an agent for another**, is a fiduciary. Special obligations are imposed when such **fiduciary relationships** are created. They demand:

- that the primary duty of the real estate agent is to **represent the interests of his client**, and his position, in this respect, should be clear to all parties concerned in a real estate transaction; that, however, the agent, in performing his duties to his client, shall treat other parties to a transaction fairly.

- that the real estate agent be faithful and observant to trust placed in him, and be scrupulous and meticulous in performing his functions.

- that the real estate agent place **no personal interest above that of his client.**

ARTICLE 2

INTEGRITY

A real estate broker or salesperson has a special obligation to exercise integrity in the discharge of his responsibilities, including employment of prudence and caution so as to avoid misrepresentation, in any wise, by acts of commission or omission.

ARTICLE 3

COMPETENCY

It is the obligation of a real estate agent **to be knowledgeable** as a real estate brokerage practitioner. He should:

- **be informed on market conditions** affecting the real estate business and be pledged to continuing education in the intricacies involved in marketing real estate for others.

- **be informed** on national, state, and local issues and developments in the real estate industry.

- **exercise judgment and skill** in the performance of his work.

The Texas Real Estate License Act and the Rules of the Texas Real Estate Commission are available on the Web at http://www.trec.state.tx.us. Download them as a part of this class. We will discuss parts of both throughout this course.

THE NEW EMPHASIS ON THE LAW OF AGENCY

All states, including Texas, have seen a renewed emphasis and focus on real estate agency. This has occurred for several reasons. The nature of the real estate business complicates the traditional application of the law of agency. Let's consider other reasons:

There has been an **increased emphasis in professionalism** in the real estate industry. "Professional" is a term that generally indicates high levels of education (e.g., doctors, lawyers, architects, and engineers never stop their education; it is an ongoing part of their business). Educational requirements at all levels have dramatically increased over the last 20 years in real estate. As early as 1974, *World Book* stated that "Real Estate work is rapidly moving toward professional status." Obviously the recognition of this process is not quite as rapid as the real estate business had hoped. It has been suggested by some authorities that it is the desire for professionalism that has caused more and more interest in and emphasis on the law of agency as it applies to the real estate business.

Increased complexity of real estate transactions requires more specialized knowledge. Even though today's salespeople are better educated and better trained than in the past, there are still problems that need to be addressed. The changing rules of real estate agents, consumer disclosure laws, and federal legislation have radically redefined real estate practices.

Litigation in agency law has increased. America is becoming a more litigious society. There have been misunderstandings, abuses, and violations of the law of agency and other related laws in the real estate business. To the licensee and the public, real estate laws become more complicated every day.

Public perception is a problem. Confusion breeds mistrust and frustration in the consumer and in the licensee. Agents, customers, and clients have all had a growing confusion of the roles, relationships, and responsibilities existing in the practice of real estate. They are all taking a new look at and questioning the wording, terminology, and semantics used by the public and the practitioner. They are questioning the use and application of terms like: "agent, subagent, dual agent, middleman, facilitator, client, and customer."

Consumers do not understand the agency relationship between themselves and the real estate broker. Studies by the **Federal Trade Commission** found that over 70 percent of the buyers incorrectly thought that the real estate agent represented them.

There has been an increased focus on consumer protection. The law is turning away from the idea of "**caveat emptor**," or "let the buyer beware." Both the Texas Deceptive Trade Practices-Consumer Protection Act and the Texas Real Estate License Act give the agent duties of discovery and of disclosure to the buyer, which has added to the agency responsibility, as have The Americans with Disabilities Act (ADA) and Fair Housing laws.

Emotion tends to cloud reactions, thoughts, and decisions. In the residential field, there has been a changing perception of a home as an investment as well as a shelter. The sale and purchase of a home is still an emotional experience for most buyers and sellers.

The number and types of **marketing systems** has increased. The trend toward more and more specialization in the real estate industry has been encouraged by the increasing body of law in each area of the business. Not only do practitioners divide themselves by types of properties such as commercial or industrial, divisions of real estate practice like property management or appraisal, physical area, or price range, licensees now specialize in parts of the sales process. There are now people who only list, show, or close. In times past, the listing agent was the agent of the seller, and the selling agent was the **subagent** of the seller. This means that both agents were working for the seller.

The emergence of buyer representation, intermediary status, and dual agency has required the industry to take a new look at agency. Agency seems to have permeated every aspect of the real estate business. It's a required course for licensure! All of the recent emphasis on agency in the profession and out of the business requires a new look at the practices of the industry as new problems arise. Better understanding and more education is needed to help resolve these problems.

DISCUSSION QUESTIONS

■ As the buyer in a real estate transaction, list the services that you would expect from the real estate licensee with whom you are dealing.

List your reasons.

■ As the seller in a real estate sale, list the services that you would expect from the real estate agent with whom you are dealing.

List your reasons.

■ Compare and contrast the answers in the preceding two questions. Do you think that the buyer and seller are naturally adversaries?

List your reasons.

CREATION OF THE AGENCY RELATIONSHIP

PURPOSE

After carefully reading Chapter 2, the student will be able to:

- List and describe ways to create agency.

- Discuss the relationship between compensation and agency and depict the problems of gratuitous agency.

- List those who must have a real estate license.

- Enumerate those who are exempted from real estate licensure.

- Define: *broker*, *actual authority*, *ostensible authority*, *implied agency*, and *ratification*.

Key Words to look for in this chapter:
1. Fiduciary
2. Middleman
3. Gratuitous Agency
4. Meeting of the minds
5. Actual authority
6. Implied authority
7. Ostensible authority
8. Real Estate Broker
9. Listing
10. Exemptions: Attorneys At Law

The law of agency is a part of the law of contracts. Agency is created by an agreement between two parties, for one party (the agent) to "stand in the shoes" of the other (the principal) and represent the principal's interest when dealing with third parties. Therefore, it takes two parties to create an agency, the principal and the agent; but for the law of agency to work, it requires three parties: the principal, the agent, and the third party.

WHEN AND HOW

When and how the agency relationship is created has been the subject of a number of lawsuits. The relationship between the principal and the agent is a **fiduciary** one that consists of trust and confidence. Logically, the fiduciary relationship arises very early in the transaction, when confidences are exchanged between the principal and the agent, which can occur prior to any employment contract or express agency relationship.

In *Wilson v. Donze*, 692 S.W.2d 734 (Tex. App.-Fort Worth 1986), the jury found that an agency relationship existed even though the principal had specifically rejected the agency earlier in the transaction.

Wilson v. Donze, 692 S.W.2d 734 (Tex. App.-Fort Worth 1986)

In May 1982, Ken Wilson, a real estate broker, called Anthony and Lena Donze and asked if their home was for sale. They told him that the sales price was $85,000. After inquiring if he were a broker, they also told him that they did not use real estate brokers, that they would not pay a commission, and that they would sell the property themselves.

Wilson, having stated that he had a couple interested in this type property, asked if he could sell their property and get his fee from the buyer. They agreed to let him look at the property and subsequently said that he could show it. Later, Wilson presented a contract to the Donzes naming Ken/Car Investments, Inc. as the purchaser. The contract was for the full asking price of $85,000. Wilson and his wife owned Ken/Car.

The day before the contract was presented, another real estate agent working with Wilson secured a contract offer from the Bullards to purchase the property for $100,000. This agent told them that he thought it would take at least $115,000 to purchase the property. They indicated that they would be willing to pay that.

On the same day that Ken/Car purchased the property from the Donzes, the agent called the Bullards telling them that their offer had been rejected and that they would need $115,000 to purchase the property. They agreed, and the agent prepared a contract for that amount, naming Ken/Car as the seller.

Later the Bullards and the Donzes talked with each other on the telephone and discovered the fact that each thought the transaction was between them, and that neither had been aware of a middleman. Subsequently, the Donzes sued Wilson.

Wilson claimed that he represented neither party (he had no employment contract with either party); and since the Donzes received their asking price and were happy with the Bullards as the new owners, they had no right to complain.

Ken Wilson appealed a judgment of $24,900 for actual damages and $35,000 in exemplary damages for the breach of Wilson's fiduciary duties as a real estate agent for the Donzes. The Court of Appeals of Texas in Fort Worth affirmed the lower court decision.

DISCUSSION QUESTIONS

■ If Wilson were the agent of neither party nor a mere middleman, could the agency have been created?

■ In this case, *when* and *how* could the agency relationship have been created?

■ How could Wilson have kept his status as a middleman?

It should be noted that in this case, the jury determined that Wilson represented the Donzes. When and how an agency relationship is created is a fact issue for the jury and not a clear question of law. It should also be noted that one should not presume that one is an agent for the seller, as the licensee can also be an agent for the purchaser. *Foster v. Cross*, 650 P.2d 406 (Alaska 1982); *Tatum v. Preston Carter Co., ante.*

Gratuitous Agency

The law of agency also applies to "gratuitous" agencies. A **gratuitous agency** is one that arises when an agent undertakes to give advice or professional service to another person for no compensation. Even though it is voluntary, and may be "free," the fiduciary duties still arise. (One should note that this is also true of lawyers. If a lawyer gives "free" legal advice, that lawyer may still be liable for malpractice.) In *Kelly v. Roussalis*, 776 P.2d 1016 (Wyoming 1989), the agent voluntarily, and for no commission, gave advice to and consulted with a consumer on certain real estate matters. When that information turned out to be incorrect, the agent was liable for breaching his duty of care.

Kelly v. Roussalis, 776 P.2d 1016 (Wyoming 1989)

John Roussalis had had several real estate transactions with Gus Kelly and McNamara Realty when Kelly showed him a home on South Poplar listed with another real estate company at $600,000. John indicated that the property cost more than he wanted to pay and that he would need to list and sell their present house before purchasing another. Kelly told Roussalis that the property owner was having financial difficulties and might lose the property through foreclosure. He indicated that a better price might be had at a forced sale.

Later Roussalis' wife read a legal notice giving a legal description of a property scheduled to be sold at public auction. The property was in the name of the owner of the South Poplar property.

Roussalis called Kelly and asked him to find out if this were the same property that had been shown him. Without checking because he "was too busy," Kelly assumed, and told the buyer, that it was the same property.

Even though McNamara had a policy against agents attending foreclosure sales, Kelly then offered to help Roussalis purchase the home at the auction. He arranged a loan of $250,000 and line of credit. He accompanied Roussalis to the auction and bid for him. When the mortgagee bid $97,000, Kelly stated that he raised the bid to $150,000 to shut out further bidding. Kelly obtained a check from the bank and paid the sheriff.

The house, bought and paid for, was not the South Poplar property. Kelly said that he would get the sale set aside. His attempt to do so failed.

John Roussalis brought action against Kelly and McNamara Realty claiming negligence by the agent. Kelly claimed that he was acting, not as a real estate agent, but as a friend. The District Court ruled in favor of Roussalis. Broker and agent appealed.

The Wyoming Supreme Court upheld the decision stating that the agent, acting as a volunteer, did not show the proper care expected of real estate agents and was negligent. It further held that the agent was representing the broker and that the broker was responsible for his salesperson's actions.

DISCUSSION QUESTIONS

■ Should an agent volunteer to help a friend?

■ In what ways could a consumer think that a friend who is a licensee is their agent?

■ In the absence of a formal agreement, what might create an agency relationship?

Again, the Kelly case is a situation where no formal agency relationship was created, but the jury found that the fiduciary duty had arisen. A similar result occurred in *Lyle v. Moore*, 599 P.2d 336 (Montana 1979), where the court found that the fiduciary relationship started prior to the listing agreement being executed. The court found that the broker did not adequately explain the terms of the listing agreement to the principal and took advantage of his superior knowledge of the marketplace to the principal's detriment.

Compensation Issues

One should also note that payment of commission does not, by itself, determine the existence of an agency relationship. The Texas Real Estate License Act addresses only compensation, not who pays it. It even allows the agent to be paid by more than one party, so long as the source of compensation is disclosed to all concerned parties (see §1101.652(b)(7); (8)). **This may be important for buyer's brokers. If getting paid by the buyer (any compensation—in any form), it needs to be disclosed if the buyer's broker is also getting a commission (or other item of value) from the seller or listing broker.**

Even though no commission is earned, an agency relationship can be created. In short, you can have the liability of being an agent, but with none of the benefits, if a licensee inadvertently allows an agency relationship to be created. Note the case of *Canada v. Kearns*, 624 S.W.2d 755 (Tex. App.-Beaumont 1981), where a sponsoring broker was held liable for an agent's misconduct even though no commission was earned.

Canada v. Kearns, 624 S.W.2d 755 (Tex. App.-Beaumont 1981)

In the summer of 1977, Ray and Elaine Canada bought a home from Louis and Virginia Bowen in Port Neches, Texas. Virginia was an agent of and bookkeeper for Gayle Kearns, Gayle Kearns Real Estate.

According to Ray Canada, he and his wife saw the house advertised for sale in the Port Arthur News under a Gayle Kearns Real Estate ad. The phone number given in the ad was the number of the agency. The home was carried as a Gayle Kearns' listing in MLS. The property had been shown to a different customer by another agent of Gayle Kearns Real Estate. There was a Kearns sign in the yard of the Bowen's house.

The Canadas called and met with Mrs. Bowen, who had already shown them another home. Virginia showed them her house. While touring the property, Ray states that he asked if the roof leaked because he saw water damage in the hall. Virginia said that the roof had leaked but was repaired and in good condition.

The Canadas went to the agency office and signed a purchase contract, which was headed with the Gayle Kearns Real Estate name. After they moved into their new home, the Canadas found that the roof was not satisfactory and had to have it repaired.

The Canadas brought action against Gayle Kearns, real estate broker, claiming misrepresentations were made by her salesperson, Virginia Bowen, about the condition of the roof of the house that they had purchased. Gayle Kearns argued that the transaction did not come under the Real Estate License Act because Virginia was selling her own home and because there was no commission or fee involved.

The jury found for the plaintiffs, but the court set aside the jury decision and granted a judgment, notwithstanding the jury verdict, for the defendant. The Canadas appealed this decision. The Court of Appeals reversed the lower court and held that the plaintiffs recover $21,400.02, all court costs and legal interest from the defendant, even though there may have been no benefit to the sponsoring broker.

DISCUSSION QUESTIONS

■ Should the sponsoring broker have immediately rejected the agent's acts, and would that have protected her?

■ What steps should be taken by a sponsoring broker to prevent a salesperson's misconduct from creating this kind of liability?

AGENCY AGREEMENTS

In addition to when and how the agency relationship is created, we also look to how the agreement of the parties establishes the agency relationship in more detail. In general, courts have held that agency relationships are created by one of three methods: actual authority, ostensible authority, or ratification.

AGENCY BY ACTUAL AUTHORITY

For an agency relationship to exist there must be some act constituting appointment of a person as an agent, as it is a consensual relationship. There must be a **meeting of the minds**, consent of both principal and agent, which may be either expressed or implied, and some control by the principal over the agent for the agency relationship to exist. *Carr v. Hunt*, 651 S.W.2d 875 (Tex. Civ. App.-Dallas 1983). Oddly enough, the actual authority can be verbal; but in order to sue the seller for a commission, the memorandum of employment must be in writing. This creates the inexplicable situation where you have the liability of the agency relationship but without the ability to sue for the commission, because there is no written listing agreement. *Schiller v. Elick*, 240 S.W.2d 997 (Tex. 1951). You may recall that an agent can be hired to represent the purchaser as well as the seller. *Tatum v. Preston Carter Co.*, 702 S.W.2d 186 (Tex. 1986).

A part of actual authority is **implied authority**. *Spring Garden 79U, Inc. v. Stewart Title Company*, 874 S.W.2d 945 (Tex. App.-Houston [1st Dist.] 1994). Implied authority is the authority an agent has because of custom in the industry. For instance, advertising is not discussed in most listing agreements, yet the agent has the implied authority to advertise the property for sale if it is common marketing custom in that area in order to accomplish the agency objective.

AGENCY BY OSTENSIBLE AUTHORITY

Agency by **ostensible authority** is also called an agency by **estoppel** or agency by **apparent authority**. It is the classic creation of the agency relationship without the agent even knowing it. This occurs when the conduct on the part of the principal would lead a reasonably prudent purchaser to believe that the agent had the authority he or she purports to exercise. In these situations, the agency relationship and all its liability is created as the agency relationship arises. *Canada v. Kearns*, supra. This is another situation where the agent would be liable to his principal for misconduct or breach of fiduciary duties, but the licensee doesn't have the right to sue for a commission. *Roquemore v. Ford Motor Co.*, 290 F. Supp 130 (N.D. Tex 1967).

In *Hall v. Halamicek Enterprises, Inc.*, 669 S.W.2d 368 (Tex. Civ. App.-Corpus Christi 1984), the court made further distinctions between apparent authority and agency by estoppel. The court held that "apparent authority" is based on estoppel, which arises from two sources: (1) the principal *knowingly* permitting an agent to hold himself out as having requisite authority; or (2) the principal may, by lack of ordinary care, lead a reasonably prudent purchaser to believe that he actually has such authority by what the agent says or does.

In order to establish an agency by estoppel, two elements must be established:

- the principal must have held the agent out in other instances, or in the particular transaction, as possessing authority to be an agent, or he must have knowingly acquiesced in the agent's authority; and

- the person dealing with the agent must have relied (*reliance* is the keyword) on the conduct of the principal to the third party's detriment.

In either case, it *requires the principal's participation* to create an ostensible agency. Declarations of the agent alone are not sufficient; it requires the actions of the principal to create the apparent authority.

Note also that this, too, can create an agency for the purchaser as well as the seller. *Foster v. Cross*, supra; *Lester v. Marshall*, 352 P.2d 786 (Colorado 1960); and *Little v. Rohauer*, 707 P.2d 1015 (Colo. App.-1985).

DISCUSSION QUESTIONS

■ List actions that a principal could do that would lead a third party to believe an agency exists.

■ List how a sponsoring broker could lead a third party to believe that a salesperson is the broker's agent.

AGENCY BY RATIFICATION

Agency by **ratification** occurs when the principal ratifies the acts of the agent after the agency function (procuring the ready, willing, and able buyer) has been performed. This may happen when a principal, although he or she had no knowledge of the unauthorized acts of his or her agent, retains the benefits of the transaction after acquiring full knowledge. *Land Title Company of Dallas, Inc. v. Stigler*, 609 S.W.2d 754 (Tex. 1980); *Cox v. Venters*, 887 S.W.2d 563 (Ky. Ct. App. 1994). The critical factor of determining the ratification is whether the principal's knowledge of the transaction legitimizes the previous act of the agent. The creation of the agency relationship is confirmed when the principal discovers the completion of the transaction and fails to repudiate the consummation of that transaction. This has also been called an agency by acquiescence. *Gillen v. Stevens*, 330 S.W.2d 253 (Tex. Civ. App.-Waco 1959 n.r.e.).

Special Rules for Real Estate Agency—Licensure

As discussed in Chapter 1, Texas initially adopted its real estate license law in 1939. The License Act is a general law that applies to all persons who engage in the real estate business. Its legislative intent is to avoid fraud on the public by requiring a license of anyone who deals in real estate for others. *Henry S. Miller Co. v. Treo Enterprises*, 585 S.W.2d 674 (Tex. 1979).

The broker or licensee occupies a status under the law that recognizes privileges and responsibilities. Under the terms of the Texas Real Estate License Act, all applicants are required to be competent, honest, and trustworthy. Other states have similar provisions, which have been upheld by their respective courts.

Ellis v. Flink, 301 So. 2d 493 (Fla. App. 1974); *Department of Employment v. Bake Young Realty*, 560 P.2d 5044 (Idaho 1977). Therefore, the real estate broker is ultimately responsible to the public.

One may logically conclude that principals have the right to trust their broker and rely on his or her experience and training. Those dealing with a licensed broker may naturally assume that person is honest and ethical. If licensees are competent as defined under the Act, they hold themselves out to the public as having particular skills and knowledge in the field of real estate. The licensee, therefore, is an expert, tested by the state and licensed because of his or her special competence. *Holloman v. Denson*, 640 S.W.2d 417 (Tex. Civ. App.-Waco 1982).

DISCUSSION QUESTIONS

■ As a consumer, what special competencies, skills, and knowledge would you expect a licensee to have?

■ What real estate–related jobs do you think should require a real estate license?

"BROKER" DEFINITION

Almost any real estate act of a licensee (as defined by §1101.002 of the Texas Real Estate License Act), when performed (1) for another, and (2) for the reasonable expectation of some valuable consideration, constitutes the practice of brokerage. Apparently, when the brokerage function is performed, the licensee is automatically the agent of someone. *Wilson v. Donze*, supra. If, however, the broker performs the function for his or her own account, or the principal earns part of a commission, it does not fall under the definition of brokerage. *Xarin Real Estate, Inc. v. Gamboa*, 715 S.W.2d 80 (Tex. App.-Corpus Christi 1986). A brokerage function is defined by the Texas Real Estate License Act as follows:

SECTION 1101.002

■ "Real estate" means a leasehold, as well as any other interest or estate in land, whether corporeal, incorporeal, freehold, or nonfreehold, and whether the real estate is situated in this state or elsewhere.

■ "Real estate broker" means a person who, for another person and for a fee, commission, or other valuable consideration, or with the intention or in the expectation or on the promise of receiving or collecting a fee, commission, or other valuable consideration from another person:

a. sells, exchanges, purchases, rents, or leases real estate.

b. offers to sell, exchange, purchase, rent, or lease real estate.

c. negotiates or attempts to negotiate the listing, sale, exchange, purchase, rental, or leasing of real estate.

d. lists or offers or attempts or agrees to list real estate for sale, rental, lease, exchange, or trade.

e. appraises, or offers or attempts or agrees to appraise, real estate.

f. auctions, or offers or attempts or agrees to auction, real estate.

g. buys or sells or offers to buy or sell, or otherwise deals in options on real estate.

h. aids, attempts, or offers to aid in locating or obtaining for purchase, rent, or lease any real estate.

i. procures or assists in the procuring of prospects for the purpose of effecting the sale, exchange, lease, or rental of real estate.

■ "Broker" also includes a person employed by or on behalf of the owner or owners of lots or other parcels of real estate, at a salary, fee, commission, or any other valuable consideration, to sell the real estate or any part thereof, in lots or parcels or other disposition thereof. It also includes a person who engages in the business of charging an advance fee or contracting for collection of fee in connection with a contract whereby the person undertakes primarily to promote the sale of real estate either through its listing in a publication issued primarily for such purpose, or for referral of information concerning the real estate to brokers, or both.

■ "Real estate salesperson" means a person associated with a Texas licensed real estate broker for the purposes of performing acts or transactions comprehended by the definition of "real estate broker" as defined in this Act.

■ "Person" means an individual or a corporation, foreign or domestic.

■ "Commission" means the Texas Real Estate Commission.

The Texas Real Estate Commission frequently revises its regulations. The current rules are always available on the TREC Web site, and what follows are some of them.

535.1

Section (§535.1) of the regulations provides that a person conducting brokerage business from another state by mail, telephone, the Internet, e-mail, or other medium is also considered acting within this state, if all of the prospective buyers, sellers, landlords, or tenants are legal residents of this state. The adoption of the amendment was necessary to narrow the application to nonresidents, who have significant contacts with the State of Texas, thus permitting regulation of their activities as real estate brokers.

If the person performing the brokerage act is unlicensed, he or she is subject to the civil and criminal penalties of the Act. The penalties are not exclusive, and additional liabilities can be incurred through any unlawful conduct (consider §1101.651(a) of the Act, and a broker in Houston who received four years in prison for paying an unlicensed person a commission).

In addition to the broad definitions in §1101.002, the Real Estate Commission's Rules and Regulations have clarified and further delineated a number of questionable areas:

535.12 GENERAL

- A person may invest in real estate or contract to purchase real estate and then sell it or offer to sell it without having a real estate license. Texas real estate licensure is not required of one who buys and sells real property only for his or her own account.

  Give an example.

- One who owns property jointly with another may sell and convey title to his interest in the property, but he or she must be licensed to act for compensation as an agent for the other owner unless otherwise exempted from the requirement of licensure.

  Give an example.

535.13 DISPOSITIONS OF REAL ESTATE

- Subleasing may be done without licensure for the sublessor's own profit but not the compensation to be paid by another unless the recipient is otherwise exempted from the requirements of licensure.

  Give an example.

■ Unless otherwise exempted by this Act, one who collects rentals for another and for compensation must be licensed if the person also rents or leases property for the owner.

Give an example.

■ Real estate broker licensure is required for the operation of a rental agency. This section does not prohibit employment of an answering service or unlicensed clerical or secretarial employees identified to callers as such to confirm information concerning the size, price, and terms of property advertised.

Give an example.

■ Real estate licensure is required for a person hired by a corporation for the purpose of selling real property owned by the corporation.

Give an example.

■ Real estate licensure is required of a subsidiary corporation, which, for compensation, negotiates in Texas for the sale of its parent corporation's real property.

Give an example.

535.15 NEGOTIATIONS

■ Locating and bringing together a buyer and seller through correspondence or telephone constitutes negotiation if done from within the borders of Texas.

How might this be done?

- Real estate licensure is required for one to negotiate in Texas for listings. **Give an example.**

535.16 Listings

- Trade associations or other organizations which provide a computerized listing service for their members, but which do not receive compensation for the sale of real estate, would not be required to be licensed under this Act.

  Give an example.

- A broker may not take net listings unless the principal insists upon a net listing and when the principal appears to be familiar with current market values of real property. When a broker accepts a listing, he enters into a fiduciary relationship with his principal, whereby the broker is obligated to make diligent efforts to obtain the best price possible for the principal. The use of a net listing places an upper limit on the principal's expectancy and places the broker's interest above his principal's interest with reference to obtaining the best possible price. Net listings should be qualified so as to assure the principal of not less than his desired price and to limit the broker to a specified maximum commission.

  Give an example.

- A real estate licensee is obligated to advise a property owner as to the licensee's opinion of the market value of a property when negotiating a listing or offering to purchase the property for the licensee's own account as a result of contact made while acting as a real estate agent.

535.17 Appraisals

- A salesperson may make, sign, and present real estate appraisals for his sponsoring broker, but the appraisals must be submitted in the broker's name and are the broker's responsibility. A real estate salesperson may not appraise real property for others and for compensation without such activity being conducted through his sponsoring broker.

Give an example.

■ This section does not cover a situation wherein a savings and loan association, mortgage bank, commercial bank, credit union, or any other financial institution, or its employees, in contemplation of making a loan, appraises a piece of property and charges and receives a fee for its services.

An example might be:

■ Except as provided by this section, appraisals of real property performed in this state by Texas real estate licensees shall be conducted in accordance with the Uniform Standards of Professional Appraisal Practice of the Appraisal Foundation in effect at the time the appraisal is performed. A real estate licensee may, for a separate fee, provide an opinion of value or comparative market analysis, which does not conform with the Uniform Standards of Professional Appraisal Practice of the Appraisal Foundation, if the licensee provides the person for whom the opinion or analysis is prepared with a written statement containing the following language: "THIS IS AN OPINION OF VALUE OR COMPARATIVE MARKET ANALYSIS AND SHOULD NOT BE CONSIDERED AN APPRAISAL. In making any decision that relies upon my work, you should know that I have not followed the guidelines for development of an appraisal or analysis contained in the Uniform Standards of Professional Appraisal Practice of the Appraisal Foundation."

■ The exception allowed by subsection does not apply to a transaction in which the Resolution Trust Corporation or a federal financial institution regulatory agency has required compliance with the Uniform Standards of Professional Appraisal Practice of the Appraisal Foundation.

Give an example.

535.19 LOCATING PROPERTY

■ Except as provided by this section a real estate license is required for a person to receive a fee or other consideration for assisting another person to locate real property for sale, purchase, rent, or lease, such as the operation of a service that finds apartments or homes.

Give an example.

■ The compilation and distribution of information relating to rental vacancies or property for sale, purchase, rent, or lease is activity for which a real estate license is required if payment of any fee or other consideration received by the person who complies and distributes the information is contingent upon the sale, purchase, rental, or lease of the property. An advance fee is a contingent fee if the fee must be returned if the property is not sold, purchased, rented, or leased.

Give an example.

■ Referring a prospective buyer, seller, landlord, or tenant to another person in connection with a proposed real estate transaction is an act requiring the person making the referral to be licensed if the referral is made with the expectation of receiving valuable consideration. For purposes of this section, the term "valuable consideration" includes, but is not limited to, money, gifts of merchandise having a retail value greater than $50.00, rent bonuses and discounts.

Give an example.

■ A person is not required to be licensed as a real estate broker or a salesperson if all the following conditions are met: (a) the person is engaged in the business of selling goods or services to the public; (b) the person sells goods or services to a real estate licensee who intends to offer the goods or services as an inducement to potential buyers, sellers, land-lords, or tenants; (c) after selling the goods or services to the real estate licensee, the person refers the person's customers to the real estate licensee; (d) the payment to the person for the goods or services is not contingent upon the consummation of a real estate transaction by the person's customers.

Give an example.

535.21 UNIMPROVED LOT SALES; LISTING PUBLICATIONS

■ Real estate licensure is required of those who advertise for others regarding real property, accept calls received in response to such advertisements, and refer the callers to the owner of the property.

An example might be:

■ A person may contract to advertise real estate for purchase, sale, lease, or rental in a publication without being licensed under the Texas Real Estate License Act, unless payment of any fee or consideration the person receives is contingent upon the purchase, sale, lease, or rental of the property advertised in the publication. For the purposes of this section an advance fee is a contingent fee if the person is obligated to return the fee if the property is not purchased sold, leased, or rented. This section shall be narrowly construed to effectuate the purposes for which this section was adopted.

Give an example.

Exemptions from Licensure

The exceptions under the Act (set out in 1101.005) are as follows:

■ an attorney at law licensed in this state or in other states.
■ an attorney in fact under a duly executed power of attorney authorizing the consummation of a real estate transaction.
■ a public official in the conduct of his official duties.
■ a person calling the sale of real estate by auction under the authority of a license issued by this state provided the person does not perform any other act of a real estate broker or salesperson as defined by this Act.
■ a person acting under a court order or under the authority of a will or a written trust instrument.

- a salesperson employed by an owner in the sale of structures and land on which said structures are situated, provided such structures are erected by the owner in the due course of his business.

- an on-site manager of an apartment complex.

- transactions involving the sale, lease, or transfer of any mineral or mining interest in real property.

- an owner or his employees in renting or leasing his own real estate whether improved or unimproved.

- transactions involving the sale, lease, or transfer of cemetery lots.

- transactions involving the renting, leasing, or management of hotels or motels.

- a person registered under Section 1101.501 of the Act [right of way sales] who sells, buys, leases, or transfers an easement or right-of-way for use in connection with telecommunication, utility, railroad, or pipeline service.

The exceptions are strictly construed. One should never presence they are exempt. Note *Shehab v. Xanadu, Inc.*, 698 S.W.2d 491 (Tex. Civ. App.-Corpus Christi 1985), and *Terry v. Allied Bancshares, Inc.*, 760 S.W.2d 45 (Tex. App.-Ft. Worth 1988):

Shehab v. Xanadu, Inc., 698 S.W.2d 491 (Tex. Civ. App.-Corpus Christi 1985)

Margaret Shehab had worked for Products, Inc. as a licensed real estate agent in Michigan. She agreed to move to Texas to become Sales Manager of Lafayette Place (apartments that were being converted to condos) after the company president said that she did not need a Texas real estate license to work in that capacity.

In a letter agreement Products confirmed her as Sales Manager and promised a 1 percent sales price compensation for each unit sold. She also received a rent-free apartment. From 1978 through 1981, she sold and received a commission on over 140 units.

During this time Products, Inc. became Liberty Financial Corp.; and Shehab introduced W.H. Clover to Xanadu, Inc., which was a part of Products/Liberty Financial. Clover negotiated with representatives of Liberty for the sale of the approximately 54 remaining units.

Clover's offer changed from an offer to purchase the units, which were real property to the purchase of Xanadu, itself. The sale concluded with Clover purchasing from Liberty all the assets of Xanadu, Inc. including the remaining units. Shehab claimed a commission on the sale, which she did not receive.

She sued for the fee claiming that she was the procuring cause of the sale and that, as the "on-site manager" of the complex, she was exempt from real estate license law requirements. (According to the TRELA, an on-site apartment manager does not have to be licensed.) She also sued for fraud in the misrepresentation of her need for a Texas license by the company president, and for the restructuring of the sale of real property to the sale of stock to preclude a commission.

The District Court granted a summary judgment for the project owner, and Shehab appealed. The Court of Appeals affirmed this judgment stating that exceptions to the general scheme and purpose (of the License Act) must be "strictly construed" so that an on-site manager of a "condominium project" was not the same as an on-site manager of an "apartment complex." Therefore, the unlicensed agent could not use the courts to collect a commission even though there was a contract to the contrary. Only a real estate licensee has the right to a commission under the TRELA.

Terry v. Allied Bancshares, Inc., 760 S.W.2d 45 (Tex. App.-Ft. Worth 1988)

Douglas L. Terry, a past officer of Allied, sued Allied Bancshares, Inc. and Allied Bank for a finder's fee. Terry was neither a real estate licensee nor an attorney.

Allied had offered a finder's fee to encourage employees to sell foreclosed properties. Terry found a purchaser for one of Allied's properties.

Shortly after the sale, Terry was appointed president of a competing bank. Allied refused to pay him a finder's fee on the completion of the sale.

The court ruled that Terry was precluded from recovering his compensation by the Texas Real Estate License Act's licensing requirements. Allied may have had a moral obligation to pay the fee, but the law precludes the enforcement of the finder's fee agreement because Terry did not hold a real estate license nor did he qualify as an exemption to the Act's licensure requirements.

DISCUSSION QUESTIONS

■ List some of the jobs that could involve the sale of real estate.

■ Which of those jobs require a real estate license?

■ Who do you trust to interpret the License Act for you?

The Rules and Regulations further clarify the Texas Real Estate Commission's interpretation of the exceptions.

535.31 EXEMPTIONS: ATTORNEYS AT LAW

■ Licensed attorneys are exempt from the requirements of the Real Estate License Act, but cannot sponsor real estate salespersons for licensure unless such attorneys are also licensed as real estate brokers.

■ Licensed attorneys are exempt from the requirements of the Real Estate License Act, but they are not eligible to qualify as designated agents for a corporation, which is licensed as a broker, unless such attorneys are otherwise qualified in accordance with the requirements of the Act.

Give an example.

■ Attorneys who desire real estate licensure must follow the same steps, which would be necessary if they were not attorneys.

What steps must they follow?

■ Is an attorney exempt? Can an attorney ask for a share of the listings broker's commission.

535.32 EXEMPTIONS: ATTORNEYS IN FACT

■ A power of attorney that is recorded in the county in which the particular real property is located and that specifically describes the real property to be sold authorizes a person to act as a real estate agent for the owner of such property without the necessity of real estate licensure. An unlicensed person cannot use the power of attorney method to engage in the real estate agency business.

An example is:

535.33 PUBLIC OFFICIALS

■ Public officials and employees are exempted from the requirement of real estate licensure while performing their duties as such.

Give an example.

535.34 EXEMPTIONS: SALESPERSONS EMPLOYED BY AN OWNER OF LAND AND STRUCTURES ERECTED BY THE OWNER

"Salesperson employed by an owner" means a person employed and directly compensated by an owner.

535.35 EXEMPTIONS: EMPLOYEES RENTING AND LEASING EMPLOYER'S REAL ESTATE

■ An owner-employer's act of withholding income and F.I.C.A. taxes from wages paid another would be evidence of employment.

Rule 53E.13 (d) also exempts employees of corporations and other business entities acting on behalf of their employers on transactions in which the employer is a principal.

The Real Estate License Act requires licensure of residential rental locators. §1101.022(6) defines a "residential rental locator as a person who offers for consideration to locate a unit in an apartment complex for lease to a prospective tenant. The term does not include an owner who offers to locate a unit in the owner's complex." This provision requires the same basic disclosures and revocation as other brokerage provisions under the statute. The Texas Real Estate Commission is required under this provision to adopt regulations and establish standards relating to permissible forms of advertising by a person licensed as a residential rental locator. These are a somewhat different set of rules than those that are established by brokers and salespersons generally. They concentrate on the availability of units and amenities and require compliance with 1101.652(b)(23) of the Real Estate License Act.

RESIDENTIAL RENTAL LOCATOR GUIDELINES

The Texas Real Estate Commission adopted advertising guidelines for residential rental locators. Failure of the licensee to comply with the guidelines is a violation of a TREC rule, punishable by reprimand, or suspension or revocation of the license, or administrative penalty.

The guidelines primarily concern advertising of one or more units in the same advertisement by general terms without describing the amenities available for a specific unit at a specific price. A licensee using such general advertising must include phrases that have equivalent meanings to those prescribed by the guidelines, such as "the rent is _____ dollars or more, depending on the features of the unit." If the advertisement appears in a printed publication, however, the licensee will be considered in compliance with the guidelines if the section of the publication in which the advertisement appears contains a notice set out in the guidelines.

An advertisement by a locator in an apartment unit by general terms is misleading unless at the time the advertisement is placed at least one unit meeting the description of the unit contained in the advertisement is available through the locator at the lowest rent stated in the advertisement, within either a time stated in the advertisement, or within thirty days after the advertisement is submitted for publication if no time is stated. See TAC 535.300.

PERTINENT CASES ON LICENSURE

More cases are getting through the courts that interpret the provisions of the Texas Real Estate License Act:

In *Collins v. Beste*, 840 S.W.2d 788 (Tex. App.-Ft. Worth 1992, writ den.), the owner of the property (Collins) hired the broker (Beste) to provide leasing and marketing services for Collins' properties. Later, Collins fired Beste. Beste sued, alleging that he was entitled to be paid. Collins defended alleging that Beste did not have a broker's license and therefore was not entitled to get a commission. The court upheld the Section 3 exemption, noting that an employee of an owner of property does not have to be licensed to lease property for the owner, but the exemption does not apply to purchases. Therefore, the employee was able to pursue his cause of action for the commission even though he was not licensed.

An excellent recovery fund case was decided in *Gamble v. Norton*, 893 S.W.2d 129 (Tex. App.-Houston [1st Dist.] 1995) wherein a broker was also an investor and managing partner of a joint venture in the same transaction. The trial court ultimately determined that he had liability to an excess of $1,600,000, and the plaintiffs proceeded to the Real Estate Recovery Fund for compensation. The court held that even though he had a commission agreement on the sale of the property, none of the acts complained of were committed in his conduct as a broker, but rather as an investor when he would not perform the acts for another as required by the Real Estate License Act. Therefore, they denied any recovery from the fund.

The Texas Real Estate License Act requires an employment agreement to be in writing in order to be enforceable. Amendments to the employment agreement, often made to accommodate the client, can be costly. In *Friendswood Development Company v. McDade + Company*, 911 S.W.2d 541 (Tex. 1996), a real estate broker representing a buyer (American Bureau of Shipping) entered into a "standard exclusive brokerage contract" that provided McDade was the sole broker and had the exclusive right to obtain a lease or purchase of premises on the buyer's behalf. The buyer informed McDade of its ongoing discussions with Friendswood and other Exxon affiliates, but Friendswood had no space available to rent at the time. McDade inserted an exception to the "standard brokerage contract" to create a broad exclusion for Friendswood from the contract, thus permitting ABS to contract with either McDade or Friendswood for office space. Thereafter, ABS accepted a Friendswood proposal for an interim lease for one year, in property that Friendswood didn't own, pending Friendswood space becoming available later on in the year. When McDade discovered that Friendswood had leased space to ABS that it didn't own, he filed a suit against ABS alleging a breach of the brokerage contract and against Friendswood for tortuously interfering with the brokerage contract.

The Texas Supreme Court held that the contract was clear on its face, contained no latent or patent ambiguities, and that Friendswood, in any capacity, was exempt and excluded from the terms of the brokerage contract. Moral: Any changes or exclusions to employment agreements should be *carefully* made.

Warner Communications, Inc. v. Keller, 928 S.W.2d 479 (Tex. 1996)

Texas Builders leased one of its commercial real estate properties to Atari, Inc. The owner began substantial improvements, but Atari had a change of plans and never occupied the building. Atari entered into an exclusive listing agreement with Keller REALTORS®. At the same time, Texas Builders (the owner of the building) was attempting to find tenants. Texas Builders refused to give Keller a key to the premises and would not allow Keller to put a sign on the building. Keller ultimately found a potential tenant, which Atari rejected. Keller then presented the tenant to Texas Builders, the owners. Texas Builders kept stalling the negotiations with Keller, while negotiating directly with the new tenant without Keller's knowledge. There was no listing agreement to Keller in this lawsuit, but Keller produced numerous bits of information (such as an informational letter sent to all local commercial brokers acknowledging the builder's willingness to pay a commission). A representative of the owner signed them. The court held that these general offers to the brokerage community were enough to satisfy the requirements of a written listing agreement in order to maintain an action for a commission. The court further held that the mere address and general description of the premises was enough to satisfy the requirement for a legal description in the listing.

The Texas Supreme Court reverted to the traditional rule that a real estate licensee cannot recover for a breach of contract if there is no written agreement, which satisfies the Texas Real Estate License Act. The court stuck to the traditional theory that "the writing must furnish, either within itself or by reference to some other existing document, the means or data by which the real estate at issue may be identified." The sufficiency of the description is the same that is necessary to satisfy the Statute of Frauds (to identify the property with reasonable certainty).

In addressing the fraud claim the court held that even if Texas Builders committed fraud, Keller couldn't circumvent the requirements of the Texas Real Estate License Act by claiming the lost commission as damages for fraud.

This creates an interesting question as a buyer's broker. It is often impossible to determine the identity of the property to be purchased at the time the Buyer's Representation Agreement is signed. How, then, can a buyer's broker maintain an action for commission? There is at least some authority from a lower court that, under these circumstances, this legal description is not necessary. (See *LA & N Interest, Inc. v. Fish*, 864 S.W.2d 745 (Tex. App. 1993).) The only other alternative would be to insert the legal description at a later date, when the property is identified. That may be a good idea.

Although one usually thinks of being employed as an agent, creation of the agency relationship can occur without express authority. The ultimate definition of brokerage is defined in the Texas Real Estate License Act, as interpreted by the Texas Real Estate Commission. The difficult part is the "in between" or the "gray" area. Interpretations and facts change from transaction to transaction. Agents need to have their role defined early. Their role must be clearly understood by all the parties (principals as well as other agents). The licensee is responsible to be sure that the agency roles in any given situation are carefully explained and that these roles are fully understood by everyone involved.

In Trammel Crow Company No. 60, et al v. William Jefferson Harkinson, 944 S.W.2d 631 (Tex. 1997)

A tenant authorized the broker to act as its exclusive representative in locating rental space. The broker found suitable space in Dallas. The owners told the broker that they would pay 4½ percent cash commission to the broker and sent the broker a commission agreement, which the broker re-drafted and sent back to the owner to execute. The owner never signed it. The tenant ultimately negotiated a lease directly with the owner, going around their buyer representative agreement, apparently assuming they would get cheaper rent. The owner paid their in-house broker a commission, but refused to pay the buyer's broker a commission, alleging that there was no agreement in writing, and therefore no right to a commission.

The court noted that the exclusive representation agreement did not specify a commission to be payable by the buyer, but only indicated that the commission would be paid by the seller. Therefore, it was not a commission agreement. With no agreement in writing, the broker then lost his right to pursue the commission. The broker also alleged tortuous interference by the broker who did receive the commission, alleging that he interfered with the broker's rights who represented the buyer. The court held that he could not sue for tortious interference if it was merely a claim for a commission, and specifically disapproved the prior case of *LA & N Associates v. Fish*, 864 S.W.2d 745 (Tex. App.-Houston [14th Dist.], 1993, no writ) to the extent that it permitted a claim for tortious interference.

There was a well-reasoned dissent, relying on contract principals of tortious interference and violations of the Real Estate License Act by the broker who received the commission. The clear import of the case, however, is that if one is to be a buyer's broker: (1) one needs to get a commission agreement in writing and signed by the person who was supposed to pay the commission, or (2) one should be sure that an alternative commission is to be paid by the buyer in the event the seller refused to pay a commission. Unfortunately, in many circumstances, the buyer is not going to support the buyer's broker who pursues the buyer's broker's commission, as the buyer thinks he or she is going to get a cheaper deal without the commission. It is a tough issue to deal with. There is a fairly easy rule, though. If a buyer is not willing to employ you or support your efforts as their broker, find a better client.

IS THE TRANSACTION A REAL ESTATE TRANSACTION?

One of the bigger issues recently litigated is whether or not a commercial transaction involves real estate as part of the business transaction.

In *Swor vs. Tapp Furniture Company,* 146 S.W.3d 778 (Tex. App. – Texarkana, 2004), a broker sued a seller to recover a fee for finding a buyer to purchase a funeral home business. The sale included all the assets of the business including the real estate. He alleged that there was an oral agreement for a "finder's fee" between the broker and seller. The court construed the definition of finder's fee as applying to real estate brokerage and therefore is addressed under the Texas Real Estate License Act. In reviewing the provisions of the Texas Real Estate License Act, the court noted that it was undisputed that there was no written agreement (as required by TRELA) and the plaintiff was not a licensed real estate broker (as required by TRELA). It's the same old story, whatever you call it, it's a commission. If it deals in real estate, it must comply with the Texas Real Estate License Act.

Note, however, that in *BBQ Blues Texas, Ltd. v. Affiliated Business Brokers, Inc. 183 SW 3rd 543* (Tex. App. – Dallas 2006, pet. denied), the business owners brought an action for declaratory judgment as to the enforceability of an oral agreement to pay business brokers a commission. The brokers filed a counterclaim alleging breach of contract, quantum meruit, promissory establin, and attorney fees. This is a classic conflict of selling of business and whether or not there is enough real estate in the transaction to bring the transaction into the Texas Occupations Code which requires a written employment agreement in order to sue for a commission. Here the Court held that there was an oral commission agreement that did not contemplate the transfer of real estate even though the buyers of the business assumed an existing lease. The core reason was that the business could have been sold without the transfer of the lease, and therefore the real estate transaction was not a significant part of the transaction.

The Court seemed to give a lot of emphasis to the fact that the jury found that the sale of the business did not contemplate a transfer of the lease, therefore, the Court held that the oral commission agreement for the sale of the business is enforceable since the jury found that the commission agreement did not involve the transfer of the real estate lease in Round Rock, Texas.

3

FIDUCIARY RESPONSIBILITY: GENERAL AND SPECIAL AGENCY

PURPOSE

After carefully reading Chapter 3, the student will be able to:

■ Describe the differences between general and special agency.

■ Understand the broker-salesperson relationship and the responsibilities involved.

■ Recognize the dangers of misrepresentation and the importance of accurate information.

Key Words to look for and define in this chapter:
1. General Agency
2. Special Agency
3. Assumption of general agency
4. Transaction broker

There are several types of agency responsibilities. For instance, agents can universally represent their principal in all things. There can also be general agencies created to give agents the authority for a range of transactions. Similarly, the agent's authority can be limited to a very special specific activity. All of these generally define the agent's scope of authority and responsibility.

There is a basic question of agency liability that considers the responsibility of the principal and the agent. For instance, an agent, without the knowledge of the principal, represents that a home has solid gold fixtures; and the principal does not know the misrepresentation is made. Does the principal have liability for that misrepresentation? Can the agent bind his or her principal by agreeing to and changing a contract? Answers to these questions are discussed in the concepts and the theories of general and special agency.

GENERAL AGENCY

In a **general agency**, the principal has complete responsibility for the acts of the agent performed within the scope of the agency (e.g., the real estate transaction). As a general agent, the agent is authorized to conduct a series of transactions involving a continuity of service. *George D. Thomas Builder, Inc. v. Timmons*, 658 S.W.2d 194 (Tex. Civ. App.-El Paso 1983); *Stortroen v. Beneficial Finance Co.*, 736 P.2d 391 (Colo. 1987).

The agent stands in the place of and under the authority of the principal in a range of related services or activities. In the concept of real estate brokerage, one may think of the sponsoring broker-salesperson relationship as being a general agency. The sponsoring broker "cloaks" the salesperson with a responsibility to represent that sponsoring broker. The broker gives the salesperson the authority to put signs in front of houses, use the office, give out business cards, represent the company at real estate trade association functions, house showings, etc. The salesperson may wear a badge with the sponsoring broker's company name on it, sign listings on behalf of the broker, and, as such, can create liability for the broker when acting within the scope of the broker's authority. In a fair housing case (discussed later in Chapter 12), the United States Supreme Court commented that the Fair Housing Act imposed liability without fault on the employer, and "in accordance with traditional agency principles" held there was vicarious liability of a broker for the broker's salespeople. *Meyer v. Holley*, 123 S.Ct. 824 (2003). Remember that in the previous chapter, in the case *Canada v. Kearns*, a sponsoring broker was held liable even though the broker received no commission.

The one exception, and it's a big exception, is when the real estate salesperson or broker associate is not acting under the control of the sponsoring broker. For instance, when a salesperson buys a new couch for his or her home and doesn't make the payments, does the broker have a liability for the misconduct of that agent? No. The agent did not buy his personal couch as a function of his licensure or real estate agency.

The more difficult areas occur when the agent may apparently be in the scope of his agency. Recall the discussion of ostensible authority in the previous chapter. If a real estate agent is buying real estate for his own account, and a misrepresentation or other misconduct occurs, is the sponsoring broker liable for that kind of conduct? In this situation, the liability issue is much more difficult to deal with, depending on how the real estate agent conducted himself in the negotiations and transactions. If the licensee participated in the transaction as an agent, it may create liability for the sponsoring broker. If the property was clearly purchased for the agent personally, it would not. Several factors are examined in making the determination, such as: (1) was the act committed within the time and space limits of the broker's sponsorship; (2) was the act committed at least in part by serving the principal; and (3) is it incidental to or part of the authorized conduct of the agent? See *Denlinger v. Mudgett*, 559 A.2d 661 (Vt. 1989).

SPECIAL AGENCY

Then there is the theory of **special agency**. Special agency has a limited scope of responsibility. As a result, the principal is not responsible for the acts of his or her agent. Special agency is created primarily to conduct a single transaction. It does not involve any continuity of service, *Stortroen*, supra. This type of agency is created in the real estate agent's typical listing or buyer's representation agreement. *Ingalls v. Rice*, 511 S.W.2d 78 (Tex. Civ. App.-Houston 1974).

In Texas, the real estate broker is primarily recognized to be a special agent, engaged by others to negotiate bargains or contracts for the sale or lease of real estate between other people for which the broker is paid a commission. *Doria v. Suchowolski*, 531 S.W.2d 360 (Tex. Civ. App.-San Antonio 1975, ref. n.r.e.). In most circumstances, the agent's authority is limited to marketing, showing, and finding a purchaser for the property. The broker, as a general rule, has no authority to consummate a sale or make representations on behalf of the seller without the seller's authority or expressed authority. *Loma Vista Development Co. v. Johnson*, 180 S.W.2d 922 (Tex. 1944).

Loma Vista Development Co. v. Johnson, 180 S.W.2d 922 (Tex. 1944)

Thomas W. Johnson and his wife sued Loma Vista Development Company for damages for fraud in the sale of a house. The Johnsons contended that Roy Jones was the general agent of the Loma Vista Development Co.

Loma Vista was a home construction company that had listed the house in question with McNeley Co., real estate brokers. Jones was a salesperson for this brokerage. Jones introduced himself to the Johnsons as the salesperson in charge when he showed them the house at an open house. Among other things, he misrepresented the foundation of the house as the best for that type of house. The Johnsons claimed that they relied on Jones' representation of construction in purchasing the house.

Loma Vista gave no authority to Jones or McNeley Co. to make any representations about the house. Jones was a special agent of Loma Vista, limited to finding a buyer not consummating the sale.

The trial court ruled for the Johnsons. The Court of Civil Appeals reversed the judgment and remanded because "there was no evidence establishing a legal measure of damages." The Texas Supreme Court reversed the decisions of both courts and rendered judgment for Loma Vista. The court ruled that the seller was not liable for an unknown and unauthorized act and that the buyers had the opportunity to check the truth of any of the agent's representations with the seller prior to the sale.

DISCUSSION QUESTIONS

■ Could a real estate agent bind the seller by making a misrepresentation as to the status of title?

■ If a broker made an outrageous representation (the house has a solid gold fireplace), could the seller be bound by such misrepresentation because he selected that broker to represent him?

In many other states, sellers are held bound by the misrepresentation or misconduct of their agents. *Mongeau v. Boutelle*, 407 N.E.2d 352 (Mass. App. 1980). At least at this time, Texas has not adopted this theory, but the "gray" areas are developing. There is one theory that if the seller receives the benefit of the fraud or misconduct, the seller should have liability at least to the extent of the benefit obtained, particularly if the seller knew or should have known of the fraud. At least one Texas case has held that the agent's misconduct created a joint and several liability for the seller and the broker if the seller received the benefit of the misrepresentation. *Century 21 Page One Realty v. Naghad*, 760 S.W.2d 305 (Tex. App.-Texarkana 1988).

Century 21 Page One Realty v. Naghad, 760 S.W.2d 305 (Tex. App.-Texarkana 1988)

Brenda Jones of Century 21 Page One Realty listed the home of Stanley Childers. The listing agreement, which went into Multiple Listing Service (MLS), stated that the house had no known defects.

In truth, the house had a latent foundation defect and a defective septic tank system. A neighbor testified that shortly after the house was listed she went to the Century 21 office and informed Jones of the septic tank problem. There is disagreement whether or not the seller disclosed the problem to the listing agent. But the listing form went unchanged after the neighbor reported the problem. Hooshang Naghad purchased the home through MLS. The septic tank leaked liquid sewage in the backyard, and water also leaked into the sunken living room.

Naghad brought action against the seller and the real estate agency. The jury found that the real estate agent "engaged in false, misleading, or deceptive acts and that the vendor and the agent were jointly and severally liable."

Century 21 Page One appealed. The Court of Appeals affirmed the judgment. It held that "express agreement" is not necessary. To be equally liable only "tacit understanding" is needed. Those who make a false representation, and those who benefit from it, commit fraud and are liable.

DISCUSSION QUESTIONS

■ What if the seller hadn't known there was a benefit resulting from the fraud?

■   What if the agent's misrepresentation had been the result of incorrect information given to him by the seller?

One should remember that stories change, memories fade, and a licensee's off-hand remark concerning the quality of an item can be taken seriously by the purchaser as a very clear and distinct representation. It is important to remember that when a seller encourages a licensee to "shade the truth" or not to mention a particular defect because it is unimportant, the seller may be creating liability for himself or herself as well as for the agent. The agent needs to be straightforward in dealing with his or her principal, stating that such conduct creates liability for both parties, not just the principal, or not just the agent!

If an agent discovers that a defect exists that wasn't disclosed, the agent needs to have a long, careful conversation with the seller. It is better to lose the listing than to expose both of you to liability. Keep notes and backup information for all such conversations and file them. Don't ever purge your file of these records. These records may be your only defense.

There is a final concern over the general versus special agency theory. One can begin a transaction as a special agent, the generally accepted principle in Texas, but one may become a general agent as the transaction develops. This can happen if the principal gives an agent the scope of control and authority to "stand in his shoes." For instance, a seemingly innocent comment such as, "take care of the property while I'm gone," or "Mr. Broker here has the authority to take care of the property while I'm gone," may create a situation where the broker can bind the principal. As the special agent becomes a general agent, the scope of control changes. In such situations, a general agency will be presumed. *Plains Builders, Inc. v. Pride Transportation Co.*, 554 S.W.2d 59 (Tex. Civ. App.-Eastland 1977). Agents should be careful not to expand unintentionally the scope of their agency. It could create more liability.

NONAGENCY?

A "nonagency" case involving a real estate broker came out of the 5th Circuit in *Moroder v. First City Bank Corporation of Texas*, 43 F.3d 953 (5th Cir. 1994). The case involved a loan from First City Bank where First City Bank required the mortgage assets to be turned over to a "fiduciary" who would oversee the sale and management of the mortgaged properties. In reality, the borrowers were required to use the fiduciary broker "selected" by First City. There was also an attorney in the transaction who represented the broker and the bank, who was also a trustee under the deed of trust. Apparently, the attorney also gave legal advice to the borrowers regarding the sale of the property. In the Moroder case, the court characterized the real estate broker's relationship as "unlike the typical broker-client relationship," as it "was imposed on the [borrowers] by a party with antagonistic interests." The court held that even though the broker may have technically acted as the borrower's broker, under the facts of this case that status alone did not result in a fiduciary relationship. The case was remanded to a lower court for further proceeding. In making its decision, the court quoted *Marriott Brothers v. Gage*, 704 F. Supp. 731, 738 (N.D. Tex. 1988) as holding that an entity cannot serve as a fiduciary to an opposing party in a transaction.

In a similar holding, a seller twice specifically rejected the agency relationship of the real estate agent while agreeing to pay the commission. This can be the best of both worlds. You have no fiduciary duty, but earn your fee. *Wordley Corporation v. Welsh*, 962 P.2d 86 (Utah Ct. App. 1998).

Colorado was one of the first states to establish "nonagency" where a State's Real Estate License Act does not presume agency in real estate transactions. In *Hoff & Leigh, Inc.* v. *Byler*, 62 P.3d 1077 (Col. App. 2002), an owner agreed to pay a real estate brokerage firm a commission if the broker "procured a purchaser for [defendant's] property...which results in the sale of the property." The parties agree that the broker would be a "transaction-broker." When the broker procured a buyer for the property, the owner refused to pay the commission, alleging the insufficiencies in the broker's performance warranted forfeiture of the commission. The trial court found in favor of the broker and awarded the commission.

The appeal centered on the statutory duties imposed on transaction brokers under Colorado law but has wide implications on whether similar legislation has been enacted by other states. The court noted that the Colorado statute was a significant departure from the traditional common law view of agency relationships in real estate transactions, and that the Colorado Act recognized a nonagent real estate professional (the transaction broker). The court noted that the transaction broker is not an agent for either party (which is presumed under Colorado law) "absent a written agency agreement or a sub-agency relationship." The court noted that while a real estate broker acting as agent owes a fiduciary duty to its principal, a transaction broker is not in a fiduciary relationship with either party to a real estate transaction. Under Colorado law, the duties of a transaction broker include: (1) presenting offers and counteroffers in a timely manner; (2) advising the parties and keeping them informed; (3) accounting for money and property received; (4) assisting the parties in complying with contractual terms and conditions; and (5) disclosing certain information. In what may be a key issue, the court noted that the Colorado Real Estate License Act does not prescribe a remedy for nonperformance of these obligations. Therefore, even if it was violated and the duties were not performed, forfeiture of the commission was not a remedy for nonperformance based on the fact that the agent was not a fiduciary. The court further noted, however, that the defendant would have a remedy for any out-of-pocket expenses he accrued as a result of the broker's inaction, but found that the seller never asserted such a claim.

This case may support the theory that a transaction broker may be legally upheld, but really creates confusion over what happens if transaction brokers breach their "duty" as outlined in the License Act. If a real estate license act does not regulate the industry for violations of the statutory duties of its licensees, what in the world is it regulating?

In another Colorado case, *Stearns vs. McGuire*, 2005 WL 3036538 (10th Cir. 2005), there was a similar result.

In October 2001, the purchasers asked the broker to locate an investment property in Boulder, Colorado for them to buy. The purchasers and the broker were long-time friends. In December 2001, the broker approached the owner of an apartment complex and stated that he might have some interested buyers for the apartment complex. Soon thereafter, the broker faxed to the seller a contract to buy and sell real estate signed by the purchasers ("Contract One"). At the end of Contract One, and after the purchasers' signature, the broker checked boxes to indicate that he was the seller's agent and a dual-agent with regard to the transaction. The seller submitted a counterproposal to Contract One, and the broker thereafter faxed a revised contract to buy and sell real estate signed by the purchasers ("Contract Two"). Contract Two gave the broker a 4% commission and indicated, at the bottom after the signature block, that the broker was the seller's agent for purposes of that transaction. The seller executed Contract Two.

The seller later refused to close on the sale of the apartment complex, citing the broker's failure to disclose pertinent information about the (1) Boulder market or the property and (2) his relationship with the purchasers. The seller was out of town and had not been to Boulder for a number of years. The relationship with the purchasers was a deep friendship dating from childhood, in addition to their prior representation in six deals. Ultimately the purchasers brought a specific performance action, and the seller settled by closing.

The broker sued the seller for his commission. The seller answered and asserted a variety of affirmative defenses, including breach of fiduciary duty, and also counterclaims for breach of fiduciary duty, negligence, negligent misrepresentation, and fraud.

The United States District Court for the District of Colorado dismissed the seller's breach of fiduciary duty claim and estoppel affirmative defenses on summary judgment. The seller appealed.

The Tenth Circuit affirmed the District Court's decision and held that the broker acted as a transaction broker and not as the seller's agent because there was no written agreement between the broker and the seller, despite the language at the bottom of Contract Two stating that the broker was the seller's agent. The Tenth Circuit held that Contract Two did not contain a true manifestation of the seller's consent for the broker to serve as his agent, because the seller's signature appeared *before* the declaration of agency relationship.

Apparently, under Colorado law agents don't have any duties, can do "nuthin", and can even get paid for it. **Does the industry want this lack of professionalism? Why would we need licensure?**

FIDUCIARY OBLIGATION—
DUTY OF CARE TO PRINCIPAL

PURPOSE

After carefully reading Chapter 4, the student will be able to:

■ Explain the fiduciary obligations between the agent and the principal.

■ List and define the generally recognized four duties of care from the agent to the principal.

■ Depict proper disclosure.

■ List reasons for TREC to suspend or revoke a license.

■ Explain why fiduciary duties may not terminate with the termination of agency.

■ Describe the problems and benefits of working with a cooperating broker.

■ Define: "double escrow, flip, closings, and cooperating broker."

Key Words to look for in this chapter:
1. OLD CAR
2. Performance
3. Reasonable care
4. Loyalty
5. Accounting
6. Section 1101.652 TRELA
7. Duty of Care: Cooperating Broker
8. Tortious interference
9. Minimum level of services

The principal and agent relationship creates a **fiduciary** obligation between the parties. The fiduciary is required to exercise fidelity and good faith toward his or her principal in all matters within the scope of his or her employment. *Chien v. Chen*, 759 S.W.2d 484, 495, n.7 (Tex. App.-Austin 1988). The agent cannot put himself or herself in a position contrary to his or her principal's interest. *NRC, Inc. v. Huddleston*, 886 S.W.2d 526 (Tex. App.-Austin 1994). The fiduciary relationship also imposes upon the agent the positive duty of communicating all information he or she may possess or acquire which is, or may be, material to his or her principal's advantage. *Barnsdall Oil Co. v. Willis*, 152 F.2d 825 (5th Cir. 1946).

In times past the real estate agent's duty has been to the seller. At one time we presumed seller agency, but with the onset of buyer brokerage and the perceived need for buyers to have representation, we have seen a developing area of law: buyer representation. The rules, however, appear to be the same regardless of who is the principal. Buyer representation merely creates new fact situations with which agents may be unfamiliar. These issues will be discussed later in this text.

Texas law has generally recognized four duties of care from the agent to the principal. These duties are performance, accounting, reasonable care, and loyalty. Some instructors like to use the acronym "OLD CAR" (obedience, loyalty, disclosure, confidentiality, accounting, and reasonable care) or "OLD CARP" (obedience, loyalty, disclosure, confidentiality, accounting, reasonable care, and performance). Anything that helps you remember, use it! The duty of care of the buyer's broker is not as well defined under Texas case law. Are they the same duties of care as those to the seller? This will be discussed in greater detail in a later chapter.

But first! – Let's talk about a recent 2005 change in the Texas Real Estate License Act. The legislature clearly restated Texas's position on agency. The Real Estate License Act, as amended, states:

> A broker who represents a party in a real estate transaction or who lists real estate for sale under an exclusive agreement for a party *is that party's agent.*

The new legislation creates a **minimum level of services**. A broker who is an agent:

■ *must* inform the party if the broker receives material information related to a transaction to list, buy, sell, or lease the party's real estate, including the receipt of an offer by the broker; and

■ *shall*, at a minimum, answer the party's questions and present any offer to or from the party.

A big issue has always been contacting a broker's principal directly. The Real Estate License Act (§110.1.652(b)(22)) says a licensee should not negotiate or attempt to negotiate with a principal with knowledge that that person is a party to an outstanding exclusive agency agreement.

This provision, however, notes that the delivery of an offer to a party does not violate the Act if that party's broker consents to the delivery, a copy of the offer is sent to the party's broker, and the person delivering the offer does not otherwise engage in activity that violates the Act. (See §1101.557(C)(3).)

This law is somewhat controversial. What if a principal doesn't want the agent to be involved (the principal is a real estate lawyer who doesn't think he needs the service)? This statute seems to indicate that these minimum services *must* or *shall* be provided. The other side of the issue is equally provocative. Shouldn't a licensed agent provide services? If not, why were they hired? Hmmm.

PERFORMANCE

Performance can be described as the agent doing his job. Texas law has said that the primary responsibility of the seller's agent is the duty of obtaining for their principal the highest price then obtainable and known to them. *Ramsey v. Gordon*, 567 S.W.2d 868 (Tex. Civ. App.-Waco 1978); *Riley v. Powell*, 665 S.W.2d 578 (Tex. Civ. App.-Ft. Worth 1984). Other states and publications have described this duty of care to be one of "obedience." See *Latten & Blum v. Richmond*, 388 So.2d 368 (La. 1980).

Riley v. Powell, *665 S.W.2d 578 (Tex. Civ. App.-Ft. Worth 1984)*

Dale Riley was the listing agent of Sylvia C. Powell when he contracted to purchase Sylvia's apartment complex. His listing on the property called for him to receive a 4 percent commission on the purchase.

Sylvia claimed that Dale owed her a fiduciary duty to protect her best interests and to get the best possible price for the property. Dale knew or had good reason to believe that the property was worth considerably more than the $450,000 that he contracted to pay for the property because, as Sylvia's broker, Dale had received an offer for about $700,000, which he failed to present.

Before closing, Dale failed to fulfill the financial obligations of the contract in that he assumed no personal liability for the loan. The seller's only recourse would be to foreclose on the property in case of default.

For these reasons, Sylvia claimed the contract with Dale void and refused to close. The eventual sale to a third party was for $700,000. Dale sued for specific performance.

One who seeks specific performance must comply with all contractual obligations. The Court of Appeals denied a rehearing of the case and affirmed the judgment of the District Court, which included withdrawal of the case from the jury and a take nothing judgment.

DISCUSSION QUESTIONS

■ Was the contract valid?

■ What agency problems can arise when the listing broker becomes the buyer?

- List the duties of care of performance for a buyer's broker (i.e., what has the buyer's broker been employed to do?).

- Can you list additional duties of care of performance that a seller's broker may have other than those designated in *Riley v. Powell*?

REASONABLE CARE

The duty of reasonable care generally implies competence and expertise on the part of the licensee. This is required because licensees have been issued a license and permitted to hold themselves out to the public to be qualified by training and experience to render a specialized service in the field of a real estate transaction. *Perkins v. Thorpe*, 676 P.2d 52 (Idaho Ct. App. 1985). Otherwise, the licensure would serve only as a foil to lure the unsuspecting public.

The licensee has a duty to disclose knowledge of material facts concerning the property and cannot become a party to any fraud or misrepresentation likely to affect the judgment of the principal. *Schroeder v. Rose*, 701 P.2d 327 (Idaho App. 1985). It is also important to note that when a special agency converts to a general agency because of the authority conferred on the agent by the principal (either ostensible or actual), the broker has a duty of care to see that there is no liability incurred on behalf of the principal. For example, in one case, the agent was found liable for preparing financial statements for his seller in the sale of a business. *Lunden v. Smith*, 632 P.2d 1344 (Ore. Ct. App. 1981). Similarly, a broker should not promise the availability of financing on a new house to encourage the sale of an old one. *Youngblood v. Wall*, 815 S.W.2d 512 (Tenn. App. 1991). A Texas court has held that an agent can't slander the title of his principal by recording a document in an effort to maintain an action for his commission. *Walker v. Ruggles*, 540 S.W.2d 470 (Tex. Civ. App.-Houston 1976).

Walker v. Ruggles, 540 S.W.2d 470 (Tex. Civ. App.-Houston 1976)

Robert L. Ruggles and his wife sued Sandra and Leonard Walker d/b/a Walker and Associates, REALTORS®, for damages because of slander of title. The court held that the broker maliciously, deliberately, and without probable cause interfered in the sale of the Ruggles' home by filing in the public records an earnest money contract, which the owners refused to sign, in part, because it had an incorrect legal description.

The court held that they had also interfered in the sale by distributing a letter to area title companies and real estate agencies falsely stating that they had a judgment against the owners. After the listing expired, the Ruggles relisted their home with another agent who was unable to sell the property after the circulation of the letter in which the

Walkers not only claimed to have a judgment against the Ruggles, but also stated their plan to collect a full commission should the property sell. The Ruggles took the house off the market and rented it.

The court awarded reasonable expenses, actual damages, and exemplary damages to the Ruggles and ordered the filed contract removed from the public record.

The Walkers appealed. The judgment of the trial court was affirmed.

DISCUSSION QUESTIONS

■ Did the Walkers have a right to a commission? Why?

■ What fiduciary duties, if any, did the Walkers breach?

Note that §1101.652(b)(1) of the TRELA enables the Texas Real Estate Commission to revoke the license of a licensee for acting negligently or incompetently as a licensee. As set out in Chapter 1, the Canons of Ethics require a real estate agent to be knowledgeable and informed of market conditions. How does a licensee keep from acting incompetently or negligently? Give good advice. Stay informed. Principals may need advice on certain real estate issues such as sales information, market data, and pertinent local topics. Common issues could include information on homeowners' associations, municipal utility districts, deed restrictions, and lead-based paint information. These issues will be discussed in greater detail in later chapters.

■ Obtain a copy of the *Real Estate Advisor* (a Texas Real Estate Commission publication available on TREC's Web site). How many brokers this month have had their licenses revoked for violation of the negligence or incompetence provision?

■ Discuss ways in which a special agent can become a general agent because activities of the principal give the agent additional authority. Does the purchaser have the right to rely on statements, such as accounting, cash flow, disclosure statements, prepared by the agent on behalf of the seller even if the agent is not competent in this area?

LOYALTY

It has been held by at least one court that the obligations imposed by the fiduciary duty of loyalty are the chief virtue required of the broker. *Rose v. Showalter*, 108 Idaho 631, 701 P.2d 251 (Idaho App. 1985). This loyalty includes the duty of care of **putting your principal's interest above that of your own**. For instance, you can't use your knowledge of the principal's pressing financial condition to encourage a low offer. *Rose v. Showalter*, supra. Article VII of the REALTORS® Code of Ethics requires that REALTORS® pledge to protect and promote the interests of their clients. The duty of loyalty is an all-encompassing duty of **full disclosure** to your principal of all material facts known to the agent. The agent must give his principal a full, fair, and timely disclosure of all facts within the agent's knowledge that are, or may be, material to the transaction and that might affect the principal's rights and interests or influence his victims (term used by the court, a Freudian slip?). *Mallory v. Watt*, 594 P.2d 629 (Wash. 1979). A material fact is one that the reasonable person might think is important in his or her choice of actions. See Texas Real Estate License Act §1101.652(b)(3) and (4) and *Foster v. Cross*, 650 P.2d 406 (Alaska 1982).

The Real Estate Commission Regulations deal with loyalty in a number of areas, but Section 535.156 (referencing Texas Real Estate License Act §1101.652(b)(2)) makes it very clear that a licensee's relationship with his principal is a fiduciary one and that the licensee must (1) put the interest of the licensee's principal above the licensee's own interest, and (2) convey to the principal all known information that would affect the principal's decision on whether to make, accept, or reject offers, unless the principal has agreed otherwise, and (3) keep the principal informed at all times of significant information applicable to the transaction.

There is an old saying that bad facts make bad law. In the issues that are about to be discussed, you will find that most reasonable agents would not have engaged in the misconduct. Nonetheless, these actions have resulted in a number of precedent-setting cases that focus on proper disclosure to the principal:

Flip Closings

An agent must disclose to the principal that there is a potential buyer, eliminating a "double escrow" or "flip" closing, where the agent profits at the expense of his principal. *Southern Cross Industries, Inc. v. Martin*, 604 S.W.2d 290 (Tex. Civ. App.-San Antonio 1980). A "flip" can occur when a broker buys his own listing at a lower price, then simultaneously sells to a buyer at a higher price. There are similar holdings in other states. *The State of Nevada, Department of Commerce, Real Estate Division v. Scholler*, 656 P.2d 224 (Nev. 1982); *Ellis v. Flink*, 301 So.2d 493 (Fla. App. 1974); *Mersky v. Multiple Listing Bureau of Olympia, Inc.*, 437 P.2d 897 (Wash. 1968); and *Jorgensen v. Beach 'N' Bay Realty*, 125 Cal. App. 3d 155 (4th Dist. 1981). Texas Real Estate

Commission regulations require a real estate licensee to advise a property owner as to the licensee's opinion of the market value of the property when offering to purchase the property for the licensee's own account as a result of a contact made while acting as a real estate agent. See 535.16(c). See also, *Ellison v. Alley*, 842 S.W.2d 605 (Tenn. 1992).

Increase in Value

A broker can breach duties of loyalty and reasonable care if he fails to disclose that the value of the property has increased during the listing period and uses that knowledge to the disadvantage to buy from his principal, *Ramsey v. Gordon*, 567 S.W.2d 868 (Tex. Civ. App.-Waco 1978), or that the value of the property would be higher if subdivided. *Ridgeway v. McGuire*, 158 P.2d 893 (Ore. 1945).

Financial Status

Seller agents have also been held liable for failing to disclose a purchaser's poor financial status when the seller is financing the transaction, *White v. Boucher*, 322 N.W.2d 560 (Minn. 1982), although the broker is not responsible for the nonperformance of a party. *Baxter & Swinford, Inc. v. Mercier*, 671 S.W.2d 139 (Tex. Civ. App.-Houston 1984); *Zwick v. United Farm Agency, Inc.*, 556 P.2d 508 (Wyo. 1976). If a broker has no control over the decisions of his principal, the broker is not responsible for that principal's direction or decision. *James Shore v. Thomas A. Sweeney & Assoc.*, 864 S.W. 2d 182 (Tex. App.-Tyler 1993, no writ). Brokers can't be held liable for the condition or nonperformance of an earnest money contract, such as the guarantee of completion of repairs. *McGinney v. Jackson*, 575 So.2d 1070 (Ala. 1991).

Potential Litigation

In a Virginia Supreme Court case, a broker was held liable for failure to disclose a dispute that occurred at the closing that ultimately involved the seller in litigation. The court held that the broker should have informed the principal of the dispute at the closing (the seller didn't attend) so that the seller could have made the decision on how to handle the conflict. *Owen v. Shelton*, 277 S.E.2d 123 (Va. 1981). A similar result occurred in Texas when a broker failed to disclose to the seller that the lender was about to foreclose on the seller's house. In this case, the seller was out of the state and did not realize that the property had been posted for foreclosure (although he realized he hadn't made his payments for several months!). The court held the broker liable for failing to disclose that the foreclosure was imminent. *Kinnard v. Homann*, 750 S.W.2d 30 (Tex. App.-Austin 1988).

Agent Is a Purchaser

An obvious failure to disclose would be the broker's failure to reveal his relationship with the purchaser, particularly if the purchaser is willing to give the broker an interest in the property as a part of his commission, *Rose v. Showalter*, supra., *Velten v. Robertson*, 671 P.2d 1011 (Colo. App. 1983); or that the broker is a relative of the purchaser, *Mersky v. Multiple Listing Bureau of Olympia, Inc.*, 437 P.2d 897 (Wash. 1968); or that the broker is a partner of the purchaser. *Nix v. Born*, 870 S.W.2d 635 (Tex. App.-El Paso 1994).

The disclosure that the broker *may* be a principal is not enough. Brokers must make the definite disclosure of their involvement with the purchaser. *Gordin v. Schuler*, 704 S.W.2d 403 (Tex. Civ. App.-Dallas 1985). This includes buyer's brokers and dual agents. Failure to inform an agent's dual capacity can also breach a fiduciary duty. *Gillmore v. Morelli*, 472 N.W.2d 738 (N.D. 1991). A California case has held it is a breach of fiduciary duty to fail to disclose that the agent was the buyer's broker while obtaining the listing. *Culver v. Jaoudi Industries*, 1 Cal. Rptr. 2nd 680 (Cal. Ct. App. 1991). On occasion, licensees have a seller who really needs to sell. The broker may think that by purchasing the property himself, the broker is doing a favor for the principal. This does not replace the fiduciary duty, though. It might not be a defense that the agent acted in the best interest of the principal, or in good faith, if he or she operates adverse to the interest of his or her principal. *Johnson Realty, Inc. v. Hand*, 377 S.E.2d 176 (Ga. App. 1988). A Florida case has held that a broker needed to disclose the broker's romantic relationship with a client's ex-spouse's divorce attorney indicating that this information was material and "might reasonably expected to influence complete loyalty of the broker to the principal's interest or that might reasonably expected to influence to the principal in negotiations." *Silverman v. Pitterman*, 574 So.2d 275 (Fla. Dist. Ct. App. 1991).

The South Carolina Supreme Court has noted that "there is repugnancy of one serving as both broker for a principal and the purchaser for that same principal." *Darby v. Furman*, 513 S.E.2d 848 (S.C. 1999). The Oklahoma Supreme Court has stated that if the broker is also the purchaser, the listing contracts become voidable. *Kincaid v. Black Angus Motel, Inc.*, P.2d (Okla. 1999).

If the agent is profiting at the expense of this principal, the extent of that profit needs to be disclosed. In *Roberts v. Lomanto* 5 Cal.Rptr.3d 866 (Cal. App. 2003), a listing agent was a purchaser and assigned her contract to a new purchaser for a substantial profit. The court held that there was a breach of fiduciary duty for failing to disclose the extent of that profit to her seller.

Culver v. Jaoudi Industries, 1 Cal. Rptr. 2nd 680 (Cal. Ct. App. 1991)

L. Byron Culver & Associates represented Del Rayo, a business entity of Gene Klein, as a buyer's broker. Culver asked one of its agents, Frank Whiteside, to contact Jaoudi, a potential seller, on February 8, 1985. Jaoudi indicated that the property was for sale but that five lots within the property were in escrow to Arthofer Industries and he was unsure if the sale would close. Jaoudi gave Culver a one-time listing for that particular property with a 3 percent commission. Culver is now employed by both buyer and seller!? Whiteside stated that he had a potential buyer and would get back with him.

On February 13th, the agent presented Jaoudi with a written offer to purchase the entire property from Del Rayo. Jaoudi countered, and they finally agreed on the price of

$1,750,000, with a contingency on the cancellation of the escrow with Arthofer. On February 15, 1985, Jaoudi signed the written offer. The separate escrow instructions for closing were signed by Jaoudi, but did not include the contingency. Jaoudi mentioned the contingency to Culver, but Culver said that he would hold escrow until after the Arthofer escrow was cancelled. Culver also denied any association between Culver and Del Rayo when the seller asked.

On February 16, 1985, Arthofer refused to cancel the escrow for the five lots. When Jaoudi contacted Culver and told him of the refusal, the agent told the seller that the deal was beyond his control because all the instruments had been signed and that it was up to Del Rayo. Jaoudi told the escrow company not to close with Del Rayo until he contacted them.

In the meantime, Arthofer had contacted Del Rayo and objected to their deal with Jaoudi. Culver recommended to Jaoudi that if he signed a deed before Arthofer filed a lis pendens, the seller would be "home free." Jaoudi signed the deed on February 20th. On March 18th, Jaoudi told the escrow company to close with Del Rayo and not to pay the commission to Culver.

Culver sued the seller for the commission. The court found that an undisclosed dual agency existed and denied recovery. The agent appealed, and the Court of Appeals upheld the lower court's ruling, holding that the evidence confirmed that the agent represented the interest of both seller and buyer without disclosure. No commission could be paid.

MLS® Burglaries

In *Moore v. Harry Norman, Inc. REALTORS®*, 404 S.E.2d 793 (Ga. Ct. App. 1991), homeowners sued the real estate broker and the multiple listing service for negligence because a burglar gained access to her home through her lockbox. The court held that the broker did breach a fiduciary duty to a homeowner by failing to disclose information regarding occurrences of other lockbox burglaries in the area. There was evidence that the services board made and delivered decisions not to communicate concerns over previous lockbox burglaries to its member brokers. The court further held that neither the service nor the broker were shielded from liability because of the indemnity clause in their listing agreement.

DISCUSSION QUESTIONS

- What did the agent do to establish dual agency?

■ What could the agent have done to remain the agent of the buyer? Could the agent have been the agent of only the seller?

Offer to Purchase

An often questioned issue is tendering offers to purchase. Although there are no recent Texas cases on point, there are two cases very much on point that all offers of purchasers must be submitted; if not, it is a failure of the fiduciary duty of loyalty. *Virginia Real Estate Commission v. Bias*, 308 S.E.2d 123 (Va. 1983). This is true even if the broker believes it is too low to warrant consideration. *Strout Realty Agency, Inc. v. Wooster*, 99 A.2d (Maine 1953).

Note that the Texas Real Estate Commission has a specific regulation [§535.156(a)] that requires a licensee to convey to the principal all known information that would affect the principal's decision on whether or not to make, accept, or reject offers. However, if the principal has agreed in writing that offers are not to be submitted after the principal has entered into a contract to buy, sell, rent, or lease the property, the licensee has no duty to submit offers to the principal after the principal has accepted an offer. A licensee also has an affirmative duty to keep the principal informed at all times of significant information applicable to the transaction or transactions in which the licensee is acting as agent for the principal.

Amended Contracts

You will recall from Chapter 2 that there was also a breach of fiduciary duty because of the broker's failing to disclose the listing agreement as an exclusive-right-to-sell listing agreement. *Lyle v. Moore*, supra. This includes any failure to disclose any changes in the listing agreement. *Rose v. Showalter*, supra.

Perhaps the most important issue of disclosure is that the **disclosure must be made**. It is not enough just to offer to disclose the information. The broker is obligated to advise his or her principal fully of all facts within the agent's knowledge that could reasonably be calculated to influence the principal's actions. *Hercules v. Robedeaux, Inc.*, 329 N.W.2d 240 (Wisconsin Civ. App. 1982).

If the broker is asked a question, he can't respond negligently. *Schroeder v. Rose*, supra. If the broker prepares two offers, he must submit both, not just the lower offer. In these situations, it is particularly important if the broker is getting a full commission on the one offer submitted while being required to split the commission on the offer not submitted. If the broker thinks another offer is on its way (promised tomorrow morning at 9:00 A.M.), the broker should also share this information with the seller so the seller can determine whether he or she wants to wait for that offer. *Jeffery Allen Industries, Inc. v. Sheldon F. Goode & Co.*, 505 N.E.2d 1104 (Ill. App. 1987); *Southern Cross Industries, Inc. v. Martin*, 604 S.W.2d 290 (Tex. Civ. App.-San Antonio 1980).

Because of the duty of disclosure, it is always dangerous to purchase the principal's property. See *Ramsey v. Gordon*, below:

Ramsey v. Gordon, 567 S.W.2d 868 (Tex. Civ. App.-Waco 1978)

Ramsey Properties and Western Real Estate sued John T. Gordon, James M. Barton Real Estate, and Joshua Real Estate for damages in a breach of sales contract and loss of a co-brokerage commission (Ramsey attempted to purchase property from Gordon for resale). Gordon filed a cross-action against Ramsey and Robertson for $90,000 actual damages and $100,000 exemplary damages.

Ramsey was in the business of buying and holding land for resale. Ramsey was a licensed real estate broker. Gordon signed an earnest money contract, dated September 1973, agreeing to sell his property to Ramsey and giving Ramsey a commission (3 percent sales price). On November 2, 1973, Gordon, through his attorney, sent a letter to Robertson stating that because of buyer's nonperformance, Gordon had decided not to convey the property to Ramsey and ultimately sold the property to another purchaser.

It was undisputed that Ramsey, the real estate broker, had engaged other negotiations to sell the property at a profit. Ramsey then sued for a commission. Gordon argued that Ramsey was only a purchaser. Although Ramsey claims he was only a purchaser in the transaction with Gordon, he testified in the trial that he was both agent and purchaser . . . that he was "a purchasing agent," confirming that he was Gordon's agent for the sale of the property that he had purchased. There was additional testimony that Ramsey knew the property had appreciated in value when the contract was made and failed to disclose that fact to Gordon.

Ramsey claimed to have lost $90,000 profit on the resale of the property and a loss of commissions because of the misconduct of the defendants. Gordon pleaded that Ramsey failed in his duty to obtain the highest price available without disclosing increasing land value and sought to purchase the property for personal gain. Gordon further argued that when an agent breaches his duty to his principal by having a personal interest, a contract is voidable at the option of the seller. The court reaffirmed the "settled rule" that "an agent in dealing with a principal on his own account owes it to the principal not only to make no misstatements concerning the subject matter of the transaction, but also to disclose to him fully and completely all material facts known to the agent that might affect the principal; and that unless this duty on the part of the agent has been met, the principal cannot be held to ratify the transaction."

After the court's hearing a take-nothing judgment was given against all parties. Ramsey alone appealed. The verdict was affirmed by the appellate court.

The agent must not take advantage of the naiveté of the consumer. Texas law has held that the consumer is "ignorant, unthinking, and credulous." *Spradling v. Williams*, 566 S.W.2d 561 (Tex. 1978). Consumers, then, are not regarded by the law as being knowledgeable and have the right to believe anything that a competent, educated, licensed real estate agent tells them.

Weitzel v. Barnes, 691 S.W.2d 598 (Tex. 1985)

Dennis and Lori Weitzel contracted to purchase a remodeled home from Barnes/Segraves Development Company. Their contract gave the buyers the right to inspect the plumbing and air conditioning systems. After signing the contract, the Weitzels attempted to move into the house prior to closing and found a "condemned" notice on the house. In spite of the notice, they did not have the house inspected. The Weitzels claimed that they did not inspect the house because of the development company's oral representations that the plumbing and air conditioning complied with Fort Worth's code requirements. After closing, the purchasers found that the equipment did not work. The seller's representations were false, misleading, and deceptive; the equipment did not meet city code specifications.

The Weitzels brought suit against the sellers for deceptive trade practices. The court found that oral representations can serve as the basis of a DTPA action, and that the defendant's representations were false and misleading. It found that, even with a contract allowing an inspection, the misrepresentations were actionable under the act. The Weitzels were awarded treble damages and attorney's fees by the trial court. On appeal the court of appeals reversed the judgment. The Supreme Court of Texas reversed that judgment and affirmed the judgment of the first court.

There was a dissenting opinion. Justice Gonzalez stated that he could not "believe that the Legislature ever intended for the Deceptive Trade Practices Act to be used to bail out an attorney (the purchaser was an attorney) who" writes the sales contract and "does not inspect the used house he purchases even though he had actual notice, prior to closing, that the city had condemned the property."

DISCUSSION QUESTIONS

■ What would have been your decision? Why?

■ Does the information in the dissenting opinion make any difference to your decision in the first question? If so, how?

ACCOUNTING

Any and all funds that come to the hands of real estate agents that belong to another are trust funds. They are supposed to be accounted for separately and deposited on or before the second banking day following the receipt of the funds in a non-interest-bearing real estate trust account, unless directed by their principal to do otherwise.

In *Kilgore v. Texas Real Estate Commission*, 565 S.W.2d 114 (Tex. Civ. App.-Ft. Worth 1978), a broker interpled money that he held into the registry of the court pending a lawsuit, contrary to the then Texas Real Estate Commission's rules to disburse it to the seller, his client. The court cited that the real estate licensure is a privilege, not a right, and upheld the Real Estate Commission's revocation of the broker's license for not properly accounting for funds in accordance with the orders of the Texas Real Estate Commission. The real holding of this case is probably that brokers should not be escrow agents for earnest money.

In the event money is misappropriated, an aggrieved person is entitled to go to the recovery fund (see Chapter 6) as a result of a court decision for violating the Texas Real Estate License Act. *Texas Real Estate Commission v. Century 21 Security Realty, Inc.*, 598 S.W.2d 920 (Tex. Civ. App.-El Paso 1980). Even a sponsoring broker can take advantage of this fund. In Century 21 Security Realty, a sponsoring broker went to the Texas Real Estate Commission to repay funds, which were misappropriated by his salesperson. Under the theory of equitable subrogation, since he had reimbursed the aggrieved parties for their misappropriated funds, the court upheld the sponsoring broker's right to be reimbursed because the Texas Real Estate Commission, upon licensing the agent, had indicated that the agent was honest and trustworthy.

LICENSE SUSPENSION AND REVOCATIONS

Section 1101.652 of the Texas Real Estate License Act provides that a license may be suspended or revoked for the following breaches of duty to the seller:

(a) The commission may suspend or revoke a license issued under this chapter or take other disciplinary action authorized by this chapter if the license holder:

(1) enters a plea of guilty or nolo contendere to or is convicted of a felony in which fraud is an essential element, and the time for appeal has elapsed or the judgment or conviction has been affirmed on appeal, without regard to an order granting community supervision that suspends the imposition of the sentence;

(2) procures or attempts to procure a license under this chapter for the license holder or a salesperson by fraud, misrepresentation, or deceit or by making a material misstatement of fact in an application for a license;

(3) engages in misrepresentation, dishonesty, or fraud when selling, buying, trading, or leasing real property in the license holder's own name;

(4) fails to honor, within a reasonable time, a check issued to the commission after the commission has sent by certified mail a request for payment to the license holder's last known business address according to commission records;

(5) fails or refuses to produce on request, for inspection by the commission or a commission representative, a document, book, or record that is in the license holder's possession and relates to a real estate transaction conducted by the license holder;

(6) fails to provide, within a reasonable time, information requested by the commission that relates to a formal or informal complaint to the commission that would indicate a violation of this chapter;

(7) fails to surrender to the owner, without just cause, a document or instrument that is requested by the owner and that is in the license holder's possession;

(8) fails to use a contract form required by the commission under Section 1101.155; or

(9) disregards or violates this chapter.

(b) The commission may suspend or revoke a license issued under this chapter or take other disciplinary action authorized by this chapter if the license holder, *while acting as a broker or salesperson:*

(1) acts negligently or incompetently;

(2) engages in conduct that is dishonest or in bad faith or that demonstrates untrustworthiness;

(3) makes a material misrepresentation to a potential buyer concerning a significant defect, including a latent structural defect, known to the license holder that would be a significant factor to a reasonable and prudent buyer in making a decision to purchase real property;

(4) fails to disclose to a potential buyer a defect described by Subdivision (3) that is known to the license holder;

(5) makes a false promise that is likely to influence a person to enter into an agreement when the license holder is unable or does not intend to keep the promise;

(6) pursues a continued and flagrant course of misrepresentation or makes false promises through an agent or salesperson, through advertising, or otherwise;

(7) fails to make clear to all parties to a real estate transaction the party for whom the license holder is acting;

(8) receives compensation from more than one party to a real estate transaction without the full knowledge and consent of all parties to the transaction;

(9) fails within a reasonable time to properly account for or remit money that is received by the license holder and that belongs to another person;

(10) commingles money that belongs to another person with the license holder's own money;

(11) pays a commission or a fee to or divides a commission or a fee with a person other than a license holder or a real estate broker or salesperson licensed in another state for compensation for services as a real estate agent;

(12) fails to specify a definite termination date that is not subject to prior notice in a contract, other than a contract to perform property management services, in which the license holder agrees to perform services for which a license is required under this chapter;

(13) accepts, receives, or charges an undisclosed commission, rebate, or direct profit on an expenditure made for a principal;

(14) solicits, sells, or offers for sale real property by means of a lottery;

(15) solicits, sells, or offers for sale real property by means of a deceptive practice;

(16) acts in a dual capacity as broker and undisclosed principal in a real estate transaction;

(17) guarantees or authorizes or permits a person to guarantee that future profits will result from a resale of real property;

(18) places a sign on real property offering the real property for sale or lease without obtaining the written consent of the owner of the real property or the owner's authorized agent;

(19) offers to sell or lease real property without the knowledge and consent of the owner of the real property or the owner's authorized agent;

(20) offers to sell or lease real property on terms other than those authorized by the owner of the real property or the owner's authorized agent;

(21) induces or attempts to induce a party to a contract of sale or lease to break the contract for the purpose of substituting a new contract;

(22) negotiates or attempts to negotiate the sale, exchange, or lease of real property with an owner, landlord, buyer, or tenant with knowledge that that person is a party to an outstanding written contract that grants exclusive agency to another broker in connection with the transaction;

(23) publishes or causes to be published an advertisement, including an advertisement by newspaper, radio, television, the Internet or display, that misleads or is likely to deceive the public, tends to create a misleading impression, or fails to identify the person causing the advertisement to be published as a licensed broker or agent;

(24) withholds from or inserts into a statement of account or invoice a statement that the license holder knows makes the statement of account or invoice inaccurate in a material way;

(25) publishes or circulates an unjustified or unwarranted threat of a legal proceeding or other action;

(26) establishes an association by employment or otherwise with a person other than a license holder if the person is expected or required to act as a license holder;

(27) aids, abets, or conspires with another person to circumvent this chapter;

(28) fails or refuses to provide, on request, a copy of a document relating to a real estate transaction to a person who signed the document;

(29) fails to advise a buyer in writing before the closing of a real estate transaction that the buyer should:
  (A) have the abstract covering the real estate that is the subject of the contract examined by an attorney chosen by the buyer; or
  (B) be provided with or obtain a title insurance policy;

(30) fails to deposit, within a reasonable time, money the license holder receives as escrow agent in a real estate transaction:
  (A) in trust with a title company authorized to do business in this state; or
  (B) in a custodial, trust, or escrow account maintained for that purpose in a banking institution authorized to do business in this state;

(31) disburses money deposited in a custodial, trust, or escrow account, as provided in Subdivision (30), before the completion or termination of the real estate transaction;

(32) discriminates against an owner, potential buyer, landlord, or potential tenant on the basis of race, color, religion, sex, national origin, or ancestry, including directing a prospective buyer or tenant interested in equivalent properties to a different area based on the race, color, religion, sex, national origin, or ancestry of the potential owner or tenant; or

(33) disregards or violates this chapter.

The commission may not investigate under this section a complaint submitted more than four years after the date of the incident involving a real estate broker or salesperson that is the subject of the complaint.

DISCUSSION QUESTIONS

■ Could the same 1101.652 items be violated when representing the buyer?

■ Since Texas law allows a broker to represent both parties as principals, how does a broker determine which information is "confidential" and can't be disclosed versus those items that may make a material difference in the other party's decision to purchase? List confidential information that, in your opinion, should not be disclosed.

An often overlooked issue concerning fiduciary duty is that the duty may not terminate. For instance, once brokers have obtained the confidence and trust of the principal, they can't turn around, shed their fiduciary obligations, and act like they were not privy to that confidential information. *Southern Cross Industries, Inc. v. Martin*, 604 S.W.2d 290 (Tex. Civ. App.-San Antonio 1980). In effect, the brokerage employment relationship may terminate, but the broker's knowledge of the confidential information still puts him or her in a distinct position of being able to take advantage of the seller's confidential information. So the fiduciary duty by itself may not end. *Swallows v. Laney*, 691 P.2d 874 (N.M. 1984).

A very tough case involved leasing of commercial office space is *Coldwell Banker v. Camelback Office Park*, 751 P.2d 530 (Arizona App. 1988):

Coldwell Banker v. Camelback Office Park, 751 P.2d 530 (Arizona App. 1988)

Camelback Office Park was a joint venture formed to develop a four-story office building, the Arboleda. Before completion of the building, Camelback entered into an exclusive lease listing agreement with Coldwell Banker. This agreement could be terminated by Coldwell Banker for any reason upon thirty days written notice. In the event of cancellation, Coldwell was to provide Camelback a list of prospects with whom the agency was "actively negotiating" at the time of termination. If anyone listed became a tenant within a period of six months from the termination date, Coldwell would be the procuring broker and would be paid according to the listing agreement.

Coldwell Banker was also the listing broker for a competing office building close to the Arboleda, the Transamerica building. When Camelback became upset because of this conflict, they were persuaded to let Coldwell continue their exclusive agency if John Amory, one of their senior brokers, were assigned to the Camelback building. Amory disclosed his major listings and explained that he felt none of these buildings would be in direct competition because of the difference in the rental rates.

Ted Gianas, an independent broker, approached Amory looking for information about possible additional office space for American Express in the Camelback area. He outlined a proposal for leasing office space in the Camelback building.

On July 21, 1982, Camelback terminated its listing with Coldwell stating that the agency was not working hard enough to find tenants. The termination took effect about August 20th. On August 23rd, Coldwell presented its list of prospective tenants. Negotiations between American Express and Camelback continued without Coldwell. On August 24th, American Express signed a letter of intent outlining the lease proposal that was recommended to the management. The letter was accompanied by a "good faith" deposit, which Camelback could keep if management did not approve the proposal.

On October 12th American Express met Amory, the broker for the Hartford Center in the Black Canyon area, and asked about space in that property.

Amory showed the Hartford building to American Express officials. American Express began negotiations with Hartford through Amory who made no effort to persuade the company to reconsider the Camelback building, nor did he make any attempt to tell Camelback.

When Camelback learned that American Express was no longer interested, they went to New York to talk with corporate management trying to get them to reconsider their rejection of the Camelback lease. Negotiations were renewed. The resulting lease was drastically different from the original proposal.

Since the lease was signed within the six-month period after their listing was terminated, Coldwell Banker asked for, and Camelback refused, to pay the commission. Coldwell filed suit for its commission. Camelback argued that they had no right to a commission because they had breached their fiduciary duties. Camelback countersued, saying that they had been damaged by Coldwell's actions regarding the potential lease between them and American Express.

The trial court found no causal relationship, so no commission was owed. The court also found that Camelback did not prove its counterclaim. Both parties appealed.

The appellate court found Camelback to be the prevailing party and awarded them attorney's fees and court costs. Otherwise, they affirmed the judgment of the trial court.

DISCUSSION QUESTIONS

- Which decision do you agree with, and why?

- In the Camelback case, was there dual agency?

- How much disclosure is enough disclosure?

A very important agency fiduciary and disclosure case involved Edina Realty, Inc.:

Dismuke v. Edina Realty, Inc., 1993 WL 327771 (Minn. Dist. Ct.)

Edina Realty, Inc. is a licensed real estate brokerage in Minnesota. Often one Edina sales associate represented the buyer and another associate represented the sellers in the same transaction, making dual agency transactions for the firm.

Edina disclosed its dual agency by using an agency disclosure statement in its standard purchase agreement or sales contract. The company required both seller and buyer to initial the disclosure statement:

AGENCY DISCLOSURE: _____
(selling agent)

STIPULATED HE OR SHE IS REPRESENTING THE _____ IN THIS TRANSACTION. THE LISTING AGENT OR BROKER STIPULATES HE OR SHE IS REPRESENTING THE SELLER IN THIS TRANSACTION. BUYER & SELLER INITIAL:

Buyer(s) _____   Seller(s)_____

In each case the sellers acknowledged that they had initialed and were aware that Edina Realty sales associates represented the sellers and the buyers. The company relied only on the disclosure statement to disclose and explain its dual agency.

Sellers sued on behalf of themselves and others in their same situation. They claimed that Edina breached its fiduciary duty of undivided loyalty to the sellers by failing "to fully and adequately disclose the consequences and effect of its dual agency status." Edina claimed that the disclosure statement satisfied disclosure requirements of the state's law.

The court found that while the disclosure appeared to comply with state statutory requirements, it was not a full or adequate disclosure of all facts required under common law. Since the "plaintiffs need not prove actual injury or intentional fraud," the "plaintiffs are entitled to judgment as a matter of law."

DISCUSSION QUESTIONS

■ What impact do you see this case having in our approach to agency disclosure?

■ What would be a "full and adequate" disclosure?

The agency duties are under new scrutiny and refinement. It is, therefore, extremely important for the real estate licensee to know and understand the fiduciary duties of care to the principal.

DUTY OF CARE OF THE COOPERATING BROKER

Definition

The cooperating broker is generally regarded as the selling broker (as distinguished from the salesperson) who is not the listing broker and has no contract with the principal. The cooperating broker is generally classified as a subagent of the principal and an agent of the listing broker. *Stortroen*, supra; *Fennell v. Ross*, 711 S.W.2d 793 (Ark. 1986). As a subagent he or she sustains no contractual relationship to the principal, *Janes v. CPR Corporation*, supra, but may have the same duty of care as the listing broker to discover and disclose defects. *Given v. Aldemeyer/Stagmon/Kaiser, Inc.*, 788 S.W.2d 503 (Ky. Ct. App. 1990). Texas addressed this issue by defining subagent by statute in 1995. Under Texas law, a subagent is a licensee who represents a principal through cooperation with and consent of a broker representing the principal and who is not sponsored by or associated with the principal's broker (see 1101.002 (8)(A), (B)).

States vary widely on the duties and liabilities of the cooperating broker. This confusion exists with respect to rights between brokers as well as with the relationship of the cooperating broker to his or her respective client. In general, the cooperating agent represents the seller as a matter of law. *Velten v. Robertson*, supra; *Fennell v. Ross*, supra. The basic premise is that a real estate brokerage firm with whom property is listed becomes the agent of the seller for the purposes of finding a purchaser. In the past, if the broker was a member of MLS®, the membership created an automatic subagency with all member brokers and their agents *if* the client has given the listing broker express authority to make the unilateral offer of subagency. Blanket unilateral subagency is no longer automatic. However, the subagency is assumed unless stated or disclosed otherwise or is withdrawn. This duty of utmost good faith and fidelity applies to all subagents as well. *Mersky v. Multiple Listing*, supra; *Stortroen*, supra.

Most states have adopted this theory in some form, unless there is a clear agreement to the contrary.

Do the listing broker and cooperating broker operate independently? There may be some authority that an "independent agency" is established, rather than a subagency, since the cooperating broker may not bind the listing broker, nor vice versa. *Sullivan v. Jefferson*, supra; *Buffington v. Haas*, supra. This theory results in a joint venture of sorts between the two brokers.

Conflicts

The agency relationship creates liability for the agent. This can be so even if the agency relationship is created by acquiescence or by actual or ostensible authority. The liability generally relies on two theories: (1) the broker's failure to carry out an express undertaking that the principal had relied on him to carry out, and (2) the broker's failure to perform a duty implied in the relationship of real estate broker and client. *Lester v. Marshall*, 352 P.2d 786 (Colo. 1960). In *Ramsey v. Gordon*, supra, both agents were held liable. It has also been held, though, that the negligence of the cooperating agent cannot be imputed to the listing agent. *Sullivan v. Jefferson*, 400 A.2d 836 (Ct. App. N.J. 1979). Alternatively, the negligence of the listing agent is also not imputed to the selling agent. *Asleson v. Westbranch Land Co.*, 311 N.W.2d 533 (N.D. 1981). However, both can be liable in any given transaction. *Easton v. Strassburger*, supra. See also *Given v. Aldemeyer/Stagmon/Kaiser, Inc.*, supra.

Many listing brokers are currently refusing to offer subagency because of the possible liabilities involved. They have no control over the cooperating broker's actions or knowledge of that broker's understanding of their agency responsibilities. The 1995 legislature may have stopped this worry. Section 15F(c) of the Texas Real Estate License Act, that became Chapter 1101, Texas Occupations Code, Sec. 1101.805 (f), provides that neither a party nor a licensee is liable under the License Act for a misrepresentation or a concealment of a material fact made by a subagent in a real estate transaction unless the party or licensee knew of the falsity of the misrepresentation or concealment and failed to disclose the party's or licensee's knowledge of the falsity of the misrepresentation or concealment.

The dilemma of the cooperating broker was outlined in the old Texas case of *Scott v. Kelso*, (Tex. Civ. App. 1910), when it stated that

> "As agent for the vendor, his duty is to sell at the highest price. As agent for the vendee, his duty is to buy at the lowest price. And even if the parties bargain for themselves, they are entitled to the skill, knowledge, and advice of the agent, and at the same time to communicate with him without the slightest fear of betrayal, so that it is hardly possible for him to be true to the one without being false to the other."

The old cases had some insight!

COMPENSATION

The vast majority of cooperating broker lawsuits deal with the ability of the cooperating broker to maintain an action for a commission. The general rule is that brokers cannot do so because there is no privity of contract with the seller. *Boyert v. Tauber*, ante. **However, recent changes in the Texas Real Estate License Act now allow a broker to sue another broker for a commission or tortious interference even though there is no written contract. See §1101.806.**

In traditional seller agency, the agreement on a commission is between the listing broker and the seller. Theoretically, the cooperating broker is not known to the principal of the transaction, and the agreement to share a commission is merely an agreement between the listing broker and the cooperating broker.

The authority of an agent (listing broker) to appoint a subagent (cooperating broker) to share commissions or perform other brokerage acts must be approved by the seller, *Janes v. CPR Corporation*, supra, and is typically contained in the agent's standard MLS® employment contract. The sharing of the commission is legal so long as it has the full knowledge and consent of both principals. *Williams v. Knight Realty, Co.*, 217 S.W. 755 (Tex. Civ. App. 1919). It has also been held that an agreement between brokers to work together and share a commission is considered a partnership. *Moore v. Sussdorf*, 421 S.W.2d 460 (Tex. Civ. App.-Tyler 1967, ref. n.r.e.).

In the absence of an agreement, the listing broker's ability to share his or her commission with another broker is legal provided there is no secret agreement between the brokers representing different principals to divide their commissions. If there is not a direct disclosure and acknowledgment of the cooperating broker's agency, it can be implied through acquiescence, as can the agent's subsequent liability. *Gillen v. Stevens*, 330 S.W.2d 253 (Tex. Civ. App.-Waco 1959, ref. n.r.e.). Secret commissions are against public policy and may deprive brokers of their right to compensation. It is not sufficient that the broker merely produced a buyer; he or she must also perform the fiduciary duty imposed by law with reasonable care and skill. *Schroeder v. Rose*, supra; *Jones v. Maestas*, 696 P.2d 920 (Idaho App. 1985). This is discussed in greater detail in Chapter 14.

5

OBLIGATIONS TO THIRD PARTIES

PURPOSE

After carefully reading Chapter 5, the student will be able to:

■ State the agent's obligations to third parties under the License Act.

■ Discuss misrepresentation.

■ List the disclosures prohibited by the Texas Real Estate License Act.

■ Explain the broker's use of the Seller Disclosure Statement.

■ Explain how the court has construed agent obligations to third parties.

■ Discuss the agent's defense from third party misrepresentation.

■ Define: *puffing, rollback taxes, a MUD, Texas Public Beaches, Coastal Area Property, CLOs, affiliated business arrangement, Resale Certification from the Condominium Owner's Association.*

Key Words to look for in this chapter:
1. Duty of care
2. Seller's Disclosure Statement
3. Puffing
4. Rollback Taxes
5. MUD Forms
6. Annexation Issues
7. Texas Public Beaches
8. Coastal Area Properties
9. Mold Assessors and Remediators
10. Seller's Disclosure of Property Condition
11. Seller's Disclosure Notice
12. Residential Condominiums
13. Seller's Disclosure Regarding Potential Annexation
14. Membership in a Property Owners' Association
15. Residential Lead-Based Paint Disclosure

The next two chapters deal with different laws that address the same or similar situations. For this reason, they may seem repetitive in places. This chapter, however, discusses fiduciary duties under the law of agency that deal with third parties. Chapter 6 deals primarily with the Texas Deceptive Trade Practices Act. While reading this chapter, one should consider how to deal with someone other than one's client.

DISCUSSION QUESTION

■ What is wrong with the following statement? "As a salesperson for ABC Seller's Agency, I listed the seller's house. At the time I listed it, I told the sellers it was way over priced. My buyers have asked if I thought it was priced too high. I told them it was."

DUTIES

The first material point in considering fiduciary duties to third parties is that there aren't any. The fiduciary duty runs between the principal and the agent, and if the third party is a customer, not a client, there is no fiduciary duty. What has evolved over the years, though, is an expanding duty of care to the third party, whether it be seller or purchaser, to make sure the third party is not deceived. The REALTORS® Code of Ethics requires that REALTORS® treat the third party honestly. The Texas Real Estate Commission's Canons of Professional Ethics and Conduct for Real Estate Licensees state that licensees "shall treat other parties to a transaction fairly." The Rules of the Texas Real Estate Commission require a Consumer Information Form 1-1 to be on public display in a prominent location in each place of business the broker maintains (see 531.18(b)) so that a party is informed as to where to file complaints against a licensee.

Traditionally, the duty of care to the third party has been one of honesty and integrity. The Texas Real Estate License Act, however, has expanded that obligation:

■ A real estate broker has the obligation to advise the purchaser in writing that the purchaser is to obtain a policy of title insurance or have an attorney of his or her choice examine an abstract of title to the property. See §§1101.555; .806.

■ The Texas Real Estate License Act also provides for license revocation or suspension for the following acts related to third parties:

a. The agent must disclose to a potential purchaser a latent structural defect or other defect known to the broker or salesperson. Latent structural defects and other defects do not refer to trivial and insignificant defects, but refer to those defects that would be a significant factor to a reasonable and prudent purchaser in making a decision to purchase. See §§1101.652(b)(3); .652(b)(4). How does a licensee determine what defects would be a significant factor to a reasonable and prudent purchaser? When in doubt, disclose!

DISCUSSION QUESTIONS

■ What defects might be or might not be significant to a purchaser?

■ How can the licensee do this?

b. The licensee must make clear to the parties which one he is acting for. §§1101.652(b)(7) & (8).

c. The licensee must not make a false promise of a character likely to influence, persuade, or induce any person to enter into a contract or agreement when the licensee could not or did not intend to keep such a promise. §1101.652(b)(5).

d. The licensee must not pursue or continue a flagrant course of misrepresentation or making of false promise through agents, salesperson, advertising, or otherwise. See §1101.652(b)(6).

e. The licensee must not solicit, sell, or offer for sale, real property under a scheme or program that constitutes lottery or deceptive practice. §§1101.652(b)(14) & (15).

f. The licensee must not negotiate or attempt to negotiate the sale, purchase, exchange, lease, or rental of real property with an owner, lessor, buyer, or tenant knowing that the owner is a party to an outstanding written contract, granting exclusive agency in connection with the property to another real estate broker. §1101.652(b)(22).

g. The licensee must not publish or cause to be published an advertisement including, but not limited to, advertising by newspaper, radio, television, or display which is misleading or which is likely to deceive the public, or which in any manner, tends to create a misleading impression, or which fails to identify the person causing the advertisement to be published as a licensed real estate broker or agent. See 1101.652(b)(23). Logically, this would specifically apply to those brokers who run ads in newspapers advertising properties for sale or lease when in fact they don't exist, but use the telephone responses as "leads" to snare unsuspecting purchasers and tenants.

h. The licensee must surrender to the rightful owner, on demand, a document relating to a real estate transaction to a person who signed the document. §1101.652(b)(28).

i. The licensee must not engage in any act or conduct that constitutes discrimination as defined under federal or state law. §1101.652(b)(32).

The case law interpreting misrepresentations has been very one-sided and has held that the misrepresentations made to third parties were actionable even though they were innocent, unknowing misrepresentations. *Kelley v. Texas Real Estate Commission*, 671 S.W.2d 936 (Tex. App.-Houston [14th Dist.] 1984). In *Henry S. Miller v. Bynum*, 797 S.W.2d 51 (Tex. App.-Houston [1st Dist.] 1990), the broker was even held liable for innocent misrepresentations in brochures that were prepared by his principal.

Henry S. Miller v. Bynum, 797 S.W.2d 51 (Tex. App.-Houston [1st Dist.] 1990)

Douglas Bynum and Starfire Engineering, Inc., d/b/a Tiffany's Hair Styles, a tenant of Wood Winds Shopping Center, brought Deceptive Trade practices claims against Henry S. Miller Company, the leasing agent, and Richard Dover and John C. Riddle Development Company owners.

Bynum, Tiffany's Hair Styles, claimed that a brochure that he received from the leasing agent Miller, prepared by John Riddle Interests, claimed that the Wood Winds Shopping Center was a "1st class" center that was almost "wholly leased out." The brochure also held out that the Center was owned (including the parking lot) by John C. Riddle and John Riddle Interests, and stated that rent was adjusted according to the quality and quantity of services. According to Bynum, the brochure promised that construction debris would be cleaned daily and that the Center would be advertised to prospective customers of Bynum.

Tiffany's Hair Styles became a tenant of Wood Winds Shopping Center and began business. Utilities were interrupted, flooding and breaks in water lines occurred, interrupting Bynum's business. Bynum claimed that the Center failed to clean up construction debris, and that there was soft, runny tar in the parking lot, which, contrary to representation, Riddle did not even own. Bynum states that, for these business reasons and as a consequence of the misrepresentations made to the company, the beauty shop had to be sold.

The District Court found that the Deceptive Trade Practices Act had been violated and express warranties breached and awarded damages. The agent, Miller, appealed.

Miller Co. claimed that they had no knowledge of misrepresentation. They stated that they did not know that the representations they gave regarding the shopping center were false; and that under DTPA, you can't be held liable for failure to disclose something you don't know.

The court found not only a failure to disclose but affirmative misrepresentation that was a procuring cause of Bynum's damages. The court held that a real estate agent is completely liable for any information the agent passes on from a principal to a customer and that it is not necessary to prove that the agent knew the statements were false or misleading. There was a strong dissenting opinion contesting that the agent is always responsible for the credible statements the agent transmits on behalf of the principal.

This is clearly a case of what the broker "should have known."

┌─────────────────────────────────┐
│   DISCUSSION   QUESTIONS   │
└─────────────────────────────────┘

■ Considering the third paragraph of the foregoing case (loss of power, water, parking), how would you have felt as Bynum/Tiffany's Hair Styles?

■ What could the broker have done to avoid liability? How important are the fine details?

■ Should a broker only prepare his or her own material?

A typical statement of fact situations was made in the Alaska case, *Bevins v. Ballard*, 655 P.2d 757 (Ala. 1982), where an Alaska Supreme Court stated that:

> "Frequently, the owners may move away, leaving their broker as the only reachable defendant. As between the broker who communicated the misrepresentation and the purchaser whose only fault was to rely on the broker, we think it preferable that the broker bear any loss caused by the misrepresentation. Broker, in turn, can protect himself from liability by investigating the owners' statement or by disclaiming knowledge, by requiring the seller to sign at the time of the listing, a statement setting forth representations which will be made, certifying that they are true and providing for indemnification if they are not."

The Texas Real Estate License Act has specific rules regarding some disclosures; however, §1101.556 of the License Act prohibits the disclosure or discussion about HIV or HIV-related illnesses as it relates to the property. The legislature also enacted a similar provision for death on the property. A real estate licensee has no duty to inquire about, disclose, or make representations concerning a death on a property, which was the result of suicide, natural causes, or accidents unrelated to the condition of the property. Apparently there still must be a disclosure as to whether murder, execution, etc. occurred on the premises.

DISCUSSION QUESTIONS

■ How will one know the cause of death without inquiring?

■ If a potential buyer asks about suicide, is there a duty to disclose?

Some comfort and protections may be obtained by the broker's use of the **Seller's Disclosure Statement**. All sellers of property with a single-family home located on it have to provide a Seller's Disclosure Statement wherein the seller makes the representation as to the condition of the property. Hopefully, this will relieve some liability for brokers who can rely on this information as being true so long as the licensee does not know or could not have known the information was false. See the Deceptive Trade Practices Act 17.505. A copy of the statutory Seller's Disclosure Notice is discussed in greater detail later and is included at the end of this chapter.

In dealing with third parties, an agent should ask if a buyer's broker represents that third party. Buyer agency is becoming a major force in the residential market, as it has been for years in commercial transactions. Buyer agency has increased, as agency disclosure has become mandatory. If one assumes that the other agent is a subagent and discloses seller's confidential information, a breach of fiduciary duty results. Never assume anything except a 3 percent mortgage. Buyer's brokerage will be discussed in greater detail in Chapter 9.

Court cases that have construed agents' obligations to third parties include the following:

■ An agent misrepresenting that a homebuilder built homes of good construction and that the builder was on "an approved builder's list." *Lakeway Real Estate Corp. v. Whittlesey*, Cause No. 9086 (Tex. Civ. App.-Texarkana, December 28, 1992).

■ An agent representing the title was free and clear on property when it was not. *Ingalls v. Rice*, supra; and *Stone v. Lawyer's Title Insurance Corp.*, 554 S.W.2d 183 (Tex. 1977).

■ An agent offering an opinion as to the future use of the adjacent property. *Trenholm v. Ratcliff*, 646 S.W.2d 927 (Tex. 1983). The Trenholm case is particularly noteworthy because it considers the value of a broker's expert opinion versus the standard of a "consumer" in Texas.

■ An agent's misrepresenting of the square footage of a house. *Cameron v. Terrell & Garrett, Inc.*, 618 S.W.2d 535 (Tex. 1981). The Cameron case is a particularly noteworthy case because it was one of the first cases decided under the Texas Deceptive Trade Practices Act, discussed in the next chapter.

- An agent representing that there were no drainage or sewage problems when there were. *McRee v. Bolstad*, 646 P.2d 771 (Wash. Civ. App. 1982). See also *Kessler v. Fanning*, discussed later.

- The agent failing to follow through on a promise to provide funds to a prospective purchaser. *McGaha v. Dishman*, 629 S.W.2d 220 (Tex. Civ. App.-Tyler 1982). This case is also noteworthy because the broker promised to produce second lien financing to facilitate the closing and then failed to do so at the closing table.

- An agent remaining silent when there should have been a representation of facts. *Smith v. National Resort Communities*, 585 S.W.2d 655 (Tex. 1979). It is important to note here that there is duty to speak if you know of a defect rather than remain silent about it.

- There has been a series of cases concerning disclosing information about the house or the property being the site of a murder. Texas statute indicates that death on a property does not have to be disclosed under certain conditions. The statute, however, is unclear as to what those specific conditions might be. Note *Reed v. King*, 193 Cal. Rptr. 130 (Cal. Ct. App. 1983), in which the house was the site of a multiple murder. It is unclear as to whether this would fall within the exceptions of the Texas Real Estate License Act. Recall that the Texas Real Estate License Act also prohibits certain disclosures concerning death, but it may still be an issue. It is certainly conceivable that such a fact could make a difference to the mind of a prudent purchaser in making his decision to purchase, creating a "latent defect" under the License Act.

- A broker who bought property for himself after knowing the seller would accept another purchaser's offer. *Sawyer v. Jarvis*, 432 N.E.2d 849 (Ill. 1982).

- An agent representing the property was free of termites while concealing a second, conflicting report. *Godfrey v. Steinpress*, 180 Cal. Rptr. 95 (Cal. App. 1982). One must never conceal an inspection report, a termite report, or any other report that may shed light or be informative as to the condition of the property. *Hernandez v. Schultz*, 15 S.W.3d 648 (Tex. App.-Dallas 2000).

- A broker misrepresenting the availability of financing through third party sources. *Danny Darby Real Estate v. Jacobs*, 760 S.W.2d 711 (Tex. App. 1988).

- Failing to disclose to the buyer that property was undergoing foreclosure procedures. *Gray v. Boyle*, 803 S.W.2d 678 (Tenn. 1990).

- There have even been some causes of action upheld for failing to disclose technical information concerning building code violations or requirements for flood insurance. In *Revitz v. Terell*, 572 So.2d 996 (Fla. Dist. Ct. App. 1990), the court held that a seller's agent knew or should have known about the requirement of flood insurance. The agent had a duty to disclose those facts.

- In one of the more amazing cases, a seller was held liable for failing to disclose that he had a particularly obnoxious neighbor. The court held that reputation and history clearly have a significant effect on the value of a piece of property, and that ill repute or "bad will" may depress the value of the property. The fact that a neighborhood contains an overtly hostile family who delights in tormenting their neighbors with unexpected noises or unending parties is not a matter that would ordinarily come to the attention of a buyer viewing the property at a time carefully selected by the seller to correspond with an anticipated lull in the "festivities." One may suppose the broker's obligations would not be far behind if the broker "should have known" of the difficulty. *Alexander v. McKnight*, 7 Cal. App. 4th 973 (Cal. App. 1992); *Shapiro v. Sutherland*, 76 Cal. Rptr. 2d 101 (Cal. App. 2d Dist. 1998).

- Recommending a building inspector who was not neutral and independent. *Johnson v. Beverly-Hanks & Associates*, 500 S.E.2d 38 (N.C. 1991). Don't recommend inspectors! Give purchasers a list; then let them pick one with whom they feel comfortable.

- When holding an open house, there may be a duty to inspect the premises, particularly if the defect is reasonably discoverable through such inspections. One court noted that the broker, if found liable, might have a cross-claim against the homeowner who fails to warn the broker of the dangers. *Hopkins v. Fox & Lazo REALTORS®*, 626 A.2d 1110 (N.J. 1993). It should be noted that there was a strong dissent in this case and we have another case that holds almost exactly the opposite way. *Zaffiris v. O'Loughlin*, 585 N.Y.S. 2d 94 (App. Div. 1992).

- Failing to disclose agency relationships in accordance with the state law and being clear about that agent's representation. *Habeeb v. Ohio Department of Commerce*, 2004 W.L. 63944 (Ohio App., 2004).

- There is also a disturbing case that indicates that a licensee may be required to disclose a matter other than physical characteristics of the property. When a purchaser learned that the prior owner of the property was facing allegations of child molestation in the house, the purchaser sued the broker for failing to disclose the truth regarding the owner of the house. The jury found that the broker knowingly engaged in false, misleading, or deceptive acts since the agent knew the prior owner's reputation and withheld the information from the buyer. *Sanchez v. Guerrero*, 885 S.W.2d 481 (Tex. App.-El Paso 1994).

Perhaps the most difficult thing about the Sanchez case is that the needs to disclose certain items are not defined well. This has brought us to a concern as to whether to disclose "stigma." Stigmatized properties are generally defined as those that bear no physical defects but have a lower value or are more difficult to sell for emotional or psychological reasons. It is difficult to know whether a purchaser would be concerned about certain things, such as violent death on the premises, haunted houses or houses with bad "karma," or the site of a horrible criminal act. While seller disclosure laws could remedy this somewhat, sellers are often not honest when dealing with their listing broker, or the licensee may be new and not aware of a house's previous history. While Texas may require brokers to disclose property with stigma, it does not require brokers to disclose property stigma such as death (discussed previously) and HIV status of a previous occupant. Other areas of stigma, though, are not addressed by statute and brokers are left with the "crystal ball" problem, resulting in imputed knowledge and liability for failure to disclose.

DISCUSSION QUESTION

■ What other examples of a broker failing to disclose can you give?

As was discussed previously, the misrepresentation can be innocent and unknowing but still hold the broker liable.

AGENTS' DEFENSES FROM THIRD PARTY MISREPRESENTATIONS

The only reported cases to exempt brokers from liability to third parties have been pretty one-sided.

■ *The agent didn't say it*—One effective defense has been when the agent never made the representations. *Newsome v. Starkey*, 541 S.W.2d 468 (Tex. Civ. App.-Dallas 1976); *Ozuna v. Delaney Realty*, 593 S.W.2d 797 (Tex. Civ. App.-El Paso 1980, writ ref'd n.r.e.); *Stagner v. Friendswood Development Co., Inc.*, 620 S.W.2d 103 (Tex. 1981).

Another potential defense is that what the agent said is not specific enough for the licensee to be held accountable. *Bischoff Realty, Inc. v. Ledford*, 562 N.E.2d 1321 (Ind. Ct. App. 1990). See also *Autohaus v. Aquilar*, 794 S.W.2d 459 (Tex. App.-Dallas 1990).

O'Hern v. Hogard, 841 S.W.2d 135 (Tex. App.-Houston [14th Dist.] 1992)

The O'Herns bought the Robinsons' home. The listing agent was Bonnie Hogard, a broker. The sellers had agreed to reduce the price of the home. The buyers agreed to a provision stating that the buyers felt the house would need extensive and ongoing maintenance because of the site positioning, foundation, and drainage; but that they would take the home "as is." After their purchase the O'Herns noticed foundation problems. They sued the sellers and the selling and listing agents alleging DTPA violations and claimed that they would not have purchased the home if the information on its condition had been disclosed. The trial court granted a summary judgment.

The Robinsons never met the O'Herns, so they had made no representations to them. The Robinsons had signed a seller disclosure indicating some minor settling problems and returned it to Hogard, who never presented the statement to the O'Herns. The O'Herns have complained of much more damage than minor settling problems.

The defendants claimed that their failure to disclose was not a producing cause of the damages. The O'Herns stated that they planned on having the property inspected regardless of what the real estate agents told them, and they had the right to have an inspection before closing. They chose Brazos Realty Inspection, Inc. to inspect the foundation. While they admitted that the report raised their comfort level, they also stated that they relied on the expertise of their own broker on soil conditions and cracks in the foundation.

The trial court found that Lewis O'Hern's testimony made it clear that he did not rely upon anyone else's advise, expertise, or judgment in purchasing the home. O'Hern also disclosed he was aware of some defects in the house before closing. The agents allege that a disclosure of the structural defects would not have stopped the purchase. The appellate court, however, found that the "appellees [Hogard] failed to prove their failure to disclose was not a producing cause of the O'Herns' damages." In effect, the court held that the real estate agent must prove that the buyer relied specifically on another's representation.

- *The licensee didn't know*—The courts will apparently not hold an agent to the duty of care for failing to reveal information that he or she does not know. *Robinson v. Preston Chrysler Plymouth, Inc.*, 633 S.W.2d 500 (Tex. 1982); *Pfeiffer v. Ebby Halliday Real Estate*, 747 S.W.2d 887 (Tex. App.-Dallas 1988); *Commercial Credit Corp. v. Lisenby*, 579 So.2d 1291 (Ala. 1991). The real estate agent has also been held not liable when the plaintiff was not relying on the real estate agent's representations because of the plaintiff's own inspection of the property prior to acquisition. *Lone Star Machinery Corp. v. Frankel*, 564 S.W.2d 135 (Tex. Civ. App.-Beaumont 1978). See also *Chicago Expert Packing Co. v. Teledyne Indus. Inc.*, 566 N.E.2d 326 (Ill. App. Ct. 1990). The same is apparently true when the consumer had information from another source that is correct, even though the agent's information was incorrect. *Mikkelson v. Quail Valley Realty*, 641 P.2d 124 (Utah 1982). The principal may still have the duty to read and understand his or her own contract. *Jones v. Maestas*, 108 Idaho 69, 696 P.2d 920, (Idaho App. 1985). But see, *Phillips v. JCM*, 666 P.2d 876 (Utah 1983); and *Wilkenson v. Smith*, 639 P.2d 768 (Wash. 1982).

In *Steptoe v. True*, 38 S.W.3d 213 (Tex. App.-Houston [14th Dist.] 2001), a buyer of beachfront property sued the listing broker for violations of the DTPA, fraudulent inducement, negligent misrepresentation, and breach of contract. While showing the property the listing broker allegedly told the buyer that the bulkhead of the property had been grandfathered by the state and the buyer was "led to believe" that the bulkhead was there to stay. In executing the earnest money contract, the buyer also executed a "Notice Regarding Coastal Area Property" and the "Addendum for Property Located Seaward of the Gulf Intracoastal Waterway" as required by the Texas Real Estate Commission, which acknowledged the beach property and the determination of the vegetation line. After the purchase of the property the State of Texas removed the bulkhead and the property subsequently subsided into the Gulf of Mexico. The buyer testified that the broker (True) never had a conversation with her about the bulkhead. He only responded in generic terms and commented that he really didn't know about a problem with beach erosion in that area, but did acknowledge that bulkheads were "nice to have." The court held that these comments were not affirmative misrepresentations as a matter of law.

The court noted that "the decisive test" is whether the seller asserts a fact of which the buyer is ignorant, or merely states an opinion or judgment on a matter of which the seller has no special knowledge and on which the buyer may be expected also to have an opinion and to exercise his or her judgment. The court held that the comments were not actionable because they merely pointed out the obvious.

The court noted the well-established rule in Texas that a defendant "has no duty to disclose material facts [of which] it *should have known*." Texas law requires that the defendant had knowledge of the information and had failed to bring it to the plaintiff's attention.

In addressing the cause of action for negligent misrepresentation, the court noted "there is no law in Texas supporting the imposition of such a duty [to inspect listed property and disclose all facts which might materially affect its value or desirability.] An imposition of this type of liability should be left to the Texas legislature."

A similar result was achieved for a seller in *Bynum v. Prudential Residential Services Ltd. Partnership,* 129 S.W.3d 781 (Tex. App.-Houston [1st Dist.] 2003), where a seller was sued for failing to disclose that the house was remodeled without getting building permits. The court noted that there was no evidence ever presented to the court that showed that the sellers knew that a building permit was never pulled. Sellers can't disclose what they don't know, and absent "actual knowledge" of the defect, the plaintiff's cause of action failed. The Court also noted in that case there was no duty to provide continuing updates as to matters within the Seller's Disclosure of Property Condition.

In another case, *Sherman v. Elkowitz,* 130 S.W.3d 316 (Tex. App.-Houston [14th Dist.] 2004), the court dismissed a cause of action against a real estate agent who passed on information contained in the Seller's Disclosure Form, holding that the broker would have a duty to come forward with information about the defect only if he had any reason to believe that the seller's disclosures were false or inaccurate. The

Court also held that if a defect has been corrected, there is no duty to disclose a corrected defect, because repairing a defect doesn't prove its continued existence. The court also held that there was no duty to disclose prior lawsuits affecting the property.

■ *The agent made a mistake*—The fact that the agent made a mere mistake that does not result from lack of honesty or from lack of diligence that a reasonable broker would employ is not a breach of fiduciary duty. *Perkins v. Thorpe*, ante; *Schroeder v. Rose*, supra. The better presumption, though, is that innocent misrepresentation is not a good defense, regardless of the sophistication of the purchaser. *Shaffer v. Earl Thacker Co., Ltd.*, 716 P.2d 163 (Int. Ct. App.-Hawaii 1986); *Henry S. Miller v. Bynum*, supra.

■ *It's not the agent's job, and just not fair*—A new, logical defense is beginning to develop in various states. If the purchaser hired someone else to do the inspections, the broker is not liable. *Pfeiffer v. Ebby Halliday*, supra. If the information is beyond the scope of real estate brokerage (technical information such as surveys), the broker is not liable. *Hoffman v. Connall*, 736 P.2d 242 (Wash. 1987); *McMullen v. Joldersma*, 435 N.W.2d 428 (Mich. 1988). A broker does not have obligations to explain a contract to a purchaser. *Haldiman v. Gosnell Development Corp.*, 748 P.2d 1209 (Ariz. App. 1987). One case has held that the broker doesn't have to know about the soil composition. *Herbert v. Soffell*, 877 F.2d 267 (4th Cir. 1989).

The agent's duty to the *seller* is to present all offers, not the purchaser! There's no duty to the *purchaser* to disclose their offers to the seller! *Allen v. Lindstrom*, 379 S.E.2d 450 (Va. 1989) cert. den. 110 S.Ct. 145 (1989).

Inaccurate financial information provided by the seller may not fall under the broker's area of expertise and was supplied by the seller, not the broker. *Burton v. Mackey*, 801 P.2d 865 (Or. Ct. App. 1990).

In *Bartlett v. Schmidt*, 33 S.W.3d 35 (Tex.App.-Corpus Christi 2000, writ denied), Schmidt bought some land from sellers, who were represented by their broker, Bartlett. Schmidt wanted the property for use as a shipbuilding facility, where he intended to build ocean-going vessels. Pursuant to the contract, Schmidt was given a title commitment. The commitment showed some restrictive covenants that affected adjacent property but that did not restrict commercial development on his property. The title company failed to show various amendments to the restrictions that, in fact, did prohibit commercial use of the property. Schmidt consulted with his lawyer, then bought the property. When he began laying the foundation for a shipbuilding enterprise, he was advised that the property had been annexed by the adjacent subdivision and was now limited to residential use only. Schmidt sued the seller, the broker, and the title company. The title company settled. The trial court held that Bartlett was liable for fraud, negligent misrepresentation, and DTPA violations.

Both fraud and negligent misrepresentation require a showing of *reliance*. Here, Bartlett argued that since Schmidt had consulted with his lawyer before buying the property, that consultation was an independent investigation that negates his claims. The decisions that support this notion are based on the notion that the buyer's decision to undertake a separate investigation indicates that he is not relying on representations about the property. Here, before he bought the property, Schmidt asked third parties to review conveyancing documents to be sure there were no restrictions on his intended use. He did this after he heard Bartlett's representations about the property, and, so the court held, therefore relied on the third parties' representations, not on Bartlett's representations. Reliance on the title company's two external assessments of the feasibility of purchasing property was held to introduce a "new and independent" cause of the buyer's damages, thus negating the producing cause element of a DTPA claim.

Another case reinforces this theory even better. In *Cendant Mobility Services Corporation v. Falconer*, 135 S.W.3d 349 (Tex.App.-Texarkana 2004, no pet.). The Gregg County house purchased by Kenneth S. Falconer turned out to be a nightmare. Falconer purchased the house in 1999 through Cendant Mobility Services Corporation, a relocation firm selling the property for the prior owners, the Gunnelses. After the purchase, and a severe drought, Falconer began to see damage to interior and exterior walls and floors revealing serious and widespread structural flaws. Falconer sued Cendant, asserting causes of action for fraud and violation of the DTPA, claiming that Cendant failed to disclose that the house's foundation had shown evidence of substantial movement in the past and that Cendant provided only a portion of the relevant engineer's report for his review. The evidence reveals, however, that Falconer's initials appear on each page of the previous homeowner's real estate disclosure and an engineer's structural inspection report.

Despite Falconer's admission that he received and initialed at least those portions of the documents describing the foundation's condition, he nevertheless maintains that he was misled by Cendant's agent. He testified he would not necessarily characterize what she affirmatively told him about the house as a misrepresentation of the information available to her, but believed she misled him by selectively informing him of certain portions of the disclosures and reports, omitting the fact that substantial movement had taken place in the past. Instead, she reportedly pointed out from the seller's disclosure statement only that minor settlement had occurred in the past and then jumped forward to the last two sentences of the engineer's report, indicating that the foundation was stable, that the house was structurally sound, and that no additional repairs were warranted. In answer to the question: "Do you expect Cendant to sit down and read each—the contract through line by line with you?" He said: "If that's what it takes."

Despite Falconer's belief that Cendant's agent should have explained every detail of the contract, including any disclosures or attached reports, this is simply not the law. Even where there exists a fiduciary relationship—which did not exist here—there is no duty under the DTPA requiring sellers to orally disclose the contents of a written contract. The information provided in the seller's disclosure and the engineers report was clear and unambiguous and subject to Falconer's review before signing. It is well settled that the parties to a contract have an obligation to protect themselves by reading what they sign. Unless there is some basis for finding fraud, the parties may not excuse themselves from the consequences of failing to meet that obligation. In this case, there was no evidence of fraud. The evidence was that Falconer had everything in front of him and didn't read it. The failure of one party to read a contract, or any of the materials appertaining to it, however, does not equate with a failure of the other party to disclose the information contained within the four corners of that contract. Absent a showing Cendant misrepresented the information disclosed in written form, Falconer was obligated to protect himself by reading the contract. He cannot now be excused from the consequences of failing to meet that obligation.

- *The purchaser ignores the defect or the information*—An excellent case in defense of brokers was decided by the Supreme Court of Ohio in 1988. *Layman v. Binns*, 35 Ohio St.3d 176. In this case the purchaser observed a defective wall that had been repaired, and bought the house anyway. Then he sued the broker. The Court held that the broker has no liability where: (1) the defective conditions are discoverable; (2) the purchaser has an opportunity for investigation without concealment or hindrance by the vendor; (3) the condition was open to observation; and (4) the vendor hasn't engaged in fraud. In the court's opinion, to decide otherwise would "invite litigation instituted by a disappointed buyer"; and the court also stated a very logical conclusion: "A duty falls upon the purchaser to make inquiry and examination."

Some states, including Alabama, still adhere to **caveat emptor**, "let the buyer beware." *Blackman v. First Real Estate Corp.*, 529 So.2d 955 (Ala. 1988); although it does not apply in an incorrect response to a direct inquiry. *Fennell Realty Co. v. Martin*, 529 So.2d 1003 (Ala. 1988). The use of the Seller Disclosure Form is no defense to an agent's misrepresentations. *Cornelius v. Austin*, 542 So.2d 1220 (Ala. 1989).

One court has held it to be a defense if the defect is disclosed, and the purchaser buys anyway. *Zak v. Parks*, 729 S.W.2d 875 (Tex. App. 1987). See also, *Connor v. Merrill Lynch Realty, Inc.*, 581 N.E.2d 196 (Ill. App. Ct. 1991).

Another case held that if the buyer knew of the fire damage and bargained for a lower purchase price because of it, the buyer can't turn around and sue the broker. *Van Gessel v. Folds*, 569 N.E.2d 141 (Ill. Ct. 1991).

■ *Helping the buyer to help the seller*—If an agent's conduct is not adverse to principal's interest, it may not be improper. For instance, an agent might act for the third party to assist in procuring financing or inspections, and doing so will not create a new agency between the broker and the purchaser. *Fowler v. Westain Enterprises, Inc.*, 906 P.2d 1053 (Wyo. 1995).

■ *Professional limitation periods*—Some states have specific statutes limiting causes of action against professionals, which may include real estate licensees. See *Tylle v. Zoucha*, 412 N.W.2d 438 (Neb. 1987). However, the Supreme Court held that real estate licensees were not "professionals." A similar result was reached in *Sumpter v. Holland Realty, Inc.*, 93 P.3d 680 (Idaho-2004), wherein the Idaho Supreme Court held that a real estate licensee was not a professional as defined under Idaho law. In that case, the Court relied on a state statute that defined professional service corporations and talked about the professionals who could incorporate as a professional corporation. The statute did not include real estate licensees. The Texas statute does not, either.

■ *A broker has no duty to inspect the property*—*Kubinsky v. Van Zandt Realtors*, 811 S.W.2d 711 (Tex. App. 1991, writ den.); the rule might be different, however, if it's a buyer's broker. *Lewis v. Long & Foster Real Estate, Inc.*, 584 A.2d 1325 (Md. App. 1991). Another case has held that the broker has the fiduciary duty to confirm that the property meets with the client's standards or should disclose that no such investigation has been made. *Salhutdin v. Valley of California, Inc.*, 29 Cal. Rptr. 2d 463 (Cal. App. 1994).

■ *A broker may not be liable for another broker's misconduct*—A New Mexico Supreme Court recently held that a listing salesperson was not liable to a buyer when another salesperson out of the same firm breach their duty. The Court held that the fiduciary duties of one real estate salesperson are not attributable to another salesperson operating under the same qualifying broker unless one salesperson is at fault in appointing, supervising, or cooperating with the other. *Moser v. Bertram*, 858 P.2d 854 (N.M. 1993). You may recall that the 1995 legislature made an attempt to limit some of this liability through an amendment to the Texas Real Estate License Act. Tort reform!

In *Hamlett v. Holcomb*, 69 S.W.3d 816 (Corpus Christi, 2002), the buyer failed to obtain financing and terminated his contract to purchase the seller's home. The seller (Hamlett) sued her listing broker (Holcomb), alleging that the broker breached a fiduciary duty to her because the broker "encouraged" the buyer to allow a breach to take place.

Holcomb counterclaimed for attorneys' fees under the listing agreement. According to the earnest money contract, buyer was allowed to terminate the contract if his financing failed and have the earnest money refunded to him. The trial court granted judgment in favor of the buyer and the broker (Holcomb) and awarded attorneys' fees and court costs to Holcomb. The court held that the contract is unambiguous under its express terms and that the buyer was entitled to repudiate the contract if his financing failed. It was uncontradicted that the lender refused to make the loan. The court held that a claim for breach of a contract defeats a claim for breach of fiduciary duty that depended on the breach of the contract; that the buyer had the right to terminate, and that this could result in no breach of fiduciary duty for the listing broker. The court upheld the award of attorneys' fees to the listing broker.

■ *A sponsoring broker has no liability if the agent doesn't*—In *Ebby Halliday Real Estate, Inc. v. Murnan*, 916 S.W.2d 585 (Tex. App.-Ft. Worth 1996), the trial court held the sponsoring broker (Ebby Halliday Real Estate, Inc.) liable for damages, but not the sales agent! (Hmm.) The jury found that the real estate licensee handling the transaction did not cause any damage to the plaintiffs, nor did the agent engage in any false, misleading, deceptive, or unconscionable act that produced damage to the plaintiffs. This court held that since the licensee was the only Ebby Halliday agent that had contact with the plaintiff, the sponsoring broker, Ebby Halliday, could not be held liable for any misconduct or damages. The court reasoned that if the agent did not engage in any misconduct, you can't impute misconduct to a sponsoring broker who had no other contact with the plaintiff. Sometimes the jury gets confused. That's why there are appellate courts.

■ *The purchaser is too smart*—In *Snyder v. Lovercheck*, 992 P.2d 1079 (Wyo. 1999), the court concluded that the clause contained in a real estate contract that disclaimed reliance on any representations by the seller precluded the buyer from recovering from the seller for negligent misrepresentation concerning the condition of certain wheat fields that the buyer acquired.

The court discussed the question of whether the buyer had a cause of action against the buyer's broker for failing to warn the buyer of the presence of the disclaimer clause in the contract so that the buyer could strike it. The buyer and his broker had conducted conversations with the seller and seller's broker concerning the presence of an adverse rye grass condition in the wheat fields. The seller had presented to the buyer that the wheat fields had been very productive in the past and that the condition affected only a small part of the total area. The crops were planted, but had not sprouted at the time of the sale, so it was difficult for the seller to assess the condition easily on his own.

The broker was fully aware that the seller had sought and obtained the representations concerning the rye grass problem. The broker was also fully aware of the language, as it was form language in the standard Wyoming real estate sale contract for property of this type.

In response, the broker cited several cases from other jurisdictions in which the court had concluded that even where a real estate broker breached his duty of care, the broker was relieved of responsibility for his error by the client's act of signing the contract.

The court rejected the theory that a broker has no responsibility with regard to explanation or disclosure of contract terms simply because the client has signed the contract. If the broker can't give such advice, the broker had a duty to advise the client to obtain it elsewhere.

The court, however, did conclude that the nature of the duty must be evaluated in the context of the client's own experience, sophistication, and opportunity to read and understand the contract himself. The court acknowledged that typically, having found the existence of a duty such as one to make a "full, fair and understandable" explanation of the contract, the court would remand to the trial court for a determination of whether the duty had been breached. But the court, simply on the basis of the record, had little patience with the buyer's claim that he was undone by the carelessness of his broker:

"[Buyer] fancies himself a sophisticated purchaser. He has bought, sold and traded various parcels of real estate several times in the past. He was negotiating the purchase of a 1,960 acre farm for $526,500.00. He was savvy enough to require that the sellers prepare a statement of condition of property. The statement provided that the Sellers [made] no other representations of any kind relating to said property. [Buyer] read the document, and expressed neither concern nor confusions about the language. [Broker] was justified in believing that a similar provision in the contract was understandable and acceptable to Snyder."

Buyer, in other words, was "too sophisticated for his own good."

A similar result was reached in the Texas case of *Larsen v. Langford & Associates, Inc.*, 41 S.W.2d 245 (Tex. App.-Waco 2001), wherein the purchaser was a real estate broker acting on his own behalf. The purchaser admitted receiving the seller's disclosure form before closing and before signing the final inspection and disclosure form. The form was incomplete but the buyer never requested that the form be finally completed. The Court held that both buyers and sellers were sophisticated parties in the real estate business. The buyer did not have the property inspected prior to the purchase even though the house was over seventy years old. The court held that the buyers did not even raise an inference that the Larsens were fraudulently induced to rely on the representations made to them by Langford's representative or those representations made in the Seller's Disclosure Notice. This case is discussed in greater detail in Chapter 6.

You may also recall in *Cendant Mobility Services Corporation v. Falconer*, 135 S.W.3d 349 (Tex. App.-Texarkana 2004, no pet.), which involved a consumer who alleged he was misled by Cendant's agent because she only pointed out what she considered to be important parts of the Homeowner's Real Estate Disclosure Instructional and Inspection Report. He further testified that he relied on his real estate agent to point out what was important in the reports. On cross-examination, however, the plaintiff admitted that he didn't read the reports that were given to him by Cendant, and that his not reading the reports was not Cendant's fault. The Court noted that

> "[even where there exists a fiduciary relationship—which we do not have here—there is no duty under the DTPA requiring sellers to orally disclose the contents of a written contract.] . . . [is well settled that the parties to a contract have an obligation to protect themselves by reading what they sign. Unless there is some basis for finding fraud, the parties may not excuse themselves from the consequences of failing to meet that obligation.] . . . [every person with legal capacity . . . is held to know what words were used in the contract, to know their meaning, and to understand their legal effect.]"

The court went on to note that the failure of one party to read a contract, or any of the materials appertaining to it, does not equate to the failure of the other party to disclose the information within the contract. The buyer is obligated to protect himself or herself by reading the contract (the inspection report).

The DTPA now provides that the licensee is not liable for misrepresentation or concealment of material fact made by a party in a real estate transaction, or made by his or her subagent in a real estate transaction, unless the licensee knew of the falsity of the misrepresentation or concealment and failed to disclose the licensee's knowledge of the falsity of the misrepresentation or concealment. §1101.805. This specifically prevails over common law and seems to impose an "actual knowledge" requirement on the broker and eliminates the ability to impute liability for what the broker "should have known." Note, however, that the new provisions do not diminish the real estate broker's liability for the broker's acts, nor the acts or admissions of the broker's salespersons.

Lewis v. Long & Foster Real Estate, Inc., 584 A.2d 1325 (Md. App. 1991)

In her home day care center business, Lynne Lewis provided care for the child of Blaine Milner, an employee and licensed sales broker of Long & Foster Real Estate. She and her husband approached Blaine to help them find a home to purchase where they could operate their day care center, which was to help pay their mortgage payments. Milner showed them a property in a townhouse complex. Milner asked about the operation of a day care in the area and relayed the information to Mrs. Lewis that she would need only to obtain a permit from the village to operate an in-house business. The Lewises contracted to purchase the property.

The real estate agent recommended a title company for the examination of the title, and it conducted all the services for settlement. There was no evidence that a specific search about in-house businesses was requested in any contract.

The Lewises remodeled their new property for their day care business. She obtained approval from the village to open and operate the business. Four months after the opening she received a letter from the townhouse homeowners' association telling her that the day care business violated subdivision restrictions.

The purchasers sued the broker, brokerage, and title company for failure to disclose. The circuit court dismissed the complaint, and the Lewises appealed.

The appellate court made some interesting observations in making its decision. The purchasers claimed that the real estate broker owed a duty of care to the buyer whom he or she represented, including the investigation of restrictions on the property that would affect the purchase and use of their property. The court found that a real estate broker should endeavor "always to be informed regarding laws."

The purpose of a real estate licensing act is to set standards of conduct for real estate licensees and to protect the public who deal with those licensees. The court stated that "as a regulated profession, much like physicians, attorneys, or certified public accountants, real estate brokers have a responsibility to the public to conduct themselves in a reputable manner. These statutes set minimum guidelines for professional conduct, their purpose being to safeguard the public."

The court recognized that a real estate licensee cannot serve two masters. The court held that usually a seller is the broker's client, but the court allowed that it is possible for a broker to be responsible to the buyer. In Maryland, an oral agreement can establish an agency relationship with a real estate broker. Milner took the job of finding a suitable property for the Lewises' day care center.

When a property sells, the listing agent and the buyer's agent divide the commission. The court stated that the "commission is a percentage of the purchase price that is paid by the buyer. When a buyer enlists the services of a real estate broker, there is an implicit understanding by all parties that the broker will receive a fee, via a commission, at the culmination of the sale. Even though a buyer's purchase money passes through several hands before reaching his broker's pocket, a buyer's broker clearly receives a fee from his client."

The appellate court confirmed the dismissal of the suit against the title company, but reversed the decision of the lower court to dismiss the purchaser's complaint holding that the real estate agent, as a buyer's agent, had a duty to investigate these items the buyer requested, and disclose those facts.

- *Puffing*—defined as an "obvious exaggeration," has been effectively wiped out as a defense in Texas. *Ridco v. Sexton*, 623 S.W.2d 792 (Tex. Civ. App.-Ft. Worth 1981).

- *No duty to successor agents?* In *Lefmark Management Co. v. Old*, 946 S.W.2d 52 (Tex. 1997), the widow of a customer killed in an armed robbery of a shopping center sued the store and the shopping center owners and managers, along with the former property manager of the shopping center. On the day of the criminal activity, however, the previous manager did not own, occupy, manage, possess, or otherwise have any control over the shopping center. The Court held that a management company does not have a duty to disclose a dangerous condition to a subsequent management company. One would think that the same theory of defense would apply to a listing broker. If a listing broker knows of a defect in the property, does he or she have a duty to disclose that defect to a successor listing broker? This case seems to indicate that there may not be a duty to do so.

■ *No defense?* A disturbing case, *McFarland v. Associated Brokers*, 977 S.W.2d 427 (Tex. App.-Corpus Christi 1998). A buyer requested an inspection of a home prior to closing in accordance with the addendum. The inspection was performed, and a leak was discovered, and the roof was repaired at the seller's expense with a warranty given by the contractor. After moving into the home, the buyer filed a suit against the broker's alleged violations of the Texas DTPA. In the trial, the broker successfully defended the case and was awarded $19,200 for legal fees. The Court of Appeals reversed the holding, however. What else could the broker have possibly done to protect himself and the purchaser? This is why lawsuits tend to be so scary.

A Texas real estate broker can also be liable for misrepresentations under the DTPA. This will be discussed in detail in Chapter 6.

Although a broker's duty of care to a third party is not a fiduciary one, one can see after reviewing the Texas Real Estate License Act and Texas cases on agency that a real estate licensee has a high duty of disclosure to purchasers and to see that they are not deceived. Two simple rules have evolved: Disclose anything you think would make a difference to a prudent purchaser in making his decision to purchase; and investigate any material that you are to deliver to the purchaser to be sure that the representations contained in that material are true.

Remember, however, that this duty is still not an easy burden when relating to third parties. The proverbial conflict exists. A seller or buyer deems that an item is confidential and requests that you not disclose it; but you, as an agent, know that it would make a material difference to the other party in making the decision to purchase. It is best for the agent, at this point, to sit down with the seller and explain his or her obligations to disclose. When defects are discovered later, the purchaser will sue both the broker and the seller, so keeping the seller well-advised on these issues prevents lawsuits for the seller also. A few of the more pertinent disclosures need to be discussed.

STATUTORY DISCLOSURE ITEMS

Rollback Taxes

The Texas Constitution [Article VIII, 1-d (Agricultural Land) and, 1-d-1 (Open Space Land)] gives a special tax benefit to qualifying owners of agricultural and open space land basing taxes on the productivity capacity of the land, not the market value. This may result in a valuation lower than market value, which brings about lower taxes for the years of eligibility. If the agriculture use of the land is changed to nonagricultural use or if the land is sold, the taxes are rolled back five years. If a change in eligibility occurs, a tax "rollback" recaptures the deferred tax. Changes in the use of ecological laboratories, timberlands, and agricultural open land roll back the taxes three years. The rollback is figured on the difference between the taxes as billed and the taxes that would have been billed without the special benefits for the preceding three years. (See Texas Promulgated Forms for the sale of farm and ranch.)

MUD Forms

The Texas legislative session placed responsibility on sellers and real estate agents to use mandatory disclosure forms to notify buyers if a property is within a Municipal Utility District (MUD). Originally MUDs were created by developers. MUDs are subdivisions politically created, a government entity, within a city or its extraterritorial jurisdiction to provide city utility services not otherwise provided by a city. The Water Commission approves the formation of a MUD.

The monies required for funding a Municipal Utility District are acquired from the sale of bonds. Taxes, in addition to regular property taxes, are levied on property within the district to fund the bonds. Prospective real estate purchasers need to be aware of the possibility of unusually high property taxes that might result from a MUD. Two notices are required by the Texas Water Code to be signed by the purchaser.

■ The first notice must be given to and signed by the buyer at or prior to the signing of a binding sales contract (Section 50.301, Texas Water Code). Notice of the obligation is given in earnest money contracts promulgated by TREC and the notice may be an attachment to the contract. The notice must relate the MUD tax rate and the district's bonded indebtedness. Among other things this notice requires the name, taxing authority, right to issue bonds, and purpose of the MUD. It must warn purchasers of possible annual standby fees for water and sewage on property that have not been connected to these facilities.

MUDs have the authority to place a standby fee on properties in the district not connected to the service and without a house, building, or other improvement that have water, sewer, sanitary, and/or drainage facilities and services available. The form also discloses the amount of the MUD fees and that the fees create a lien on the property (Section 50.3011a).

If the property is located in a " area," the disclosure must contain the amount of taxes assessed on the "designated area" above those on the rest of the MUD. Certain areas in a MUD covering more than 1,500 acres may be designated for special benefits not available to the rest of the district. Only these designated areas must pay for the special services and benefits by another tax assessment (Section 54.812(b)). All of this information must be filed by the MUDs in the deed records (Section 50.302(b)(8)).

If the MUD notice is not signed by the buyer, the sales contract may not be valid since it may be terminated by the buyer. If the notice is not signed at all, there may be liability on the part of the seller and the broker for damages. If the buyer resells, the buyer loses the right to sue for failure to receive the notice.

■ The second notice must be given at closing. This notice must be a separate document, signed and acknowledged by the buyer and recorded in the deed records (see Disclosure Form 2, Section 50.301, Texas Water Code).

Another notice may be necessary to advise the purchaser of any contract between the MUD and the city concerning water and waste water rates that was a contingency for the city's allowing the creation of the MUD (Section 54.016(h)(4)(A)).

Annexation Issues

Any person who proposes to sell or convey real property located in a Municipal Utility District must also give the purchaser written notices relating to annexation. The notices apply in three circumstances:

1. Districts located in whole or in part of the extraterritorial jurisdiction on one or more municipalities and not located within the corporate boundaries of a municipality.

2. Districts located in whole or in part within the corporate boundaries of a municipality.

3. Districts that are not located in whole or in part within the corporate boundaries of a municipality or the extraterritorial jurisdiction of one or more home ruled municipalities.

Texas Public Beaches

Texas is an open beach state where property beyond the natural vegetation line toward the ocean or Gulf is an easement under state protection "as recognized in law and custom." This beach easement changes size as the vegetation line moves. This can be effected by a hurricane. No one can build on the beach without special permission from the state of Texas.

On March 1, 1995, TREC promulgated contract addenda for mandatory use in the Texas coastal regions: TREC No. 33-0, Addendum for Coastal Area Property, Figure 5-1, and TREC No. 34-1, Addendum for Property Located Seaward of the Gulf Intracoastal Waterway, Figure 5-2 (see 61.025 Texas Natural Resources Code). These addenda contain caveats for people purchasing in the Gulf Coast areas. The sale of properties located elsewhere is not affected by the addenda.

Coastal Area Properties

If the property abuts and shares a common boundary with the tidally influenced submerged lands of Texas, Section 33.135, Texas Natural Resources Code mandates a notice (TREC No. 33-0, Figure 5-1) regarding coastal property to be

FIG 5-1   ADDENDUM FOR COASTAL AREA PROPERTY

PROMULGATED BY THE TEXAS REAL ESTATE COMMISSION (TREC)   04-23-07

ADDENDUM FOR
COASTAL AREA PROPERTY
(SECTION 33.135, TEXAS NATURAL RESOURCES CODE)

TO CONTRACT CONCERNING THE PROPERTY AT

_____
(Address of Property)

NOTICE REGARDING COASTAL AREA PROPERTY

1. The real property described in and subject to this contract adjoins and shares a common boundary with the tidally influenced submerged lands of the state. The boundary is subject to change and can be determined accurately only by a survey on the ground made by a licensed state land surveyor in accordance with the original grant from the sovereign. The owner of the property described in this contract may gain or lose portions of the tract because of changes in the boundary.

2. The seller, transferor, or grantor has no knowledge of any prior fill as it relates to the property described in and subject to this contract except:_____
_____
_____.

3. State law prohibits the use, encumbrance, construction, or placing of any structure in, on, or over state-owned submerged lands below the applicable tide line, without proper permission.

4. The purchaser or grantee is hereby advised to seek the advice of an attorney or other qualified person as to the legal nature and effect of the facts set forth in this notice on the property described in and subject to this contract. Information regarding the location of the applicable tide line as to the property described in and subject to this contract may be obtained from the surveying division of the General Land Office in Austin.

_____   _____
Buyer   Seller

_____   _____
Buyer   Seller

This form has been approved by the Texas Real Estate Commission for use with similarly approved or promulgated contract forms. Such approval relates to this form only. TREC forms are intended for use only by trained real estate licensees. No representation is made as to the legal validity or adequacy of any provision in any specific transactions. It is not suitable for complex transactions. Texas Real Estate Commission, P.O. Box 12188, Austin, TX 78711-2188, 1-800-250-8732 or (512) 459-6544 (http://www.trec.state.tx.us) TREC No. 33-1. This form replaces TREC No. 33-0.

TREC No. 33-1

Reprinted by permission from the Texas Real Estate Commission.

FIG 5-2   ADDENDUM FOR PROPERTY LOCATED SEAWARD OF THE GULF INTRACOASTAL WATERWAY

PROMULGATED BY THE TEXAS REAL ESTATE COMMISSION (TREC)   12-10-07

ADDENDUM FOR
PROPERTY LOCATED SEAWARD OF THE
GULF INTRACOASTAL WATERWAY
(SECTION 61.025, TEXAS NATURAL RESOURCES CODE)

TO CONTRACT CONCERNING THE PROPERTY AT

_____

(Address of Property)

DISCLOSURE NOTICE CONCERNING LEGAL AND ECONOMIC RISKS OF PURCHASING COASTAL REAL PROPERTY NEAR A BEACH

WARNING: THE FOLLOWING NOTICE OF POTENTIAL RISKS OF ECONOMIC LOSS TO YOU AS THE PURCHASER OF COASTAL REAL PROPERTY IS REQUIRED BY STATE LAW.

- READ THIS NOTICE CAREFULLY. DO NOT SIGN THIS CONTRACT UNTIL YOU FULLY UNDERSTAND THE RISKS YOU ARE ASSUMING.
- BY PURCHASING THIS PROPERTY, YOU MAY BE ASSUMING ECONOMIC RISKS OVER AND ABOVE THE RISKS INVOLVED IN PURCHASING INLAND REAL PROPERTY.
- IF YOU OWN A STRUCTURE LOCATED ON COASTAL REAL PROPERTY NEAR A GULF COAST BEACH, IT MAY COME TO BE LOCATED ON THE PUBLIC BEACH BECAUSE OF COASTAL EROSION AND STORM EVENTS.
- AS THE OWNER OF A STRUCTURE LOCATED ON THE PUBLIC BEACH, YOU COULD BE SUED BY THE STATE OF TEXAS AND ORDERED TO REMOVE THE STRUCTURE.
- THE COSTS OF REMOVING A STRUCTURE FROM THE PUBLIC BEACH AND ANY OTHER ECONOMIC LOSS INCURRED BECAUSE OF A REMOVAL ORDER WOULD BE SOLELY YOUR RESPONSIBILITY.

The real property described in this contract is located seaward of the Gulf Intracoastal Waterway to its southernmost point and then seaward of the longitudinal line also known as 97 degrees, 12', 19" which runs southerly to the international boundary from the intersection of the centerline of the Gulf Intracoastal Waterway and the Brownsville Ship Channel. If the property is in close proximity to a beach fronting the Gulf of Mexico, the purchaser is hereby advised that the public has acquired a right of use or easement to or over the area of any public beach by prescription, dedication, or presumption, or has retained a right by virtue of continuous right in the public since time immemorial, as recognized in law and custom.

The extreme seaward boundary of natural vegetation that spreads continuously inland customarily marks the landward boundary of the public easement. If there is no clearly marked natural vegetation line, the landward boundary of the easement is as provided by Sections 61.016 and 61.017, Natural Resources Code.

Much of the Gulf of Mexico coastline is eroding at rates of more than five feet per year. Erosion rates for all Texas Gulf property subject to the open beaches act are available from the Texas General Land Office.

State law prohibits any obstruction, barrier, restraint, or interference with the use of the public easement, including the placement of structures seaward of the landward boundary of the easement. OWNERS OF STRUCTURES ERECTED SEAWARD OF THE VEGETATION LINE (OR OTHER APPLICABLE EASEMENT BOUNDARY) OR THAT BECOME SEAWARD OF THE VEGETATION LINE AS A RESULT OF PROCESSES SUCH AS SHORELINE EROSION ARE SUBJECT TO A LAWSUIT BY THE STATE OF TEXAS TO REMOVE THE STRUCTURES.

The purchaser is hereby notified that the purchaser should: (1) determine the rate of shoreline erosion in the vicinity of the real property; and (2) seek the advice of an attorney or other qualified person before executing this contract or instrument of conveyance as to the relevance of these statutes and facts to the value of the property the purchaser is hereby purchasing or contracting to purchase.

_____   _____
Buyer   Seller

_____   _____
Buyer   Seller

TREC No. 34-3

Reprinted by permission from the Texas Real Estate Commission.

included in the sales contract. (Information on the location of the tide lines may be obtained from the survey division of the Texas General Land Office.) An addendum either promulgated by TREC or required by the parties should be used. The notice states that the boundary is subject to change and that the owner may lose or gain parts of the land because of changes in the boundary. Boundaries can be defined accurately only by a survey of the property made by a licensed state land surveyor following the original grant. State law forbids any structure in, on, or over state-owned submerged lands below the tide line without specific permission.

Mold Assessors and Remediators

The 2003 Legislature created a new chapter (1958) to the Occupations Code to regulate mold related activity such as mold remediation and mold assessments. The statute requires the Texas Board of Health to promulgate rules by April 1, 2004 for minimum specific standards and work practices for conducting a mold assessment or remediation, safety standards, a public education program, a code of ethics, licensing and registration requirements, examination, training, and continuing education. The statute exempts: (1) an owner or tenant from licensure, so an owner may perform assessment or remediation on his or her own property; and (2) contaminated areas of less than 25 contiguous square feet.

In general terms, this statute requires a license for either (1) mold assessment or (2) mold remediation. A Texas Board of Health licensee who intends to perform **mold assessment** on a mold remediation project must prepare a work analysis for the project. The work analysis must specify: (1) the rooms or areas were the work will be performed, (2) the quantities and materials to be removed or cleaned at the project, (3) the proposed methods for each type of remediation and each type of area in the project, and (4) the proposed clearance criteria for each type of remediation in each type of area in the project.

If the Texas Board of Health licensee intends to perform **mold remediation,** he or she must prepare a work plan providing instructions for the remediation and efforts to be performed. For the remediation efforts to be performed for the mold or remediation project, the licensee must provide a work plan to the client before the mold remediation begins. Not later than the fifth day before the date on which the licensee starts the mold remediation, the licensee must notify the Texas Department of Health in writing about the project. If it is an emergency, then notice to the Department of Health may be verbal but made not later than the next business day after the licensee identifies the emergency.

This may be a huge help for consumers. The statute provides that not later than the tenth day after the date the licensee completes mold remediation to the property, he or she must provide a certificate of mold remediation to the property owner. The certificate must include a statement by the mold assessment licensee that the project has been remediated as outlined in the mold management plan. If the mold assessment licensee determines that the underlying cause of the mold has been remediated and is reasonably certain that the mold will not return from that remediated cause, the mold assessment licensee shall indicate on the certificate that the underlying cause of the mold has been remediated. If the property owner sells the property, the property owner is required to provide the buyer with a copy of each certificate that has been issued for the property under the statute. Get this! The statute provides that the **property owner is not liable for damages related to mold remediation** on the property if: (1) a certificate of mold remediation has been issued, and (2) damages accrued on or before the date of the issuance of the certificate. See Section 1958.303.

In addressing the insurance issue, the statute provides that insurer may not make an underwriting decision regarding a residential property insurance policy based on previous mold damage or a claim for mold damage if: (1) the applicant for insurance coverage has property eligible for coverage under a residential property policy, (2) the property has had mold damage, (3) mold remediation has been performed on the property, and (4) the property was (a) remediated (as evidenced by the certification of mold remediation) or (b) has been inspected by an independent assessor or adjuster who determined, based on the inspection, that the property does not convey any evidence of mold damage. See Insurance Code, Article 21.21-11.

To prevent conflicts of interest, the license holder may not perform both mold assessment and mold remediation on the same project (Section 1958.155(a)).

Do we need it?

A study by the Institute of Medicine (an entity of the National Academy of Sciences, which is chartered by Congress) has concluded that mold does not cause cancer, fatigue, gastrointestinal problems, or neurological disorders, as many had believed in the past. The study found that there are many factors in indoor environments that can intermingle to produce allergic reactions, but that the mold alone cannot be held responsible for causing such severe illnesses. Note report dated June 1, 2004, in www.GlobeSt.com.

The Importance of a Home Inspection

HUD requires that the borrower, in any transaction involving FHA Insurance, be provided with a notice of acknowledging the importance of a home inspection before the execution of a contract. (Mortgage Letter 96-10.) A copy of TAR® Form 1928 follows (see Figure 5-3). If the notice is not provided to a prospective purchaser before the execution of the contract, HUD will require reexecution of the contract before processing the loan.

The notice states that HUD does not warrant the condition of the property and that it is important that a buyer have a home inspection to identify any possible defects. The borrower may finance up to $200 of the inspection costs.

Seller's Disclosure of Property Condition

All sellers of residential property in Texas, with some obvious exceptions, must provide the buyers with a Seller's Disclosure of **Property Condition** form. The "notice" is required by Section 5.008 of the Property Code.

FIG 5-3   TAR® FORM 1928

**U.S. Department of Housing
and Urban Development (HUD)**
Federal Housing Administration (FHA)

OMB Approval No: 2502-0538
(exp. 06/30/2006)

For Your Protection: Get a Home Inspection

Name of Buyer (s) _____

Property Address _____

_____

Why a Buyer Needs a Home Inspection

A home inspection gives the buyer more detailed information about the overall condition of the home prior to purchase. In a home inspection, a qualified inspector takes an in-depth, unbiased look at your potential new home to:

- evaluate the physical condition: structure, construction, and mechanical systems;
- identify items that need to be repaired or replaced; and
- estimate the remaining useful life of the major systems, equipment, structure, and finishes.

Appraisals are Different from Home Inspections

An appraisal is different from a home inspection. Appraisals are for lenders; home inspections are for buyers. An appraisal is required to:

- estimate the market value of a house;
- make sure that the house meets FHA minimum property standards/requirements; and
- make sure that the house is marketable.

FHA Does Not Guarantee the Value or Condition of your Potential New Home

If you find problems with your new home after closing, FHA can not give or lend you money for repairs, and FHA can not buy the home back from you.

Radon Gas Testing

The United States Environmental Protection Agency and the Surgeon General of the United States have recommended that all houses should be tested for radon. For more information on radon testing, call the toll-free National Radon Information Line at 1-800-SOS-Radon or 1-800-767-7236. As with a home inspection, if you decide to test for radon, you may do so before signing your contract, or you may do so after signing the contract as long as your contract states the sale of the home depends on your satisfaction with the results of the radon test.

Be an Informed Buyer

It is your responsibility to be an informed buyer. Be sure that what you buy is satisfactory in every respect. You have the right to carefully examine your potential new home with a qualified home inspector. You may arrange to do so before signing your contract, or may do so after signing the contract as long as your contract states that the sale of the home depends on the inspection.

I/we understand the importance of getting an independent home inspection. I/we have considered this before signing a contract with the seller for a home. Furthermore, I/we have carefully read this notice and fully understand that FHA will not perform a home inspection nor guarantee the price or condition of the property.

_____ **I/We choose to have a home inspection performed.**

_____ **I/We choose <u>not</u> to have a home inspection performed.**

X_____   X_____

Signature & Date   Signature & Date

form **HUD-92564-CN** (12/04)

The form provided in the Property Code is shown in Figure 5-4. There is also another, more complete form available through the Texas Association of REALTORS®, shown in Figure 5-5. Note that the TAR form is in much greater detail, but either form is acceptable.

If this form is not delivered to the buyers before the sales contract, the buyers have seven days from receipt of the notice to cancel the contract for any reason. The form, therefore, should be readily available to anyone working with the buyer. It is a disservice to the seller, as well as the buyer, for the purchaser not to have this notice in hand before making an offer.

Additionally, good real estate practice dictates that the notice should be filled out and signed **by the seller** at or before the time of the listing. It is vital that the seller understands his or her responsibilities and the extreme importance for truth and accuracy in completion of this form.

The Seller's Disclosure of Property Condition is not required in the following circumstances:

- pursuant to a court order or foreclosure sale.
- by a trustee in bankruptcy.
- to a mortgage by a mortgagor or successor in interest, or to a beneficiary of a deed of trust by a trustor or successor in interest.
- by a mortgagee or a beneficiary under a deed of trust who has acquired the real property at a sale conducted pursuant to a power of sale under a deed of trust or a sale pursuant to a court ordered foreclosure or has acquired the real property by a deed in lieu of foreclosure.
- by a fiduciary in the course of the administration of a decedent's estate, guardianship, conservatorship, or trust.
- from one co-owner to one or more other co-owners.
- made to a spouse or to a person or persons in the lineal line of consanguinity of one or more of the transferors.
- between spouses resulting from a decree of dissolution of marriage or a decree of legal separation or from a property settlement agreement incidental to such a decree.
- to or from any governmental entity.
- transfers of new residences of not more than one dwelling unit that have not previously been occupied for residential purposes.
- transfers of real property where the value of any dwelling does not exceed five percent (5 percent) of the value of the property.

Residential Condominiums

Buyers of a residential condominium must receive pertinent information from the seller as required by Section 82.157 of the Texas Property Code.

FIG 5-4   SELLER'S DISCLOSURE OF PROPERTY CONDITION

APPROVED BY THE TEXAS REAL ESTATE COMMISSION (TREC)

09-01-07

SELLER'S DISCLOSURE OF PROPERTY CONDITION

(SECTION 5.008, TEXAS PROPERTY CODE)

CONCERNING THE PROPERTY AT_____
(Street Address and City)

THIS NOTICE IS A DISCLOSURE OF SELLER'S KNOWLEDGE OF THE CONDITION OF THE PROPERTY AS OF THE DATE SIGNED BY SELLER AND IS NOT A SUBSTITUTE FOR ANY INSPECTIONS OR WARRANTIES THE PURCHASER MAY WISH TO OBTAIN. IT IS NOT A WARRANTY OF ANY KIND BY SELLER OR SELLER'S AGENTS.

Seller ☐ is ☐is not occupying the Property. If unoccupied, how long since Seller has occupied the Property?

1. The Property has the items checked below [Write Yes (Y), No (N), or Unknown (U)]:

__ Range	__ Oven	__ Microwave
__ Dishwasher	__ Trash Compactor	__ Disposal
__ Washer/Dryer Hookups	__ Window Screens	__ Rain Gutters
__ Security System	__ Fire Detection Equipment	__ Intercom System
__ TV Antenna	__ Smoke Detector	__ Satellite Dish
__ Ceiling Fan(s)	__ Smoke Detector-Hearing Impaired	__ Exhaust Fan(s)
__ Central A/C	__ Carbon Monoxide Alarm	__ Wall/Window Air Conditioning
__ Plumbing System	__ Emergency Escape Ladder(s)	__ Public Sewer System
__ Patio/Decking	__ Cable TV Wiring	__ Fences
__ Pool	__ Attic Fan(s)	__ Spa __ Hot Tub
__ Pool Equipment	__ Central Heating	__ Automatic Lawn Sprinkler System
__ Fireplace(s) & Chimney (Woodburning)	__ Septic System	__ Fireplace(s) & Chimney (Mock)
__ Gas Lines (Nat./LP)	__ Outdoor Grill	__ Carport
__ Garage: __ Attached __ Not Attached	__ Sauna	__ Water Supply __ City __ Well __ MUD __ Co-op
__ Garage Door Opener(s):__ Electronic __ Controls	__ Pool Heater __ Water Heater: __ Gas __ Electric	

Roof Type: _____ Age: _____ (approx)

Are you (Seller) aware of any of the above items that are not in working condition, that have known defects or that are in need of repair? ☐ Yes ☐ No ☐ Unknown If yes, then describe. (Attach additional sheets if necessary): _____

_____

2. Does the property have working smoke detectors installed in accordance with the smoke detector requirements of Chapter 766, Health and Safety Code? ☐ Yes ☐ No ☐ Unknown

If the answer to the question above is no or unknown, explain. (Attach additional sheets if necessary):

_____

_____

_____

FIG 5-4 *(continued)*

Seller's Disclosure Notice Concerning the Property at_____ Page 2   09-01-07
                                                                    (Street Address and City)

3. Are you (Seller) aware of any known defects/malfunctions in any of the following?

   Write Yes (Y) if you are aware, write No (N) if you are not aware.

   ___ Interior Walls   ___ Ceilings   ___ Floors

   ___ Exterior Walls   ___ Doors   ___ Windows

   ___ Roof   ___ Foundation/Slab(s)   ___ Basement

   ___ Walls/Fences   ___ Driveways   ___ Sidewalks

   ___ Plumbing Sewers/Septics   ___ Electrical Systems   ___ Lighting Fixtures

   ___ Other Structural Components (Describe) _____

   _____

   _____

4. Are you (Seller) aware of any of the following conditions? Write Yes (Y) if you are aware, write No (N) if you are not aware.

   ___ Active Termites (includes wood   ___ Termite or Wood Rot Damage   ___ Previous Termite Damage
       destroying insects)   Needing Repair

   ___ Previous Termite Treatment   ___ Previous Flooding   ___ Improper Drainage

   ___ Water Penetration   ___ Located in 100-Year   ___ Present Flood Insurance
                                               Floodplain   Coverage

   ___ Previous Structural or Roof Repair ___ Hazardous or Toxic Waste   ___ Asbestos Components

   ___ Urea-formaldehyde Insulation   ___ Radon Gas   ___ Lead Based Paint

   ___ Aluminum Wiring   ___ Previous Fires   ___ Unplatted Easements

   ___ Landfill, Settling, Soil Movement, Fault Lines   ___ Subsurface Structure or Pits

   ___ Previous Use of Premises for Manufacture of Methamphetamine

5. Are you (Seller) aware of any item, equipment, or system in or on the Property that is in need of repair? ☐ Yes (iIf you are aware) ☐ No (if you are not aware). If yes, then describe. (Attach additional sheets if necessary)

   _____

   _____

   _____

6. Are you (Seller) aware of any of the following? Write Yes (Y) if you are aware, write No (N) if you are not aware.

   ___ Room additions, structural modifications, or other alterations or repairs made without necessary permits or not in compliance with building codes in effect at that time.

   ___ Homeowners' Association or maintenance fees or assessments.

   ___ Any "common area" (facilities such as pools, tennis courts, walkways, or other areas) co-owned in undivided interest with others.

   ___ Any notices of violations of deed restrictions or governmental ordinances affecting the condition or use of the Property.

   ___ Any lawsuits directly or indirectly affecting the Property.

   ___ Any condition on the Property which materially affects the physical health or safety of an individual.

   If the answer to any of the above is yes explain. (Attach additional sheets if necessary):

   _____

   _____

   _____

TREC No. OP-H

FIG 5-4 *(continued)*

Seller's Disclosure Notice Concerning the Property at_____ Page 3 09-01-07
(Street Address and City)

7. If the property is located in a coastal area that is seaward of the Gulf Intracoastal Waterway or within 1,000 feet of the mean high tide bordering the Gulf of Mexico, the property may be subject to the Open Beaches Act or the Dune Protection Act (Chapter 61 or 63, Natural Resources Code, respectively) and a beachfront construction certificate or dune protection permit may be required for repairs or improvements. Contact the local government with ordinance authority over construction adjacent to public beaches for more information.

_____   _____
Date   Signature of Seller   Date   Signature of Seller

The undersigned purchaser hereby acknowledges receipt of the foregoing notice and acknowledges the property complies with the smoke detector requirements of Chapter 766, Health and Safety Code, or, if the property does not comply with the smoke detector requirements of Chapter 766, the buyer waives the buyer's rights to have smoke detectors installed in compliance with Chapter 766.

_____   _____
Date   Signature of Purchaser   Date   Signature of Purchaser

FIG 5-5   SELLER'S DISCLOSURE NOTICE

TEXAS ASSOCIATION OF REALTORS®

SELLER'S DISCLOSURE NOTICE
©Texas Association of REALTORS®, Inc. 2007

Section 5.008, Property Code requires a seller of residential property of not more than one dwelling unit to deliver a Seller's Disclosure Notice to a buyer on or before the effective date of a contract. **This form complies with and contains additional disclosures which exceed the minimum disclosures required by the Code.**

CONCERNING THE PROPERTY AT _____

THIS NOTICE IS A DISCLOSURE OF SELLER'S KNOWLEDGE OF THE CONDITION OF THE PROPERTY AS OF THE DATE SIGNED BY SELLER AND IS NOT A SUBSTITUTE FOR ANY INSPECTIONS OR WARRANTIES THE BUYER MAY WISH TO OBTAIN. IT IS NOT A WARRANTY OF ANY KIND BY SELLER, SELLER'S AGENTS, OR ANY OTHER AGENT.

Seller ❏ is ❏ is not   occupying the Property. If unoccupied (by Seller), how long since Seller has occupied the Property? ❏ _____ or ❏ never occupied the Property

Section 1. The Property has the items marked below: (Mark Yes (Y), No (N), or Unknown (U).)
This notice does not establish the items to be conveyed. The contract will determine which items will & will not convey.

Item	Y	N	U	Item	Y	N	U	Item	Y	N	U
Cable TV Wiring				Gas Lines (Nat/LP)				Pump: ❏ sump ❏ grinder			
Carbon Monoxide Det.				Hot Tub				Rain Gutters			
Ceiling Fans				Intercom System				Range/Stove			
Cooktop				Microwave				Roof/Attic Vents			
Dishwasher				Outdoor Grill				Sauna			
Disposal				Patio/Decking				Smoke Detector			
Emergency Escape Ladder(s)				Plumbing System				Smoke Detector – Hearing Impaired			
Exhaust Fans				Pool				Spa			
Fences				Pool Equipment				Trash Compactor			
Fire Detection Equip.				Pool Maint. Accessories				TV Antenna			
French Drain				Pool Heater				Washer/Dryer Hookup			
Gas Fixtures				Public Sewer System				Window Screens			

Item	Y	N	U	Additional Information
Central A/C				❏ electric ❏ gas number of units: _____
Evaporative Coolers				number of units: _____
Wall/Window AC Units				number of units: _____
Attic Fan(s)				if yes, describe: _____
Central Heat				❏ electric ❏ gas number of units: _____
Other Heat				if yes describe: _____
Oven				number of ovens: _____ ❏ electric ❏ gas ❏ other: _____
Fireplace & Chimney				❏ wood ❏ gas logs ❏ mock ❏ other: _____
Carport				❏ attached ❏ not attached
Garage				❏ attached ❏ not attached
Garage Door Openers				number of units: _____ number of remotes: _____
Satellite Dish & Controls				❏ owned ❏ leased from _____
Security System				❏ owned ❏ leased from _____
Water Heater				❏ electric ❏ gas ❏ other: _____ number of units: _____
Water Softener				❏ owned ❏ leased from _____
Underground Lawn Sprinkler				❏ automatic ❏ manual areas covered: _____
Septic / On-Site Sewer Facility				if yes, attach Information About On-Site Sewer Facility (TAR-1407)

(TAR-1406) 7-2-07   Initialed by: Seller: _____,_____ and Buyer: _____, _____   Page 1 of 5

FIG 5-5   *(continued)*

Concerning the Property at _____

Water supply provided by: ❑ city ❑ well ❑ MUD ❑ co-op ❑ unknown ❑ other:_____
Was the Property built before 1978? ❑ yes ❑ no ❑ unknown
    (If yes, complete, sign, and attach TAR-1906 concerning lead-based paint hazards).
Roof Type: _____ Age: _____(approximate)
Is there an overlay roof covering on the Property (shingles or roof covering placed over existing shingles or roof covering)? ❑ yes ❑ no ❑ unknown

Are you (Seller) aware of any of the items listed in this Section 1 that are not in working condition, that have defects, or are need of repair? ❑ yes ❑ no If yes, describe (attach additional sheets if necessary): _____
_____
_____
_____

Section 2. Are you (Seller) aware of any defects or malfunctions in any of the following?: (Mark Yes (Y) if you are aware and No (N) if you are not aware.)

Item	Y	N	Item	Y	N	Item	Y	N
Basement			Floors			Sidewalks		
Ceilings			Foundation / Slab(s)			Walls / Fences		
Doors			Interior Walls			Windows		
Driveways			Lighting Fixtures			Other Structural Components		
Electrical Systems			Plumbing Systems					
Exterior Walls			Roof					

If the answer to any of the items in Section 2 is yes, explain (attach additional sheets if necessary): _____
_____
_____
_____
_____

Section 3. Are you (Seller) aware of any of the following conditions: (Mark Yes (Y) if you are aware and No (N) if you are not aware.)

Condition	Y	N	Condition	Y	N
Aluminum Wiring			Previous Roof Repairs		
Asbestos Components			Other Structural Repairs		
Diseased Trees: ❑ oak wilt ❑ _____			Radon Gas		
Endangered Species/Habitat on Property			Settling		
Fault Lines			Soil Movement		
Hazardous or Toxic Waste			Subsurface Structure or Pits		
Improper Drainage			Underground Storage Tanks		
Intermittent or Weather Springs			Unplatted Easements		
Landfill			Unrecorded Easements		
Lead-Based Paint or Lead-Based Pt. Hazards			Urea-formaldehyde Insulation		
Encroachments onto the Property			Water Penetration		
Improvements encroaching on others' property			Wetlands on Property		
Located in 100-year Floodplain			Wood Rot		
Present Flood Insurance Coverage (If yes, attach TAR-1414)			Active infestation of termites or other wood-destroying insects (WDI)		
Previous Flooding into the Structures			Previous treatment for termites or WDI		
Previous Flooding onto the Property			Previous termite or WDI damage repaired		
Previous Fires			Termite or WDI damage needing repair		
Previous Foundation Repairs			Previous Use of Premises for Manufacture of Methamphetamine		

FIG 5-5   *(continued)*

Concerning the Property at _____

If the answer to any of the items in Section 3 is yes, explain (attach additional sheets if necessary): _____
_____
_____
_____
_____
_____

Section 4.   Are you (Seller) aware of any item, equipment, or system in or on the Property that is in need of repair, which has not been previously disclosed in this notice?   ❏ yes ❏ no   If yes, explain (attach additional sheets if necessary): _____
_____
_____
_____
_____
_____

Section 5.   Are you (Seller) aware of any of the following (Mark Yes (Y) if you are aware. Mark No (N) if you are not aware.)

Y   N
❏   ❏   Room additions, structural modifications, or other alterations or repairs made without necessary permits or not in compliance with building codes in effect at the time.

❏   ❏   Homeowners' associations or maintenance fees or assessments. If yes, complete the following:
Name of association:_____
Manager's name: _____ Phone:_____
Fees or assessments are: $_____ per _____ and are: ❏ mandatory ❏ voluntary
Any unpaid fees or assessment for the Property? ❏ yes ($_____) ❏ no
If the Property is in more than one association, provide information about the other associations below or attach information to this notice.

❏   ❏   Any common area (facilities such as pools, tennis courts, walkways, or other) co-owned in undivided interest with others. If yes, complete the following:
Any optional user fees for common facilities charged? ❏ yes ❏ no If yes, describe: _____
_____

❏   ❏   Any notices of violations of deed restrictions or governmental ordinances affecting the condition or use of the Property.

❏   ❏   Any lawsuits or other legal proceedings directly or indirectly affecting the Property.

❏   ❏   Any death on the Property except for those deaths cause by: natural causes, suicide, or accident unrelated to the condition of the Property.

❏   ❏   Any condition on the Property which materially affects the health or safety of an individual.

❏   ❏   Any repairs or treatments, other than routine maintenance, made to the Property to remediate environmental hazards such as asbestos, radon, lead-based paint, urea-formaldehyde, or mold.
If yes, attach any certificates or other documentation identifying the extent of the remediation (for example, certificate of mold remediation or other remediation).

If the answer to any of the items in Section 5 is yes, explain (attach additional sheets if necessary): _____
_____
_____
_____
_____
_____

(TAR-1406) 7-2-07   Initialed by: Seller: _____,_____ and Buyer: _____, _____   Page 3 of 5

FIG 5-5 *(continued)*

Concerning the Property at _____

Section 6. Seller ❑ **has** ❑ **has not attached a survey of the Property.**

Section 7. Within the last 4 years, have you (Seller) received any written inspection reports from persons who regularly provide inspections and who are either licensed as inspectors or otherwise permitted by law to perform inspections? ❑ yes ❑ no If yes, attach copies and complete the following:

Inspection Date	Type	Name of Inspector	No. of Pages

Note: A buyer should not rely on the above-cited reports as a reflection of the current condition of the Property. A buyer should obtain inspections from inspectors chosen by the buyer.

Section 8. Check any tax exemption(s) which you (Seller) currently claim for the Property:
❑ Homestead   ❑ Senior Citizen   ❑ Disabled
❑ Wildlife Management   ❑ Agricultural   ❑ Disabled Veteran
❑ Other:_____   ❑ Unknown

Section 9. Have you (Seller) ever received proceeds for a claim for damage to the Property (for example, an insurance claim or a settlement or award in a legal proceeding) and not used the proceeds to make the repairs for which the claim was made? ❑ yes ❑ no If yes, explain:_____
_____
_____
_____

Section 10. Does the property have working smoke detectors installed in accordance with the smoke detector requirements of Chapter 766 of the Health and Safety Code?* ❑ unknown ❑ no ❑ yes. If no or unknown, explain. (Attach additional sheets if necessary): _____
_____
_____

*Chapter 766 of the Health and Safety Code requires one-family or two-family dwellings to have working smoke detectors installed in accordance with the requirements of the building code in effect in the area in which the dwelling is located, including performance, location, and power source requirements. If you do not know the building code requirements in effect in your area, you may check unknown above or contact your local building official for more information.

Seller acknowledges that the statements in this notice are true to the best of Seller's belief and that no person, including the broker(s), has instructed or influenced Seller to provide inaccurate information or to omit any material information.

_____   _____   _____   _____
Signature of Seller   Date   Signature of Seller   Date
Printed Name: _____   Printed Name: _____

FIG 5-5   *(continued)*

Concerning the Property at _____

ADDITIONAL NOTICES TO BUYER:

(1) The Texas Department of Public Safety maintains a database that the public may search, at no cost, to determine if registered sex offenders are located in certain zip code areas. To search the database, visit www.txdps.state.tx.us. For information concerning past criminal activity in certain areas or neighborhoods, contact the local police department.

(2) If the property is located in a coastal area that is seaward of the Gulf Intracoastal Waterway or within 1,000 feet of the mean high tide bordering the Gulf of Mexico, the property may be subject to the Open Beaches Act or the Dune Protection Act (Chapter 61 or 63, Natural Resources Code, respectively) and a beachfront construction certificate or dune protection permit may be required for repairs or improvements. Contact the local government with ordinance authority over construction adjacent to public beaches for more information.

(3) If you are basing your offers on square footage, measurements, or boundaries, you should have those items independently measured to verify any reported information.

(4) The following providers currently provide service to the property:

Electric:_____   Sewer:_____

Water:_____   Cable:_____

Trash:_____   Natural Gas:_____

Local Phone:_____   Propane:_____

(5) This Seller's Disclosure Notice was completed by Seller as of the date signed. The brokers have relied on this notice as true and correct and have no reason to believe it to be false or inaccurate. YOU ARE ENCOURAGED TO HAVE AN INSPECTOR OF YOUR CHOICE INSPECT THE PROPERTY.

The undersigned Buyer acknowledges receipt of the foregoing notice and acknowledges the property complies with the smoke detector requirements of Chapter 766, Health and Safety Code, or, if the property does not comply with the smoke detector requirements of Chapter 766, the buyer waives the buyer's rights to have smoke detectors installed in compliance with Chapter 766.

_____   _____
Signature of Buyer   Date   Signature of Buyer   Date
Printed Name: _____   Printed Name: _____

(TAR-1406) 7-2-07   Page 5 of 5

This includes copies of the condominium's Declaration, By-Laws, and any Rules of the Association. It also requires a Resale Certificate from the Condominiums Owners' Association stating its financial condition and prepared no more than three months before the delivery date to the buyer's or the seller's affidavit that he or she has requested the information from the association. As provided in the promulgated residential condominium earnest money contract for resale, if the seller has not provided this information prior to contract offer, the buyer may cancel the contract before the sixth day after the date he or she receives the material. The buyer may void the contract by hand delivery or written notice of cancellation to the seller by certified United States mail, return receipt requested.

Seller's Disclosure Regarding Potential Annexation

A person who sells an interest in real property located in the extraterritorial jurisdiction of a city is now required to give the purchaser of the real property a written notice that his or her property is located outside the limits of the municipality. See Property Code Sec.5.011.

The seller must deliver the notice to the purchaser before the date of the execution of the earnest money contract for sale.

Seller's Notice of Obligations Related to Membership and Property Owners' Association

If a seller of residential real property is subject to membership in a property owners' association, and the property comprises not more than one dwelling unit, the seller is now required to give to the purchaser of the property a written statement indicating that the purchaser is obligated to be a member of the property owners' association. See Property Code Sec. 5.012.

The seller must deliver the notice to the purchaser before the date the contract is executed. This is also discussed in greater detail in Chapter 1.

Property Owners' Association Disclosures

State law also requires the property owners' association, not later than the tenth day after the date of the written request for subdivision information is received from an owner, owner's agent, or title insurance company or its agent acting on behalf of the owner, to deliver to the owner, owner's agent, or title insurance company or its agent current copies of the restrictions and a copy of the bylaws and rules to the property owners' association.

Residential Lead-Based Paint Hazard Reduction Act of 1992

Lead is a soft and malleable metal. For years it was used for paint bases and for plumbing pipes. Leaded and lead-based paint in drinking water are a special concern.

Lead is poisonous and an irritant to the brain. Babies and young children are more susceptible to the effects of lead than adults. The younger the child, the greater the effect of the poison. The levels of lead can cause behavioral and learning problems in children because of neurological damages. High levels of lead exposure can cause convulsions, retardation, and death. The Centers for Disease Control has indicated that research shows lead blood levels for children need to be as low as ten micrograms per deciliter to be an acceptable level.

Recognizing the need to control exposure to lead-based paint hazards, Congress passed the Residential Lead-Based Paint Hazard Reduction Act of 1992. The main purpose of the Act was to develop the infrastructure and standards necessary to reduce lead-based paint hazards in housing.

In general, the Act requires sellers and lessors, or any agent acting on their behalf, of most residential housing built before 1978 to provide purchasers and lessees with all information known to the seller, lessor, or agent of the presence of lead-based paint and lead-based paint hazards. The Act does not require the disclosures for transfers due to foreclosure sales or informal rental agreements, which do not involve a lease and renewals of existing leases.

INTERESTING NOTE! A housing group calling itself the National Multi-Housing Council is dedicating a portion of its legislative agenda to fight new proposals concerning lead-based paint, apparently contending that little, if any, good has come from the laws already on the books. The organization noted that the problem of childhood lead poisoning was well on its way out long before the disclosures were mandated in 1996. According to the Centers for Disease Control, the presence of elevated lead levels in the general population decreased 94 percent between 1988 and 1994. The incidence of lead poisoning has dropped even more dramatically, with just 0.4 percent of young children reported as having lead poisoning.

What caused the lead poisoning to drop? The organization notes that the decline in blood levels through the 1990s was the result of eliminating lead from most gasoline products, eliminating lead solder from food and beverage cans and water supply pipes, and limiting the admission of lead from industrial facilities. The organization notes that "Regulations on housing providers embody a costly and cumbersome regulatory approach that increases the cost of and threatens the supply of affordable housing and has little impact on the overall incidence of childhood lead poisoning" (*Real Estate Intelligence Report*, Spring 2000).

6

Deceptive Trade—Practices, Fraud, and Real Estate Recovery Fund

Purpose

After carefully reading Chapter 6, the student will be able to:

- Understand the key terms from DTPA.
- Explain the idea of "caveat emptor" and how the DTPA has affected it.
- Discuss the importance of *Cameron v. Terrell & Garrett, Inc.*
- Identify the causes of action for a consumer under DTPA.
- Define latent defects.
- Give examples and applications of the "laundry list."
- List statutory defenses and case law defenses under the DTPA.
- Identify ways agents have been found guilty of real estate fraud.
- Explain the importance and application of the Real Estate Recovery Fund.

Key Words to look for in this chapter:
1. Caveat Emptor
2. Goods
3. Services
4. Consumer
5. Unconscionable action or course of action
6. Knowingly
7. Waiver
8. Mere opinion
9. Real Estate Fraud
10. Real Estate Recovery Fund

The previous chapter dealt with duties to third parties as a real estate agency relationship. This chapter deals with a specific statute on how a licensee must deal with the public, both sellers and buyers, and in many cases, both.

There is a Latin phrase, **caveat emptor**, which literally means, "Let the buyer beware." This concept governed the responsibilities, or lack of them, between the buyer and the seller. Under this theory a purchaser buys at his or her own risk. The idea is as old as its Latin language indicates; and for many years it regulated real estate transactions.

There are exceptions to caveat emptor, however, which include expressed or implied warranties, misrepresentation involved in the sale, misleading information, or fraud. Notwithstanding these exceptions, consumer advocates insist on greater consumer protection. Their claim is that consumers are ignorant, gullible, and purchase without proper consideration or thought.

DISCUSSION QUESTION

■ Under what circumstance have you felt ignorant and credulous as a consumer?

Laws were passed to require that sellers divulge "latent defects," those defects not readily detected by the purchaser. A seller who fails to warn the buyer about these defects or lies about the condition of the real estate can be guilty of misrepresentation. The sellers can be guilty by omission or by commission, by what they don't say, and by what they do say.

As an agent, the real estate licensee can also be just as guilty because of what he or she said or did not say. The Texas Supreme Court has ruled that a real estate purchaser is a consumer of the broker's services. *Cameron v. Terrell & Garrett, Inc.*, 618 S.W.2d 535 (Tex. 1981).

In Texas the consumer is also protected by §1101.652(b)(3) and (4) of the Real Estate License Act, Fraud in Real Estate and Stock Transactions Statute (Art. 27.01 of the Texas Business and Commerce Code), and the **Texas Deceptive Trade Practices-Consumer Protection Act (DTPA)**. The DTPA virtually eliminates the caveat emptor concept in Texas.

The DTPA makes "false, misleading, or deceptive acts or practices" in the selling, advertising, or leasing of real property illegal. The DTPA has been a leading basis of lawsuits against real estate practitioners in Texas. A real estate licensee can be liable for damages whether he or she acted knowingly or unknowingly. In some cases, treble (triple) damages and attorneys' fees can be awarded.

Now it's the real estate agents who should beware. All licensees should take extreme care in the handling of each document or instrument involving a real estate transaction. Errors and omissions insurance offers some protection to licensees; one should note, however, that most errors and omissions insurance policies do not cover more than just the actual damages for violations of the

Texas Deceptive Trade Practices Act (which can award multiple damages, attorneys' fees, and court costs). In addition to being held liable for damages under the DTPA, real estate brokers and salespeople can have their licenses revoked by TREC for the same conduct that violates the DTPA.

KEY DEFINITIONS FROM THE DTPA— APPLICABLE TO REAL ESTATE BROKERS

- ■ "Goods" are defined as tangible chattels or real property [emphasis supplied] purchased for lease or use, Sec. 17.45 (1);

- ■ "Services" mean work, labor, or services purchased or leased for purchase, including services furnished in connection with the sale or repair of goods, Sec. 17.45 (2);

- ■ "Consumer" means an individual, partnership, corporation, or governmental entity who seeks or acquires by purchase of lease, any goods or services, Sec. 17.45 (4);

- ■ "Unconscionable action or course of action" means an act or practice, which, to a consumer's detriment takes advantage of the lack of knowledge, ability, experience, or capacity of a person to a grossly unfair degree;

- ■ "Knowingly" means actual awareness of a falsity, deception, or unfairness of the act or practice giving rise to the consumer's claim or, in an action brought under a breach of an express or implied warranty as provided in Sec. 17.50, actual awareness of the act or practice constitutes the breach of warranty, but actual awareness may be inferred where objective manifestations indicate the person acted with actual awareness.

CAUSES OF ACTION

A consumer may maintain a DTPA action where one or more of the following from Section 17.50 is a producing cause of damages:

- ■ the use or employment by any person of a false, misleading, or deceptive act or practice that is specifically enumerated in a subdivision of Subsection (b) of Section 17.46 (commonly known as the "laundry list") of the subchapter;

- ■ breach of an express or implied warranty;

- ■ any unconscionable action or course of action by any person; or

- ■ the use or employment by any person of an act or practice in violation of Article 21.21, Texas Insurance Code, as amended.

DISCUSSION QUESTION

■ What example of one of these "causes of damages" can you think of?

There is a general exclusion, though, provided in Section 17.49(f) of the DTPA for a claim arising out of a written contract if the contract relates to a transaction involving total consideration by the consumer of more than $100,000, the consumer is represented by legal counsel, and the contract does not involve the consumer's residence. Similarly, the Act also exempts claims arising from a transaction, a project, or a set of transactions relating to the same project, involving total consideration by the consumer of more than $500,000, other than a cause of action involving a consumer's residence, even if the consumer is not represented by a legal counsel. This provides a huge defense for commercial real estate brokers, but not for a licensee who sells homesteads.

OTHER IMPORTANT PROVISIONS UNDER THE DECEPTIVE TRADE PRACTICES ACT

I. SEC. 17.42

A waiver is valid and enforceable if (1) the waiver is in writing and is signed by the consumer; (2) the consumer is not in a significantly disparate bargaining position; and (3) the consumer is represented by legal counsel in seeking or requiring the goods and services, Section 17.42(a)(1).

To be effective, the waiver must be: (1) conspicuous and in boldface of at least ten points in size; and (2) identified by the heading "Waiver of Consumer Rights," or words of similar meaning; and (3) substantially in the following form:

> "I waive my rights under the Deceptive Trade Practices-Consumer Protection Act, Section 17.41 et seq., Business & Commerce Code, a law that gives consumers special rights and protections. After consultation with an attorney of my selection, I voluntarily consent to this waiver."

The statute does not require the signature of the consumer's attorney. This waiver is seldom utilized, as an attorney is reluctant to let his or her client waive such significant rights.

2. SEC. 17.44

This subchapter shall be liberally construed and applied to promote its underlying purposes, which are to protect consumers against false, misleading, and deceptive business practices, unconscionable action, and breaches of warranty and to provide effective and economical procedures to secure such protection.

3. SEC. 17.46

Specific applications of the 17.46 "laundry list" of deceptive trade practice violations, which are particularly applicable to real estate transactions, are:

- representing that goods are original or new if they are deteriorated, reconditioned, reclaimed, used, or secondhand, Sec. 17.46(B)(6); when selling real property *nothing* is new; Don't say it.

- representing that goods or services are of a particular standard, quality, or grade, or that goods are of a particular style or model, if they are of another, Sec. 17.46(B)(7);

- disparaging the goods, services, or business of another by false or misleading representation of facts, Sec. 17.46(B)(8);

- making false or misleading statements of fact concerning the reasons for existence of, or amount of price reductions, Sec. 17.46(B)(11);

- representing that an agreement confers or involves rights, remedies, or obligations that it does not have or involve or that are prohibited by law, Sec. 17.46(B)(12);

- knowingly making false or misleading statements of fact concerning the need for parts, replacement, or repair service, Sec. 17.46(B)(13);

- misrepresenting the authority of a salesperson, representative, or agent to negotiate the final term of a consumer transaction, Sec. 17.46(B)(14);

- representing that work or services have been performed on or parts replaced in goods when the work or services were not performed nor the parts replaced, Sec. 17.46(B)(22);

- failing to disclose information concerning goods or services that was known at the time of the transaction. The failure to disclose such information was intended to induce the consumer into a transaction into which the consumer would not have entered had the information been disclosed, Sec. 17.46(B)(24).

DISCUSSION QUESTIONS

- List some examples of real estate activities that might violate the "laundry list."

■ How and why might these be violations?

■ The court cannot suspend or revoke a broker's license under the DTPA, but there are a number of pertinent corresponding provisions of the Real Estate License Act. These provisions provide that a licensee can have his or her license revoked or suspended for:

a. soliciting, selling, or offering for sale real property under a scheme or program that constitutes a lottery or deceptive practice, §1101.652(b)(14); (15);

b. making a material misrepresentation, or failing to disclose to a potential purchaser any latent structural defect or any other defect known to the broker or salesperson. A latent structure defect and other defects do not refer to trivial or insignificant defects but refer to those defects that would be a significant factor to a reasonable and prudent purchaser in making a decision to purchase, §1101.652(b)(3); (4);

c. pursuing a continued and flagrant course of misrepresentation or making a false promise through agents, salespersons, advertising, or otherwise, §1101.652(b)(6);

d. failing to make clear, to all parties to a transaction, which party he is acting for, or receiving compensation from more than one party except with full knowledge and consent of all parties, §1101.652(b)(7); (8);

e. inducing or attempting to induce a party to a contract of sale or lease to break the contract for the purpose of substituting in lieu thereof a new contract, §1101.652(b)(21);

f. guaranteeing, authorizing, or permitting a person to guarantee that future profits will result from a resale of real property, §1101.652(b)(17);

g. acting in the dual capacity of broker and undisclosed principal in a transaction, §1101.652(b)(16);

h. accepting, receiving, or charging an undisclosed commission, rebate, or direct profit on expenditures made for a principal, §1101.652(b)(13);

i. failing to disclose information concerning goods or services that was known at the time of the transaction. The failure to disclose such information was intended to induce the consumer into a transaction into which the consumer would not have entered had the information been disclosed, Sec. 17.46(B)(24).

BROKERAGE CASES INTERPRETING THE DTPA

There is no doubt as to the trend of the courts in Texas under the Deceptive Trade Practices Act. The consumer has been held to have a duty of care of being ignorant, unthinking, and credulous. *Spradling v. Williams*, 566 S.W.2d 561 (Tex. 1978). Brokers, on the other hand, have been tested (by the state) and held to provide the services of an expert. In other words, consumers must be protected from brokers who are considered real estate experts. *Holloman v. Denson*, 640 S.W.2d 417 (Tex. Civ. App.-Waco 1982).

■ *Property management services.* The seller can sue the broker for misrepresentation of services either for sale or management of the property. *Lerma v. Brecheisen*, 602 S.W.2d 318 (Tex. Civ. App.-Waco 1980).

■ *Lack of contract.* In *Cameron v. Terrell & Garrett, Inc.*, 618 S.W.2d 535 (Tex. 1981), the Texas Supreme Court also held the purchaser could sue the broker for misrepresentation even though there is no contract between them.

■ *Material omission.* Agents can be guilty by omission as well as commission, by what they do not say as well as what they do say. Silence is not a defense to a violation of the act, if in fact there was a duty to speak because of the agent's superior knowledge in the subject matter. Cases now establish very clear criteria for an agent's liability for "failing to disclose." In order to maintain the cause of action, the plaintiffs must prove:

a. the defendant knew of the information at the time of the transaction;

b. the defendant failed to disclose the information;

c. the failure to disclose was intended to induce the plaintiff into a transaction; and

d. the plaintiff would not otherwise have entered into the transaction.

The failure to disclose the information was the producing cause of damages in *Sanchez v. Guerrero*, 885 S.W.2d 487 (Tex. App.-El Paso 1994).

■ *Mere opinion.* Although not a deceptive trade practices case, *Trenholm v. Ratcliff*, 646 S.W.2d 927 (Tex. 1983) wiped out any defense of a broker maintaining "mere opinion" as a defense. Everybody is entitled to an opinion. *Ballow v. Charter Realty ERA*, 603 So.2d 877 (Ala. 1992); *Carpenter v. Merrill Lynch Realty Operating Partnership, L.P.*, 424 S.E.2d 178 (N.C. App. 1993). There is a concern, however, when a consumer can construe that opinion to be a representation of fact, or, if the opinion is delivered to the consumer with the intention of inducing the consumer to make a purchase, it will be construed as a misrepresentation, particularly in light of the fact that brokers are generally considered to be experts. *Hinkley v. Vital*, (1992 Mass. App. Div. 92); *Robertson v. United New Mexico Bank at Roswell*, 14 F.3d 1076 (5th Cir. 1994).

- *Exaggeration.* Exaggerations can also create a cause of action against the agent. *Ridco v. Sexton*, supra. This case also eliminates any defense of mere "puffing" as a defense under the Act.

- *I'm a principal.* Being a party to the transaction does not excuse the actions of a licensee. *Ramsey v. Gordon*, supra, wipes out any defense of an agent by claiming that he or she has "changed position" and that he or she is now a principal in a transaction.

- *No compensation.* A broker can act as a volunteer and still be liable. *Canada v. Kearns*, supra, held the broker liable even though the broker received no fee.

- *Salesperson liability.* If the sponsoring broker is not sued, though, there's a different result! In *Miller v. Keyser*, 90 S.W.3d 712 (Tex. 2002), the Court was determining whether an agent or a disclosed principal could be held liable for passing along false representations. The Court held that, since the DTPA allows a consumer to bring suit against "any person," the agent can be held personally liable for the misrepresentation he makes when acting within the scope of his employment.

The case revolves around the sale of lots in Pearland, Texas that backed up to Brazoria County's Drainage District, located on the back 20 feet of each lot. Each buyer knew that the drainage easement was on the lot, but the agent (salesperson) represented to the homeowners that the lots were oversized and that they were in fact larger than the lots of a competing builder in the subdivision. The homeowners paid a premium for these "oversized" lots. After building their homes, the buyers received a letter from the Brazoria County Drainage District, telling them that all fences in the easement must be removed at the owner's expense. As a result, the homeowners sued. Through a series of procedural maneuvers, the only defendant left as a defendant was the salesperson, Barry Keyser, who argued that a corporate agent cannot be held personally liable for company misrepresentations (apparently assuming, under the Texas law, that everything he did was on behalf of the corporation that held his license).

The Court disagreed noting that Keyser personally made the representations about the size of the lot and the location of the fence. He was the only person with whom the homeowners had any contact. Based on the plain language of the statute, Keyser is liable for his own DTPA violations.

Keyser then claimed that his misrepresentations were innocent (apparently relying on information given to him by the sponsoring broker). The Court noted, however, that the DTPA does not require the consumer to prove employee acted knowingly or intentionally in order to create liability. Keyser was liable even if he did not know his representations were false or even if he did not intend to deceive anyone. The Court held that they did have a right to seek indemnification from the employer and therefore could have sued the employer, brought them into the case as part of their defense.

■ *I didn't know.* An innocent misrepresentation also creates liability even though the agent had no knowledge of the falsity. *Guilbeau v. Anderson,* 841 S.W.2d 517 (Tex. App.-Houston [14th Dist.] 1992, no writ); *Henry S. Miller v. Bynum,* 797 S.W.2d 41 (Tex. App.-Houston [1st Dist.] 1990).

■ *Unconscionable acts.* More cases seem to be concerned with the issue of "unconscionability." Note that Section 17.45(5), discussed earlier, is almost perfectly suited for a real estate transaction, particularly when a real estate agent is dealing with first-time home buyers who trust that agent and rely on his or her expertise to guide them through the home-buying process. In *Chastain v. Koonce,* the Texas Supreme Court established the criterion for "unconscionable action," or course of action, under 17.45(5). The criterion requires "taking advantage of a consumer's lack of knowledge to a grossly unfair degree, thus, requires a showing of intent, knowledge, or a conscious indifference" at the time the misrepresentation was made. *Chastain v. Koonce,* 700 S.W.2d 579 (Tex. 1985). Considering the consumer is "ignorant, unthinking, and credulous," and a licensee is "an expert, tested by the State and found to be competent," the trend of the courts under this statute is predictable. Most buyers ask questions of the agent, expecting true and accurate responses. *Sanchez v. Guerrero,* supra.

One of the first DTPA cases involved the sale of real property and assured that real estate purchasers and practices were covered by the Act:

Cameron v. Terrell & Garrett, Inc., *618 S.W.2d 535 (Tex. 1981)*

Jerry and Jo Ann Cameron sued the listing real estate agent, Terrell & Garrett, Inc. for triple damages because of a misrepresentation of the square footage in the house that they purchased in Arlington, Texas. The real estate company had put the listing in the local multiple listing service. The information stated that the house contained 2,400 square feet.

The Camerons were looking for a house with their own agent when they found the house in question. Their agent showed them the square footage information in the listing service. They claim that their agreement to buy the house for $52,957.04 was based on the price of $22.06 per square foot.

After moving in, the buyer found that their house had only 2,245 square feet of heated and cooled area; if the garage, porch, and wall space were included, there would have been 2,400 square feet. They claimed actual damages of $3,419.30. They sought treble damages, reasonable attorney fees, and court costs. As agents of the sellers, Terrell and Garrett claimed that the Camerons were not their consumers since they didn't furnish goods or services for the Camerons.

Therefore the primary question was whether the Camerons were consumers under the DTPA. The jury returned a verdict for the Camerons. The trial court disregarded these findings disputing sufficient legal evidence and rendered a take-nothing judgment for Terrell and Garrett.

The Camerons appealed. The court of appeals affirmed the trial court's decision, but on different grounds. It held that the Camerons were not consumers of Terrell and Garrett's services (they represented the seller); and therefore, they could not bring a private suit. The Supreme Court reversed these judgments holding that the Camerons were consumers and that there was some evidence to support the jury's decision. The Camerons were entitled to treble damages, attorney's fees, and costs as the DTPA authorizes. Damages were based on the value of the improvements and the land.

The Court stated that the Deceptive Trade Practices-Consumer Protection Act was designed to protect consumers from deceptive trade practice in the purchase or lease of any goods or services. The person need not seek or receive goods or services furnished by the seller or vendor of goods to be a consumer.

The criterion for a violation of the Act appears to be the existence of circumstances where the knowledge of the agent, combined with the consumer's relative ignorance, acts to make even the slightest divergence from mere praise a representation of fact. *Chrysler-Plymouth City, Inc. v. Guerrero*, 620 S.W.2d 700 (Tex. Civ. App.-San Antonio 1981).

It has also been held that the cause of action is not limited to the "laundry list" of Sec. 17.46(b). Where an unlisted act is alleged as a violation of the DTPA, there must be two factual findings:

■ that the act or practice occurred; and

■ that it was a deceptive trade practice. *Spradling v. Williams*, supra; *Ybarra v. Saldana*, 624 S.W.2d 948 (Tex. Civ. App.-San Antonio 1981).

DEFENSES UNDER THE DTPA

1. Statutory Defenses

WAIVER

There are several defenses to damages under the Deceptive Trade Practices Act. Some of these defenses involved the defendant's relying on written information from a third party.

For DTPA causes of action arising after September 1, 1995, the absolute bar to waiver in a residential transaction has been removed. Section 17.42(a) provides:

Any waiver by a consumer of the provisions of this subchapter is contrary to public policy and is unenforceable and void; provided, however, that a waiver is valid and enforceable if:

■ the waiver is in writing and is signed by the consumer;

■ the consumer is not in a significantly disparate bargaining position; and

■ the consumer is represented by legal counsel in seeking or acquiring the goods or services.

RELIANCE ON OTHER SOURCES

- Sec. 17.505—If the defendant can prove that before consummation of the transaction [emphasis supplied] he gave reasonable and timely notice to the plaintiff of the defendant's reliance on:

  a. written information relating to the particular goods and service in question obtained from official government records, if the written information was false or inadequate and the defendant did not know and could not reasonably have known of the falsity or inaccuracy of the information;

  b. written information relating to the particular goods or service in question obtained from another source if the information was false or inaccurate and the defendant did not know and could not reasonably have known of the falsity or inaccuracy of the information; or

  c. written information concerning a test required or prescribed by government agency, if the information from the test was false or inaccurate and the defendant did not know and could not reasonably have known of the falsity or inaccuracy of the information.

Apparently the term "and could not reasonably have known of the falsity or inaccuracy" imposes upon the real estate broker the duty of care to at least investigate the information to determine whether it was true. See *Henry S. Miller v. Bynum*, supra.

There is also no definition that applies to "consummation of the transaction." One interpretation is that it must be prior to the "execution of any agreements" that can apparently mean the earnest money contract rather than the closing. If this is the case, an agent must give the various parties notice for inspections and representations very early in the transaction for this defense to apply.

OFFER OF SETTLEMENT

- Sec. 17.505—There is a DTPA requirement that a consumer must give the defendant a specific complaint and the amount of actual damages at least 60 days prior to filing the lawsuit. If the lawsuit is filed without the 60-day notice, the effect of filing the petition is the same as providing the written notice, as it gives the defendant 60 days from filing the lawsuit to offer to settle.

  a. The notice required apparently does not have to meet any formal requirements as it is to purely "inform the seller of the consumer's complaint and thus therefore provide an opportunity for the parties to settle the matter without litigation." *North American Van Lines v. Bauerele*, 678 S.W.2d 229 (Tex. Civ. App.-Ft. Worth 1984). The "specific complaint" can be relatively general in description. *Jim Walters Homes, Inc. v. Valencia*, 690 S.W.2d 239 (Tex. 1985);

b. The notice, however, must state a specific monetary amount of damages. *Sunshine Datsun v. Ramsey*, 687 S.W.2d 652 (Tex. Civ. App.-Amarillo 1984);

c. If the defendant gives a tender offer to settle the property within the time allowed, it is a defense to the potential treble damage exposure [DTPA Sec. 17.506(d)]. It should also be noted that any offer to settle made by the defendant during the 60 days must also include the attorney's fees in addition to the actual damages claimed by the plaintiff. *Cail v. Service Motors, Inc.*, 660 S.W.2d 814 (Tex. 1983).

CONTRIBUTION AND INDEMNITY

■ Sec. 17.555—This provision extends indemnity and contribution under the Act to encompass all possible damages under the Act. It can be considered as a very effective defense under the rights to the facts situation. The statute provides that the defendant may seek contribution or indemnity from one who, under statute law or common law, may have liability for the damaging event of which the consumer complains. This would allow the defendant to implead the seller, property inspector, or other person who the court may determine to have the ultimate liability. The statute also provides for the defendant to get reimbursement for reasonable attorney's fees and costs.

The real facts are that the broker may have to cross-file against a friend, another broker, or inspector to save their own neck! It is a hard rule, but a real test of liability.

MANDATORY MEDIATION

■ Sec. 17.5051 and 17.5052—The 1995 changes to the DTPA also provide for mediation and offers of settlement through mediation. Under this new procedure, a party may, not later than the ninetieth day after the date of service of the pleading, file a motion to compel mediation in a dispute. After the motion is filed, the court must, not later than 30 days after the motion is filed, sign an order setting the time and place of the mediation. The mediation must be held within 30 days after the date the order is signed, unless the parties agree otherwise. A party, however, may not compel mediation if the amount of economic damages claimed is less than $15,000, unless the party seeking to compel the mediation agrees to pay the cost of the mediation. Offers made during the mediation are treated very similarly to those under 17.505.

PROFESSIONAL SERVICES

A new amendment to Section 17.49 now prohibits a claim for damages based on the rendering of a professional service, the essence of which is the providing of advice, judgment, opinion, or similar professional skill. Logically, this could apply to real estate brokers as a very broad exemption. The exemption does not apply, however, to (1) an express misrepresentation of the material fact; (2) an unconscionable action or course of action, the failure to disclose information and violation of 17.46(b)(24); or (3) a breach of an express warranty that cannot be characterized as advice, judgment, or opinion. See Section 17.49(c). The effect of this defense seems to hinge on whether a real estate licensee will be held by the courts to be a "professional." Note the cases cited under "Professional Limitation Periods" in Chapter 5.

2. Case Law Defenses Under the DTPA

There are very few precedents to use in a broker's defense. The only reported cases to exempt brokers from liability have been one-sided cases.

- *Never said it.* The agent never made this representation. *Newsome v. Starkey*, 541 S.W.2d 468 (Tex. Civ. App.-Dallas 1976); *Ozuna v. Delaney Realty*, 593 S.W.2d 797 (Tex. Civ. App.-El Paso 1980, writ ref'd n.r.e.); *Stagner v. Friendswood Development Co., Inc.*, 620 S.W.2d 103 (Tex. 1981); *McCrea v. Cubilla Condominium Corp.*, 685 S.W.2d 755 (Tex. Civ. App.-Houston 1985). *Always* pass on the information given to you, and cite the source. Don't say it yourself. Reference the source! Note *Sherman v. Elkowitz*, supra.

- *Didn't know it.* With some exceptions, the courts will not penalize an agent for failing to reveal information he/she did not know. The courts will apparently not hold an agent to the duty of care of failing to reveal information that he or she does not know. *Robinson v. Preston Chrysler Plymouth, Inc.*, 633 S.W.2d 500 (Tex. 1982). This will depend upon whether the licensee could reasonably have known (remember 17.505) of the falsity or inaccuracy of the information.

- *The plaintiff relied on someone else.* Also, the real estate agent has not been held liable when the plaintiff was not relying on the real estate agent's representations because of the plaintiff's own inspection of the property before purchase. *Lone Star Machinery Corp. v. Frankel*, 564 S.W.2d 135 (Tex. Civ. App.-Beaumont 1978). See also *Bartlett v. Schmidt*, discussed earlier.

  Another exception may be available when the purchaser knows the correct information from another source, and thought the agent's information was incorrect. *Mikkelson v. Quail Valley Realty*, 641 P.2d 124 (Utah 1982). The courts have also ruled that the principal still has the duty to read and understand his or her own contract. *Jones v. Maestas*, supra; but see *Phillips v. JCM*, supra; *Wilkenson v. Smith*, supra; *Gillis v. First City Mortgage Company*, 694 S.W.2d 144 (Tex. App.-Houston [14th Dist.] 1985, writ ref'd n.r.e.).

- *Mistake.* A mere mistake, which does not result from lack of honesty or from lack of diligence that a reasonable broker would employ, is not a breach of fiduciary duty. *Perkins v. Thorpe*, ante; *Schroeder v. Rose*, supra.

■ *Relied on the licensed real property inspectors.* The Real Estate License Act provides for licensing of inspectors to inspect and report on the condition of real property. In the event a licensed inspector engages in conduct that constitutes fraud, misrepresentation, deceit, or false pretenses, there are statutory procedures for recovering money from either the inspector or the Real Estate Commission required Recovery Fund. This provides a "safe harbor" for real estate agents. They can refer the purchaser to a licensed real property inspector, to check out the technical, mechanical defects in the property. Essentially, the real estate agent can say "not my fault–not my job–not my area of expertise." It also gives him or her a third party to rely on under §1101.652(b)(3) & (4) of the Real Estate License Act and 17.555 of the DTPA since a consumer would rely on the representations of the inspector rather than the representations of the real estate agent, *Ozuna* and *Stagner*, supra.

There is a possibility, however, that the recommendation of a particular inspector may result in liability. *Diversified Human Resources Group, Inc. v. PB-KBB, Inc.*, 671 S.W.2d 634 (Tex. Civ. App.-Houston 1984); *Johnson v. Beverly-Hanks & Assoc.*, 500 S.E.2d 38 (N.C. 1991). Although the better reasoning seems to support the fact that the agent is not a guarantor of a third party's performance, professionals frequently make recommendations to their clients but don't accept responsibility for that third party's performance. See *Sparks v. RE/MAX Allstar Realty*, Lexis 131 (Ky. App. 2000).

Strong support was given to the inspector defense in the case of *Kubinsky v. Van Zandt Realtors*, 811 S.W.2d 711 (Tex. App.-Ft. Worth 1991, writ den.), wherein the court held that the agent did not have a duty to inspect or make any affirmative investigations beyond asking the sellers if defects existed. Real estate inspection is a separate and distinct discipline requiring licensure by the Texas Real Estate Commission, and real estate brokers are prohibited by law from blending the functions of real estate brokerage and real estate inspections. A similar holding was made in *Hagans v. Woodruff*, 830 S.W.2d 732 (Tex. App.-Houston [14th Dist.] 1992, no writ), wherein the court held that a broker does not have a duty to inspect listed property and disclose all facts that momentarily affect the value or desirability of the property. Similarly, there is no duty for the broker to disclose that there have been repairs made to the property, or to disclose defects if the defects have been repaired. *Pfeiffer v. Ebby Halliday Real Estate, Inc.*, 747 S.W.2d 887, 890 (Tex. App.-Dallas 1988, no writ). The Ebby Halliday case also noted that "common knowledge" was not enough to impose liability on a broker under the DTPA and that proof of actual knowledge of a defect of condition was needed to impose liability.

While the foregoing three cases seem to limit the liability of the real estate agent, it must be emphasized that these cases, standing on their own, are not an absolute defense to causes of action. An agent should always exercise good judgment in determining whether a defect or corrected defect may make a material difference to the purchaser making his or her decision to purchase. It is often difficult to balance the buyer's concerns versus the role of representing the seller in determining the quality of the house.

- *Who, me?* The broker is not a party to the earnest money contract. He or she will not be held responsible for his principal's default or misconduct. *Baxter & Swinford, Inc. v. Mercier*, 671 S.W.2d 139 (Tex. Civ. App.-Houston 1984). The same may be true when a broker follows the orders of his or her principal, and the agent has no control over the principal's conduct or decision making. *Shore v. Thomas A. Sweeney & Associates*, 864 S.W.2d 182 (Tex. App.-Tyler 1993, no writ).

- *As is.* The subject of "as is" was addressed by the Texas Supreme Court in *Prudential Insurance Company of America v. Jefferson Associates, Ltd.*, 896 S.W.2d 156 (Tex. 1995), discussed next.

Prudential Insurance Company of America v. Jefferson Associates, Ltd., 896 S.W.2d 156 (Tex. 1995)

The Prudential Insurance Company of America sold a four-story office building in Austin, Texas, to F. B. Goldman, who later conveyed to Jefferson Associates, Ltd., a limited partnership of which Goldman was a partner. Goldman was an experienced investor and had bought and sold several large investment properties on an "as is" basis. Before bidding on the building, Goldman had it inspected by his maintenance supervisor, his property manager, and an independent professional engineering firm. Prudential's representative told Goldman that the building was "superb," "superfine," and "one of the finest little properties in the city of Austin." Goldman's original architects reviewed the specifications in 1987, some three years after the sale, and saw nothing to indicate that the building contained asbestos. The building, however, had a fireproofing material called Mono-Kote® that contained asbestos. There was no evidence that Prudential actually knew before Goldman filed the lawsuit that the Jefferson building contained asbestos.

In the contract to purchase the building, there were the following provisions:

1. As a material part of the consideration for this Agreement, seller and purchaser agree that purchaser is taking the Property "AS IS with any and all latent and patent defects and that there is no warranty by seller that the property is fit for a particular purpose. Purchaser acknowledges that it is not relying upon any representation, statement or other assertion with respect to the property condition, but is relying upon its examination of the property. Purchaser takes the property under the express understanding that there is no express or implied warranties (except for limited warranties of title set forth in the closing documents). Provisions of this Section 15 shall survive the Closing;" and
2. Purchaser hereby waives any action under the Texas Deceptive Trade Practices Act.

The Texas Supreme Court held that by agreeing to purchase something "as is," a buyer agrees to make his own appraisal of the property and to accept the risk that he may be wrong. The court noted that the sole cause of buyer's injury in said circumstances, by his own admission, is the buyer himself, as he has agreed to take the full risk of determining the value of the purchase. Rather than pay more, a buyer may choose to rely entirely upon his own determination of the condition and value of the purchase. In making this choice, he removes the possibility that the seller's conduct will cause this damage. The court qualified its holding, though, that the "as is" language is not determinative in every circumstance, and would not apply if: (1) the buyer is induced to make a purchase because of fraudulent representation or concealment of information by the seller; (2) the buyer is impaired by the seller's conduct, such as obstructing an inspection; and (3) the "as is" clause is an important basis of the bargain, not an incidental or "boilerplate" provision.

The court also noted that there was no evidence that Prudential actually knew of the asbestos, and restated Texas law as it relates to the Deceptive Trade Practices Act: (1) a seller has no duty to disclose facts he does not know; (2) a seller is not liable for failing to disclose what he only should have known; and (3) a seller is not liable for failing to disclose information he did not actually know.

Concerning the statements made by the Prudential representative, the court held that they were merely puffing and could not constitute fraud, unless the maker knew it was false when he made it or made it recklessly without knowledge of the truth. The court also noted that the problems of asbestos had been well known and publicly discussed for years when Goldman bought the building, and therefore, Goldman's agreement to buy the building "as is" precluded him from recovering damages against Prudential.

As to the Deceptive Trade Practices Act, the court noted that the "as is" provision does not violate the prohibition against consumer's waiver under the DTPA, noting that "Goldman's agreement does not say he cannot sue Prudential for violating the DTPA; it says he cannot win the suit. He cannot win because he has asserted facts which negate proof of causation required for recovery."

Justice Gonzales noted that the court "returns to reason by reinstating reliance as an essential part of producing cause in a DTPA claim premised on a representation." This case may give considerable relief to real estate professionals.

Does this theory apply to home sellers and buyers? Probably so.

In *Smith v. Levine*, 911 S.W.2d 427 (Tex. App.-San Antonio 1995), the Smiths leased a house to Mr. Grissom, who was interested in buying the house. Grissom hired an inspection company to do a foundation analysis. It reflected that the foundation was defective. Grissom discussed the report with Mr. Smith and offered to give him a copy in exchange for paying part of the fee. The seller refused, indicating that the report "would have no value to us." The Smiths later listed the house with a real estate agent and did not mention the defective foundation on the agent's questionnaire. After the listing agreement expired, the Smiths put the house on the market themselves, describing the house as being in "excellent" condition. When showing the house, the Smiths also assured the purchasers that visible cracks were superficial. The purchasers (Mitchells) hired an engineer to do a "walk through" inspection, which also indicated that the cracks were minor and superficial.

The Mitchells later listed the house with a REALTOR® who secured a contract with a new purchaser. This second purchaser hired the same inspector who did the original inspection showing the foundation as being defective. (What a coincidence!)

The jury found that the Smiths knowingly engaged in a "false, misleading or deceptive act or practice," as well as "unconscionable acts or course of action," both of which were the producing cause of damages to the Mitchells. The court affirmed that the jury was entitled to find that the Smiths knew the foundation was defective because of the original inspection.

The earnest money contract also contained an "as is" provision. The Court held, however, citing the Prudential case, that "as is" is not a defense to a cause of action where a party is induced to enter into the contract because of fraudulent misrepresentation or concealment of information by the seller.

"As Is"; Non Reliance

Larsen v. Langford & Associates, Inc., supra, involves the second "as is" case out of the Waco Court of Appeals. A real estate broker (Larsen) and his wife who had access to the Multiple Listing Service were looking for a house in Corsicana, Texas. The house was described as historic, built in 1913, and that the home needed work. The property was listed with Carlene Langford & Associates, Inc. The broker, representing himself, requested to see the home. No one from the Langford office accompanied the Larsens to the home. They ultimately entered into a residential Earnest Money Contract to purchase the home for $65,000.00 through an assumption of the Seller's loan. Langford was the Seller's broker. The Buyer's broker represented himself. The Buyers admitted learning of problems with the home before closing and also agreed to receiving a Seller's Disclosure Form before the closing and before signing the final inspection. The Sellers did not fill out some parts of the Seller's Disclosure Form. The Buyer, however, never requested that they complete the form.

After closing, the Broker/Buyer alleged common law fraud, statutory fraud, negligent misrepresentation and violations of the DTPA. The court noted that all four causes of action were predicated on the reliance of the Buyer on a representation made by the Seller or the Seller's agent. The court further noted that the box 7.D.1 was checked which indicated that the home was purchased "as is." The listing Broker also prepared another document that was signed by the Buyers at closing and included the following clauses:

"I/We have been advised by the named Realtor/Real Estate Company to make any and all inspections of the subject property either by myself or anyone that I wish to employ, such as a licensed real estate inspector.

I have made all inspections or have had an employee of my choice to make them for me. I accept the property in its present condition and am satisfied with the inspections and any repairs that were required.

Brokers and sales associates shall not be liable or responsible for any inspections or repairs pursuant to this Contract and Addendum even in an event of a problem that has been overlooked by any or all parties involved in this transaction."

The Court noted that enforceability of the "as is" agreement is determined according to: (1) the sophistication of the parties; (2) the terms of the "as is" agreement; (3) whether the "as is" clause is freely negotiated; (4) whether it was an arm's length transaction; and (5) whether there was a knowing misrepresentation or concealment of a known fact. The Court noted that the transaction was conducted at arm's length, that both parties were similarly knowledgeable and sophisticated parties in the real estate business, *particularly in light of the fact that the Buyer acted on his own behalf as a broker.* The Court also noted that the "as is" language was found in two separate documents, the preprinted Earnest Money Contract and the Final Inspection and Disclosure form. The Court held that by signing both agreements, the Larsens (Buyers) explicitly agreed that they would accept the property in its present condition without requiring any repairs by the Seller, that they had made their own inspection and, further, relinquishing Langford of any liability for the repairs known or unknown by the Seller. The relevant contract provisions were clearly unambiguously demonstrated. The Larsens' agreement to rely solely upon themselves, their own inspections or inspectors they chose and that the agreement affirmatively negated the element of each claim that the Langfords' conduct caused them any harm; the Court further found that there is no inducement for the Buyer to buy the house based on representations made by the Broker and that the "as is" language effectively waived their rights to prevail under an allegation under the Deceptive Trade Practices Act.

Similarly, in *Cherry v. McCall* 138 SW 3rd 35 (Tex. App. San Antonio 2004), the court reinforced this "as is" defense even though one of the parties was somewhat less sophisticated than the other. The Court held that there was no evidence that the parties entered into the contract from unequal bargaining positions or that the transaction was not made at arm's length. The court further noted that because the Plaintiffs contracted to accept the property "as is," they cannot, as a matter of law, prevail on their breach of contract. See also *Sherman v. Elkowitz, supra* and *Bynum v. Prudential Residential Properties, supra.*

In *Cole v. Johnson*, 157 S.W.2d 856 (Tex. App.-Ft. Worth 2005), purchasers sued a seller for nondisclosure of certain information regarding the foundation of their home. At closing, the purchaser signed a document indicating that the sales price was being lowered $2,000 in lieu of foundation repairs, agreed that the sellers would be held harmless for any present or future repairs, and further agreed that the property was being purchased in an "as-is" condition. Other documents were provided to buyers at or prior to closing, totaling 55 pages of documentation relating to the foundation repairs. In the Seller's Disclosure Notice form, the seller represented that they were not aware of any undisclosed defective conditions, and that they were unaware of any current defective conditions to the drainage on the property. After the closing, there was a telephone conversation between the buyers and the sellers in which the seller indicated that the foundation work had failed. The buyers sued the seller based solely on this verbal allegation of nondisclosure.

The trial court awarded a summary judgment to the sellers, including attorney's fees. The court found that the purchasers were aware that there was no foundation warranty on the premises; they were aware that the property had an extensive history of foundation problems and foundation work. The court further found that they were aware that the foundation work had not cured the foundation problems because the foundation had continued to move and that there were numerous references in the reports given to the buyer that indicated there were continuing slab problems. The court noted the seller of a house is charged only with disclosing such material facts as to put a buyer exercising reasonable diligence on notice of a condition of the house, and that it was obvious, even to a layperson, that the foundation had not corrected all of the problems and that they were ongoing at the time of the inspection reports that had been given to the buyer.

The court further noted that the use of the "as-is" provision is enforceable depending on the "totality of the circumstances" surrounding the agreement and that absent fraud, the "as-is" agreement is enforceable. The court found no fraud in this transaction at all.

Could Statutory Preemption Help?

In *Robinson v. Grossman*, 57 Cal. App.-4th 634 (Cal. App. 1997), owners represented that they were unaware of any significant defects in the foundation, exterior walls, windows, ceiling, or other components of the home. The inspector noted hairline stucco cracks but reassured by the sellers that they were cosmetic cracks. The inspector noted, "I see nothing to contradict what Seller has mentioned." There were also signs of water infiltration, which the seller alleged had been remedied.

The purchaser engaged the services of the buyer's broker, who made the following remarks on the disclosure statement. "My visual inspection found numerous cracks in the house. Buyer's agent recommends Buyer to have property inspected by professional home inspector and have the land checked by a geologist." The buyer's inspector indicated that there was no significant problem with the home. The court noted the statutory changes in California law, effectively, overruling *Easton v. Strassburger*, 152 Cal. App.3d 90, 199 Cal. Rptr. 383, creating the requirement of a statutory Real Estate Transfer Disclosure Statement to the Buyer. The court held that under the post-Easton statutory scheme, once the sellers and their agents made required disclosures, it is incumbent upon the particular purchasers to investigate and make informed decision based thereon.

Amyot v. Luchini, 932 P.2d 244 (Alaska 1997) involved a suit by a purchaser of property because of an innocent misrepresentation made by the seller. The sellers, in putting the house on the market, had an inspection done on the property, which determined that the frame foundation of the property was satisfactory and that with normal maintenance the building would easily have a remaining life for over 35 years. The purchaser, upon moving into the property, discovered that the property was defective. He hired a professional engineer to inspect the house who tendered a repair estimate of approximately $100,000. The original inspector who had inspected the house for the sellers had indicated that he could repair it for $4,000. The purchasers sued the sellers for the cost of repairs under innocent, negligent, and intentional misrepresentation theories. After a two-week trial, the jury determined that the sellers were not negligent and awarded the sellers $26,087.60 in attorney's fees.

In *Nobrega v. Edison Glen Assoc.,* 2001 N.J. LEXIS 527 (May 22, 2001), the New Jersey legislature enacted the New Residential Real Estate Off-Site Conditions Disclosure Act (the "Disclosure Act") in 1995, which requires persons who own, lease, or maintain potentially dangerous off-site conditions to provide the municipal clerk of each municipality in which the conditions exist a list of those conditions and their location, and to update the list annually. The law also requires the seller of new real estate construction to provide the prospective purchaser with a notice of the availability of the lists of off-site conditions in the municipal clerk's office and to inform the buyer that he or she has the right to cancel the contract within five days of its execution. Parties who comply with the law may not be sued under the state Consumer Fraud Act.

In 1987, the Edison Glen constructed a condominium complex containing 315 units located near federal Superfund sites. Two of those sites are located within two miles of the Edison Glen complex. In 1997, 90 purchasers of the units filed a suit against the developer for negligence, fraud and misrepresentation, breach of contract, breach of warranty, and violation of the Consumer Fraud Act when the owners learned from an appraiser that the market value of their units had declined by 40% because of the proximity of the Superfund sites to the complex. The plaintiffs alleged that the defendant developer knew or should have known of the nearby Superfund sites and of the hazardous conditions, but failed to disclose that information to them before they purchased the condominiums. The defendants filed a motion to dismiss on the grounds that the claims were barred by the Disclosure Act.

The New Jersey Supreme Court found that the Disclosure Act was enacted to respond to an earlier decision by that court that *Strawn v. Caruso* held that a builder-developer of residential real estate or a broker representing it is liable to a purchaser for nondisclosure of off-site physical conditions known to it and unknown and not readily observable by the buyer if the existence of those conditions is of sufficient materiality to affect the habitability, use, or enjoyment of the property so as to render the property substantially less desirable or valuable to the objectively reasonable buyer. The Court then ruled that the Disclosure Act prospectively precludes plaintiffs from suing sellers and developers of real estate under the Consumer Fraud Act for failure to disclose off-site conditions, provided that the sellers and developers satisfy their off-site disclosure responsibilities under the Planned Real Estate Development Full Disclosure Act and the Air Safety and Zoning Act of 1983.

Maybe the Texas real estate industry needs to lobby the legislature!

Damages Under the DTPA

The statutory damages recoverable under the Deceptive Trade Practices Act include:

■ The amount of economic damages found by the trier of fact (the judge or jury). If the trier of fact finds that the conduct of the defendant was committed knowingly, the trier of fact may award not more than three times the amount of the economic damages.

■ An order enjoining such acts or failure of act.

■ Orders necessary to restore to any part of the suit any money or property, real or personal, that may have been acquired in violation of this subchapter.

■ Any other relief that the court deems proper, including the appointment of a receiver or the revocation of a license or certificate authorizing the person who engages in business in this state if the judgment has not been satisfied within three months of the date of final judgment. The court may not revoke or suspend a license to do business in the state or appoint a receiver to take over the affairs of the person who has failed to satisfy judgment if the person is a licensee of or regulated by a state agency that has the statutory authority to revoke or suspend a license or to appoint a receiver or trustee.

Damages under the DTPA have changed a lot. Section 17.50 provides for "economic" damages. The amount of economic damages is found by the trier of fact (jury, or judge if there is no jury).

"Economic damages" means compensatory damages for pecuniary loss, including costs of repair and replacement. The term does not include exemplary damages or damages for physical pain and mental anguish, loss of consortium, disfigurement, physical impairment, or loss of companionship and society.

If the trier of fact finds that the conduct of the defendant was committed "knowingly," the consumer may also recover damages for mental anguish, as found by the trier of fact, and the trier of fact may award not more than three times the amount of economic damages.

If the trier of fact finds the conduct was committed "intentionally," the consumer may recover damages for mental anguish, as found by the trier of fact, and the trier of fact may award not more than three times the amount of damages for mental anguish and economic damages. "Intentionally" is defined under the statute as actual awareness of, or flagrant disregard of, prudent and fair business practices.

REAL ESTATE FRAUD

There are two claims for fraud in Texas: (1) common law fraud, and (2) statutory fraud. To recover an action from common law fraud, the plaintiff must show that:

(1) a material representation was made;

(2) which was false;

(3) which was known to be false when made or was made recklessly as a positive assertion without knowledge of its truth;

(4) which was intended to be relied upon;

(5) which was relied upon; and

(6) which caused injury.

Green Intern., Inc. v. Celeste, 951 S.W.2d 384, 390 (Tex. 1997).

Statutory fraud can be claimed under Section 27.01 of the Business & Commerce Code by showing:

(1) a representation of a material fact;

(2) which was false;

(3) made to induce a person to enter into a contract;

(4) which was relied upon by that person in entering the contract; and

(5) which causes injury.

Scott v. Sebree, 986 S.W.2d 364 (Tex. App.-Austin 1999, pet. denied). The statutory cause of action differs from the common law only that it does not require perfect knowledge or recklessness as a prerequisite to the recovery of actual damages.

Agents have been held liable for real estate fraud for a number of different issues:

- representing that title was unencumbered. *Stone v. Lawyer's Title Insurance Corp.*, 554 S.W.2d 183 (Tex. 1977);

- failing to follow through on a promise to provide funds to a prospective purchaser. *McGaha v. Dishman*, 629 S.W.2d 220 (Tex. Civ. App.-Tyler 1982);

- remaining silent; silence is a positive misrepresentation of the facts. *Smith v. National Resort Communities*, 585 S.W.2d 655 (Tex. 1979).

REAL ESTATE RECOVERY FUND

If a real estate licensee cannot or will not pay damages or if the injured party wishes, that party can be compensated from the Real Estate Recovery Fund, which was set up to protect the consumer. *Texas Real Estate Commission v. Century 21 Security Realty, Inc.,* 598 S.W.2d 920 (Tex. Civ. App.-El Paso 1980). The recovery fund is also liable for attorney's fees. *Texas Real Estate Commission v. Hood,* 617 S.W.2d 838 (Tex. Civ. App.-Eastland 1981). Any valid claim against the fund may result in suspension of the broker or salesperson's license (see TRELA 1101.655). A new 2007 change the license act now states that the license will not be reinstated until that licensee has repaid the recovery fund in full, plus interest at the current legal rate. The recovery fund is limited to the aggregate of $50,000, including attorney's fees, in the same transaction or $100,000 against any one licensed real estate broker or salesperson. A discharge in bankruptcy, however, will relieve a person from the penalties and disabilities provided for under the Real Estate License Act, §1101.607(3). Only actual damages (not treble damages) may be recovered out of the fund. *State v. Pace,* 640 S.W.2d 432 (Tex. Civ. App.-Beaumont 1982).

To summarize, one should focus on the fact that agents owe fiduciary duties to their principal but also have certain responsibilities to third parties. The Canons of Ethics require fairness. Both the DTPA and the Texas Real Estate License Act require disclosures and create liability for misrepresentations to third parties by omissions or commissions. It's a tough world out there!

TERMINATION OF THE AGENCY RELATIONSHIP

PURPOSE

After carefully reading Chapter 7, the student will be able to:

■ List ways to terminate agency.

■ Discuss reasons for the termination of agency.

■ Apply the reasons to terminate agency to "real-world" situations.

■ Define: *express agreement, revocation, renunciation, operation of law,* and *supervening illegality*.

Key Words to look for in this chapter:
1. Express Agreement
2. Accomplishment of Agency Objective
3. Time
4. Revocation by Principal
5. Renunciation by Agent
6. Death of Either Party
7. Insanity of Either Party
8. Supervening Illegality

Sometimes the agency relationship works well; everyone is happy. Sometimes it needs to be terminated, as the "fit" may not be quite right to accomplish the objective. An agency can be terminated in many ways, but there are two basic ways that the termination of the agency relationship can be accomplished: either by (1) "acts of the parties," which includes an express agreement to terminate, time, accomplishment of the agency objective, revocation by the principal, or renunciation by the agent; or (2) "operation of law," which includes death, insanity, or supervening illegality.

ACTS OF PARTIES

Express Agreement

The agency can be terminated by acts of the parties when an express agreement between the parties is executed, prior to the expiration of the listing or buyer/tenant representation agreement and before the sale. In this situation, the parties agree the relationship isn't working as it should. The relationship also terminates when the listing or the buyer/tenant representation agreement expires. The Texas Real Estate License Act 1101.652(b)(12) provides for license revocation if employment contracts don't have a termination or expiration date.

The listing or buyer/tenant representation agreement must contain a definite period of employment. If it doesn't, one court has held that the employment agreement violates the license act, so it is void. *Perl v. Patrizi*, 20 S.W.3d 76 (Tex. App.-Texarkana 2000). The statute forbids the automatic renewal of a listing or buyer/tenant representation agreement into perpetuity.

BUT WAIT!....

In *Northborough v. Cushman & Wakefield of Texas, Inc.*, 162 S.W.3d 816 (Tex. App.-Houston [14th Dist.] 2005) (discussed briefly in Chapter 1), a real estate brokerage firm brought a cause of action against an owner of an office building contending it was due brokerage commissions under agreement reached with the building's previous owner. The facts in this case are somewhat complicated. The original owner was Alliance. It ultimately sold the property to Northborough. Alliance entered into an agreement to pay commissions with Cushman & Wakefield. Those agreements were specifically assumed by Northborough as a part of the sale transaction between Alliance and Northborough.

The primary commission that was agreed to be paid involved a tenant (Texaco) or any of its affiliates, or subsidiaries. The schedule of commissions provided that if the lease was renewed or extended, or if a tenant leased additional space, the building owner would pay an additional commission to Cushman. Texaco assigned its office lease to Star Enterprises which was a joint venture of Texaco. Star Enterprises ultimately assigned its interest to Equiva, also a joint venture of Texaco, and it was the renewal of Equiva's lease that became the basis for charging the commission.

The owner alleged two primary defenses. The first is that the Cushman commission agreement was void because it lacks a definite termination date in violation of the Texas Real Estate License Act. The second was that the final lease to Equiva was a "new arrangement" that superseded the Star lease and extinguished Northborough's obligations to pay the commissions (it was not extended and renewed).

The court quickly rejected the building owner's argument that express terminations is statutory required as a prelude to recovery of the commission.

Specifically citing *Perl v. Patrizi*, the court "declined to follow" *Perl* because: (1) the section relied on under the *Perl* court has nothing to do with the enforceability of a broker's commission agreement; it relates solely to the suspension or revocation of a broker's real estate license; and (2) nothing in the section of the Real Estate License Act (1101.652) references the broker's ability to maintain a cause of action. The court acknowledged that it disagreed with the *Perl* decision and held exactly the opposite way of the *Perl* court.

In dealing with the extension and renewal provisions of the commission agreement, the court noted that even though the space involved different parties and an agent did not participate in the negotiations, there was no evidence to suggest that the lease was ever cancelled and that, in fact, Equiva assumed Star's position in the Star lease through an Assignment and Amendment of Lease. The Court affirmed a lower court's summary judgment in favor of Cushman & Wakefield.

There will be more to come on this issue!

CAVEAT: Just because the employment relationship is terminated doesn't mean that the fiduciary duty has also terminated. The confidential information the agent obtained while the property is listed must still remain confidential. An agent cannot use the confidential information to adversely affect the interest of the former client without liability. *Swallows v. Laney*, supra.

Accomplishment of the Agency Objective

The agency also terminates when the purpose for that agency contract has been performed (the sale of the property). *Jones v. Allen*, 294 S.W.2d 259 (Tex. Civ. App.-Galveston 1956, ref. n.r.e.).

The best way for your real estate agency to end is to accomplish the agency objective and put a "sold" or "leased" sign on the property. Of course, you want a successful end to your efforts, happy customers and clients, and money in your pocket.

Stortroen v. Beneficial Finance Co., 736 P.2d 391 (Colo. 1987)

In October 1983, Beneficial Finance Company gave an exclusive right to sell listing on a house that they owned to Olthoff Realty Company, who put the property in a multiple listing service. The Stortroens wanted to sell their home and buy a larger one. They listed their home with Foremost Realty, whose agent showed them prospective houses to purchase after consulting the local multiple listing service.

In January 1984, Foremost showed the Stortroens the Beneficial house and helped them to prepare a contract offer of $105,000. Although the sale was contingent on the sale of the Stortroens' home, the offer provided for the Beneficial property to remain on the market; and if there was another offer on the house, the Stortroens had 72 hours to remove their contingency.

Beneficial went over the contract with Olthoff and countered, offering to sell at $110,000. The counteroffer states that acceptance would be "evidenced by the Purchaser's signature hereon; and if seller receives notice of such acceptance on or before 9 P.M. 2-3-84," the counter would become a contract.

Meanwhile, the Carellis, third party plaintiffs and defendants, were shown the home by another brokerage firm. They submitted an offer of $112,000 to Olthoff in the afternoon of February 3, 1984. After informing Beneficial of the offer, Olthoff told the Carelli's agent to take the offer directly to Beneficial. Having received their offer, Beneficial called Olthoff telling him that Beneficial wanted to accept the higher offer and to withdraw the counteroffer to the Stortroens.

When he was unable to reach Foremost, Olthoff left telephone messages at their office and residence saying that Beneficial had withdrawn the counteroffer. After Beneficial was informed of these messages, it accepted the Carelli offer in writing.

Unaware of the withdrawal, Foremost presented Beneficial's counter to the Stortroens. They signed their acceptance at about 4:10 P.M. Foremost discovered the message from Olthoff when she returned to her office. On the next Monday, Foremost delivered the counter, signed on February 3rd, and a document withdrawing the contingency clause, written on February the 4th, to Olthoff. The Stortroens later filed the contract with the county clerk. As a result of this cloud on the title, the Carellis refused to close their transaction, but they moved into the property with a month-to-month lease.

On April 26, 1984, the Stortroens sued Beneficial and the Carellis claiming breach of contract and seeking specific performance and damages and an order requiring the Carellis to vacate the property. The Carellis cross-filed against Beneficial and added a complaint against Olthoff.

The District Court ruled that Foremost was the buyer agent of the Stortroens so their delivery of the written acceptance of the counter to Foremost did not constitute notice of acceptance to Beneficial. The Court granted summary judgment on behalf of Beneficial. The parties then filed a joint motion with the Supreme Court for a decision on whether the selling broker, Foremost, was the agent of the buyers or the agent of the seller.

The Supreme Court considered that under the listing agreement the subagent of the listing broker is the subagent of the seller. Their decision was that "the listing broker's act of listing the property with the multiple listing service constitutes an offer of subagency by the listing broker to other [service] members to procure a buyer in exchange for a percentage of the sale commission." They felt that, in the "inherently ambiguous circumstance of a residential sale," the broker "operating within a multiple listing service is clearly in a chain of agency to the seller . . ."

Although Foremost may have been an agent of the Stortroens for the sale of their home, she was a subagent of Olthoff Realty because of the multiple listing service and therefore a subagent to Beneficial for the sale of Beneficial's property. This agency was seen as independent of and separate from her seller agency with the Stortroens.

Thus, the notice given to Foremost of the Stortroens' acceptance was notice to the listing broker and the seller making a binding purchase contract between the Stortroens and Beneficial. For these reasons, the judgment of the District Court was reversed.

Time

Agency can be terminated by the expiration of time. In absence of any express writing or accomplishment of the agency objective, the agency can last for a reasonable period of time. *Bouldin v. Woosley*, 525 S.W.2d 276 (Tex. Civ. App.-Waco 1975, no writ). Remember, employment agreements cannot automatically renew forever. In light of 1101.652(b)(12) and the Perl case referred to previously, this theory has little application under Texas law today.

Jones v. Allen, 294 S.W.2d 259
(Tex. Civ. App.-Galveston 1956, ref. n.r.e.)

In January 1948, Duncan Allen, a licensed real estate broker, listed the property of Leonard Jones for a 5 percent commission. On February 13th of that year, the lister found a buyer, W. V. Ratcliff, who contracted for the purchase of the property. He offered $13,500, $3,500 down and a ten year note at 4 percent interest for the rest. The earnest money was supposed to be $500. The lister presented this as a good price for the property. Jones, the seller, requested that the deferred payment be incorporated into the contract.

On February 16, 1948, C. H. Jones, another broker, came to Allen's office representing that he had a purchaser for the property at $19,000 cash. He presented an earnest money contract from C. H. Jones and D. E. McAughan with $1,000 in earnest money. That same day Allen secured a written agreement from Ratcliff to sell the property for $15,000. And at the same time and day, Jones agreed to accept the entire $13,500 for the property in cash rather than finance part of the money. Allen concealed the prearranged sale at a price of $19,000 and the fact Ratcliff had arranged to sell the property for $15,000 from Jones.

Subsequently, a representative of the title company, acting as trustee, was deeded the property. A fee charged by the title company for the title policy and the commission was paid out of the proceeds. Immediately, the trustee executed a deed for the property to Henry Kaplan and D. E. McAughan. Ratcliff received the difference between his purchase price and the amount for which he had agreed to sell to Hubbard. Allen received the difference between $15,000 and $19,000 minus a title fee of $13.75. This second title fee was the difference between the $90.75 for the $13,500 policy and the price of a $19,000 policy.

On January 7, 1953, claiming that they had heard the facts within the last six months, Jones filed suit against Allen alleging that breach of trust had occurred and that Ratcliff was a dummy purchaser acting for Jones. The broker pleaded the four year statute of limitations and a general denial. The verdict was a take-nothing judgment.

On appeal, Allen argued that the duty of full disclosure is imposed only during the course of the agency relationship and that the agency relationship ended when Jones and Ratcliff contracted the property and the seller became obligated to convey. Jones claimed that the agency continued until the actual transfer of title occurred. The appellate court ruled that Allen was under no legal duty to Jones, that the seller was legally obligated to sell under the terms of the contract, that the appellant was free to deal for himself, and that the "appellant was defrauded," but it had no bearing on this decision. The judgment of the lower courts was affirmed.

Revocation by the Principal

If the agent has no interest in the property, the principal always has the unilateral right to revoke the contract, provided it doesn't breach the terms of the employment contract. *Sunshine v. Manos*, 496 S.W.2d 195 (Tex. Civ. App.-Tyler

1973, ref. n.r.e.). No one has the right to force their services on a principal who doesn't want those services. If it is unilaterally revoked, however, the agent has the ability to sue for damages, and if the agent has produced a buyer, sue for the full commission. Please note that while the court can award the agent damages if there is revocation by the principal, the agent must sue the principal for the damages and run the risk that the court will award them. Texas courts have fairly loosely interpreted this. Even if it is a breach of the contract terms to revoke the agency, if the principal's best interest is served, the courts will uphold the revocation of the agency and just award the agent damages. *Cahn v. Pye*, 429 S.W. 630 (Tex. Civ. App.-ref. n.r.e.). This may be true even though the agency agreement provides that the agency is irrevocable. *Brigham v. Cason*, 233 S.W. 530 (Tex. Civ. App.-Ft. Worth 1921, no writ). **If your services are terminated by the principal, but you keep your sign up, you might violate §1101.652(b)(7) and (8) of the License Act. See Chapter 4.**

Agency can be terminated at any time by a breach of the fiduciary relationship. There are no restrictions at all on the revocation of the agency by the principal because of any breach of duty of care by the agent. *Woodward v. General Motors Corp.*, 298 F.2d 121, (Cert. Den. 369 U.S. 887). The real estate agent has no right to a commission if he or she breaches the contract. If the agency is a general agency, however, the principal is still liable for the agent's acts until third parties have notice of the termination of the agency or until there is a timely repudiation of the agency by the principal.

So we have the logical result. If an agent sues for a commission, the agent should expect a countersuit for breach of fiduciary duty, as a defense to the agent's recovery.

DISCUSSION QUESTIONS

■ You listed property for $95,000. You are very excited about this property because it is a very good listing. You put the property in a multiple listing service and advertise it in the local newspaper's classified section. You host an agents' open house, where you serve brunch to your fellow agents. With the sellers' permission, you video tape the property to show to prospects, and show the video to several prospective buyers. One of the buyers is very interested in the property when the seller withdraws the listing, revoking your agency. All that time and money is expended.

What do you do?

■ The Cosbys listed their home with you because the company Mrs. Cosby works for told her that she was being transferred to Long Beach, California, within 90 days. Today Mrs. Cosby found out that she was not going to be transferred. The Cosbys want you to take their home off the market, but another real estate company has just brought you a contract offer on the property. Should you sue for a commission? How might enforcing your legal rights be a bad business decision?

■ Remembering that enforcing your legal rights may be a bad business decision, would you reconsider your answers to the previous two questions? If so, how?

Renunciation by the Agent

The agent can renounce the agency relationship, subject to the agent's liability for damages if the principal is damaged. *Walter E. Heller & Co. v. Barnes*, 412 S.W.2d 747 (Tex. Civ. App.-El Paso 1967); *Tatum v. Preston Carter Co.*, supra.

The agent can, and should, terminate the agency if the principal requests the agent to perform an illegal act, or an act that would result in harm or cause damages to another. Some principals are so demanding and unreasonable that they simply are not worth the effort. This is almost always a "people" problem, not a legal problem. Personalities sometimes clash too much to create an effective marketing effort. For the real estate licensee's protection, any termination should be in writing with the reason stated.

DISCUSSION QUESTION

■ List reasons why an agent might withdraw from a transaction and terminate the agency relationship.

TERMINATION BY OPERATION OF LAW

Termination by operation of law generally consists of death, insanity, and supervening illegality. It has even been held that marriage of the principal can terminate the agency relationship (the spouse wouldn't agree to sell!).

Death of Either Party

At the death of a real estate broker, all his or her listings terminate and all the salespeople that he or she sponsors must have a new sponsor before they can actively engage in real estate. All the listings that they procured for their old broker will have to be renewed for the new brokerage relationship. Obviously, a dead real estate agent cannot sell property (it's too difficult to market effectively), nor can a dead person hold title to real estate (he or she can't be a principal).

Before the sale of a property can take place, the will of the deceased owner must be probated; or there must be an administration of the estate in determination of heirship to determine the owners of the property. Then the executor under a will, or the administrator under an intestate succession, can execute documents on behalf of the decedent and consummate the sale. Remember, death does not terminate the seller's performance under an earnest money contract, but it does terminate the agency relationship.

The same is true by the use of Powers of Attorney. A deed is inoperative if it is executed by an attorney in fact, acting as agent after the principal's death. It is void and conveys no title. *Wall v. Lubbock*, 118 S.W. 886. This is true even if the agent is unaware of the principal's death. *Cleveland v. Williams*, 29 Tex. 204 (1867).

Insanity of Either Party

The same theory holds true for insanity of the principal. *Harrington v. Bailey*, 351 S.W.2d 946 (Tex. Civ. App.-Waco 1961), and the agent/broker. Differing from death, however, a durable power of attorney can survive the insanity of either party.

DISCUSSION QUESTION

■ Lidia Marsh looks to be about 65 years old. When you took Lidia's listing, you noticed that she seemed forgetful about some things, but you thought it was because of her nervousness over the seriousness of listing her home that you had to repeat yourself so many times. When you went back to your office to share the new property listing with your co-workers, several of the agents called your seller senile. One agent referred to her as "crazy as a loon." You begin to question seriously the lister's mental competency.

What do you do now?

Supervening Illegality

Agency can be terminated by change of law. If the agency is legal at the inception, but a change of law makes it illegal, the agency is terminated. For instance, if you have an agreement to manage a massage parlor, and the county declares massage parlors illegal, the agency is terminated. Note the Centex case described next.

Centex Corp. v. Dalton, 840 S.W.2d 952 (Tex. 1992)

In 1988, Texas was in a period of economic recession that had a devastating affect on thrift institutions. The Federal Home Loan Bank Board (FHLBB) and other financial regulatory agencies decided it was in the best interest of the public to close, merge, or sell thrift institutions under the "Southwest Plan."

In November of that year, David Quinn, executive vice president of Centex, a company involved in residential and commercial construction and related financing services, asked John Dalton, a real estate broker, to help Centex purchase some of the thrifts available through the Southwest Plan.

While in Washington, D.C., making an unsuccessful attempt to purchase a group of thrifts for his company, Dalton heard of four other central Texas institutions for sale. These four became known as the "Lamb Package." In December, Centex entered into a letter agreement with Dalton promising him $750,000 if Centex acquired the Lamb Package. Before the agreement was signed David Quinn met with the FHLBB, which told him that the fee to Dalton would be all right if Centex, and not any of the thrift institutions, paid the money.

The night before the purchase, Quinn learned that the Bank Board probably would not allow Dalton's fee. Centex went ahead with the acquisition through Texas Trust Saving Bank, a Texas Trust it formed for this purpose. This acquisition was approved on December 29, 1988. There was a condition that forbid Texas Trust to pay directly or indirectly a finder's fee. Through an amendment, the Bank Board made it specific that the prohibition was also against any affiliate of Texas Trust. Although Dalton performed his duties, Centex refused to pay him because of the prohibition. Dalton sued for his fee. The court decided in favor of Centex. Dalton appealed.

In August 1989, the Financial Institutions Reform, Recovery and Enforcement Act (FIRREA) replaced the Bank Board. It created the Office of Thrift Supervision (OTS) with the powers that had been the Bank Board's. December 11th, while this case was being appealed, the OTS issued an order to prevent Centex or Texas Trust from paying any fees to Dalton. The appellate court reasoned that the prohibition applied only to Texas Trust, and not Centex. It ruled in favor of Dalton.

Centex appealed. Although the Court recognized an injustice, the Supreme Court held that Centex was excused from paying the fee by the doctrine of impossibility.

As a final thought, sometimes the agency relationship simply doesn't work properly. In that event, one or both parties need to simply elect to terminate their agency agreement to prevent further liability down the road. Some call this "gut reaction," in that you just feel uncomfortable with the relationship when a party makes comments or reacts to situations that make the agent feel that there's trouble ahead. In those situations, it is just easier to gracefully recommend another agent. One lawsuit eats up a lot of commissions! It may be easier just to pass that commission and work on your next transaction.

8

PRACTICING LAW AND REAL ESTATE BROKERAGE

PURPOSE

After carefully reading Chapter 8, the student will be able to:

■ Understand the history of, and need for, promulgated contracts and the exceptions to their use.

■ Understand the Texas Real Estate Broker-Lawyer Committee.

■ Discuss the lack of real estate license requirements for attorneys.

■ Determine why a real estate licensee cannot give legal advice or practice law.

■ Know how an attorney can practice real estate and the problems that might arise.

■ Understand how lawyers cannot participate in any real estate commission without a license.

Key Words to look for in this chapter:
1. Required Forms
2. Texas Real Estate Broker-Lawyer Committee
3. TREC promulgated forms
4. Suspension or revocation of license

Real estate involves a lot of contract law. A real estate licensee uses and/or must be familiar with escrow and employment agreements, sales contracts, and contracts for deed, leases, options, and wills.

One of the oldest controversies in real estate is the disagreement between attorneys and real estate licensees over what constitutes practicing real estate versus what is practicing law, particularly in the area of writing contracts. Strict guidelines have been given to licensees regarding their authority to write or prepare contracts for their customers and clients.

Some states recognize and allow licensees to prepare contracts. In Texas, it is unlawful for a licensee to practice law or to give legal advice unless that licensee is also an attorney. Still, there remains the question of whether writing real estate sales contracts constitutes practicing law.

In 1972, the Texas Real Estate Commission requested the state Attorney General's opinion on this question. The Attorney General responded that the Commission could sanction the use of a contract form. He stated that such a form, "duly promulgated (published and required for use) by the Commission," could be used by licensees without violation of statute or the illegal practice of law. He also said that in the absence of such a form clearly sanctioned by the Commission, drawing up or supplying of any contract form, or the filling in the blanks for the parties of any contract form by a real estate licensee might "reasonably be deemed suspect and possibly [be] in violation of" the Texas Real Estate License Act, according to existing state court decisions on the subject.

This decision was a partial basis for the Commission to establish the Texas Real Estate Broker-Lawyer Committee. The Committee consists of twelve members, six appointed by the State Bar of Texas and six appointed by the Commission. This Committee has the job of drafting and revising uniform contract and other forms (such as mediation agreements and addendums) that are required for use by all licensees in the practice of real estate.

A contract promulgated or approved by the Commission must be used unless an attorney draws up a contract (see discussion to follow) or the parties insist on using another form. Other exceptions are discussed later in the chapter. This would allow a practitioner to insist on a particular contract if that licensee were a party to the real estate transaction. A licensee may not make any changes to the contract except for business details and statements of fact for conforming the contract to the wishes and intent of the parties and the disclosure of pertinent information. These changes must be at the direction of the buyer and/or the seller and initialed by them. To make any changes otherwise would be considered practicing law. It may be more prudent to have the principal actually write the provision himself or herself so that the broker cannot be faced with a practicing law allegation because the licensee wrote in the provisions.

Please note that the agent should not make any suggestions to the buyer or seller. To do so might be a violation of fiduciary duty. Inserting language in the base contract to take the place of another promulgated form, such as the Property Condition Addendum or a buyer's or seller's lease, is illegal. The principal should initiate any changes. The correct form or addendum must be used.

The Texas Real Estate License Act was amended in 1983 to require the use of the promulgated contract forms.

REQUIRED FORMS

SEC. 1101.654

Sec. 1101.654 of the Act provides that the completion of contract forms that bind the sale, exchange, option, lease, or rental of any interest in real property by a real estate broker or salesperson incident to the performance of the acts of a broker does not constitute the unauthorized or illegal practice of law in this state, provided:

- the forms have been promulgated for use by the Texas Real Estate Commission for the **particular kind of transaction involved;** or the forms have been prepared by an attorney at law licensed by this state and approved by said attorney for the **particular kind of transaction involved** (can a party prepare his or her own standard forms for many different transactions? i.e., buyer's broker using his or her personal standard form for a national chain store).

- the forms have been prepared by the property owner or prepared by an attorney and required by the *property owner*. (QUERY: What about forms required by the buyer?)

SEC. 1101.155

The Texas Real Estate Commission adopts rules and regulations requiring real estate brokers and salespeople to use contract forms that have been prepared by the Texas Real Estate Broker-Lawyer Committee and promulgated by the Texas Real Estate Commission; provided, however, that the Commission shall not prohibit a real estate broker or salesperson from using a contract form or forms binding the sale, exchange, option, or lease, that have been prepared by the *property owner* or an attorney, and required by the *property owner* [emphasis supplied]. Contract forms prepared by the Texas Real Estate Broker-Lawyer Committee appointed by the Commission and the State Bar of Texas and promulgated by the Commission prior to the effective date of the Act are deemed to have been prepared by the Texas Real Estate Broker-Lawyer Committee. The Commission may suspend or revoke a license issued under the provisions of this article when it has determined that the licensee failed to use a contract form required by the Commission pursuant to this section.

The Rules and Regulations of the Real Estate Commission deal in greater detail and expand TREC's interpretation of practicing law to add these exceptions when requiring TREC promulgated forms:

- transactions in which the licensee is functioning solely as a principal, not as an agent.

- transactions in which an agency of the United States government requires a different form to be used.

- when using forms made available by TREC for trial use. TREC Rules and Regulations, Sec. 537.11(b).

In using the TREC promulgated forms, the licensee is limited to filling in the blanks of the form. A licensee may not add to or strike matter from such forms, except that licensees shall add factual statements and business details desired by the principals and shall strike only such matter as is desired by the principals and as is necessary to conform the instrument to the intent of the principals. TREC Rules and Regulations, Sec. 537.11(d).

The licensee is also allowed to disclose pertinent information, including such facts that might affect the status of or title to real estate, protection, and proof of disclosure in Sec. 537.11(c) of the TREC Rules, and §1101.654 of the TRELA that also prohibits the licensee from advising as to the validity of title to real estate.

LAWYERS AS REAL ESTATE BROKERS

Section 1101.005 of the Texas Real Estate License Act exempts from licensure "an attorney at law licensed in this state or any other state."

This creates two possible interpretations:

- Any or all attorneys, licensed in any state, can operate as *real estate brokers* in Texas, which is a literal interpretation of the exemption.

  Problems:

  a. Can a patent lawyer, licensed in North Dakota, be expected to engage competently in or give legal advice concerning the real estate business in Texas? Can a criminal lawyer in Texas?

  b. A lawyer cannot employ salespeople, as they must have and be compensated through their sponsoring broker, Occupations Code, §1101.651.

  c. Who has jurisdiction over misconduct? The Texas Real Estate Commission has jurisdiction over licensees, which the lawyer is not. The State Bar of Texas will be reluctant to force its jurisdiction over a lawyer who is not practicing law.

  The attorney may very well be practicing law in a real estate transaction. At least one recent case has held that an attorney who is also a licensed REALTOR® could not avoid regulatory requirements imposed on licensees merely because attorneys are exempt from licensing requirements. *Shanlian v. Faulk*, 843 P.2d 535 (Wash. App. 1992).

- An attorney at law is not required to have a real estate license to negotiate a transaction.

  All attorneys who deal in real estate engage in conduct that constitutes brokerage for another person and for a fee as defined in Sec. 1101.002 of the TRELA. In the case of *Sherman v. Bruton*, ante, decided under the previous statute, the court held that an attorney, solely by virtue of his or her license to practice law, is not authorized to engage generally in the business of a real estate brokerage.

Problems:

Actually, none. Without this exemption, all attorneys negotiating real estate contracts would be required to have a real estate license. This exception implies that the legal services are incidental to his law practice. *Sherman v. Bruton*, 497 S.W.2d 216 (Tex. Civ. App.-Dallas 1973, no writ). In the Sherman case, it was also held the attorney could not sue for a commission without an agreement in writing as specified by the TRELA.

Conflicts of interest?

a. In the past, the Statement of Principles originally adopted by the State Bar of Texas and the Texas Real Estate Commission contained no prohibition for a person to be an attorney and real estate agent in the same transaction. This Statement of Principles was abrogated in July 1982, and the basic conflict has not been addressed in any other forum. Can a lawyer look after the best interest of his client in preparing documentation and avoiding pitfalls when he stands to lose a substantial real estate commission if the deal doesn't close? Is he then acting as a real estate broker or a lawyer? What about deceptive trade practice or failure to disclose? Is he paid by the seller? Does he represent the buyer? Is he a cooperating broker?

b. Is it fee splitting to reduce a client's fee if receiving another fee from the seller? There are significant authorities, including the Dallas Bar Association, that question the ethics and legality of performing both functions, including the taking of referral fees. See Sanford, "Ethical, Statutory, and Regulatory Conflicts of Interest in Real Estate Transaction," *St. Mary's Law Journal*, Vol. 17, No. 1, (1985), and cases cited therein.

The Texas Real Estate License §1101.652(b)(11) subjects a licensee to license suspension or revocation for paying a commission or fee to or dividing a commission or fee *with anyone not licensed as a real estate broker or salesperson in this state or in any other state.* This provision subjects licensees to disciplinary action if they split their fee with anybody (including a lawyer licensed in this state or any other state) for performing brokerage services for another, if that person is not licensed as a real estate broker or salesperson. Please note that there is still no restriction for splitting a fee with another principal, so long as the principal is not performing brokerage acts for another person.

Section 1101.651 of the License Act was also amended to make it unlawful for a licensed broker to employ or compensate a person for performing an act enumerated in the definition of "real estate broker" if that person is not a licensed broker or a licensed salesperson in Texas. The amendment eliminated the reference (and therefore makes it illegal) to compensate directly or indirectly an attorney at law licensed in this state or any other state if he or she is not a licensed real estate broker or salesperson in this state. These provisions are apparently aimed at lawyers who felt that the law authorized them to split commissions with licensees, even when no brokerage function was performed!

One case, *Elin v. Neal*, 720 S.W.2d 224 (Tex. App.-Houston [14th Dist.] 1986, writ ref'd n.r.e.), seems to indicate that all lawyers were exempt from real estate licensure for any and all functions. This restates the obvious problem. The Texas Real Estate Commission has no jurisdiction over lawyers, although the license act now prohibits a licensee from fee splitting if no brokerage services are performed. The State Bar of Texas probably has no jurisdiction over a lawyer while engaging in real estate brokerage functions. Is there an answer to this? Not really. Unprincipled people and "loopholes" have always existed. The key is to recognize the situation and rise above it.

9

AGENCY DISCLOSURE/BUYER AGENCY, SINGLE AGENCY, AND DUAL AGENCY

PURPOSE

After carefully reading Chapter 9, the student will be able to:

■ Interpret the Agency Information Statement.

■ Explain exclusive buyer (tenant) agency, its procedures, duties of care, and compensation.

■ Define: *single agency*, *agency disclosure*, and *buyer agency*.

■ Discuss dual agency, its problems, and conflicts of interest.

Key Words to look for in this chapter:
1. Agency Disclosures
2. Substantive dialogue
3. Exclusive Buyer (Tenant) Agency
4. Information About Brokerage Services
5. Agency Policy of Listing Agents
6. Need for Advice
7. Initial Interview
8. Earning the Commitment
9. Duties of Care
10. Inspectors
11. Single Agency
12. Dual Agency
13. Intermediary

There are several alternatives to the traditional seller agency relationship that have received increased interest and discussion and in many market areas are already established. These alternatives have required the public and real estate licensees take a new look at the way real estate is practiced, particularly residential real estate.

This new look demands the answers to some new questions. Should buyer/tenants have someone represent them? Does the real estate licensee have to represent either the buyer/tenant or the seller/landlord? Can the real estate practitioner represent both? Can the real estate licensee represent neither the buyer nor the seller? How can you confirm if the buyer already has employed a broker? When and to whom is agency disclosed?

AGENCY DISCLOSURES

The Initial Disclosure/Information About Brokerage Services

Initial disclosure is still required at first contact with a party. The licensee is required to furnish a party in a real estate transaction, at the time of the first *substantive dialogue* with the party, the following written statement in 10-point type:

"Before working with a real estate broker, you should know that the duties of a broker depend on whom the broker represents. If you are a prospective seller or landlord (owner) or a prospective buyer or tenant (buyer), you should know that the broker who lists the property for sale or lease is the owner's agent. A broker who acts as a subagent represents the owner in cooperation with the listing broker. A broker who acts as a buyer's agent represents the buyer. A broker may act as an intermediary between the parties if the parties consent in writing. A broker can assist you in locating a property, preparing a contract or lease, or obtaining financing without representing you. A broker is obligated by law to treat you honestly."

"IF THE BROKER REPRESENTS THE OWNER: The broker becomes the owner's agent by entering into an agreement with the owner, usually through a written listing agreement, or by agreeing to act as a subagent by accepting an offer of subagency from the listing broker. A subagent may work in a different real estate office. A listing broker or subagent can assist the buyer but does not represent the buyer and must place the interests of the owner first. The buyer should not tell the owner's agent anything the buyer would not want the owner to know because an owner's agent must disclose to the owner any material information known to the agent."

"IF THE BROKER REPRESENTS THE BUYER: The broker becomes the buyer's agent by entering into an agreement to represent the buyer, usually through a written buyer representation agreement. A buyer's agent can assist the owner but does not represent the owner and must place the interests of the buyer first. The owner should not tell a buyer's agent anything the owner would not want the buyer to know because the buyer's agent must disclose to the buyer any material information known to the agent."

"IF THE BROKER ACTS AS AN INTERMEDIARY: A broker may act as an intermediary between the parties if the broker complies with the Texas Real Estate License Act. The broker must obtain the written consent of each party to the transaction to act as an intermediary. The written consent must state who will pay the broker and, in conspicuous bold or underlined print, set forth the broker's obligations as an intermediary. The broker is required to treat each party honestly and fairly and to comply with the Texas Real Estate License Act. A broker who acts as an intermediary in a transaction: (1) shall treat all parties honestly; (2) may not disclose that the owner will accept a price less than the asking price unless authorized in writing to do so by the owner; (3) may not disclose that the buyer will pay a price greater than the price submitted in a written offer unless authorized in writing to do so by the buyer; and (4) may not disclose any confidential information or any information that a party specifically instructs the broker in writing not to disclose unless authorized in writing to disclose the information or required to do so by the Texas Real Estate License Act or a court order or if the information materially relates to the condition of the property. With the parties' consent, a broker acting as an intermediary between the parties may appoint a person who is licensed under the Texas Real Estate License Act and associated with the broker to communicate with and carry out instructions of one party and another person who is licensed under that Act and associated with the broker to communicate with and carry out instructions of the other party. 'If you choose to have a broker represent you, you should enter into a written agreement with the broker that clearly establishes the broker's obligations and your obligations. The agreement should state how and by whom the broker will be paid. You have the right to choose the type of representation, if any, you wish to receive. Your payment of a fee to a broker does not necessarily establish that the broker represents you. If you have any questions regarding the duties and responsibilities of the broker, you should resolve those questions before proceeding.'"

The information about brokerage services is required at the time of the first substantive dialogue. What is substantive dialogue? Substantive dialogue is defined by the Real Estate License Act as a meeting or written communication that involves a substantive discussion relating to specific real property. It does not include a meeting that occurs at a property held open for prospective purchasers or tenants or a meeting that occurs after the parties of the transaction have signed the contract to sell, buy, rent, or lease the real property concerned. A copy of the form is shown as Figure 9-1.

A licensee is not required to provide this written information if:

- the proposed transaction for a residential lease is not more than one year and no sale is being considered; or
- the licensee meets with the party who is represented by another licensee.

It is debatable as to whether this would impute knowledge back to the party who is represented by the licensee.

The Next Disclosure

The Information About Brokerage Services is just that, information. There is another disclosure that must be made in a transaction. A licensee who represents a party in a proposed real estate transaction must disclose that representation at the time of the licensee's first contact with: (1) another *party* [emphasis supplied] to the transaction; or (2) another licensee who represents another party to the transaction. The disclosure may be orally or in writing. It would seem to be a prudent business practice, however, to disclose in writing so that the agent could confirm that the disclosure was properly made. Including it in the agent's next correspondence is a good idea.

Exclusive Buyer (Tenant) Agency

There is an age-old position that **"no man can serve two masters."** Buyers and sellers, while their interests seem to be the same (to buy/sell the property), are in adversarial positions, particularly pertaining to agency. Many people feel

FIG 9-1   INFORMATION ABOUT BROKERAGE SERVICES

Approved by the Texas Real Estate Commission for Voluntary Use

Texas law requires all real estate licensees to give the following information about brokerage services to prospective buyers, tenants, sellers and landlords.

Information About Brokerage Services

Before working with a real estate broker, you should know that the duties of a broker depend on whom the broker represents. If you are a prospective seller or landlord (owner) or a prospective buyer or tenant (buyer), you should know that the broker who lists the property for sale or lease is the owner's agent. A broker who acts as a subagent represents the owner in cooperation with the listing broker. A broker who acts as a buyer's agent represents the buyer. A broker may act as an intermediary between the parties if the parties consent in writing. A broker can assist you in locating a property, preparing a contract or lease, or obtaining financing without representing you. A broker is obligated by law to treat you honestly.

IF THE BROKER REPRESENTS THE OWNER:
The broker becomes the owner's agent by entering into an agreement with the owner, usually through a written - listing agreement, or by agreeing to act as a subagent by accepting an offer of subagency from the listing broker. A subagent may work in a different real estate office. A listing broker or subagent can assist the buyer but does not represent the buyer and must place the interests of the owner first. The buyer should not tell the owner's agent anything the buyer would not want the owner to know because an owner's agent must disclose to the owner any material information known to the agent.

IF THE BROKER REPRESENTS THE BUYER:
The broker becomes the buyer's agent by entering into an agreement to represent the buyer, usually through a written buyer representation agreement. A buyer's agent can assist the owner but does not represent the owner and must place the interests of the buyer first. The owner should not tell a buyer's agent anything the owner would not want the buyer to know because a buyer's agent must disclose to the buyer any material information known to the agent.

IF THE BROKER ACTS AS AN INTERMEDIARY:
A broker may act as an intermediary between the parties if the broker complies with The Texas Real Estate License Act. The broker must obtain the written consent of each party to the transaction to act as an intermediary. The written consent must state who will pay the broker and, in conspicuous bold or underlined print, set forth the broker's obligations as an intermediary. The broker is required to treat each party honestly and fairly and to comply with The Texas Real Estate License Act. A broker who acts as an intermediary in a transaction:

   (1) shall treat all parties honestly;
   (2) may not disclose that the owner will accept a price less than the asking price unless authorized in writing to do so by the owner;
   (3) may not disclose that the buyer will pay a price greater than the price submitted in a written offer unless authorized in writing to do so by the buyer; and
   (4) may not disclose any confidential information or any information that a party specifically instructs the broker in writing not to disclose unless authorized in writing to disclose the information or required to do so by The Texas Real Estate License Act or a court order or if the information materially relates to the condition of the property.

With the parties' consent, a broker acting as an intermediary between the parties may appoint a person who is licensed under The Texas Real Estate License Act and associated with the broker to communicate with and carry out instructions of one party and another person who is licensed under that Act and associated with the broker to communicate with and carry out instructions of the other party.

If you choose to have a broker represent you,
you should enter into a written agreement with the broker that clearly establishes the broker's obligations and your obligations. The agreement should state how and by whom the broker will be paid. You have the right to choose the type of representation, if any, you wish to receive. Your payment of a fee to a broker does not necessarily establish that the broker represents you. If you have any questions regarding the duties and responsibilities of the broker, you should resolve those questions before proceeding.

Real estate licensee asks that you acknowledge receipt of this information about brokerage services for the licensee's records.

_____   _____
Buyer, Seller, Landlord or Tenant   Date

01A   TREC No. OP-K

Reprinted by permission from the Texas Real Estate Commission.

that agency law dictates a policy of single agency practice in all cases, and that dual agency (discussed later) is impossible because of the duties of care under the law of agency. Therefore, they argue that an agent must be an exclusive agent and must represent either the buyer or the seller; thus, the birth of exclusive buyer/tenant agency.

Long a recognized, viable agency option in commercial real estate, representation of the buyer has now replaced listing broker subagency as a prevailing method of working with buyers. More customers/consumers are becoming better informed about agency alternatives and the need for buyer representation. Traditional agents (owner agents) may find it almost impossible to work with and meet the needs of the buyer/tenant without jeopardizing their agency with the owners, so more agents are also becoming representatives of the buyer or the tenant.

Buyer/tenant agency gives a different dimension to the practice of real estate. Buyers and tenants have the same opportunity for representation as the seller/landlord. Buyers and tenants with their own agents can freely disclose their needs. They can ask for and receive information about market conditions such as market value, the sales history of an area or a property, and answers to specific questions and concerns from their agent, who has no conflicting fiduciary duty to the seller.

There is a concern, however, that many real estate agents have never been trained to be a buyer's broker. Historically, the MLS® system and most state laws on agency encouraged agents to be trained as seller's brokers or cooperating brokers. Texas license laws and broker regulations were originally drafted with exclusive seller agency as the norm. Innovative business owners always outpace legislatures and create "the cutting edge" in new trends. Therefore, statutory change is always somewhat behind business practices. This is certainly true of the real estate brokerage industry.

DISCUSSION QUESTIONS

- You have just successfully helped a seller negotiate the sale of his home, which you have listed. Just after he signs the sales contract, he turns to you and says, "Now that you have sold my house, you will have to find me a new home to buy." Do you see any possible agency problems?

- Who can you think of that should have buyer/tenant representation? What relationships or circumstances would dictate the need for a buyer/tenant agent?

Who Could You Represent as a Buyer's Agent?

There are people who probably should be represented by buyer or tenant agents because of their relationship to the agent, such as:

- family members;

- people that you work with in business or who are clients in another area of your life;

- business partners;

- neighbors;

- friends; and

- acquaintances such as members of churches and clubs to which you belong.

You may want to consider the people that you have worked with in past transactions.

There are also those who, because of their vulnerable position, may have difficulty with a licensee's exclusive representation of the seller/landlord, such as:

- first-time buyers/renters;

- out-of-town buyers/renters;

- clients who want to remain anonymous; and

- buyers/tenants who want to be or insist upon being represented by their own agents.

Commercial Transactions

The relationship between agent and owner is better understood in a commercial transaction. Parties tend to be more knowledgeable, and perhaps more adversarial, in commercial transactions. They also tend to negotiate harder about a lot of technical issues and are usually represented by counsel. Often a "tenant's representative" seeks out a "good deal" for the tenant but is paid by the landlord. The agency is clearly disclosed, but the landlord is willing to pay a commission to get the tenant. In these transactions, buyer/tenant agency reduces the possibility of subagency confusion. It can greatly reduce the possibility of unintentional, undisclosed dual agency, thus reducing many problems and adverse consequences. With buyer/tenant agency, it can be easier for all parties to understand who represents whom. Not only can this understanding reduce confusion, it can also avoid conflict. In many ways, buyers may get better service, as the buyer's broker focuses on an acceptable product to buy, not just "doing the deal," which is the traditional marketing effort for seller's agents.

Residential Transactions—Agency Policy of Listing Agents

In a residential environment, the buyers and sellers may not be so sophisticated. Some residential listing brokers still question whether to cooperate (not share their commissions) with buyer agents. Listing brokers should not make the decision to refuse to work with buyer agents without the sellers' participating in the decision. Company policy should state whether any distinctions are made when dealing with buyer broker/agents. Seller agents should be sure their sellers understand the advantages and disadvantages of dealing with a buyer's agent at the time the listing agreement is signed. This is automatically made possible in some prepared forms such as the TAR® MLS® form. It is also necessary for the seller and the listing/seller agent to know immediately if the showing/selling agent is a buyer agent.

The question becomes, "Is it in the seller's best interest to refuse buyer agency?" If a seller refuses to work with or compensate a buyer's broker, a potential purchaser is eliminated. It can also benefit the seller if these represented buyers are better informed, more serious, and more committed to purchase. These buyers can be more eligible and better qualified prospects. Some listing brokers are even refusing to offer subagency and insist upon working with buyer agents. Since buyer agency can eliminate questions of who represents whom, it can also help eliminate the fear of accidental dual agency and misrepresentation. Buyer agents can save a seller agent's time and efforts as they represent their clients. They can reduce some of the listing broker's risks. Each agent is working toward their respective clients' goals and toward a successful end to the transaction, without the conflict of representing both.

PROCEDURE

The practice of real estate changes when buyer agency is involved. Here, the contract that sets up the relationship between the principal and the agent will not be a Listing Agreement, but a Buyer/Tenant Representation Agreement. There will also be a reversal of the nomenclature. The buyer will be the "client" and the seller the "customer."

Buyers' agents must be sure to disclose their agency status immediately when contacting a listing agent to request a showing. Recall that TREC requires that a real estate licensee furnish a party (seller or buyer) in a real estate transaction, at the time of the first substantive dialogue with the party, the Information About Brokerage Services. If another broker represents that party, the disclosure must be given to the other licensee. If the buyer's agent is paid by both parties (or is given a bonus), it should be disclosed (preferably in writing) to avoid violating §1101.652(b)(13) of the License Act by sharing "secret" commissions.

NEED FOR ADVICE

It is argued that consumers, particularly as purchasers, want and need advice in making important decisions. Buyer's brokerage may be the easiest answer to this consumer request as it does not create unexpected (and misunderstood) complications that may arise through dual agency or intermediary status. The procedures for a buyer's broker will be significantly different from those of a seller's broker. The buyer's broker might pursue property that is not on the market and should have a significant knowledge of the "for sale by owner" (FSBO) market, Web sites, and other sources for potential sales that are not in the traditional MLS® listing. In representing the buyer, the agent may also perform other services, such as: (1) preparing an extensive comparative market analysis for the market that the buyer is attempting to locate in, pointing out factors in market trends and historical appreciation (or depreciation) factors in the neighborhood; (2) making a special effort to be sure that offers are presented to owners; (3) having studies available concerning inspections, financing, and environmental hazards in special hazard areas, such as flood-prone areas, earthquake zones, fault lines, and so on; and (4) making special provisions for a walk-through prior to closing.

INITIAL INTERVIEW

It has been suggested that in representing buyers, one should take as much care in interviewing and counseling the buyer as a listing agent typically does in preparing for the initial listing appointments. This may include a "buyer's kit," which would contain community information, standard documentation for a real estate transaction, financing information, and inspection information. The better part of the counseling session probably would be devoted to determining the buyer's wants and needs for the product. In developing a priority list for determining the buyer's needs, the buyer's financial qualifications should also be examined in depth to determine the amount of down payment, closing costs, and debt service that the buyer can handle. Many buyer's brokers use a buyer information checklist for the buyer to sign, acknowledging that the buyer has received all of this information.

Sample Interview Checklist

I. Discuss Broker/Salesperson Qualifications

- Education
- Agency classes
- Experience
- Agency issues
  a. Company policy
  b. Relationships to other buyers and sellers

    c. Agency disclosures

    d. Fiduciary obligations

    e. Explanation of role in the transaction (to help buyer make a good decision)

2. Discuss Buyer's Wants and Needs

- Visualize your last home.
- Visualize home where you grew up.
- List desires and necessities.
- Develop priority list for those desires and necessities.

    a. Give me your top three desires in a house.

    b. Give me your top three things that you do not like in a house.

- Stigma issues?
- Unusual concerns or problems with prior homes or locations

3. Present the Buyer's Kit

- Community information
- Standard documents
- Financing information

    a. Copy of loan application

    b. Cards for loan officers

    c. Loan types

    d. Loan procedures

       1. Application

       2. Cost

       3. Credit report

4. Know the Property

- History of insurance claims
- Inspection information
- Inspection rules and regulations
- Survey information, if available
- Appraisal information, if available
- Prior inspections, if available
- Home warranties, if available
- Termites
- Lead-based paint
- Flood-prone areas

- Foundation problems

- Homeowner's association assessments and fees

- Police and fire department location

- School locations

- Zoning and/or deed restriction information

5. Discuss Buyer Issues

- Source of buyer contract

- How long have you been looking for a house?

- Have any other agents shown you homes?

- Do you have any contracts with them?

- Did you see anything that you particularly liked?

- Did you make an offer? What happened? What is your negotiating strategy? Is it realistic in this market?

- Are any of your relatives or friends real estate agents?

- Remind buyers to refer open house signs, if interested.

- History of insurance claims on prior residences

DISCUSSION QUESTION

- Can you think of other questions?

6. Discuss Financial Qualification

- Down payment

- Monthly payments

    a. Job stability

    b. Sources of income

- Closing costs

- Debt

EARNING THE COMMITMENT

It is also important that the buyer's broker develop a relationship with the client to be sure that the broker is protected as the client looks for property. Brokers have often discovered that when operating as a cooperating broker (under the subagency rules) it may be very difficult to keep the buyer's commitment and loyalty, particularly when it comes to compensation. A prudent agent should ultimately complete the initial consultation by having the buyer(s) execute a Buyer/Tenant Representation Agreement. A fully professional attitude and approach by the buyer's broker should result in a better commitment and rapport so that the broker's efforts don't go uncompensated.

As a buyer's broker, different skills are also required.

SHOWING PROPERTY WHILE REPRESENTING BUYER

- Determine which properties buyer wants to see, which could include properties for sale by Owner, not on the market, and available through sources other than MLS®.

- Disclose agency status to seller (which can be verbal under Texas law if it is listed). A prudent agent should use the Information About Brokerage Services Form.

- Counsel buyer on how to react while viewing the property (don't look excited and enthusiastic—it may change the seller's negotiating strategy).

- Gather information and history about the property that is being shown and the neighborhood.

- Be critical; point out negatives in the property that may be of concern to the Buyer.

- Determine seller motivation to strategize the negotiation process, if possible.

WRITING THE OFFER AND NEGOTIATING

- Do a thorough comparative market analysis to determine a good range of offers.

- Utilize proper TREC forms—special issues to address: earnest money, special title issues (special uses), option provisions, and inspection provisions.

- Warranties to be assigned at closing, or to be paid for by the seller as a part of the transaction.

- Reserve the buyer's right to walk through, prior to closing, to confirm that the repairs have been made (and nothing has been removed).

- Determine upper limits which buyer could pay before getting into a different housing market where other homes may be available.

- Personally present the offer, in a very positive, realistic manner.

- Confirm zoning and deed restrictions for intended use.

DUE DILIGENCE ISSUES

- Zoning
- Deed restrictions

- Flood-prone areas

- Schools, shopping, neighbors

- Inspectors, lead-based paint, radon, and utility capacity and availability issues

- Survey

- Availability of financing to the buyer

- Ad valorem taxes going up? Tax rollbacks?

- MUD (Municipal Utility District) District Notice?

- Annexation

- Project owner's association

- Well and septic systems

CLOSING ISSUES

- Review of settlement statement

- Walk-through prior to closing

- Utility changes and/or certificates of occupancy

- Bill of sale for personal items

- Keys

- Homeowner's insurance and flood insurance, if applicable

- Is title OK? (title commitment issues); but remember, you can't give legal advice

- Provide good funds

- Homeowner's warranty

FOLLOW-UP

- Contact buyer at one week, three months, and yearly intervals to determine satisfaction and to continue building your rapport with the buyer

- Rekey the house at broker's expense, if permitted

- Introduction to neighbors, if possible

- Housewarming gift (something terribly expensive usually works)

DISCUSSION QUESTION

- What differences do you see in the practice of seller agency and buyer agency?

Buyer's Agent—Duties of Care—What Are They?

We must take a new look at the buyer's agent's duties. Loyalty will be to the buyer. For example, CMAs (Comparative Market Analysis) will be for the buyers to make and to support their offers. Duties of care might be the same (performance, accounting, reasonable care, loyalty) but will follow the legal dictates of the buyer. There must be reasonable care and diligence in previewing and showing to best meet the buyer's needs. There may be a new approach to accounting for earnest monies to the seller or the seller's agent. There will be new questions of confidentiality and a new focus on the duties of a buyer's agent to inquire about property use and condition. Recall the case of *Lewis v. Long & Foster* in Chapter 5, wherein a buyer's agent was held responsible for determining use restrictions on the buyer's property, and the *Salhutdin* case, also in Chapter 5, where the court held that a broker has the fiduciary duty to confirm that the property meets the client's standards, or should disclose that no such investigation has been made. In *Wyrick v. Tillman & Tillman Realty*, discussed later, it was held that an agent should have been more diligent in helping find a "quiet and safe" neighborhood.

To date, however, there is very little case law that outlines the duties of the buyer's broker. Let's consider some of that "gray" area.

INSPECTORS

What if the buyer requests the "toughest" inspector? To assist the buyer, you would probably provide the buyer with a list of inspectors you knew to be good and would represent the buyer's interest in doing quality inspections. Let the buyer make the decision as to whom to choose. Make sure the buyer understands it is the *buyer's* decision. Remember, the focus of the buyer's broker is not to "do the deal," but to make sure the buyer gets the product he or she has bargained for.

CONFLICT WITH BUYERS

Another complicating issue develops if a real estate agent represents Buyer 1, who submits an offer on a house. Then if Buyer 2 (also represented by the same real estate agent) wants to submit another offer on that same house, can the buyer's broker adequately represent both buyers? At first glance, it would appear that it would be no different than having two similar houses listed for sale—the agent simply introduces the buyer to both houses and hopes an acceptable offer is submitted.

As a buyer's broker, one may assume that the agent would simply submit both buyer's contracts to the seller and let the seller make the decision, but there is a deeper problem. What if Buyer 1 learns of Buyer 2's offer and says, "I want to out bid that offer at all costs!" Do brokers have a duty of care to disclose all that they know to the buyer that they represent even if it is confidential information of another buyer? Do you have a duty to disclose that there is a competing bid? If so, how much can you disclose? Do competing buyers that you represent have a right to know anything about the other offer? Can either buyer rely on the buyer's broker's 100 percent loyalty, and full disclosure, in such a situation?

SUPERFLUOUS CONTINGENCIES

What if the buyer wants a special "out" drafted in the Earnest Money Contract so he or she can continue to look for other properties? This is not an unusual request in commercial real estate transactions, and it may become an issue in residential real estate transactions now that the TREC contract forms allow for termination options. We have traditionally thought that both listing and "other" broker encourage the sale of the property and market them for the benefit of the seller. The buyer's agent may now introduce a more adversarial process to the residential brokerage business.

DISCLOSING SUBAGENCY

Agents must not only immediately identify themselves as the buyer's agent at first contact with the seller or the seller's agent before any pertinent information can be given that will have to be disclosed, they must also disclaim subagency if subagency is offered or expected. A listing agent may frequently get a phone call to show property and, asking the other broker who he or she represents, get a confused response. In such situations, always anticipate that the other agent will be a buyer's agent; in doing so you eliminate the possibility of confidential information being disclosed unintentionally. The listing agent should also be cautioned that the agent calling today as a subagent may call tomorrow as a buyer's agent on the same property. It's safer for listing brokers to assume that the other agent is always a buyer's broker!

DISCLOSURES TO THE PRINCIPAL

What about unintentional disclosures? Recall that agents must disclose to their principal everything they know. If a buyer's agent is operating in a real estate office that also takes listings, is the buyer's agent to be excluded from sales meetings where confidential information may be discussed? Should you have separate fax machines for confidential faxes that may be transmitted? Should discussions be held behind closed doors when the agent and principal are discussing specific seller's and/or buyer's needs so that the confidential information cannot be overheard by other agents? Since some new listing forms allow sellers to specify the types of agency that they will accept (i.e., subagent or dual agent), there can be no problem limiting lockbox use to only those types of agents.

The Law of Agency and previous case law has given us very little guidance in this area. As stated previously, buyer brokerage is a relatively new concept and there have not been very many cases on duties of care at this point. The easiest alternative is to get out of the transaction. Any other alternative could breach a fiduciary duty for the party you chose not to represent (i.e., you chose to represent one client against the other).

COMPENSATION

Compensation of the buyer's broker is another issue. There has never been a concern about paying any broker or a broker getting paid from both sides so long as the commissions are disclosed and there is no "secret" commission paid. Note that in the TAR® Residential Buyer/Tenant Representation Agreement (Form 1501), Paragraph 11 enables broker's compensation to be paid under at least six possible scenarios: (1) commission; (2) construction fees; (3) a Service Provider fee; or (4) "other" including without limitation (5) hourly fees; and (6) retainers. Under our traditional agency relationships, sellers have been liberal about allowing listing brokers to share commissions with the other broker (presumably including buyer's brokers) so, from a practical standpoint, if the system doesn't change, we will come to expect normal seller compensation for both listing and buyer's brokers. Note, however, that under the TAR® Exclusive Right to Sell Listing Agreement (Form 1101), the seller has the right to restrict payment to a buyer's broker under Paragraph 8.A. Logically, listing agents may want to point out to sellers that if they do not wish to pay a buyer's broker, they may be eliminating a substantial part of the buying market, as buyer's brokers will prefer not to show a listing in which they may not be compensated from the seller (particularly if this is a requirement by the buyer under the buyer's representation agreement).

Consider a problem, though. If the buyer thinks he or she saves money by going directly to the seller, that buyer may be encouraged to "dump" the agent when the going gets tough!

PRESENTING OFFERS

Another issue arises as to whether the buyer's broker should be with the listing broker when offers are presented. The issues presented here are rather predictable. The seller's broker wants to be protected and doesn't want to give another broker access to the seller. There may be another problem in creating an adversary relationship, which the listing broker and seller may not be comfortable with. The other side of the issue is that the broker wants to represent the buyer effectively and make sure that the buyer's position is presented positively to the seller.

The key thing to remember, however, is that who pays the commission is not determinative. Contrary to what you might have heard, the law of agency does not necessarily follow the money. A broker can represent either party, get paid by either party or both parties, provided that all commissions are disclosed. Some sellers may argue that they are paying the commission and expect the brokers to represent them. The buyer's counterargument is that the seller is including the broker's commission in the sales price, and therefore the buyer is paying it indirectly. If the seller has built a commission payment in the sales price, who gets that commission should logically not be of concern since the property is marketed and the deal is made. The split of commissions between the brokers is merely that: agreements between brokers. The seller and buyer are not traditionally a part of that agreement to split the commission. But remember that the new TAR® listing forms with choice of agency can limit with whom the lister shares the commission.

DISCUSSION QUESTIONS

■ What problems can arise if a brokerage has a house listed by an agent that it sponsors, and another agent that the company sponsors sells the listed property as a subagent?

■ Is the answer different if the other agent works for another sponsoring broker?

■ What agency problems have arisen for the listing broker if an agent for the listing broker represents the buyer?

A few other cases are surfacing for buyer's brokers:

In *Lee Hawkins Realty Inc. v. Moss*, 724 So.2d 1116 (Miss. App. 1998), the purchasers brought suit against other parties to a transaction alleging that they were misled to believing there was a warranty on the home they purchased. The lower court awarded damages to be paid to the plaintiff by their realty company, Lee Hawkins Realty (a buyer's broker), but against no other party.

The sellers owned a home in Brandon, Mississippi, and listed their home for sale. The purchasers moved to Mississippi from North Carolina and contacted Lee Hawkins Realty and informed the broker that they were only interested in purchasing a home that had a 2-10 (two year builder defect-10 year structural defects) homeowner's warranty policy. The Davises informed the purchaser that the home was in fact covered by 2-10 warranty. The buyer requested a copy of the 2-10 warranty and, relying on the escrow officer's representation that such a warranty existed while in the closing, the buyer proceeded with the closing. He was later informed that the warranty was never in existence.

The court noted that the seller's agent had no duty to disclose to the buyer unless she knew there was a misrepresentation; that she could rely on the veracity of her principal, who had apparently indicated that the warranty existed. As to the buyer's agent, however, the court had a much different approach. The court noted that Lee Hawkins Realty negligently allowed Moss to proceed with the sale without first verifying the accuracy of the warranty, determining whether there was a warranty, and relying on oral representations derived from another person's telephone conversation. Since this affects the legal rights of the purchaser, is this practicing without a license? I doubt it. It is simply enforcing the terms of the contract that were agreed to, which could be confirmed by obtaining the warranty.

In *Field v. Century 21 Klowden-Forness Realty*, 73 Cal. Rptr.2d 784, the purchaser of the real estate brought a claim for breach of fiduciary duty against their exclusive buyer's broker based upon the broker's alleged failure to inspect related title documents to determine the scope of an easement and to determine correctly the acreage of the tract. The plaintiffs claimed that the brokers falsely represented that the easement holder had an easement only for use of his driveway. In fact, the easement prevented the Fields from exclusively using a major portion of their property. In addition, the acreage of the property was less than was represented by the broker. The buyer's agent was aware of the easement but neither verified the extent of the easement or the represented acreage of the property, nor did she advise the buyers to do so. The conduct of the agent implied both the acreage and the extent of the easement were as erroneously represented. In addition, the broker did not recommend inspection of the septic system of code compliance or alert the buyers to signs of obvious physical defects.

In *Brown v. Roth*, 514 S.E.2d 294 (N.C. Ct. App. 1999), the Roths, sellers, owned the house and hired the defendant Lakeway Properties, Ltd., as the real estate agent to sell their property. On the Multiple Listing Form the broker represented that the Roth house contained 3,484 square feet of heated living area. This information was received from a well-known and highly respected appraiser. The broker did not otherwise verify the information prior to preparing the Multiple Listing Form. Another agent of the broker represented Dr. Brown on the purchase of the property as a buyer's agent, entering into a "Dual Agency Agreement."

In an attempt to refinance, another appraiser indicated that the house contained only 3,108 square feet. The buyer sued his agent for (1) breach of fiduciary duty, (2) negligent misrepresentation, (3) fraud, and (4) unfair and deceptive trade practices. The agent crossed claimed against the first appraiser for erroneous representation as to square footage. The court granted summary judgement for the broker holding that the broker could reasonably rely on the measurements of the house by a trained professional appraiser.

The appeals court acknowledged that a broker may act as an agent for two parties with adverse interests with the full knowledge and consent of both. And further held that the broker had a fiduciary obligation to make a full and truthful disclosure to plaintiff (buyer) of all material facts with regard to the property, known by it or discoverable with reasonable diligence. The heat of the square footage of the Roths' house was a material fact and was discoverable by the broker with reasonable diligence and thus should have been disclosed by the broker to the buyer. The court noted that the guideline established by the North Carolina Real Estate Commission suggested that real estate agents are expected to measure personally all properties they list and calculate the square footage accurately. They must not rely on tax records, information from a previous listing, or representations of the seller or others. North Carolina may have created an additional duty of care as a result of that guideline.

If the buyer requests a "peaceful" house, the buyer's broker better deliver it! In *Wyrick v. Tillman & Tillman Realty, Inc.* (No. 03-00-00061-CV, Tex. App.-Austin 2001), a buyer brought a cause of action against Tillman Realty, who acted as the buyer's agent for the purchase of property in New Braunfels. The purchaser anticipated moving to New Braunfels and requested that Tillman represent her. He agreed to represent her solely as a buyer's agent. The buyer explained that she was moving away from San Antonio to escape the city life, noise, and traffic. Tillman showed her a home and said it was in a quiet and safe neighborhood. Due to an illness, she only visited New Braunfels twice before the closing date and did not move in for several months. Near the end of her first month of occupancy (September 1996), the buyer discovered that the railroad right-of-way was near the house, and a meat processing plant was a block away.

In 1988, the railroad temporarily discontinued the use of the railway for train traffic, but the railroad retained the right to reopen the right-of-way to rail traffic, and did so in November 1998. The broker admitted that he knew the ongoing issues of the right-of-way and knew that it had not been resolved when he found the house for the buyer. It was further noted that the meat processing plant discharged fumes and odors and created a high volume of traffic from the trucks going to and from the plant. The broker alleged that: (1) he had no duty to disclose facts not known to the real estate agent, (2) there is no duty to disclose facts regarding other properties, and (3) the buyer is deemed to have relied on her own investigation. The trial court granted a summary judgment for the broker.

The buyer appealed, alleging that the broker had a duty to disclose these two facts because they materially affect her property. The broker told the buyer that the neighborhood in which the house was located was then, and historically had been, a quiet and safe neighborhood. Broker defended by saying the statements were true at the time they were made (1996), but there was no guarantee they would be true in the future. The Court relied on the Canons of Professional Ethics and Conduct of the Texas Real Estate Commission in defining a fiduciary relationship and confirmed that a broker's contract of employment calls for the utmost good faith on the part of the broker and that he is bound to disclose to his principal all material facts within his knowledge affecting the transaction. The court held that a buyer's agent has a duty to perform his work in a competent, skillful, and professional manner, and has a duty to disclose all material facts that have a bearing on the decision to purchase, and that, viewed in the context of the contract between the broker and his client, would have an effect on the client's satisfaction of the property. The court confirmed the fact that the broker already knew the existence of the railroad right-of-way and meat processing plant.

As for the buyer's duty to inspect the property, the court held that the evidence tended to show that the railroad tracts were difficult to discover and that her visits to the house were in the evening and when it was often dark, and therefore may not have been aware of the railroad right-of-way or the meat processing plant. The summary judgment was reversed, and the case was remanded for further proceedings, so we may hear more about this case in the future.

In *Saiz v. Horne* 668 N.W.2d 332 (S.D.-2003), the South Dakota Supreme Court held that a buyer's broker had a duty to advise the buyer about the rules and procedures involved in a real estate transaction (very similar to the Texas Real Estate Commission Code of Ethics) including advising the buyer to obtain the required Seller's disclosure form.

In *Sumpter v. Holland Realty, Inc.* 93 P.3d 680 (Idaho-2004), the Idaho Supreme Court held that the duties of a buyer's agent (which was set out in their contract) included: (1) to exercise reasonable skill and care; (2) to promote the best interest of the client in good faith, honesty, and fair dealing; (3) to disclose any adverse material facts the agent actually knows or reasonably should have known; (4) to conduct a reasonable investigation of the property and material representations about the property made by the seller or seller's agent; and (5) when appropriate, to advise the client to obtain professional inspections of property or to seek appropriate tax, legal, and other professional advice and counsel. When compared to the Texas Real Estate Commission Rules, there is very little difference between the Idaho's Supreme Court's interpretation of very similar rules.

SINGLE AGENCY

So far, we have discussed two forms of agency: an exclusive seller agency and an exclusive buyer agency. Texas law now provides other alternatives. One of these is the concept of single agency, representing the seller or the buyer, but not both, in any given transaction. This gives the real estate brokerage company the flexibility of representing buyers and sellers, but not having the conflict of interest of representing both. Utilizing the single agency concept, the agent would get the representation agreement from the buyer or the seller. When representing the seller and utilizing the TAR® Form No. 1101, check box 9.B.(1). If representing the buyer and utilizing the TAR® Form No. 1501, check paragraph 8.B.(1). Your company's policy may vary, though. The standard form just doesn't fit all situations. See TAR® Forms 1101 and 1501 in Figures 9-2 and 9-3.

Procedures

This can create conflicts in office policy. If there are in-house listings, **there can be no in-house buyer broker,** as the same company would represent both parties and create a dual agency. Suggested procedures could be as follows:

WHEN REPRESENTING THE BUYER

■ Do not sign an agreement to be a buyer's representative until the buyer has seen and rejected all of the in-house listings. If the buyer chooses an in-house listing, you remain as a subagent and don't represent the buyer.

■ After the in-house listings have been rejected, you are free to represent the buyer in acquiring other properties. If the buyer decides he or she likes a listed property after viewing the other properties, you can refer the buyer to another broker or terminate your buyer's agency and handle the transaction as an agent of the seller. CAUTION: REMEMBER THAT YOU CANNOT USE CONFIDENTIAL INFORMATION OBTAINED BY THE BUYER AGAINST THE BUYER'S BEST INTEREST IN THE EVENT THE BUYER BEGINS TO NEGOTIATE ON ONE OF YOUR IN-HOUSE LISTINGS.

■ When a potential for an in-house listing exists but is not yet engaged (no listing agreement has been signed), the agent should be sure that the buyer sees that parcel of real estate before the listing is obtained. Therefore, if the seller calls the office and requests a listing appointment, and the potential listing fits the buyer's profile, you should show that product to the buyer before you take the listing in order to prevent the conflict. In addition, there is no listing, no right to a commission, virtually nothing that protects the broker's interest. This potential conflict needs to be addressed very early in any transaction.

WHEN REPRESENTING THE SELLER

Deal with all buyers as customers and retain your status as an agent/subagent for in-house company listings. (If another agent signs a buyer representation agreement that fits your company's profile, you may not show that property.)

FIG 9-2   RESIDENTIAL REAL ESTATE LISTING AGREEMENT EXCLUSIVE RIGHT TO SELL

TEXAS ASSOCIATION OF REALTORS®

RESIDENTIAL REAL ESTATE LISTING AGREEMENT
EXCLUSIVE RIGHT TO SELL

USE OF THIS FORM BY PERSONS WHO ARE NOT MEMBERS OF THE TEXAS ASSOCIATION OF REALTORS® IS NOT AUTHORIZED.
©Texas Association of REALTORS®, Inc. 2003

1. **PARTIES:** The parties to this agreement (this Listing) are:

Seller: _____
_____
Address: _____
City, State, Zip: _____
Phone:_____Fax: _____
E-Mail: _____

Broker: _____
Address: _____
City, State, Zip: _____
Phone:_____Fax: _____
E-Mail: _____

Seller appoints Broker as Seller's sole and exclusive real estate agent and grants to Broker the exclusive right to sell the Property.

2. **PROPERTY:** "Property" means the land, improvements, and accessories described below, except for any described exclusions.

A. <u>Land:</u> Lot_____, Block_____, _____
_____ Addition, City of_____,
in _____ County, Texas known as _____
_____ (address/zip code),
or as described on attached exhibit. *(If Property is a condominium, attach Condominium Addendum.)*

B. <u>Improvements:</u> The house, garage and all other fixtures and improvements attached to the above-described real property, including without limitation, the following permanently installed and built-in items, if any: all equipment and appliances, valances, screens, shutters, awnings, wall-to-wall carpeting, mirrors, ceiling fans, attic fans, mail boxes, television antennas and satellite dish system and equipment, heating and air-conditioning units, security and fire detection equipment, wiring, plumbing and lighting fixtures, chandeliers, water softener system, kitchen equipment, garage door openers, cleaning equipment, shrubbery, landscaping, outdoor cooking equipment, and all other property owned by Seller and attached to the above-described real property.

C. <u>Accessories:</u> The following described related accessories, if any: window air conditioning units, stove, fireplace screens, curtains and rods, blinds, window shades, draperies and rods, controls for satellite dish system, controls for garage door openers, entry gate controls, door keys, mailbox keys, above-ground pool, swimming pool equipment and maintenance accessories, and artificial fireplace logs.

D. <u>Exclusions:</u> The following improvements and accessories will be retained by Seller and excluded: _____
_____.

E. <u>Owners' Association:</u> The property ❏ is ❏ is not subject to mandatory membership in an owners' association.

FIG 9-2   *(continued)*

Residential Listing concerning _____

3. **LISTING PRICE:** Seller instructs Broker to market the Property at the following price: $_____ (Listing Price). Seller agrees to sell the Property for the Listing Price or any other price acceptable to Seller. Seller will pay all typical closing costs charged to sellers of residential real estate in Texas (seller's typical closing costs are those set forth in the residential contract forms promulgated by the Texas Real Estate Commission).

4. **TERM:**

   A. This Listing begins on _____ and ends at 11:59 p.m. on _____.

   B. If Seller enters into a binding written contract to sell the Property before the date this Listing begins and the contract is binding on the date this Listing begins, this Listing will not commence and will be void.

5. **BROKER'S FEE:**

   A. <u>Fee</u>: When earned and payable, Seller will pay Broker a fee of:

   ❑ (1) _____% of the sales price.

   ❑ (2) _____.

   B. <u>Earned</u>: Broker's fee is earned when any one of the following occurs during this Listing:
       (1) Seller sells, exchanges, options, agrees to sell, agrees to exchange, or agrees to option the Property to anyone at any price on any terms;
       (2) Broker individually or in cooperation with another broker procures a buyer ready, willing, and able to buy the Property at the Listing Price or at any other price acceptable to Seller; or
       (3) Seller breaches this Listing.

   C. <u>Payable</u>: Once earned, Broker's fee is payable either during this Listing or after it ends at the earlier of:
       (1) the closing and funding of any sale or exchange of all or part of the Property;
       (2) Seller's refusal to sell the Property after Broker's Fee has been earned;
       (3) Seller's breach of this Listing; or
       (4) at such time as otherwise set forth in this Listing.

       Broker's fee is <u>not</u> payable if a sale of the Property does not close or fund as a result of: (i) Seller's failure, without fault of Seller, to deliver to a buyer a deed or a title policy as required by the contract to sell; (ii) loss of ownership due to foreclosure or other legal proceeding; or (iii) Seller's failure to restore the Property, as a result of a casualty loss, to its previous condition by the closing date set forth in a contract for the sale of the Property.

   D. <u>Other Fees</u>:

       (1) <u>Breach by Buyer Under a Contract</u>: If Seller collects earnest money, the sales price, or damages by suit, compromise, settlement, or otherwise from a buyer who breaches a contract for the sale of the Property entered into during this Listing, Seller will pay Broker, after deducting attorney's fees and collection expenses, an amount equal to the lesser of one-half of the amount collected after deductions or the amount of the Broker's Fee stated in Paragraph 5A. Any amount paid under this Paragraph 5D(1) is in addition to any amount that Broker may be entitled to receive for subsequently selling the Property.

       (2) <u>Service Providers</u>: If Broker refers Seller or a prospective buyer to a service provider (for example, mover, cable company, telecommunications provider, utility, or contractor) Broker may receive a fee from the service provider for the referral. Any referral fee Broker receives under this Paragraph 5D(2) is in addition to any other compensation Broker may receive under this Listing.

FIG 9-2 *(continued)*

Residential Listing concerning _____

      (3) <u>Transaction Fees or Reimbursable Expenses</u>: _____

_____

_____ .

E. <u>Protection Period</u>:

    (1) "Protection period" means that time starting the day after this Listing ends and continuing for _____ days. "Sell" means any transfer of any interest in the Property whether by oral or written agreement or option.

    (2) Not later than 10 days after this Listing ends, Broker may send Seller written notice specifying the names of persons whose attention was called to the Property during this Listing. If Seller agrees to sell the Property during the protection period to a person named in the notice or to a relative of a person named in the notice, Seller will pay Broker, upon the closing of the sale, the amount Broker would have been entitled to receive if this Listing were still in effect.

    (3) This Paragraph 5E survives termination of this Listing. This Paragraph 5E will not apply if:
        (a) Seller agrees to sell the Property during the protection period;
        (b) the Property is exclusively listed with another broker who is a member of the Texas Association of REALTORS® at the time the sale is negotiated; and
        (c) Seller is obligated to pay the other broker a fee for the sale.

F. <u>County</u>: All amounts payable to Broker are to be paid in cash in _____
_____ County, Texas.

G. <u>Escrow Authorization</u>: Seller authorizes, and Broker may so instruct, any escrow or closing agent authorized to close a transaction for the purchase or acquisition of the Property to collect and disburse to Broker all amounts payable to Broker under this Listing.

6. LISTING SERVICES:

❑ A. Broker will file this Listing with one or more Multiple Listing Services (MLS) by the earlier of the time required by MLS rules or 5 days after the date this Listing begins. Seller authorizes Broker to submit information about this Listing and the sale of the Property to the MLS.

    <u>Notice</u>: MLS rules require Broker to accurately and timely submit all information the MLS requires for participation including sold data. Subscribers to the MLS may use the information for market evaluation or appraisal purposes. Subscribers are other brokers and other real estate professionals such as appraisers and may include the appraisal district. Any information filed with the MLS becomes the property of the MLS for all purposes. **Submission of information to MLS ensures that persons who use and benefit from the MLS also contribute information.**

❑ B. Broker will not file this Listing with a Multiple Listing Service (MLS) or any other listing service.

7. ACCESS TO THE PROPERTY:

A. <u>Authorizing Access</u>: Authorizing access to the Property means giving permission to another person to enter the Property, disclosing to the other person any security codes necessary to enter the Property, and lending a key to the other person to enter the Property, directly or through a keybox. To facilitate the showing and sale of the Property, Seller instructs Broker to:
    (1) access the Property at reasonable times
    (2) authorize other brokers, their associates, inspectors, appraisers, and contractors to access the Property at reasonable times; and
    (3) duplicate keys to facilitate convenient and efficient showings of the Property.

B. <u>Scheduling Companies</u>: Broker may engage the following companies to schedule appointments and to authorize others to access the Property: _____ .

(TAR-1101) 10-16-03   Initialed for Identification by Broker/Associate _____ and Seller _____, _____   Page 3 of 8

FIG 9-2   *(continued)*

Residential Listing concerning _____

C. Keybox: **A keybox is a locked container placed on the Property that holds a key to the Property. A keybox makes it more convenient for brokers, their associates, inspectors, appraisers, and contractors to show, inspect, or repair the Property. The keybox is opened by a special combination, key, or programmed device so that authorized persons may enter the Property, even in Seller's absence. Using a keybox will probably increase the number of showings, but involves risks (for example, unauthorized entry, theft, property damage, or personal injury). Neither the Association of REALTORS® nor MLS requires the use of a keybox.**

(1) Broker ❑ is ❑ is not   authorized to place a keybox on the Property.

(2) If a tenant occupies the Property at any time during this Listing, Seller will furnish Broker a written statement (for example, TAR No. 1411), signed by all tenants, authorizing the use of a keybox or Broker may remove the keybox from the Property.

D. Liability and Indemnification: When authorizing access to the Property, Broker, other brokers, their associates, any keybox provider, or any scheduling company are not responsible for personal injury or property loss to Seller or any other person. Seller assumes all risk of any loss, damage, or injury. **Except for a loss caused by Broker, Seller will indemnify and hold Broker harmless from any claim for personal injury, property damage, or other loss.**

8. **COOPERATION WITH OTHER BROKERS:** Broker will allow other brokers to show the Property to prospective buyers. Broker will offer to pay the other broker a fee as described below if the other broker procures a buyer that purchases the Property.

A. MLS Participants: If the other broker is a participant in the MLS in which this Listing is filed, Broker will offer to pay the other broker:
(1) if the other broker represents the buyer: _____% of the sales price or $_____; and
(2) if the other broker is a subagent: _____% of the sales price or $_____.

B. Non-MLS Brokers: If the other broker is not a participant in the MLS in which this Listing is filed, Broker will offer to pay the other broker:
(1) if the other broker represents the buyer: _____% of the sales price or $_____; and
(2) if the other broker is a subagent: _____% of the sales price or $_____.

9. **INTERMEDIARY:** *(Check A or B only.)*

❑ A. Intermediary Status: Broker may show the Property to interested prospective buyers who Broker represents. If a prospective buyer who Broker represents offers to buy the Property, Seller authorizes Broker to act as an intermediary and Broker will notify Seller that Broker will service the parties in accordance with one of the following alternatives.

(1) If a prospective buyer who Broker represents is serviced by an associate other than the associate servicing Seller under this Listing, Broker may notify Seller that Broker will: (a) appoint the associate then servicing Seller to communicate with, carry out instructions of, and provide opinions and advice during negotiations to Seller; and (b) appoint the associate then servicing the prospective buyer to the prospective buyer for the same purpose.

(2) If a prospective buyer who Broker represents is serviced by the same associate who is servicing Seller, Broker may notify Seller that Broker will: (a) appoint another associate to communicate with, carry out instructions of, and provide opinions and advice during negotiations to the prospective buyer; and (b) appoint the associate servicing the Seller under this Listing to the Seller for the same purpose.

(3) Broker may notify Seller that Broker will make no appointments as described under this Paragraph 9A and, in such an event, the associate servicing the parties will act solely as Broker's intermediary representative, who may facilitate the transaction but will not render opinions or advice during negotiations to either party.

(TAR-1101) 10-16-03   Initialed for Identification by Broker/Associate _____ and Seller _____, _____   Page 4 of 8

FIG 9-2   *(continued)*

Residential Listing concerning _____

☐ B. <u>No Intermediary Status</u>: Seller agrees that Broker will not show the Property to prospective buyers who Broker represents.

Notice: **If Broker acts as an intermediary under Paragraph 9A, Broker and Broker's associates:**
- **may not disclose to the prospective buyer that Seller will accept a price less than the asking price unless otherwise instructed in a separate writing by Seller;**
- **may not disclose to Seller that the prospective buyer will pay a price greater than the price submitted in a written offer to Seller unless otherwise instructed in a separate writing by the prospective buyer;**
- **may not disclose any confidential information or any information Seller or the prospective buyer specifically instructs Broker in writing not to disclose unless otherwise instructed in a separate writing by the respective party or required to disclose the information by the Real Estate License Act or a court order or if the information materially relates to the condition of the property;**
- **may not treat a party to the transaction dishonestly; and**
- **may not violate the Real Estate License Act.**

10. **CONFIDENTIAL INFORMATION:** During this Listing or after it ends, Broker may not knowingly disclose information obtained in confidence from Seller except as authorized by Seller or required by law. Broker may not disclose to Seller any confidential information regarding any other person Broker represents or previously represented except as required by law.

11. **BROKER'S AUTHORITY:**

A. Broker will use reasonable efforts and act diligently to market the Property for sale, procure a buyer, and negotiate the sale of the Property.

B. In addition to other authority granted by this Listing, Broker may:
   (1) advertise the Property by means and methods as Broker determines, including but not limited to creating and placing advertisements with interior and exterior photographic and audio-visual images of the Property and related information in any media and the Internet;
   (2) place a "For Sale" sign on the Property and remove all other signs offering the Property for sale or lease;
   (3) furnish comparative marketing and sales information about other properties to prospective buyers;
   (4) disseminate information about the Property to other brokers and to prospective buyers, including applicable disclosures or notices that Seller is required to make under law or a contract;
   (5) obtain information from any holder of a note secured by a lien on the Property;
   (6) accept and deposit earnest money in trust in accordance with a contract for the sale of the Property;
   (7) disclose the sales price and terms of sale to other brokers, appraisers, or other real estate professionals;
   (8) in response to inquiries from prospective buyers and other brokers, disclose whether the Seller is considering more than one offer, provided that Broker will not disclose the terms of any competing offer unless specifically instructed by Seller;
   (9) advertise, during or after this Listing ends, that Broker "sold" the Property; and
   (10) place information about this Listing, the Property, and a transaction for the Property on an electronic transaction platform (typically an Internet-based system where professionals related to the transaction such as title companies, lenders, and others may receive, view, and input information).

C. Broker is not authorized to execute any document in the name of or on behalf of Seller concerning the Property.

(TAR-1101) 10-16-03   Initialed for Identification by Broker/Associate _____ and Seller _____, _____   Page 5 of 8

FIG 9-2   *(continued)*

Residential Listing concerning _____

12. SELLER'S REPRESENTATIONS: Except as provided by Paragraph 15, Seller represents that:
   A. Seller has fee simple title to and peaceable possession of the Property and all its improvements and fixtures, unless rented, and the legal capacity to convey the Property;
   B. Seller is not bound by a listing agreement with another broker for the sale, exchange, or lease of the Property that is or will be in effect during this Listing;
   C. any pool or spa and any required enclosures, fences, gates, and latches comply with all applicable laws and ordinances;
   D. no person or entity has any right to purchase, lease, or acquire the Property by an option, right of refusal, or other agreement;
   E. there are no delinquencies or defaults under any deed of trust, mortgage, or other encumbrance on the Property;
   F. the Property is not subject to the jurisdiction of any court;
   G. all information relating to the Property Seller provides to Broker is true and correct to the best of Seller's knowledge; and
   H. the name of any employer, relocation company, or other entity that provides benefits to Seller when selling the Property is: _____.

13. SELLER'S ADDITIONAL PROMISES: Seller agrees to:
   A. cooperate with Broker to facilitate the showing, marketing, and sale of the Property;
   B. not rent or lease the Property during this Listing without Broker's prior written approval;
   C. not negotiate with any prospective buyer who may contact Seller directly, but refer all prospective buyers to Broker;
   D. not enter into a listing agreement with another broker for the sale, exchange, or lease of the Property to become effective during this Listing;
   E. maintain any pool and all required enclosures in compliance with all applicable laws and ordinances;
   F. provide Broker with copies of any leases or rental agreements pertaining to the Property and advise Broker of tenants moving in or out of the Property;
   G. complete any disclosures or notices required by law or a contract to sell the Property; and
   H. amend any applicable notices and disclosures if any material change occurs during this Listing.

14. LIMITATION OF LIABILITY:

   A. If the Property is or becomes vacant during this Listing, Seller must notify Seller's casualty insurance company and request a "vacancy clause" to cover the Property. Broker is not responsible for the security of the Property nor for inspecting the Property on any periodic basis.

   B. **Broker is not responsible or liable in any manner for personal injury to any person or for loss or damage to any person's real or personal property resulting from any act or omission not caused by Broker's negligence, including but not limited to injuries or damages caused by:**
      (1) **other brokers, their associates, inspectors, appraisers, and contractors who are authorized to access the Property;**
      (2) **acts of third parties (for example, vandalism or theft);**
      (3) **freezing water pipes;**
      (4) **a dangerous condition on the Property; or**
      (5) **the Property's non-compliance with any law or ordinance.**

   C. **Seller agrees to protect, defend, indemnify, and hold Broker harmless from any damage, costs, attorney's fees, and expenses that:**
      (1) **are caused by Seller, negligently or otherwise;**
      (2) **arise from Seller's failure to disclose any material or relevant information about the Property; or**
      (3) **are caused by Seller giving incorrect information to any person.**

(TAR-1101) 10-16-03   Initialed for Identification by Broker/Associate _____ and Seller _____, _____   Page 6 of 8

FIG 9-2 *(continued)*

Residential Listing concerning _____

15. SPECIAL PROVISIONS:

16. **DEFAULT:** If Seller breaches this Listing, Seller is in default and will be liable to Broker for the amount of the Broker's fee specified in Paragraph 5A and any other fees Broker is entitled to receive under this Listing. If a sales price is not determinable in the event of an exchange or breach of this Listing, the Listing Price will be the sales price for purposes of computing Broker's fee. If Broker breaches this Listing, Broker is in default and Seller may exercise any remedy at law.

17. **MEDIATION:** The parties agree to negotiate in good faith in an effort to resolve any dispute related to this Listing that may arise between the parties. If the dispute cannot be resolved by negotiation, the dispute will be submitted to mediation. The parties to the dispute will choose a mutually acceptable mediator and will share the cost of mediation equally.

18. **ATTORNEY'S FEES:** If Seller or Broker is a prevailing party in any legal proceeding brought as a result of a dispute under this Listing or any transaction related to or contemplated by this Listing, such party will be entitled to recover from the non-prevailing party all costs of such proceeding and reasonable attorney's fees.

19. **ADDENDA AND OTHER DOCUMENTS:** Addenda that are part of this Listing and other documents that Seller may need to provide are:
- [X] A. Information About Brokerage Services;
- ☐ B. Seller Disclosure Notice (§5.008, Texas Property Code);
- ☐ C. Seller's Disclosure of Information on Lead-Based Paint and Lead-Based Paint Hazards (required if Property was built before 1978);
- ☐ D. MUD, Water District, or Statutory Tax District Disclosure Notice (Chapter 49, Texas Water Code);
- ☐ E. Request for Information from an Owners' Association;
- ☐ F. Request for Mortgage Information;
- ☐ G. Information about On-Site Sewer Facility;
- ☐ H. Information about Special Flood Hazard Areas;
- ☐ I. Condominium Addendum to Listing;
- ☐ J. Keybox Authorization by Tenant;
- ☐ K. Seller's Authorization to Release and Advertise Certain Information; and
- ☐ L. _____
  _____.

20. AGREEMENT OF PARTIES:

A. <u>Entire Agreement</u>: This Listing is the entire agreement of the parties and may not be changed except by written agreement.

B. <u>Assignability</u>: Neither party may assign this Listing without the written consent of the other party.

FIG 9-2 *(continued)*

Residential Listing concerning _____

C. <u>Binding Effect</u>: Seller's obligation to pay Broker an earned fee is binding upon Seller and Seller's heirs, administrators, executors, successors, and permitted assignees.

D. <u>Joint and Several</u>: All Sellers executing this Listing are jointly and severally liable for the performance of all its terms.

E. <u>Governing Law</u>: Texas law governs the interpretation, validity, performance, and enforcement of this Listing.

F. <u>Severability</u>: If a court finds any clause in this Listing invalid or unenforceable, the remainder of this Listing will not be affected and all other provisions of this Listing will remain valid and enforceable.

G. <u>Notices</u>: Notices between the parties must be in writing and are effective when sent to the receiving party's address, fax, or e-mail address specified in Paragraph 1.

21. **ADDITIONAL NOTICES:**

A. **Broker's fees or the sharing of fees between brokers are not fixed, controlled, recommended, suggested, or maintained by the Association of REALTORS®, MLS, or any listing service.**

B. **Fair housing laws require the Property to be shown and made available to all persons without regard to race, color, religion, national origin, sex, disability, or familial status. Local ordinances may provide for additional protected classes (for example, creed, status as a student, marital status, sexual orientation, or age).**

C. **Seller may review the information Broker submits to an MLS or other listing service.**

D. **Broker advises Seller to remove or secure jewelry, prescription drugs, and other valuables.**

E. **Statutes or ordinances may regulate certain items on the Property (for example, swimming pools and septic systems). Non-compliance with the statutes or ordinances may delay a transaction and may result in fines, penalties, and liability to Seller.**

F. **If the Property was built before 1978, Federal law requires the Seller to: (1) provide the buyer with the federally approved pamphlet on lead poisoning prevention; (2) disclose the presence of any known lead-based paint or lead-based paint hazards in the Property; (3) deliver all records and reports to the buyer related to such paint or hazards; and (4) provide the buyer a period up to 10 days to have the Property inspected for such paint or hazards.**

G. **Broker cannot give legal advice. READ THIS LISTING CAREFULLY. If you do not understand the effect of this Listing, consult an attorney BEFORE signing.**

_____   _____   _____   _____
Broker's Printed Name   License No.   Seller   Date

By:_____   _____   _____   _____
     Broker's Associate's Signature   Date   Seller   Date

(TAR-1101) 10-16-03   Page 8 of 8

TEXAS ASSOCIATION OF REALTORS®
RESIDENTIAL BUYER/TENANT REPRESENTATION AGREEMENT
USE OF THIS FORM BY PERSONS WHO ARE NOT MEMBERS OF THE TEXAS ASSOCIATION OF REALTORS® IS NOT AUTHORIZED.
©Texas Association of REALTORS®, Inc. 2006

1. PARTIES: The parties to this agreement are:

Client: _____
  Address: _____
  City, State, Zip: _____
  Phone:_____Fax: _____
  E-Mail: _____

Broker: _____
  Address: _____
  City, State, Zip: _____
  Phone:_____Fax: _____
  E-Mail: _____

2. APPOINTMENT: Client grants to Broker the exclusive right to act as Client's real estate agent for the purpose of acquiring property in the market area.

3. DEFINITIONS:
  A. *"Acquire"* means to purchase or lease.
  B. *"Closing"* in a sale transaction means the date legal title to a property is conveyed to a purchaser of property under a contract to buy. *"Closing"* in a lease transaction means the date a landlord and tenant enter into a binding lease of a property.
  C. *"Market area"* means that area in the State of Texas within the perimeter boundaries of the following areas:_____
  _____
  _____
  _____.
  D. *"Property"* means any interest in real estate including but not limited to properties listed in a multiple listing service or other listing services, properties for sale by owners, and properties for sale by builders.

4. TERM: This agreement commences on _____ and ends at 11:59 p.m. on _____.

5. BROKER'S OBLIGATIONS: Broker will: (a) use Broker's best efforts to assist Client in acquiring property in the market area; (b) assist Client in negotiating the acquisition of property in the market area; and (c) comply with other provisions of this agreement.

6. CLIENT'S OBLIGATIONS: Client will: (a) work exclusively through Broker in acquiring property in the market area and negotiate the acquisition of property in the market area only through Broker; (b) inform other brokers, salespersons, sellers, and landlords with whom Client may have contact that Broker exclusively represents Client for the purpose of acquiring property in the market area and refer all such persons to Broker; and (c) comply with other provisions of this agreement.

7. REPRESENTATIONS:
  A. Each person signing this agreement represents that the person has the legal capacity and authority to bind the respective party to this agreement.
  B. Client represents that Client is not now a party to another buyer or tenant representation agreement with another broker for the acquisition of property in the market area.

(TAR-1501) 4-14-06   Initialed for Identification by: Broker/Associate _____, and Client _____   Page 1 of 4

FIG 9-3   *(continued)*

Buyer/Tenant Representation Agreement between _____

C. Client represents that all information relating to Client's ability to acquire property in the market area Client gives to Broker is true and correct.

D. Name any employer, relocation company, or other entity that will provide benefits to Client when acquiring property in the market area: _____.

8. INTERMEDIARY: *(Check A or B only.)*

❑ A. <u>Intermediary Status</u>: Client desires to see Broker's listings. If Client wishes to acquire one of Broker's listings, Client authorizes Broker to act as an intermediary and Broker will notify Client that Broker will service the parties in accordance with one of the following alternatives.

(1) If the owner of the property is serviced by an associate other than the associate servicing Client under this agreement, Broker may notify Client that Broker will: (a) appoint the associate then servicing the owner to communicate with, carry out instructions of, and provide opinions and advice during negotiations to the owner; and (b) appoint the associate then servicing Client to the Client for the same purpose.

(2) If the owner of the property is serviced by the same associate who is servicing Client, Broker may notify Client that Broker will: (a) appoint another associate to communicate with, carry out instructions of, and provide opinions and advice during negotiations to Client; and (b) appoint the associate servicing the owner under the listing to the owner for the same purpose.

(3) Broker may notify Client that Broker will make no appointments as described under this Paragraph 8A and, in such an event, the associate servicing the parties will act solely as Broker's intermediary representative, who may facilitate the transaction but will not render opinions or advice during negotiations to either party.

❑ B. <u>No Intermediary Status</u>: Client does not wish to be shown or acquire any of Broker's listings.

Notice: **If Broker acts as an intermediary under Paragraph 8A, Broker and Broker's associates:**
- **may not disclose to Client that the seller or landlord will accept a price less than the asking price unless otherwise instructed in a separate writing by the seller or landlord;**
- **may not disclose to the seller or landlord that Client will pay a price greater than the price submitted in a written offer to the seller or landlord unless otherwise instructed in a separate writing by Client;**
- **may not disclose any confidential information or any information a seller or landlord or Client specifically instructs Broker in writing not to disclose unless otherwise instructed in a separate writing by the respective party or required to disclose the information by the Real Estate License Act or a court order or if the information materially relates to the condition of the property;**
- **shall treat all parties to the transaction honestly; and**
- **shall comply with the Real Estate License Act.**

9. COMPETING CLIENTS: Client acknowledges that Broker may represent other prospective buyers or tenants who may seek to acquire properties that may be of interest to Client. Client agrees that Broker may, during the term of this agreement and after it ends, represent such other prospects, show the other prospects the same properties that Broker shows to Client, and act as a real estate broker for such other prospects in negotiating the acquisition of properties that Client may seek to acquire.

10. CONFIDENTIAL INFORMATION:

A. During the term of this agreement or after its termination, Broker may not knowingly disclose information obtained in confidence from Client except as authorized by Client or required by law. Broker may not disclose to Client any information obtained in confidence regarding any other person Broker represents or may have represented except as required by law.

B. Unless otherwise agreed or required by law, a seller or the seller's agent is not obliged to keep the existence of an offer or its terms confidential. If a listing agent receives multiple offers, the listing agent is obliged to treat the competing buyers fairly.

(TAR-1501) 4-14-06   Initialed for Identification by: Broker/Associate _____, and Client _____,_____   Page 2 of 4

FIG 9-3 *(continued)*

Buyer/Tenant Representation Agreement between _____

11. BROKER'S FEES:

A. <u>Commission</u>: The parties agree that Broker will receive a commission calculated as follows: (1) ____% of the gross sales price if Client agrees to purchase property in the market area; and (2) if Client agrees to lease property in the market a fee equal to *(check only one box)*: ❏ _____% of one month's rent or ❏ ____% of all rents to be paid over the term of the lease.

B. <u>Source of Commission Payment</u>: Broker will seek to obtain payment of the commission specified in Paragraph 11A first from the seller, landlord, or their agents. If such persons refuse or fail to pay Broker the amount specified, Client will pay Broker the amount specified less any amounts Broker receives from such persons.

C. <u>Earned and Payable</u>: A person is not obligated to pay Broker a commission until such time as Broker's commission is *earned and payable*. Broker's commission is *earned* when: (1) Client enters into a contract to buy or lease property in the market area; or (2) Client breaches this agreement. Broker's commission is *payable*, either during the term of this agreement or after it ends, upon the earlier of: (1) the closing of the transaction to acquire the property; (2) Client's breach of a contract to buy or lease a property in the market area; or (3) Client's breach of this agreement. If Client acquires more than one property under this agreement, Broker's commissions for each property acquired are earned as each property is acquired and are payable at the closing of each acquisition.

D. <u>Additional Compensation</u>: If a seller, landlord, or their agents offer compensation in excess of the amount stated in Paragraph 11A (including but not limited to marketing incentives or bonuses to cooperating brokers) Broker may retain the additional compensation in addition to the specified commission. Client is not obligated to pay any such additional compensation to Broker.

E. <u>Acquisition of Broker's Listing</u>: Notwithstanding any provision to the contrary, if Client acquires a property listed by Broker, Broker will be paid in accordance with the terms of Broker's listing agreement with the owner and Client will have no obligation to pay Broker.

F. In addition to the commission specified under Paragraph 11A, Broker is entitled to the following fees.
    (1) <u>Construction</u>: If Client uses Broker's services to procure or negotiate the construction of improvements to property that Client owns or may acquire, Client ensures that Broker will receive from Client or the contractor(s) at the time the construction is substantially complete a fee equal to: _____
    (2) <u>Service Providers</u>: If Broker refers Client or any party to a transaction contemplated by this agreement to a service provider (for example, mover, cable company, telecommunications provider, utility, or contractor) Broker may receive a fee from the service provider for the referral.
    (3) <u>Other</u>: _____
_____
_____.

G. <u>Protection Period</u>: "Protection period" means that time starting the day after this agreement ends and continuing for _____ days. Not later than 10 days after this agreement ends, Broker may send Client written notice identifying the properties called to Client's attention during this agreement. If Client or a relative of Client agrees to acquire a property identified in the notice during the protection period, Client will pay Broker, upon closing, the amount Broker would have been entitled to receive if this agreement were still in effect. This Paragraph 11G survives termination of this agreement. This Paragraph 11G will not apply if Client is, during the protection period, bound under a representation agreement with another broker who is a member of the Texas Association of REALTORS® at the time the acquisition is negotiated and the other broker is paid a fee for negotiating the transaction.

H. <u>Escrow Authorization</u>: Client authorizes, and Broker may so instruct, any escrow or closing agent authorized to close a transaction for the acquisition of property contemplated by this agreement to collect and disburse to Broker all amounts payable to Broker.

I. <u>County</u>: Amounts payable to Broker are to be paid in cash in _____ County, Texas.

FIG 9-3   *(continued)*

Buyer/Tenant Representation Agreement between _____

12. MEDIATION: The parties agree to negotiate in good faith in an effort to resolve any dispute that may arise related to this agreement or any transaction related to or contemplated by this agreement. If the dispute cannot be resolved by negotiation, the parties will submit the dispute to mediation before resorting to arbitration or litigation and will equally share the costs of a mutually acceptable mediator.

13. DEFAULT: If either party fails to comply with this agreement or makes a false representation in this agreement, the non-complying party is in default. If Client is in default, Client will be liable for the amount of compensation that Broker would have received under this agreement if Client was not in default. If Broker is in default, Client may exercise any remedy at law.

14. ATTORNEY'S FEES: If Client or Broker is a prevailing party in any legal proceeding brought as a result of a dispute under this agreement or any transaction related to this agreement, such party will be entitled to recover from the non-prevailing party all costs of such proceeding and reasonable attorney's fees.

15. LIMITATION OF LIABILITY: Neither Broker nor any other broker, or their associates, is responsible or liable for Client's personal injuries or for any loss or damage to Client's property that is not caused by Broker. Client will hold broker, any other broker, and their associates, harmless from any such injuries or losses. Client will indemnify Broker against any claims for injury or damage that Client may cause to others or their property.

16. ADDENDA: Addenda and other related documents which are part of this agreement are:
- ☑ Information About Brokerage Services
- ☐ Protecting Your Home from Mold
- ☐ Information Concerning Property Insurance
- ☐ General Information and Notice to a Buyer
- ☐ Protect Your Family from Lead in Your Home
- ☐ Information about Special Flood Hazard Areas
- ☐ For Your Protection: Get a Home Inspection
- ☐ _____

17. SPECIAL PROVISIONS:

18. ADDITIONAL NOTICES:

A. Broker's fees and the sharing of fees between brokers are not fixed, controlled, recommended, suggested, or maintained by the Association of REALTORS® or any listing service.

B. Broker's services are provided without regard to race, color, religion, national origin, sex, disability or familial status.

C. Broker is not a property inspector, surveyor, engineer, environmental assessor, or compliance inspector. Client should seek experts to render such services in any acquisition.

D. If Client purchases property, Client should have an abstract covering the property examined by an attorney of Client's selection, or Client should be furnished with or obtain a title policy.

E. Buyer may purchase a residential service contract. Buyer should review such service contract for the scope of coverage, exclusions, and limitations. The purchase of a residential service contract is optional. There are several residential service companies operating in Texas.

F. Broker cannot give legal advice. This is a legally binding agreement. READ IT CAREFULLY. If you do not understand the effect of this agreement, consult your attorney BEFORE signing.

Broker's Printed Name	License No.	Client	Date

By:_____

Broker's Associate's Signature	Date	Client	Date

(TAR-1501) 4-14-06   Page 4 of 4

Reprinted by permission of Texas Association of REALTORS®, Inc.

Refer that buyer to another broker, or terminate the buyer agency and handle the transaction as an agent of the seller.

Clearly, most serious conflicts occur when representing the buyer, since the agent may choose to represent that buyer and later have to withdraw from the representation. This situation usually would not occur when representing the seller.

DISCUSSION QUESTION

- What scenarios can you think of where you are representing the seller and because of change in circumstances, you might need to represent the buyer as well?

Showings

The single agency concept also creates another conflict. In the event an agent represents the buyer and goes to a property that is an in-house listing, the agent also needs to call the office and ask how the seller filled in Paragraph 8 of the TAR® Exclusive Right to Sell Listing Agreement to determine whether the seller will agree to pay a buyer's broker or if the commission is restricted to subagents of the broker. When taking the listing, a logical approach would be to make sure that the third box in Paragraph 8.A. is the seller's choice in order to prevent the conflict on payment of commissions.

Single agency has an advantage in that it forces real estate agents to focus on their agency relationships with buyers and sellers on a regular basis. This enables them to clarify their role in each transaction and maintain rapport with the parties.

DUAL AGENCY

One may think that dual agency only has historical significance. The 1995 Texas legislature amended §1101.558 of the Texas Real Estate License Act so that it now contains no reference to dual agency. This does not eliminate dual agency (the statute did not declare it illegal). A new 2005 amendment to the Real Estate License Act, however, added a provision that a broker **must agree** to act as an intermediary if the broker agrees to represent in a transaction a buyer or a tenant and a seller or a landlord. The big question is whether or not this provision requires all licensees to be intermediaries and, if so, does it eliminate dual agency? What is the difference between an intermediary who is not appointed to represent the parties and a dual agent? As a practical matter, they are probably the same. Any agent who engages in a practice of dual agency would have to rely on the common law agency principles as they apply to duty of care and liability. Almost any legal scholar will tell you that relying on common law agency rules is like testing a light socket with your tongue to make sure the power is on. Even when dual agency was specifically authorized by statute, some considered it a very risky practice. The tougher question is: Does the new intermediary provision eliminate this problem?

Traditionally, real estate brokers have represented the sellers, and real estate brokerage was generally concerned with a marketing concept helping the seller get the highest price in the market place. There is no conflict if you treat that buyer as a customer. You may recall from Chapter 5 that you can be very helpful to the buyer, very informative to the buyer, make the buyer feel very comfortable about that transaction but not have a fiduciary relationship with that buyer. Real estate has been marketed under this concept for years. However, when the listing broker sees the buyer "slip away" because the principal requests buyer representation, the agent may think the only alternative is dual agency. That is, the agent represents and has a fiduciary relationship to both the buyer and the seller.

The advent of buyer brokerage has developed a niche in the marketplace for buyers who feel like they want representation, or for buyers who have particularly close relationships with real estate brokers, such that a buyer agency is almost presumed (business partner, relative, etc.). Most real estate brokers are gregarious, enthusiastic, and build their businesses by networking with friends and associates. There may be a special relationship with a buyer who buys several investment homes or parcels of property with a particular broker while not requesting buyer representation. The buyer in today's market may have been a seller of a previous tract when a fiduciary relationship with a broker was created during the sale. An even more sensitive topic is a buyer coming to a real estate broker's office and requesting assistance, perhaps requesting buyer representation, and the broker feels restricted on showing in-house listings because of the conflict of interest. Is there a conflict? One would have to answer "yes."

Generally, the interests of the buyer and seller are adverse. The courts have held that a real estate licensee may not represent these adversarial parties without the knowledge and consent of those parties. The position of all parties would have to be fully and adequately explained and understood. Therefore, both disclosure and informed consent are necessary to authorize a legal dual agency.

Duties of Care

A dual agent has an unusual (and not well defined) standard of care. How can you give 100 percent of your loyalty to two parties? In dual agency, you place yourself in the position of representing potentially adverse parties, and there are many possible conflicts of interests. You must scrupulously fulfill your duties to both without divulging confidential information to either. It would seem obvious that some sort of legal limitations on the agent's responsibilities in this agency relationship are needed.

In Texas, a real estate agent may be a dual agent as long as all parties to the transaction have prior knowledge and consent. *Hughes v. Miracle Ford, Inc.*, 676 S.W.2d 642 (Tex. App.-Dallas 1984, ref. n.r.e.); *Phillips v. Campbell*, 480 S.W.2d 250 (Tex. App.-Houston [14th Dist.] 1972). It is possible for dual agency to be either intended or unintended (i.e., for dual agency to exist accidentally because of the actions of the real estate licensee). Undisclosed dual agency happens when a listing agent or subagent did or said something that indicated or implied that the agent also represented the buyer; or the agent of the buyer said or did something that indicated or implied that the agent also represented the seller, without stating that agency relationship to the parties. This can happen without salespeople realizing that they have created, or meaning to establish, dual agency. Recall Chapter 2 on the creation of agency.

If there is a dual agency, there is the question of conflict of interest. Buyers and sellers are considered by law to have competitive and adverse interests. Is it possible for agents to represent both the buyer and seller without putting the entire transaction in jeopardy? There is the question of giving 100 percent loyalty to two different principals. There is the question of the degree of disclosure necessary, the duty of loyalty, compensation, and disclosure of pertinent facts. One court has held that an agent owes a high degree of loyalty to his or her principal, including a duty of full disclosure of material facts. This is especially true of dual agency. *Guisinger v. Hughes*, 362 S.W.2d 861 (Tex. Civ. App.-Dallas 1962, ref. n.r.e.). It would appear that if you are going to be a dual agent in Texas, you can only offer a limited range of services, not 100 percent of your loyalty to either side.

It is important to note that dual agency was an important change in the Texas Real Estate License Act and was authorized before intermediary status (discussed in the next chapter). On September 1, 1993, the Texas Real Estate License Act was amended to allow dual agency. The Act prohibited dual agency except where the statutory requirements were met. In order to do so, the agent was required to:

- provide the parties with Information About Brokerage Services.

- obtain the written consent of all parties to the transaction.

- disclose the source of expected compensation to all parties.

All of these disclosures could have been made in the broker's listing agreement or by a representation agreement that authorized a broker to act as agent to more than one party to a transaction, provided that the agreement set forth the dual agency conflict in conspicuous bold or underlined print.

A real estate broker who acts as an agent for more than one party to a transaction shall:

■ not disclose to the buyer or tenant that the seller or landlord will accept a price less than the asking price unless otherwise instructed in a separate writing by the seller or landlord.

■ not disclose to the seller or landlord that the buyer or tenant will pay a price greater than the price submitted in a written offer to the seller or landlord unless otherwise instructed in a separate writing by the buyer or tenant.

■ not disclose any confidential information or any information a party specifically instructs the real estate broker in writing not to disclose unless otherwise instructed in a separate writing by the respective party or required to disclose such information by law.

■ treat all parties to the transaction honestly and impartially so as not to favor one party or work to the disadvantage of any party.

The Act also required, "the real estate broker shall use due diligence to assist the parties in understanding the consents, agreements, or instructions under . . . which the real estate agent is permitted to represent more than one party to a transaction." [TRELA, §1101.558]. It should be noted that the Act did not distinguish between the salesperson or broker when referencing dual agency.

In Minnesota, a court ruled in a landmark case that although a real estate firm's disclosures of dual agency relationships complied with state laws on agency disclosure, the firm's disclosure was inadequate because it failed to meet the requirements of common law. In *Dismuke v. Edina Realty, Inc.*, a group of listing sellers sued Edina claiming there was no informed consent to the dual agency. They complained that the firm's statement in its usual purchase contract concerning dual agency had not adequately informed them of the company's potential conflict while utilizing dual agency in their transactions. Edina had adopted the policy that the listing agent represented the seller and that the selling agent acted as an independent contractor representing the buyer. This policy was stated on their sales contracts. Since there is a major problem of public misconception, licensees might be well advised to refrain from engaging in dual agency.

At this time dual agency is not addressed by HUD/FHA. There being no prohibitions, one might assume agreement. The VA, Department of Veterans Affairs, allows dual agency, but not if the buyer is required to pay the commission.

Is dual agency dead? No. The historical role of statutory dual agency is important to lay the foundation for the new intermediary concept in the current Texas Real Estate License Act. Even under the new statute, certain conduct of an intermediary may result in dual agency. Only now we have no statutory guidelines nor do we have applicable disclosure forms. Dual agency status is not even discussed in the new agency information form. We're back to common law dual agency, subject to the courts' interpretations of the 2005 statutory mandate of intermediary status.

DISCUSSION QUESTIONS

■ What if a principal instructs a real estate broker in writing not to disclose certain items, but the broker knows that item will make a material difference to the purchaser in making his decision to purchase (i.e., he has obtained information that there was a death on the premises that may have been suicide, and the buyer has very strong feelings against buying a house in which somebody has died)?

■ What similar conflicts can you list?

■ Even though a principal may have agreed to dual agency, can a broker treat a principal "impartially" when one of the principals is the broker's mother, husband, or very close friend? Explain your answer.

Recall the case of *Dismuke v. Edina Realty, Inc.* Note the following two paragraphs in the court's decision:

> "In the instant matter, Edina Realty concedes it engaged in dual agency transactions with plaintiffs. The only disclosure Edina Realty made to plaintiff concerning its dual agency status was the disclosure statement contained in the purchase agreements. While this disclosure statement appears to satisfy Edina Realty's statutory disclosure obligation to plaintiffs under Minn. Stat. Sec. 82.19, Subd. 5, it cannot be characterized as either a full or adequate disclosure of all the facts under common law.
>
> Edina Realty's failure to furnish plaintiffs with a full and adequate disclosure of facts concerning its dual agency is a breach of its fiduciary duty to plaintiffs. As plaintiffs need not prove actual injury or intentional fraud, there are no factual issues to submit to a jury. Accordingly, plaintiffs are entitled to judgment as a matter of law, and there is no need to reach Edina Realty's motion for partial summary judgment."

This was clearly a dual agency case. The agents complied with state law for disclosure purposes, but the court obviously didn't feel that the disclosures were sufficient to constitute "informed consent." Obviously, at least one of the parties to that case felt like they had not been treated impartially.

It should also be pointed out that many courts have indicated that "no man can serve two masters," which was quoted in the *Lewis v. Long & Foster* case, discussed earlier in Chapter 5. Similarly, in the *Coldwell Banker v. Camelback Office Park* case, the Court stated:

> "A broker occupies a confidential and fiduciary relationship with his principal, and hence is held to the highest ethical standards of fair and honest dealings.
>
> An agent has a duty not to act for a competitor of his principal unless this is permitted by the understanding of the parties.
>
> We hold that by breaching its duty of good faith to Camelback by competing with it and in failing to disclose that it was doing so, Coldwell forfeited its right to a commission from Camelback."

A New Jersey case, *Baldasarre v. Butler*, 604 A.2d 112 (N.J. Sup. 1992), involved a case of a real estate lawyer who represented both parties, wherein the Court stated:

> ". . . plaintiffs' execution of the 'conflict of interest' letter did not cure the conflict and that [the attorney's] dual representation was the genesis of the underlying dispute between the parties.
>
> . . . the representation of a buyer and a seller in connection with the preparation and execution of a contract of sale of real property is so fraught with obvious situations where a conflict may arise that one attorney shall not undertake to represent both parties in such a situation . . . a conflict of interest will exist and consent to continue representation is immaterial."

In an Idaho case, *Enright v. Jonassen*, 931 Pac.2d 1212 (Idaho 1997), the Idaho Supreme Court held that a real estate broker acting as both a listing and selling agent owed a duty to disclose to the purchaser that the property was in the flood plain and avalanche overlay area.

Perhaps the best explanation of the dual agency issue was set out in *Harry Brown v. F.S.R. Brokerage, Inc.*, 72 Cal. Rptr.2d 828, wherein the court started out its decision with the following statement: "Common sense and ancient wisdom join the law in teaching that an agent is not permitted to simultaneously serve two principles whose interest conflict about the matter served—at least, not without full disclose and consent of both." In this case the seller felt that the agent was "working exclusively for me, and only had my interest in mind." After the closing, he discovered he had signed an agreement consenting to dual agency. The facts indicated that the listing agent was trying to hold for a higher price while the selling agent was trying to bargain the seller down to make a more attractive purchase for the purchaser. This sets up your classic conflict of two agents, same brokerage company, different advice. Does the statutory and enactment of intermediary relationships solve this age-old problem?

In *Bazol v. Rhines*, 600 N.W.2d 327 (Iowa App. 1999), a broker and its affiliated companies had developed the subdivision in which sellers owned a home, and consequently sellers selected broker as their agent to sell their home. Palma, an agent for broker, procured a buyer. Both buyer and seller then signed a dual agency consent and the brokerage appointed another of its agents to serve as seller's agent. At the time Palma was well aware that the buyers had a need for a place suitable for their four dogs, and in fact identified seller's home in part because of its suitability for this purpose.

A few weeks later, a lawyer examining title determined that a restrictive covenant existed limiting dog ownership to one per dwelling. The lawyer notified broker and suggested that the broker (which, remember, had developed the subdivision through an affiliate) obtain a waiver of the restriction or find another solution to the conflict. The sale did not close.

By this time, it was mid-October and the selling season in Iowa was nearing an end. Although sellers relisted with broker, the home was not sold until mid-March, and for a price $10,000 less than the prior sale. In the meantime, sellers had moved into a new home and were carrying the two properties. The sellers sued the broker for the reduced selling price and the cost of paying interest and taxes on the unsold property.

The trial court found, and the Iowa Court of Appeals agreed, that the brokerage and the selling broker were liable for a breach of fiduciary duty. The court relies on ethical duties established by the National Association of REALTORS® as well as the language of the listing agreement itself to establish that the broker had a duty of disclosure both to buyers and sellers of problems known to it that affected the transaction.

The court responded that the failure to disclose resulted in the property being taken off the market for a period of over two months in prime selling season. Further, the court reasoned that sellers might have found a solution to the problem with the dog restriction had they known of the problem when it first arose, and that in any event the broker itself had a duty to seek a waiver of the restriction.

As you can see, while the practical aspects of dual agency may be a little simpler than the single agency concept, we have a number of court cases that indicate a strong leaning against the theory of dual agency. Of the basic concepts of agency (exclusive seller's agency, exclusive buyer's agency, single agency, and dual agency) dual agency probably has the highest potential for conflict.

The overwhelming concern in selecting any form of agency is that the office policy for your company should be complete and deal clearly with alternatives to minimize risks. Another important concern is communication. Principals tend to bring lawsuits as a result of conflict and miscommunication. If a broker is electing dual agency as an office policy, open and honest rapport with principals is an absolute necessity at every stage of the transaction. The best advice is to disclose, disclose, disclose, disclose, educate, and be friendly, return your phone calls, and be honest.

Contracts for Sale

There could be a number of conflicts for the dual agent in the sales contract. When a buyer asks how much earnest money should be put at risk, how does the agent respond? When representing the seller, you always want a lot of earnest money; when representing the buyer, you want to submit as little earnest money as possible. Other paragraphs of the contract contain contingencies. In representing the seller, you want no contingencies in the contract; when representing the buyer, you want all the contingencies you can get. When both parties rely on you for advice as to whether these contingencies should be included, do you respond in favor of the buyer, in favor of the seller, or "let them decide" with no advice? The same is true of the inclusion of a number of the alternative TREC promulgated addenda. Some strongly favor the buyer rather than the seller. How does the broker advise parties on using these forms and still remain impartial?

CLASS EXERCISE

■ Prepare a script for how you would present the Information About Brokerage Services to buyers and sellers for their signature if you were the buyer's agent. After reading the next chapter, prepare the script as you were a salesperson for an intermediary broker.

■ Circle the references to agency and agency relationships in Figure 9-2.

10

INTERMEDIARY STATUS AND ALTERNATIVES

PURPOSE

After carefully reading Chapter 10, the student will be able to:

- Explain the TRELA definitions of intermediary status.
- Discuss how the intermediary status applies in a real estate transaction.
- Illustrate the appointment process.
- Discuss the alternatives to the traditional seller agency relationship.

Key Words to look for in this chapter:
1. Intermediary = Sponsoring Broker
2. The Appointment Process
3. The Notification Form
4. Limited Agency
5. Facilitator
6. Nonagent
7. FAQs About Being an Intermediary and Disclosure of Agency

The 1995 Texas legislature introduced a new concept of agency representation into Texas real estate brokerage law, effective January 1, 1996, called an intermediary. An intermediary is defined under the Texas Real Estate License Act as "a broker who is employed to negotiate a transaction between the parties . . . and for that purpose may be an agent to the parties to the transaction." Please note that only the sponsoring broker (the intermediary broker) will most likely act as an intermediary, although the function can be delegated to others.

Intermediary = Sponsoring Broker

The statute provides that a real estate broker may act as an intermediary between the parties if:

- the real estate broker obtains written consent from each party to the transaction for the real estate broker to act as an intermediary in the transaction; and

- the written consent of the parties states the source of any expected compensation to the real estate broker. See §1101.559.

A written employment agreement, which also authorizes the real estate broker to act as an intermediary, is sufficient to establish that written consent if the written agreement sets forth, in conspicuous bold or underlined print, the real estate broker's obligations. Sound like the old dual agency?

A real estate broker who acts as an intermediary between the parties:

- may not disclose to the buyer or tenant that the seller or landlord will accept a price less than the asking price unless otherwise instructed in a separate writing by the seller or landlord.

- may not disclose to the seller or landlord that the buyer or tenant will pay a price greater than the price submitted in a written offer to the seller or landlord unless otherwise instructed in a separate writing by the buyer or tenant.

- may not disclose any confidential information or any other information parties specifically instruct the real estate broker in writing not to disclose unless otherwise instructed in a separate writing by the prospective party or required to disclose such information by this Act [the Real Estate License Act] or a court order, or if the information materially relates to the condition of the property.

- shall treat all parties to the transaction honestly. §1101.651.

    Note that another provision of the statute also requires that the intermediary be required to

    "act fairly so as not to favor one party over the other." See §1101.551; .559.

THE APPOINTMENT PROCESS

If a real estate broker obtains the consent of the parties to act as an intermediary, the broker may (it is not required) appoint, by providing written notice to the parties, one or more licensees associated with the broker to communicate with and carry out instructions of one party and one or more other licensees associated with the broker to communicate with and carry out instructions of the other party or parties. The parties must consent and authorize the broker to make the appointment, which may be set out in the listing agreement.

There are no guidelines in the statute for one-broker offices. Can they be intermediaries? Yes. However, they would not be able to:

- go through the appointment process.
- give advice or opinions.

During negotiations, an appointed licensee may provide opinions and advice to the party to whom the licensee is appointed.

The Texas Real Estate Commission has taken the position that an intermediary broker may not appoint himself or herself as an agent for either party. Therefore, a working sponsoring broker, even though it is his or her listing, must appoint other agents to represent the parties in the transaction. The Commission has also determined that the broker can appoint another broker (or brokers) to make the appointments. Other pertinent questions as to intermediary status have been published by the Commission and are included at the end of this chapter.

The statute also provides that the duties of a licensee acting as an intermediary supersede or are in lieu of the licensee's duties under common law or any other law, however, no duties are defined under the statute other than the previously referenced five duties (which are really no different than those required of a dual agent, discussed previously). Depending on the appointment process, an intermediary may become an undisclosed dual agent!

In effect, one may say that the intermediary status is nothing more than the old dual agency. The duties and responsibilities of an intermediary are very similar to, if not the same as, the dual agent under the previous statute. If the sponsoring broker is an intermediary, however, an appointed licensee can give advice and opinions, which is more services than could be provided as a dual agent. The intermediary broker is not allowed to give advice and opinion. TAR® revised 12 forms for use by its members to conform with the new intermediary status. Summarized, the intermediary "check list" should work as follows:

- disclose agency relationships at first contact.
- provide the required written information about brokerage services to any party you are working with (or to a party that is not represented) at your first face-to-face meeting (it would be prudent to have it executed; note Figure 9-1).
- when engaging employment either as a buyer's representative or as a listing broker, the listing broker should be sure that, when utilizing the TAR® Form No. 1101 (Residential Exclusive Right to Sell Form), Figure 9-2, that box 9.A.(1) or 9.A.(2) is checked. When representing the buyer

(TAR® Form 1501, Figure 9-3), box 8.A.(1) or 8.A.(2) should be checked. **THERE MUST BE A WRITTEN AGREEMENT BY BOTH PRINCIPALS TO BE AN INTERMEDIARY.**

■ inform everyone else in the transaction (parties and licensees) who you represent at first contact (while the statute doesn't require this disclosure to be in writing, it is good business practice).

■ if the real estate firm (and your employment contract) authorizes an intermediary relationship, the agent should:

   a. remind parties that the firm will act as an intermediary when an in-house sale is apparent (see new TAR® Form, discussed later).

   b. should choose whether to make appointments of both associated licensees at the time the in-house sale becomes apparent.

   c. if appointments are made, **provide written notice** to the parties.

In the intermediary situation, the complications of presentation that we have under the single agency concept don't arise, as both parties have already agreed and consented to the intermediary status. Recall TAR® forms 1101 and 1501 mentioned earlier in the previous chapter. Go to Figures 9-2 and 9-3 and fill them in now as if you were an intermediary. There are other TAR® Forms if the transaction is commercial (No. 1301, 1302, 1502) or Farm and Ranch (No. 1201). Remember, you must be a member of TAR® to use these forms.

The Real Estate License Act has created three "window periods" that a licensee will go through to create intermediary status:

The first window period is the exclusive agency wherein the licensee has an exclusive right to sell and an exclusive buyer's representation agreement. During this phase there is a 100 percent fiduciary duty and a 100 percent disclosure to the principal that the agent represents.

The second window period is that time when the buyer and the seller, both represented by the same broker, are going into the same transaction. When this potential conflict arises, the licensee is a dual agent (or an unappointed intermediary, whatever that is) until the intermediary process has been completed.

The third window period is when the buyer and seller have been notified and have accepted that notification that they now have an agent that represents them. At that point, the appointed agent can give advice and opinion. Presumably, during the second window period (as a dual agent) the agent cannot give advice and opinion. Is it a 100 percent fiduciary to both? Probably not. What percentage would you fill in? Is a whole fee being charged for less than 100 percent fiduciary duty?

From a liability standpoint, the trick seems to be to keep the second window period as narrow as possible (i.e., as soon as the potential for conflict arises, the agent diligently pursues the intermediary appointments).

The following chart may help visualize this issue.

1st Window Period		2nd Window Period		3rd Window Period
Exclusive Buyer/Tenant and Exclusive Seller/Tenant Representation 100% Fiduciary Duty Can give advice and opinion	uh oh! →	Buyer/Tenant and Seller/Landlord both Represented by Same Broker want to do a deal Dual Agency? Unappointed Intermediary No advice or opinion Get consent?	"may" appoint agent to represent both parties →	Seller and Buyer Notified of Intermediary Status Appointed agent can give advice and opinion ?% fiduciary duty Can give advice and opinion

It does leave the lingering question: If the broker is defined as an "intermediary" but doesn't go through the appointment process, what is that broker's status? An intermediary without appointment? A dual agent? Is there a difference?

DISCUSSION QUESTIONS

- Should a broker discuss with the seller, at the time employment is engaged, that the broker can only offer a limited scope of services, and that the seller should not disclose items to the broker that are confidential because the broker may "change horses" and represent the buyer at a later date? Explain your answer.

■ What is "informed" consent? Can the licensee explain these agency relationships without practicing law? Explain your answer.

THE NOTIFICATION FORM

There is always a potential for conflict. The law has always emphasized "informed" consent. TREC has the approved agency information form, and when the intermediary relationship arises, TAR® has created a new form that can be utilized by its members. These forms reeducate the seller and/or buyer at the time that the intermediary status arises, reminding them of the terms of their respective employment agreements and that the intermediary relationship has, in fact, arisen. See TAR® Form 1409, Figure 10-1.

Note with particular concern the third paragraph of the "Notification of Intermediary Relationship" Form. This is a very important paragraph. In the event both parties have agreed to intermediary status in their representation employment agreements, and the intermediary status actually arises later (the following month), the real estate licensee now reintroduces that intermediary status issue to both parties. In a typical, arm's length transaction, this should presume no problems.

The concern, however, is if there is a "special" relationship with one of the parties. How does the other party react? For instance, the intermediary status relationship arises and it is later discovered that the buyer is not only the real estate broker's wife, but also a board-certified real estate lawyer/investor who is coming in to "low ball" the offer. Will the seller feel that the agent can treat him or her impartially and fairly? If the situation is reversed, the buyer's representative is showing a home to the buyer, and it turns out that the home is the broker's home, does the buyer feel that the broker can be impartial to the buyer?

In either circumstance, the principal will have to make the decision. If the principal doesn't feel like he or she can be treated impartially because of the peculiar circumstance, it is suggested that the real estate broker allow the buyer or seller to terminate the employment relationship, rather than create an irreconcilable conflict between the broker and the principal.

DIFFICULT QUESTIONS

■ Does a party have to consent to the particular licensee who is appointed to represent him or her? What if the sponsoring broker (intermediary) appoints a licensee to work with a party and they don't get along? Presumably, sponsoring broker could simply appoint another licensee, if

FIG 10-1   INTERMEDIARY RELATIONSHIP NOTICE

TEXAS ASSOCIATION OF REALTORS®

INTERMEDIARY RELATIONSHIP NOTICE

USE OF THIS FORM BY PERSONS WHO ARE NOT MEMBERS OF THE TEXAS ASSOCIATION OF REALTORS® IS NOT AUTHORIZED.
©Texas Association of REALTORS®, Inc. 2004

To: _____ (Seller or Landlord)

and _____ (Prospect)

From: _____ (Broker's Firm)

Re: _____ (Property)

Date: _____

A. Under this notice, "owner" means the seller or landlord of the Property and "prospect" means the above-named prospective buyer or tenant for the Property.

B. Broker's firm represents the owner under a listing agreement and also represents the prospect under a buyer/tenant representation agreement.

C. In the written listing agreement and the written buyer/tenant representation agreement, both the owner and the prospect previously authorized Broker to act as an intermediary if a prospect who Broker represents desires to buy or lease a property that is listed by the Broker. When the prospect makes an offer to purchase or lease the Property, Broker will act in accordance with the authorizations granted in the listing agreement and in the buyer/tenant representation agreement.

D. Broker ❑ will ❑ will not appoint licensed associates to communicate with, carry out instructions of, and provide opinions and advice during negotiations to each party. If Broker makes such appointments, Broker appoints:

_____ to the owner; and

_____ to the prospect.

E. By acknowledging receipt of this notice, the undersigned parties reaffirm their consent for broker to act as an intermediary.

F. Additional Information: *(Disclose material information related to Broker's relationship to the parties, such as personal relationships or prior or contemplated business relationships.)*

The undersigned acknowledge receipt of this notice

_____   _____   _____   _____
Seller or Landlord   Date   Prospect   Date

_____   _____   _____   _____
Seller or Landlord   Date   Prospect   Date

(TAR-1409) 1-7-04   Page 1 of 1

there is one in that broker's office. What if the sponsoring broker isn't available when the appointment needs to be made?

■ Can the broker refuse to appoint? The listing agent who has met a new prospect may not want to split the commission. Sound like dual agency? What if that party wants advice?

■ Should the sponsoring broker inform the parties that the intermediary appointments are not made and that the parties shouldn't expect advice?

(Does it then create a dual agency?) The statute clearly doesn't require it, but it may be prudent to do so.

■ What is the liability of a sponsoring broker who has appointed one agent to represent the buyer and another to represent the seller (the statute doesn't allow the broker to appoint the same agent for both parties), and the agents give conflicting advice? For instance, the seller's agent advises "don't take the offer, it is worth far more than that!," while the buyer's agent advises the buyer "they are asking for too much, it isn't worth it." Did the seller obtain the services bargained for under the listing agreement?

■ What is the sponsoring broker's role if the appointed agents ask the sponsoring broker for advice?

■ Can an intermediary appoint a licensed assistant as an agent? It would be illogical to do so. The assistant may be under the control of another licensee.

■ Can the intermediary appoint spouses to different sides? It is probably not a good idea. The income is community property.

■ Can the intermediary appoint an agent with 30 years of experience to represent one party, and a licensee with only 30 minutes of experience to represent the other? Would you put your best agent to negotiate against the newest, least experienced agent? Is it fair?

DISCUSSION QUESTIONS

■ Assume you have a listing with sellers you have known for years. They are on hard times, need to move, and you are an agent for an intermediary. The sellers are asking $210,000; the buyer presents a low-ball offer of $150,000. You know the buyer will go as high as $200,000 (he has told you so). Your sellers are confiding that they will accept the $150,000 but will have to sell their two cars, the last of their stock, and utilize all of their savings to do so. Do you feel comfortable with this situation?

■ Since you know that the buyer is attempting to take advantage of the sellers in the previous situation, what is your duty as an intermediary? Would the sellers think you are treating them impartially when they later discover the true facts?

An important thought on this issue: The intermediary must comply with all aspects of the statute in order to take advantage of its benefits. If any of the requirements are not met, it seems that the intermediary status almost certainly converts to dual agency status. If an appointed agent resigns, or dies, it will also terminate intermediary status. One cannot be too careful.

Another argument also comes into focus. It has been argued that intermediary status is a method by which the broker is allowed to be on everyone's (or no one's) side at once and keep the entire commission. Note the second question just referenced. This is not consumer protection. Courts may find the same concern for intermediary status that some courts found for dual agency. The jury is still out!

After all of these legislative changes were enacted, TREC still notes that the "enforcement division deals repeatedly" with real estate agent disclosure requirements for "failing to make clear to all parties in a transaction, which party the licensee is acting for."

OTHER ALTERNATIVES

A Limited Form of Agency

Some legally limited form of agency might be an alternative to the forms of agency recognized in the past. Agreeing that the industry should be ever mindful of improving the profession, is the growing pile of paperwork, red tape, and paranoia an unnecessary complication to the practice of real estate?

Some real estate licensees feel that this is an attempt to erode their role, reduce their effectiveness and their service. Others feel that this attempt to protect the consumer is in actuality encouraging disputes and strained relations and could be even more costly to the parties involved. Could a well-defined, newly recognized form of agency be recognized that would actually allow real estate licensees to practice real estate as the consumer seems to have accepted or perceived it in the past? At least one state (Georgia) has made limited agency statutory. Texas has adopted the intermediary status.

DISCUSSION QUESTIONS

■ What possible problems can you see for the buyers, sellers, and agents involved in a limited form of agency?

■ Can agents represent both buyer and seller in any way without putting the sale in jeopardy?

Facilitator

Acting as a **middleman, facilitator, independent contractor, transactional broker, mediator, consultant,** or **practitioner** rather than as an agent to either party is being considered by many as an alternative to agency. The legislators of several states have been encouraged by their constituents to consider drafting legislation about facilitator alternatives. These choices are opening whole new areas of questioning, discussion, and thinking.

There are some questions about semantics. The terms "middleman" and "broker" have long been associated with agency. Real estate agents are often independent contractors working with their brokers. "Mediator" and "consultant" are terms often used in other connotations. The term "practitioner" has been questioned as applicable to real estate licensees because of the degree of professionalism that is sometimes connected with this term.

"Facilitator" appears to be the word of choice at the moment, but it is a word that seems to have no accepted meaning, at least when applied to real estate licensees. How do we define "facilitator"? A common theory seems to be that facilitators do not establish agency relationships with any parties to the transaction. They owe no fiduciary duties to anyone. They act as intermediaries rather than as agents.

The question now might become: Can practitioners disclaim any and all agency? Proponents of this alternative claim that it is the law itself that makes it impossible for the real estate licensee to be a "true" agent. The TREC Rules provide that the Texas Real Estate License Act is an agency law (see 535.1(c)). Notwithstanding this, the proponents' position seems to indicate that all our years of court-precedented fiduciary duties in agency law can be similarly discarded and become nonexistent—a true middleman concept wherein the broker merely brings the parties together. *Burleson v. Earnest*, 153 S.W.2d 869 (Tex. Civ. App.-Amarillo 1941). Is this the kind of relationship that professional organizations have been encouraging over the last 60 years? Opponents to the facilitator concept think not.

Proponents also believe that one can be a middleman but provide services for both the buyer and the seller that make the transaction go smoother. For instance, the broker can assist the buyer in applying for a loan seeking good mortgage rates, provide comparable sales data, provide access to MLS® information, and provide TREC forms for offers. Brokers can provide seller advertising services and hold open houses and other similar services, which are quality professional services, but not create an agency relationship.

Opponents argue that in the facilitator status, the licensee is providing no services that aren't readily available from other sources. After all, real estate brokerage is a service business, and if you are providing no special services for the buyer or seller, we've effectively dissolved the business. It has been pointed out that limited service brokerage, or flat-fee brokerage, or discount brokerage, where fewer services are provided, often meets with very poor acceptance from the public in general. If real estate brokers give even fewer services than that, what does this do for the brokerage business?

Perhaps the biggest question, however, is: How many services can a broker provide before creating an agency relationship by ostensible authority? How does a licensee provide professional-quality services without establishing a relationship of trust and confidence that, then, may result in a fiduciary relationship? Similar difficulty exists between the two parties. If the licensee provides services for one party, but not the other, does the appearance of impropriety exist such that the agent may not be impartial or, even worse, becomes the agent for the other party?

The facilitator concept appears to be an easy, low-risk alternative. You may recall, however, that real estate licensure was created to protect the public. It develops into an agency relationship because of the trust and confidence that the agency relationship merits. Being a mere "facilitator" seems to run contrary to our accepted concepts of the real estate business. Does a facilitator offer fewer services but still charge a full fee?

It is extremely important that a real estate company have a written policy on agency and the types of agency that it will accept. This policy should carefully lay out the required responsibilities of each agent and the sponsoring broker. It should list the required disclosure forms and when they are required. If a company represents both buyers and sellers, early disclosure to buyer and to seller that there is a possibility of dual agency is imperative. See *Gillmore v. Morelli*, 472 N.W.2d 738 (N.D. 1991).

Nonagent

Recall the discussion of nonagency in Chapter 3. This is probably not an alternative in Texas, since the Texas Canons of Ethics clearly establish the license as an agent. See § 531.1

West v. Touchstone, 620 S.W.2d 687 (Tex. Civ. App.-Dallas 1981)

Owners of real property entered into an exclusive listing agreement with the broker to sell a parcel of real estate. The listing agreement was terminated a year later. Another year later, the broker was contacted by a party who had seen the property during the listing period and was now interested in purchasing the property.

During negotiations, it was determined that another potential deal was pending with the City of Dallas. The agent contacted the City of Dallas, allegedly as an interested citizen, and told the City of Dallas that the proposed sale was at too high a price. Subsequently the City of Dallas failed to purchase the property. The seller sued the broker alleging breach of fiduciary duty. The broker defended claiming that he was a mere "middleman" and that he had no fiduciary duty to the seller. The court concluded that even though a broker may be a "middleman," he may nevertheless be an agent if he undertakes to perform services on behalf of an owner. The broker then contended that he had a right to contact the City of Dallas as a citizen. The court further held that such a right as a citizen does not extend to excuse the violation of the agent's duty of loyalty to his principal.

DISCUSSION QUESTIONS

■ What should the real estate agent in the *West* case have done to prevent a breach of fiduciary duty?

■ List the ways that you can stay a middleman if you undertake to perform services on behalf of either party.

■ You may recall Colorado's effort at creating "nonagency" (see page 37). Is this a good alternative for Texas?

FREQUENTLY ASKED QUESTIONS ABOUT BEING AN INTERMEDIARY AND DISCLOSURE OF AGENCY

The following 48 questions and answers have been developed to assist licensees in complying with Section 15C [§1101.558] of The Real Estate License Act. These answers are intended to address general situations only and are not intended as legal opinions addressing the duties and obligations of licensees in specific transactions. What licensees say and do in a specific transaction may cause these general answers to be inapplicable or inaccurate. Licensees should consult their own attorneys for legal advice concerning the law's effect on their brokerage practices.

Q: Explain how a typical intermediary relationship is created and how it would operate.

A: At their first face-to-face meeting with a seller or a prospective buyer, the salespersons or brokers associated with a firm would provide the parties with a copy of the statutory information about agency required by The Texas Real Estate License Act (TRELA). The statutory information includes an explanation of the intermediary relationship. The brokerage firm would negotiate a written listing contract with a seller and a written buyer representation agreement with a buyer. In those documents, the respective parties would authorize the broker to act as an intermediary and to appoint associated licensees to work with the parties in the event that the buyer wishes to purchase a property listed with the firm. At this point, the broker and associated licensees would be still functioning as exclusive agents of the individual parties. The listing contract and buyer representation agreement would contain in conspicuous bold or underlined print the broker's obligations set forth in Section 15C(j) [1101.651] of TRELA. When it becomes evident that the buyer represented by the firm wishes to purchase property listed with the firm, the intermediary status would come into play, and the intermediary may appoint different associates to work with the parties. The intermediary would notify both parties in writing of the appointments of licensees to work with the parties. The associates would provide advice and opinions to their respective parties during negotiations, and the intermediary broker would be careful not to favor one party over the other in any action taken by the intermediary.

Q: What is the difference between a dual agent and an intermediary?

A: A dual agent is a broker who represents two parties at the same time in accordance with common law obligations and duties. An intermediary is a broker who negotiates the transaction between the parties subject to the provisions of Section 15C of the Texas Real Estate License Act. The intermediary may, with the written consent of the parties, appoint licensees associated with the intermediary to work with and advise the party to whom they have been appointed. In a dual agency situation in which two salespersons are sponsored by the same broker but are working with different parties, the broker and the salespersons are considered to be agents of both parties, unable to act contrary to the interests of either party.

Q: In what way does Section 15C [1101.558] prohibit or permit disclosed dual agency?

A: Disclosed dual agency is not specifically addressed in Section 15C. Since disclosed dual agency is not prohibited, licensees may, with appropriate disclosure and consent of the parties, act as dual agents.

Q: What is the advantage for the broker in acting as an intermediary?

A: If the broker and associates are going to continue to work with parties they have been representing under listing contracts or buyer representation agreements, the intermediary role is the only statutorily addressed vehicle for handling "in-house" transactions, providing both parties the same level of service.

Q: If a salesperson or associated broker lists a property and has also been working with a prospective buyer under a representation agreement, how can the salesperson or associated broker sell this listing under Section 15C [1101.558]?

A: There are three alternatives for the brokerage firm and the parties to consider:

(1) The firm, acting through the salesperson or associated broker, could represent one of the parties and work with the other party as a customer rather than as a client (realistically, this probably means working with the buyer as a customer and terminating the buyer representation agreement).

(2) If the firm has obtained permission in writing from both parties to be an intermediary and to appoint licensees to work with the parties, the salesperson or associated broker could be appointed by the intermediary to work with one of the parties. Note: **Another licensee would have to be appointed to work with the other party under this alternative. The law does not permit an intermediary to appoint the same licensee to work with both parties.**

(3) If the firm has obtained permission in writing from both parties to be an intermediary, but does not appoint different associates to work with the parties, the salesperson or broker associate could function as a representative of the firm. Since the firm is an intermediary, the salesperson and associated

broker also would be subject to the requirement not to act so as to favor one party over the other.

Q: If a salesperson may provide services to a party under Section 15C without being appointed, why would a broker want to appoint a salesperson to work with a party?

A: Appointment following the procedures set out in Section 15C would permit the salesperson to provide a higher level of service. The appointed salesperson may provide advice and opinions to the party to whom the salesperson is assigned and is not subject to the intermediary's statutory duty of not acting so as to favor one party over the other.

Q: Is an intermediary an agent?

A: Yes, but the duties and obligations of an intermediary are different than for exclusive, or single, agents.

Q: What are the duties and obligations of an intermediary?

A: Section 15C requires the intermediary to obtain written consent from both parties to act as an intermediary. A written listing agreement to represent a seller/landlord or a written buyer/tenant representation agreement that contains authorization for the broker to act as an intermediary between the parties is sufficient for the purposes of Section 15C [1101.558] if the agreement sets forth, in conspicuous bold or underlined print, the broker's obligations under Section 15C(j) [1101.651] and the agreement states who will pay the broker.

If the intermediary is to appoint associated licensees to work with the parties, the intermediary must obtain written permission from both parties and give written notice of the appointments to each party. The intermediary is also required to treat the parties fairly and honestly and to comply with TRELA. The intermediary is prohibited from acting so as to favor one party over the other, and may not reveal confidential information obtained from one party without the written instructions of that party, unless disclosure of that information is required by TRELA, court order, or the information materially relates to the condition of the property. The intermediary and any associated licensees appointed by the intermediary are prohibited from disclosing without written authorization that the seller will accept a price less than the asking price or that the buyer will pay a price greater than the price submitted in a written offer.

Q: Can salespersons act as intermediaries?

A: Only a broker can contract with the parties to act as an intermediary between them. In that sense, only a broker can be an intermediary. If, however, the broker intermediary does not appoint associated licensees to work with the parties in a transaction, any salesperson or broker associates of the intermediary who function in that transaction would be required to act just as the intermediary does, not favoring one party over the other.

Q: *Can there be two intermediaries in the same transaction?*

A: No.

Q: *Can a broker representing only the buyer be an intermediary?*

A: Ordinarily, no; the listing broker will be the intermediary. In the case of a FSBO or other seller who is not already represented by a broker, the broker representing the buyer could secure the consent of both parties to act as an intermediary.

Q: *May an intermediary appoint a subagent in another firm to work with one of the parties?*

A: Subagency is still permitted under the law, but a subagent in another firm cannot be appointed as one of the intermediary's associated licensees under the provisions of Section 15C [1101.558].

Q: *May the same salesperson be appointed by the intermediary to work with both parties in the same transaction?*

A: No; the law requires the intermediary to appoint different associated licensees to work with each party.

Q: *May more than one associated licensee be appointed by the intermediary to work with the same party?*

A: Yes.

Q: *How should an intermediary complete Paragraph 8 of the TREC contract forms?*

A: Brokers who are acting as intermediaries after January 1, 1996, should use the TREC addendum approved for that purpose in lieu of completing Paragraph 8.

Q: *May a broker act as an intermediary prior to January 1, 1996, the effective date of the TRELA amendment?*

A: No.

Q: *What is the difference between an appointed licensee working with a party and a licensee associated with the intermediary who has not been appointed to work with one party?*

A: During negotiations the appointed licensee may advise the person to whom the licensee has been appointed. An associated licensee who has not been appointed must act in the same manner as the intermediary, that is, not giving opinions and advice and not favoring one party over the other.

Q: Who decides whether a broker will act as intermediary, the broker or the parties?

A: Initially, the broker, in determining the policy of the firm. If the broker does not wish to act as an intermediary, nothing requires the broker to do so. If the broker's policy is to offer services as an intermediary, both parties must authorize the broker in writing before the broker may act as an intermediary or appoint licensees to work with each of the parties.

Q: When must the intermediary appoint the licensees associated with the intermediary to work with the parties?

A: This is a judgment call for the intermediary. If appointments are going to be made, they should be made before the buyer begins to receive advice and opinions from an associated licensee in connection with the property listed with the broker. If the broker appoints the associates at the time the listing contract and buyer representation agreements are signed, it should be clear that the appointments are effective only when the intermediary relationship arises. **The intermediary relationship does not exist until the parties who have authorized it are beginning to deal with each other in a proposed real estate transaction; for example, the buyer begins to negotiate to purchase the seller's property.** Prior to the creation of the intermediary relationship, the broker will typically be acting as an exclusive agent of each party. It is important to remember that **both** parties must be notified in writing of **both** appointments. If, for example, the listing agent is "appointed" at the time the listing is taken, care must be taken to ensure that the buyer is ultimately also given written notice of the appointment. When a buyer client begins to show interest in a property listed with the firm and both parties have authorized the intermediary relationship, the seller must be notified in writing as to which associate has been appointed to work with the buyer.

Q: Can the intermediary delegate to another person the authority to appoint licensees associated with the intermediary?

A: The intermediary may delegate to another licensee the authority to appoint associated licensees. **If the intermediary authorizes another licensee to appoint associated licensees to work with the parties, however, that person must not appoint himself or herself as one of the associated licensees, as this would be an improper combination of the different functions of intermediary and associated licensee. It is also important to remember that there will be a single intermediary even if another licensee has been authorized to make appointments.**

Q: *May a broker act as a dual agent after January 1, 1996?*

A: Dual agency is not prohibited, but the broker who attempts to represent both parties may be subject to common law rules if the broker does not act as an intermediary. Brokers who do not wish to act as exclusive agents of one party should act as a statutory intermediary as provided by §15C [1101.558] and call themselves "intermediaries" rather than "dual agents."

Q: *What are the agency disclosure requirements for real estate licensees after January 1, 1996?*

A: To disclose their representation of a party upon the first contact with a party or a licensee representing another party.

Q: *Is disclosure of agency required to be in writing?*

A: After January 1, 1996, the disclosure may be oral or in writing.

Q: *Will use of TREC 3 be required after January 1, 1996?*

A: No, TREC has repealed the rule requiring use of TREC 3.

Q: *Will licensees be required to provide parties with written information relating to agency?*

A: Yes. Section 15C [1101.558] will require licensees to provide the parties with a copy of a written statement, the content of which is specified in the statute. The form of the statement may be varied, so long as the text of the statement is in at least 10-point type.

Q: *Are there exceptions when the statutory statement is not required?*

A: Yes; the statement is required to be provided at the first face-to-face meeting between a party and the licensee at which substantive discussion occurs with respect to specific real property. The statement is **not** required for either of the following:

(1) a transaction that is a residential lease no longer than one year and no sale is being considered; or

(2) a meeting with a party represented by another licensee.

Q: *Are the disclosure and statutory information requirements applicable to commercial transactions, new home sales, farm and ranch sales, or transactions other than residential sales?*

A: Except as previously noted, the requirements are applicable to all real estate transactions. Licensees dealing with landlords and tenants are permitted by the law to modify their versions of the statutory statement to use the terms "landlord" and "tenant" in place of the terms "seller" and "buyer."

Q: *What are the penalties for licensees who fail to comply with Section 15C?*

A: Failure to comply is a violation of TRELA, punishable by reprimand, by suspension or revocation of a license, or by an administrative penalty (fine).

Q: *In what way does Section 15C [1101.558] prohibit or permit disclosed dual agency?*

A: Section 15C [1101.558] does not prohibit disclosed dual agency, so licensees may act as dual agents with appropriate disclosure and consent.

Q: *Is the licensee required under any circumstance to provide the "written statement" to buyer prospects at properties held open for prospective buyers?*

A: An encounter at an open house is not a meeting for the purposes of Section 15C. A licensee would not be required to provide the statutory statement at the open house. However, at the first face-to-face meeting thereafter with the buyer regarding a specific property and during which substantive discussions occur, the licensee will be required to provide the statement.

Q: *When acting as an appointed licensee what "'agency" limitations does the Licensee have when communicating with a buyer/tenant or seller/ landlord that an agent representing one party only doesn't have?*

A: The appointed licensee may not, except as permitted by Section 15C(j) [1101.651] of TRELA, disclose to either party confidential information received from the other party. A licensee representing one party would not be prohibited from revealing confidential information to the licensee's principal, and if the information were material to the principal's decision, would be required to reveal the information to the principal.

Q: *If a buyer's agent is required to disclose that licensee's agency status to a listing broker when setting up an appointment showing, must the listing broker also disclose to the buyer's agent that the listing broker represents the seller?*

A: Yes, on the first contact with the licensee representing the buyer.

Q: *Does the TREC encourage brokerage companies to act for more than one party in the same transaction?*

A: No.

Q: Must the intermediary broker furnish written notice to each party to a transaction when the broker designates the appointed licensees?

A: Yes.

Q: How is a property "showing" different from a proposed transaction?

A: The question appears to be: "May an associate show property listed with the associate's broker while representing the buyer without first being appointed by the intermediary, and if so, why?" Yes. Only showing property does not require the associate to be appointed, because it does not require the licensee to give advice or opinions (only an appointed associate may offer opinions or advice to a party). If no appointments will be made, of course, the associate will be working with the party and will not be authorized to provide opinions or advice.

Q: Does TREC recommend that licensees provide a written disclosure of agency?

A: It is the licensee's choice as to whether disclosure is in writing or oral, just as it is the licensee's choice as to whether proof of disclosure will be easy or difficult.

Q: Our company policy requires all buyers and sellers to agree to the intermediary practice before commencing to work with them. Does the law permit a broker employment agreement to specify this practice only?

A: If by "broker employment agreement" you mean a listing contract or buyer representation agreement, yes.

Q: What are the differences between the duties provided to the seller or landlord by the intermediary broker and the duties provided to the buyer or tenant by the appointed licensee?

A: The intermediary and the appointed licensees do not provide duties; they perform services under certain duties imposed by the law. The intermediary is authorized to negotiate a transaction between the parties, but not to give advice or opinions to them in negotiations. The appointed licensee may provide advice or opinions to the party to which the licensee has been appointed. Both intermediary and appointed licensee are obligated to treat the parties honestly and are prohibited from revealing confidential information or other information addressed in Section 15C(j) of TRELA.

Q: Must each party's identity be revealed to the other party before an intermediary transaction can occur?

A: Yes. If associates are going to be appointed by the intermediary, the law provides that the appointments are made by giving written notice to both parties. To give notice, the intermediary must identify the party and the associate(s) appointed to that party. The law does not require notice if no appointments are going to be made. The law provides that the listing contract and buyer representation agreement are sufficient to establish the written consent of the party if the obligations of the broker under Section 15C(j) [1101.651] are set forth in conspicuous bold or underlined print.

Q: *As a listing agent I hold open houses. If a buyer prospect enters who desires to purchase the property at that time, can I represent that buyer and, if so, must my broker designate me as an appointed licensee and provide the parties with written notice before I prepare the purchase offer?*

A: As a representative of the seller, you would be obligated to disclose your representation to the buyer at the first contact. The disclosure may be in writing or oral. As an associate of the listing broker, you can enter into a buyer representation agreement for your broker to act as an intermediary in a transaction involving this buyer and the owner of the property. If the owner has similarly authorized the broker to act as an intermediary, it will depend on the firm's policy whether appointments are to be made. If appointments are not going to be made, you may proceed in the transaction as an unappointed licensee with a duty of not favoring one party over the other. If appointments are going to be made, the parties must both be notified in writing before you may provide opinions or advice to the buyer in negotiations.

Q: *I have a salesperson's license through a broker and I also have a licensed assistant. Can that assistant be an appointed licensee under me as an intermediary?*

A: Your broker, not you, will be the intermediary. The intermediary may appoint a licensed associate to work with a party. If the licensed assistant is an associate of the broker, the licensed assistant could be appointed by the intermediary to work with one of the parties. If the licensed assistant is not an associate of the broker, the licensed assistant cannot be appointed. Note: **If the licensed assistant is licensed as a salesperson, the licensed assistant must be sponsored by, and acting for a broker to be authorized to perform any act for which a real estate license is required. If the licensed assistant is sponsored by a broker who is not associated with the intermediary, the licensed assistant would not be considered an associate of the intermediary either.**

Q: *I am a listing agent and a buyer prospect wants to buy the property I have listed. How can I sell my own listing?*

A: See the three alternatives discussed in the related question on page 2. You could alter the agency relationships and only represent one party, you could be appointed to work with one party and another associate could be appointed to work with the other party, or no appointments would be made, or you could work with the parties being careful not to favor one over the other or provide advice or opinions to them.

Q: *Must the respective appointed licensees each provide an opinion of value to the respective buyer prospect and seller prospect?*

A: At the time a property is listed, the licensee is obligated to advise the owner as to the licensee's opinion of the market value of the property. Once appointments have been made, the appointed associates are permitted, but not required, to provide the party to whom they have been appointed with opinions and advice during negotiations.

Q: *How can the intermediary broker advise the seller or buyer on value, escrow deposit amount, repair expenses, or interest rates?*

A: When the listing contract or buyer representation agreement has come into existence, and no intermediary status yet exists, the broker may advise the parties generally on such matters. Offers from or to parties not represented by the intermediary's firm may have made the parties knowledgeable on these matters. Once the intermediary status has been created, however, the intermediary broker may not express opinions, or give advice during negotiations. Information about such matters that does not constitute an opinion or advice may be supplied in response to the question. For example, the intermediary could tell the buyer what the prevailing interest rate is without expressing an opinion or giving advice. The seller's question about the amount of earnest money could be answered with the factual answer that in the broker's experience, the amount of the earnest money is usually $1,500 to $2,000, depending on the amount of the sales price. If the buyer asks what amount of money should be in the offer, the intermediary could respond with the factual statement that in the intermediary's experience, those offers closest to the listing price tend to be accepted by the seller. The intermediary also could refer the party to an attorney, accountant, loan officer, or other professional for advice.

Q: *I was the listing agent for a property that didn't sell but was listed by another broker after the expiration of my agreement. I now have a buyer client who wants to see that same property. Must the new broker, or my broker, designate me as an appointed licensee or how may I otherwise act?*

A: Assuming an agreement with the listing broker as regards cooperation and compensation, you may represent the buyer as an exclusive agent. You cannot be appointed by the intermediary because you are not an associate of the listing broker, and from the facts as you describe them, no intermediary status is going to arise. Confidential information obtained from the seller when you were acting as the seller's agent, of course, could not be disclosed to your new client, the buyer.

Q: *How is the intermediary broker responsible for the actions of appointed licensees when a difference of opinion of property value estimates is provided?*

A: Brokers are responsible for the actions of their salespersons under TRELA. Opinions of property values may be different and yet not indicative of error or mistake by the salespersons. If a salesperson makes an error or mistake, the sponsoring broker is responsible to the public and to TREC under Section I(c) of TRELA.

Q: *Although both the buyer and the seller initially consented to the intermediary broker practice at the time each signed a broker employment agreement, must each party consent again to a specific transaction to ensure there are not potential conflicts?*

A: TRELA does not require a second written consent. TRELA does require written notice of any appointments, and the written notice would probably cause any objection to be resolved at that point. A broker would not be prohibited from obtaining a second consent as a business practice, so that potential conflicts are identified and resolved. The sales contract, of course, would typically identify the parties and show the intermediary relationship if the broker completes the "Broker Identification and Ratification of Fee" at the end of the TREC contract form.

Q: *In the absence of the appointed licensees, can the intermediary broker actually negotiate a purchase offer between the parties?*

A: Yes. See the answer to the question relating to the duties of an intermediary.

Q: *May a licensee include the statutory statement in a listing agreement or buyer representation agreement, either in the text of the agreement or as an exhibit?*

A: Yes, but the licensee should provide the prospective party with a separate copy of the statutory statement as soon as is practicable at their first face-to-face meeting.

FEDERAL LEGISLATION AFFECTING REAL ESTATE BROKERS—PART I

PURPOSE

After carefully reading Chapter 11, the student will be able to:

- Discuss federal legislation affecting real estate.

- Explain the applications of the Real Estate Settlement Procedures Act.

- Recognize the differences in selling a security (SEC) verses real estate.

- Define: *FIRPTA, TIL, taking, wetlands, UST, EPA, CFC, EMF, CERCLA*.

- Recount the problems of land use legislation.

- Disclose environmental problems and relate their application to real estate transactions.

Key Words to look for in this chapter:
1. RESPA
2. HUD
3. Computerized Loan Origination
4. Controlled Business Arrangements
5. Securities and Exchange Commission
6. FIRPTA
7. Federal Truth-in-Lending
8. Regulation Z
9. APR
10. The "Taking" Issue/Condemnation
11. Wetlands Legislation
12. Endangered Species Act
13. EPA
14. UST
15. Asbestos
16. Lead-Based Paint
17. Chlorofluorocarbon (CFC) Emissions
18. Electromagnetic Fields (EMFs)
19. CERCLA

Federal law is also imposing requirements on real estate brokers. This includes misrepresentation of facts concerning properties and nondisclosure that causes damage to the purchaser of real property. There is liability even though there is no fiduciary relationship between the broker and the purchaser. Traditionally, the broker had liability for misconduct where a building suffered some structural defects, is subjected to flooding, or is infested by termites. Recent expansion of case and statutory law governing numerous aspects of real estate transactions at the federal level requires that real estate brokers, more than ever before, need to keep current with legal developments that may impose new or potential legal duties and liabilities.

Liability now extends to negligence, negligent misrepresentation, innocent misrepresentation, fraud, conspiracy, and failure to exercise due diligence or to inform or disclose information to the purchaser in maintaining standards imposed by the real estate brokerage business and the law of agency. Chapters 11, 12, and 13 will focus on federal legislation affecting real estate brokers. This information includes the Real Estate Settlement Procedures Act (RESPA), the Foreign Investment Real Property Tax Act of 1980 (FIRPTA), Federal Truth-in-Lending Legislation (TIL), Land Use Legislation, and the Internal Revenue Code. The chapters will also look at the Comprehensive Environmental Response Compensation and Liability Act (CERCLA), the American Disabilities Act (ADA), the Fair Housing Act, the Interstate Land Sales Full Disclosure Act, Condominium Cooperative Relief Act, the Flood Disaster Protection Act, Securities and Exchange Commission (SEC), and antitrust laws affecting real estate brokers.

THE REAL ESTATE SETTLEMENT PROCEDURES ACT

RESPA was originally enacted to correct abused practices that caused unnecessarily high real estate settlement or closing costs to be incurred by consumers. This Act creates certain requirements of lenders and escrow agents in transactions involving one- to four-family residences, such as "good faith" estimates of closing costs and special information booklets. It also prohibits certain practices. Real estate brokers come within the scope of RESPA because they provide a settlement service and are therefore subject to the anti-kickback provisions of RESPA.

Section 2607 of RESPA prohibits (in connection with a federally related mortgage loan) the giving or acceptance of any **kickback** fee or other payment in return for the referral of business in the giving or accepting of any part of the settlement service charge except for services actually performed. There are similar prohibitions against controlled business operations in which a broker may receive a referral fee that is prohibited under RESPA without the required disclosures to the consumer.

This may directly affect real estate brokers who engage in **Computerized Loan Origination** (called CLO) and own an interest in affiliated entities that may relate to the settlement process, whether it be through mortgage companies, title companies, or other related services for which the broker may get a fee or some beneficial interest as a result of his or her ownership. The provisions of RESPA, however, do exempt a transaction where a real estate broker directly or indirectly referred a mortgage loan transaction to an affiliated mortgage company, provided that the required disclosure was made to the mortgagor. (See Chapter 5.)

While RESPA has encountered more focus on enforcement lately, the rule remains the same. Any affiliated interest in a business, which may affect settlement services, must be disclosed to the consumer under the federal statutes and regulations relating to the real estate settlement procedure.

Originally, there were eight exceptions to the application of RESPA. The Housing and Community Development Act of 1992, however, limited those exceptions to:

- farms of 25 acres or more.
- home equity line of credit transactions.
- transactions involving only modification of existing obligations (excluding new obligations created to satisfy an existing obligation or loans for increased amounts).
- "bridge" loans.
- assumptions, if no lender approval is required.
- temporary financing such as a construction loan.
- secondary market transactions.

The coverage of RESPA was also extended to subordinate loans for all the one-to four-family residences, loans for cooperatives or time share interests, and to a manufactured home, including the land upon which it will be situated. RESPA also now applies to refinancing. It is important to note that there is no exemption for a business-purpose loan made to a natural person (rather than a legal entity). Therefore, RESPA may apply to a loan to a corporation, trust, or partnership if an individual is involved in the obligation. See 59 Fed. Reg. 28 at 6008.

Needed disclosures also underwent modification. The HUD Special Information Booklet is required to be given only to purchasers of a one- to four-family residential structure (not to refinancings), and a good faith estimate is required for every transaction, except for home equity loans.

The disclosure of fees was greatly expanded under the Housing Community Development Act of 1992. Mortgage broker fees for any amount, however denominated, paid directly or indirectly, must be disclosed on both the good faith estimate and the HUD-1 settlement statement. Real estate brokers who engage in the mortgage brokering business should be acutely aware that this may create additional obligations for them and the fee should be disclosed on one of the "800" series blank lines. A mortgage broker who has nonexclusive representation of a lender, and receives a loan application, is also required to give a good faith estimate.

HUD published a "final rule" addressing controlled business arrangements, referral fees, computerized loan origination systems, and other related issues under RESPA. The final rule is accompanied by three "Statements of Policy" 1996-1, 1996-2, and 1996-3.

The 1992 rules created broad exemptions for payment of referral fees. The new final rule withdrew these broad exemptions and then created new exemptions for payments to "managerial employees" and employees who do not provide settlement services. A "managerial employee" is one who does not routinely deal directly with consumers and who hires, directs, assigns, promotes, or rewards other employees or independent contractors, or is in any position to formulate, determine, or influence the policies of the employer.

The exemption, in general terms, provides that employees who are not in a position of "trust" to the consumer and therefore are not in the position to exert influence or steer the consumer to a related entity. In addition, the only payments that can be made are from the employer to the employee. An affiliated company may not make these referral fee payments.

Statement of Policy 1996-1: Computer Loan Origination Systems (CLOs)

The final rule withdrew the existing blanket exemption for CLOs. The rule eliminated the disclosure requirement of the 1992 rule, as well as the exemption for borrower payments to CLOs. The statement of policy does not define a CLO, but refers to it as "a computer system that is used by or on behalf of a consumer to facilitate a consumer's choice among alternative products or settlement service providers in connection with the particular RESPA-covered real estate transaction." The rule merely attempts to describe the existing practices of service providers. The technology is evolving so rapidly that it is difficult to provide guidance.

Any payments made to a CLO must bear a reasonable relationship to the value of the goods, facilities, or services provided. RESPA places no restrictions on the pricing structure of a CLO as long as the payments are not referral fees and are reasonably related to the services provided.

When a CLO is used in a controlled business arrangement (CBA), the RESPA regulation to control business arrangements applies. A controlled business arrangement does not violate RESPA if three conditions are met:

■ When consumers are referred from one business entity to an affiliated business entity, a written disclosure of the affiliated relationship must be provided, see the new Figure 11-1.

■ There can be no required use of the affiliated company.

■ The only thing of value is received by one business entity from other business entities in the controlled business arrangement, is a return on an ownership interest or franchise relationship.

FIG 11-1   APPENDIX D TO PART 3500

CONTROLLED BUSINESS ARRANGEMENT DISCLOSURE STATEMENT FORMAT
NOTICE

To:_____   Property: _____

From: _____   Date:_____
       (Entity making Statement)

   This is to give you notice that [referring party] has a business relationship with [provider receiving referral]. [Describe the nature of the relationship between the referring party and the provider, including percentage of ownership interest, if applicable.] Because of this relationship, this referral may provide [referring party] a financial or other benefit.

   Set forth below is the estimated charge or range of charges by [provider] for the following settlement services:

_____: $ _____

_____: $ _____

_____: $ _____

You are NOT required to use [provider] as a condition for [settlement of your loan on] [or] [purchase, sale, or refinance of] the subject property. THERE ARE FREQUENTLY OTHER SETTLEMENT SERVICE PROVIDERS AVAILABLE WITH SIMILAR SERVICES. YOU ARE FREE TO SHOP AROUND TO DETERMINE THAT YOU ARE RECEIVING THE BEST SERVICES AND THE BEST RATE FOR THESE SERVICES.

   [A lender is allowed, however, to require the use of an attorney, credit reporting agency, or real estate appraiser chosen to represent the lender's interest.]

ACKNOWLEDGEMENT

   I/we have read this disclosure form, and understand that [referring party] is referring me/us to purchase the above-described settlement services from [provider receiving referrals], and may receive a financial or other benefit as the result of this referral.

_____
Signature

Statement of Policy 1996-2:
Sham Affiliated Business Arrangements (AfBAs)

This statement makes it clear that Congress did not intend for the affiliated business arrangement (AfBA) to be used to promote referral fee payments to sham arrangements or sham entities. If the entity is not a bona fide provider of settlement services, then the arrangement does not meet the definition of a AfBA. In determining whether a AfBA is a "sham," the Department of Housing and Urban Development weighs ten factors in light of the specific facts to decide whether an entity is a bona fide provider.

To decide a permissible return on an ownership interest or franchise relationship, the Department of Housing and Urban Development considers roughly four factors.

This portion of the rule is basically simple. In a true controlled business relationship, disclosed fees are specifically allowed. If one attempts to set a "sham" relationship with an affiliated company that doesn't provide legitimate services and may attempt to disguise referral fees under "returns on ownership" it will be disallowed as a violation of RESPA.

Statement of Policy 1996-3:
Rental of Office Space, Lock-Outs, and Retaliation

In this statement, HUD acknowledges that the rental payment that is higher than the ordinary rental paid for facilities can constitute a kickback in the violation of the Section 8 of prohibition of referral fees. When HUD is faced with a complaint that a person is renting space to a person who is referring business to that person, HUD examines the facts to determine whether the rental payment bears a reasonable relationship to the market value of the rental space provided or as a disguised referral fee. The market value of the rental space may include an appropriate proportion of the cost for all the services actually provided as a tenant, such as secretarial services, utilities, telephones, and other office equipment. HUD interprets the existing regulations to require a "general market value" as a basis for the analysis. If the rental payments paid by the tenant exceed the general market value of the space provided, HUD will consider the excess amount to be to the referral of business in violation of Section 8(a) of RESPA.

Another form of referral fee can be a lock-out. A lock-out arises where a settlement service provider prevents other providers from marketing their services within a setting under that provider's control. For instance, a situation where the rental rate to a particular settlement service provider (title company) could lead to other settlement service providers being "locked out" from access to the referrals of business or from reaching the consumer would be a violation.

A third prohibition includes retaliation. Retaliations occur when a settlement service provider raises negative consequences for an agent to refer business to another settlement service provider. For example, a real estate broker who imposes quotas or referrals to a particular lender or Title Company on its agents, under the threat of dismissal, is engaging in retaliation. See 61 FR 111.

It is safe to say that the 1994 rule will probably be revised. As times change, business practices change, and settlement services become more competitive. The only thing constant is change!

Another regulation is Statement of Policy 1996-4, which sets out HUD's interpretation of Section 8 of RESPA involving payments of a fee by a title company to their appointed agent. Of particular concern were payments to an attorney of the buyer or seller as compensation for being a title agent. In order for the attorney to receive this compensation, the attorney must perform core title agent services (for which liability arises), separate from attorney services, including the evaluation of the title search to determine the insurability of title, the clearance of underwriting objections, the actual issuance of the policy or policies on behalf of the title insurance company, and, where customary, the issuance of the title commitment, and the conducting of the title search and closing. In performing the core title services, the title insurance agent must be liable to the title insurance company for any negligence in performing the services. In considering liability, HUD will examine the following type of indicia: the provisions of the agency contract, whether the agent has errors and omissions, insurance or malpractice insurance, whether a contract provision regarding an agent's liability for claiming a loss as ever enforced, whether an agent is financially able to pay a claim, and any other factors the Secretary (HUD) may consider relevant. HUD interprets this Section 8 requirement to mean that the title insurance company must charge a title insurance agency fee for title evidence, but it is not a disguised referral fee given in exchange for the referral of title business.

Texas title insurance companies are now in the fight! HUD has decided to beef up its enforcement division for title companies in Texas. On May 13, 2003, HUD sent out a letter to several title companies in the Austin market warning companies to comply with Section 8, which is the antirebate, kickback section of RESPA. Last summer, several title companies in Austin were investigated by HUD for allegedly violating Section 8 in relation to virtual home tours. HUD has received numerous complaints that indicate the practice may still be continuing, as well as complaints that title companies may be providing brochures, flyers, and other materials to real estate agents for free or below cost. If this practice continues, HUD is threatening to pursue a more formal investigation. Any person found in violation of Section 8 of RESPA may be fined up to $10,000.00, subject to imprisonment of one year, or both. The settlement agreement between HUD and the seven title companies in Austin required the title companies to pay $130,000.00 in fines and give up the free virtual tours. In the past year, HUD has tripled it's RESPA enforcement staff from 10 to 30.

In a state like Texas, where the title insurance rates are regulated by the Texas Department of Insurance, HUD looks at these "freebies" as indirect kickbacks that result in higher prices to the consumer (i.e., if the title company can afford to make business expenditures for REALTORS®, they're charging too much!). The Texas Department of Insurance has issued several memorandums on this topic, and one can never be too careful when dealing either with the Department of Insurance or the federal government. If they both come after you, the Texas Real Estate Commission can't be far behind.

SECURITIES AND EXCHANGE COMMISSION

The Securities and Exchange Commission (SEC) regulates certain forms of land use, which, in their opinion, involve securities, investment contracts, or sale of equity interests. Thus, the SEC has been very effective in regulating real estate investment trusts, real estate syndications, and certain types of condominium offerings that involve investments, interstate sales promotions, and sales made with a promise of profit or a high rate of return. One case has held that even the existence of an investment opportunity in the form of a condominium rental pool constituted a security transaction. *Hocking v. Dubois, Vitousek, & Dick Realtors*, 885 F.2d 1149 (9th Cir. 1989).

In the eyes of the SEC, virtually any investment scheme or contract to purchase real estate with the expectation of profit makes that particular real estate transaction a security and requires certain disclosures pursuant to the **Securities and Exchange Acts of 1933 and 1934.** There are only two provisions of the 1934 Act that exempt real estate investment transactions from being classified as securities. These are:

Section 4(a)2 of the Act, which exempts offerings that are made only to close friends, business associates, family relations, and other close offerings that are not made to the public in general.

Section 3(a)11 of the Act, which exempts offerings that do not go interstate, but are kept wholly as an intrastate offering. This means that the sales promotion cannot use any of the means of interstate commerce (the telephone, newspaper advertising, the U.S. mail, etc.).

The SEC has severely curtailed certain investment schemes and syndication offerings that became very common in Texas in the early 1970s. The expense of registering a security to comply with the Securities and Exchange Act is so great that most developers now prefer to restrict their offerings, or to go into a different type of real estate development altogether, instead of complying with the securities regulations. If any real estate offering has even the possibility of being considered a security, and the exemption may be in question, the real estate broker should work very closely with a lawyer well qualified in the area of real estate and securities laws.

DISCUSSION QUESTIONS

■ Can the sale of a single house constitute a securities violation?

■ What about the sales of "investments" in single-family houses to out-of-state investors?

■ How might this happen?

FOREIGN INVESTMENT REAL PROPERTY TAX ACT (FIRPTA)

FIRPTA was originally enacted to eliminate tax advantages for foreign investors. The statute requires withholding by the purchaser of 10 percent of the proceeds to the sale of the United States Real Estate Interest by a foreign person or entity. The only exception is property used as a residence selling for less than $300,000. The taxpayer or a member of the taxpayer's family must have definite plans to reside at the property for at least 50 percent of the number of days the property is used by any person during each of the first two twelve-month periods following the acquisition.

The law also requires a real estate broker representing a foreign seller to notify the purchaser and the IRS that withholding the taxes may be required. The statute assumes that the broker knows he or she is working for a foreign entity (a foreign corporation). Failure to provide the purchaser and the IRS with the required notices subjects the broker to the duty to withhold taxes. The broker is liable for the tax up to the amount of the compensation used or received. The broker may also incur civil liability to the purchaser for failure to properly notify the purchaser of the seller's foreign status, and may also be subject to criminal sanctions under the conspiracy laws.

Again, the rule is relatively simple for real estate brokers at or before closing. Obtain an affidavit from the seller that he or she is not a foreign person, or require that the purchaser withhold the 10 percent of the sales price to be forwarded to the Internal Revenue Service, or the burden may fall upon the broker to do so.

FEDERAL TRUTH-IN-LENDING

The Federal Truth-in-Lending Act is administered by the Federal Reserve Board of Governors. The part of these regulations commonly known as **Regulation Z** (Reg Z) requires disclosures that enable the consumer to see the total dollar payments for the life of the loan, the total finance charge. The TIL also deals with certain elements of broker advertising and the disclosure of the assumability of loans.

Since most real estate sales are financed, the broker needs to be familiar with the TIL as it involves: (1) credit that is offered or extended to consumer; (2) credit offered to be extended regularly; (3) finance charges made by the creditor to be paid in more than four installments; and (4) credit primarily for personal, family, or household purposes.

The Act applies to an "arranger of credit," which means that it applies to all transactions, including one involving a real estate broker who assisted a seller in financing a home. In effect, this would make the broker liable for truth-in-lending disclosure. However, brokers were specifically excluded from the definition "arranger of credit" under the 1980 revision of the Act, but a licensee who offers to extend credit should have concerns about disclosures. For instance, if a real estate broker regularly offers or extends credit out of commissions advanced to assist in the completion of closings, the Truth-in-Lending Act is applicable to such situations, as this conduct would clearly constitute credit extended for personal, family, or household services. The required disclosures are lengthy and involved and must be made before the consummation of the transaction "generally at the closing when the consumer becomes obligated on the credit transaction." If a broker, as a creditor, regularly extends consumer credit more than five times a year in the acquisition of homes and the extension of credit involves a security interest in the dwelling, then that broker comes under the TIL requirements. A TIL violation involves both criminal and civil penalties.

The TIL also mandates requirements that apply to the advertising made to promote or assist a loan subject to the Federal Truth-in-Lending Act. Only those credit terms that are actually available, may be advertised, and the credit must be disclosed as an **annual percentage rate** (APR) as defined by the Federal Truth-in-Lending Act. This includes the use of certain advertising terms, commonly referred to as the "trigger terms." Those terms include: (1) the amount of percentage of any down payment; (2) the number of payments or period of repayment; (3) the amount of any payment; and (4) the amount of any finance charge. If any of the trigger terms are used, the creditor (real estate broker) must also include additional disclosure in the advertisement: (1) the amount or percentage of any down payment; (2) the terms of repayment; (3) the annual percentage rate; and (4) disclosure of any variable rate features.

LAND USE LEGISLATION

The federal legislation affecting land use is overwhelming. It is overwhelming to developers, it is overwhelming to owners, and it is equally overwhelming to real estate brokers who are assisting both of these people in their normal day-to-day operations of selling property. **The National Flood and Insurance Program** restricts development in the flood plain. **The Federal Endangered Species Act** restricts development in designated critical habitats or other areas in which endangered species may be present. The **Safe Drinking Water Act** is enacted in counties located at the top of any aquifer recharge area and establishes wellhead protection areas. The **Clean Water Act** creates a well preservation program by restricted development in wetlands areas. The **Comprehensive Environmental Response Compensation and Liability Act** (CERCLA) relates to on-site conditions that create restrictions on land use, regulating the deposited materials or imposing liens to remediate sites through required clean-up programs. The **National Historic Preservation Act** requires maintenance of registered historic places significant in American history. Land use regulation through **Zoning Coastal Management** and other regulatory procedures control one's ability to develop or redevelop areas on coastal plains.

When a broker is marketing properties, he or she must be acutely aware of these federal laws. There will be buyers who will ask about the application of these laws in specific instances (this may create greater responsibility for buyer's brokers). It creates liability for nondisclosure if these laws are applicable, and liability for misrepresentations, however innocent they may be. All of these issues will not be discussed in great detail, but some of the more pertinent ones follow.

The "Taking" Issue/Condemnation

Waterfront property has been an emphasis in the United States Supreme Court over the last few years concerning regulation of coastal and beach front properties. In these cases, the Coastal Zone Management authority tends to restrict or totally prohibit redevelopment of properties on the beach because the public is entitled to a view of or access to the beach. In *Nollan v. California Coastal Commission*, 107 S. Ct. 3141 (1987), the U.S. Supreme Court defended real properties rights as they pertained to water. The Nollan court held that when a land use permit contains a provision that adds substantially to its intent, a taking occurs. Nollan leased a beach front lot with an option to purchase. Before acquisition, the California Coastal Commission granted a permit subject to the condition that the Nollans grant an easement laterally along the front beach of their lot between the side boundary lines, because the house would block the view of the ocean and prevent the public from realizing that a stretch of beach existed that they could enjoy. The Court held that such a restriction was a "**taking**" and was not land use regulation. If the California Coastal Commission were going to restrict that type of use, it would be condemnation; and they would have to pay the property owner for it.

The new rule appears to be that the Court must determine whether an "essential nexus" (good legal term, meaning "relationship") exists between legitimate state interest and the condition of the permit to be granted by the municipality. If the legitimate state interest does exist, then it must be decided whether the degree of the exactions demanded by the principle condition bears the required relationship to the projected impact of the proposed development. In a recent case, the United States Supreme Court indicated that the city had the right to require a green belt be dedicated for purposes of effecting proper drainage, but indicated that there was no need for the green belt to be "public property" and it could have remained in private ownership with the same result. *Dolan v. City of Tigard*, 114 S. Ct. 2309 (1994).

A similar result in *Lucas v. South Carolina Coastal Council*, 112 S. Ct. 2886 (1992), wherein Mr. Lucas paid $975,000 for two single-family residential beach-front lots in 1986. The South Carolina legislature adopted a statute that prevented new construction on beach front sites along the state's Atlantic coastline. The lower courts held that it was in the state's police power to enact land use restrictions to prevent serious harm to beaches and to prevent "noxious" uses. The U.S. Supreme Court, however, reversed and held that a re-striction is a taking when it renders the property valueless and is therefore a condemnation, requiring payment to the property owner for the value of the property. One of the significant holdings of the Court was if the regulation runs the value of the property to zero, it constitutes a taking regardless of the intent of the regulatory land use.

In *Kelo v. City of New London*, 545 U.S. 1158 (2005), the United States Supreme Court, once again, looked at the takings issue in light of redevelopment plans of the City. In 2000, the City of New London, Connecticut, approved a de-velopment plan that was projected to create an increase of 1,000 jobs, to increase tax and other revenues, and to revitalize an economically distressed city, includ-ing its downtown and water front areas. In assembling the land needed for this project, the city's development agent purchased property from willing sellers and proposed to use the power of eminent domain to acquire the remainder of the property from unwilling owners in exchange for just compensation.

The city council held a series of neighborhood meetings to educate the public about the process. In May, the city council authorized the New London Development Corporation (a private non-profit entity established some years earlier to assist the city in planning and economic development) to formally submit its plans to the relevant state agencies for review. Pfizer had already announced it would build a 300 million dollar research facility adjacent to the re-development area, two years before. The Supreme Court of Connecticut held that all the city's proposed takings were valid and authorized by Con-necticut's Municipal Development Statute. The plaintiffs alleged that the city had failed to adduce clear and convincing evidence of the economic benefits of the plan. The Supreme Court, citing *Berman v. Parker*, 348 U.S. 26 (1954), held that the economic development qualified as a valid public use under both fed-eral and state constitutions. Then, it further cited *Hawaii Housing Authority v. Metcalf*, 467 U.S. 229 (1984), noting that the State's purpose of eliminating the social and economic ills of the land oligopoly qualified as a valid public use.

More importantly, the Supreme Court noted that those who govern the city were entitled to deference. The city invoked a state statute that specifically authorizes the use of eminent domain to promote economic development. The court noted that the plan unquestionably serves a public purpose, and that the takings chal-lenged here satisfied the public use requirement of the Fifth Amendment. The Court further noted that promoting economic development is a traditional and long-accepted function of government, and that public ownership is not the sole method of promoting the public purposes of community re-development projects.

The Court further stated that it declined to second-guess the City's considered judgment about the efficacy of the development plan, and its determinations as to what lands it needed to acquire in order to effectuate the project. The amount incurred for the plan to be taken for the project and the need for a particular tract to complete the integrated plan rest in the discretion of the legislative branch.

In fact, the U.S. Supreme Court did nothing but ratify and affirm an existing state law and local ordinance. There was no "legislating from the bench," and there was nothing new about this type of holding. Another strange novelty of the case is that while wresting land from a private owner and putting it in the hands of another private owner to raise tax revenue (through no expense of the government, with the developer taking all the required risks), seems to be an entrepreneurial, capitalistic, and conservative idea, yet the conservative justices voted against it and the liberal judges voted for it.

Texas has had similar cases, none of which were decided by the Supreme Court. In all of the Texas cases, the state court held that the restriction for redevelopment of properties along Galveston's beach was valid under the Natural Resources Code [Sec. 61.025, Natural Resources Code], and the U.S. Supreme Court refused to review the case. *Matcha v. Maddox*, 711 S.W.2d 95 (Tex. App.-Dallas 1984).

Wetlands Legislation

Wetlands legislation is the popular name given to the provisions of the **Clean Water Act**, which administers the program that regulates activities in wetland areas for the United States Corps of Engineers with oversight by the **Environmental Protection Agency**. Specifically, sections of the Clean Water Act require permits for discharging filled material from a point source into the navigable waters. The statute defines navigable waters very broadly. The definition "wetlands" are those areas that are saturated by a surface or ground water at a frequency sufficient to support, and that under normal circumstances do support a vegetation typically adapted for life in saturated soil conditions. Wetlands generally include swamps, marshes, bogs, and similar areas, but a lot of other areas (not generally swampy) have been designated as wetlands.

The delineation of a wetland is still confusing, as the tract can be dry most of the year. Courts have also held that the adjacent wetlands, isolated wetlands, and human-made artificial wetlands are within the jurisdiction of the wetlands legislation. The Act prohibits any discharge from a point source into the waters of the United States, which includes such seemingly trivial activity as bulldozers, back hoes, and dump trucks. Therefore, any kind of levees, any type of grading, paving, road construction, and utility lines would be regulated activities.

More simply stated, any raw land marketed by a real estate broker should have a Phase I Environmental Assessment to determine whether there are any areas on the property that support vegetation that is unique to wetlands areas. This definitely will occur in any areas close to lakes, creeks, rivers, bays, or swamp areas. Once the Army Corps of Engineers determines which of the areas in the land are to be considered wetlands, they cannot be developed at all unless there is another wetlands developed in another part of the property, so that there is no "net loss" of wetland area. This has been held as not constituting a "taking." *Tabb Lakes, Ltd. v. United States*, 10 F.3d 796 (Fed. Cir. 1993). One case, however, has held the opposite way. *Bowles v. U.S.*, 31 Fed. Cl. 37 (1994). Even the development done on the properties that are adjacent to the wetlands will have to be carefully permitted and monitored to be sure that the additional runoff does not adversely affect the wetlands areas. There are a number of residential subdivisions along the Gulf Coast that have such restrictions applicable to individual lots in those subdivisions. The penalties for violating the wetlands legislation are unusually severe.

The Endangered Species Act

The Federal Endangered Species Act was originally enacted in 1973. The species to be protected includes any species of animal or plant life that are endangered. Subspecies of fish or wildlife or plant and any distinct population of a pedigree species are also included. Individual animals are also protected, as the Act prohibits taking of an animal's habitat. This includes any activity that would harass the animals or disturb their environments so that they don't want to occupy the area. The 1988 amendments to the Act create a violation under the Act for removal and reduction of any such species from the area of federal jurisdiction, maliciously damaging or destroying any such species on any such area, or removing, cutting, digging up, or damaging and destroying any such species in knowing violation of new law or regulation. There are both civil and criminal remedies for violating the Act.

In real terms, this means that if an area to be developed is a habitat for any kind of endangered species as determined by the federal government, all development in the area will be stopped. There are a large number of areas in Texas that have identified endangered species, particularly areas around Austin, the Gulf Coast, and East Texas. There was one case in Montana where a hunter shot an attacking bear to save his own life, yet he was prosecuted under the Endangered Species Act for harassing the animal in its normal habitat! One project in Houston was put on "hold" because it was thought that an endangered woodpecker inhabited the forest. Imagine the broker, the developer, the lender, and all the employees and other contractors awaiting the arrival of a woodpecker!

It is becoming imperative that real estate agents know about, and to some extent understand, the environmental problems that will have an increasing impact on the buying, selling, and market value of real property. The new Texas Seller Disclosure Notice form for residential property includes information on many environmental hazards. There are forms available for sellers of commercial properties. More and more people are entering this inspection area. Disclosure of these hazards is surely pertinent to the buyer's decision to purchase.

Underground Storage Tanks

Hundreds of thousands of storage tanks are buried all over the United States. Many of these underground storage tanks are leaking hydrocarbons and lead contaminants into the soil. Cities, states, and the federal government have enacted courses to give protection against the danger to the environment.

The Resource Conservation and Recovery Act of 1976 has been amended to require the **Environmental Protection Agency** (EPA) to develop a preventive program designed to prevent or detect and correct any leakage from underground tanks. An **Underground Storage Tank** (UST) is described by the Environmental Protection Agency as any tank with 10 percent or more of its capacity below ground, which contains hazardous substances. Farm and residential tanks with a capacity of 1,100 gallons or less holding fuel for noncommercial purposes, septic tanks, basement wastewater collection and storage systems, and tanks containing heating oil for on-premises use are exempted from federal regulations but may be covered by state or local laws.

Owners of these tanks must take safety precautions that include monthly checking of possible leaks, tightness of tanks, spill and overflow testing, and corrosion protection. All tanks installed prior to 1988 are covered as of December 1993. All new tanks must be installed, and old tanks removed, by qualified contractors according to the legal requirements.

There are reporting and recordkeeping requirements of owners' compliance with the regulations. Owners and operators are responsible for corrective actions and for the ability to compensate for injury or property damage according to the number of tanks owned. Property managers, lessors, lenders, and buyers of properties with tanks must be sure that they are in compliance with the regulations.

Approximately 95 percent of the estimated two million underground storage tanks are used to contain petroleum. This is an even larger problem in Texas and other major oil-producing states.

DISCUSSION QUESTION

■ Where might you find underground storage tanks?

Asbestos

Asbestos is a white, fibrous mineral that is found in about 20 percent of our older public and commercial buildings. Asbestos is found in some insulations, sidings, roofing, and floor coverings. Use of asbestos has been limited since the 1970s, but millions of American workers have been exposed to asbestos. Exposure can lead to illness and death.

Disease symptoms can range from troubled breathing to death. An estimated 365,000 people will die from related diseases by 2030 (Mount Sinai School of Medicine, study in 1982). Illnesses include cancers and tumors, scarring of the lungs, and thickening of the lung lining membranes.

Apparently, it is the asbestos fibers that cause most health problems. Therefore, compressed asbestos, such as shingles, would be less a problem than the asbestos in walls or ceilings. At first it was thought that the best remedy was to remove all asbestos. This released fibers into the air. It is now thought that containment may well be a better treatment.

Asbestos lawsuits are more likely found where heavy industry flourishes. Asbestos is a local issue for house sales, also. Note that the Texas Real Estate Commission has a form to make asbestos investigation a contingency (see TREC No. 28-0).

Lead-Based Paint

The final rule has been issued from the Environmental Protection Agency concerning lead-based paint disclosures. To facilitate compliance with the federal rules, the Texas Real Estate Broker-Lawyer Committee has developed a contract addendum for use with TREC-promulgated contract forms. A copy is shown in Figure 11-2.

WHAT IS REQUIRED?

Before the buyer or tenant becomes obligated under the contract for sale or lease:

■ Sellers and landlords must disclose known lead-based paint and lead-based paint hazards and provide available reports to buyers or tenants.

■ Sellers and landlords must give buyers and renters the pamphlet titled Protect Your Family From Lead In Your Home.

■ Homebuyers will get a 10-day period to conduct a lead-based paint inspection or risk assessment at their own expense, if desired. The number of days can be changed by mutual consent. This inspection period is not required for prospective tenants.

■ Sales contracts and leasing arrangements must include certain language to ensure that disclosure and notification actually take place.

FIG 11-2   ADDENDUM FOR SELLER'S DISCLOSURE OF INFORMATION ON LEAD-BASED PAINT
AND LEAD-BASED PAINT HAZARDS AS REQUIRED BY FEDERAL LAW

APPROVED BY THE TEXAS REAL ESTATE COMMISSION   02-09-2004

ADDENDUM FOR SELLER'S DISCLOSURE OF INFORMATION ON LEAD-BASED PAINT AND LEAD-BASED PAINT HAZARDS AS REQUIRED BY FEDERAL LAW

CONCERNING THE PROPERTY AT _____
(Street Address and City)

A. **LEAD WARNING STATEMENT:**   "Every purchaser of any interest in residential real property on which a residential dwelling was built prior to 1978 is notified that such property may present exposure to lead from lead-based paint that may place young children at risk of developing lead poisoning. Lead poisoning in young children may produce permanent neurological damage, including learning disabilities, reduced intelligence quotient, behavioral problems, and impaired memory. Lead poisoning also poses a particular risk to pregnant women.   The seller of any interest in residential real property is required to provide the buyer with any information on lead-based paint hazards from risk assessments or inspections in the seller's possession and notify the buyer of any known lead-based paint hazards. A risk assessment or inspection for possible lead-paint hazards is recommended prior to purchase."
NOTICE: Inspector must be properly certified as required by federal law.

B. **SELLER'S DISCLOSURE:**
   1. PRESENCE OF LEAD-BASED PAINT AND/OR LEAD-BASED PAINT HAZARDS (check on box only):
      ☐(a) Known lead-based paint and/or lead-based paint hazards are present in the Property (explain): _____
      _____ .
      ☐(b) Seller has no actual knowledge of lead-based paint and/or lead-based paint hazards in the Property.
   2. RECORDS AND REPORTS AVAILABLE TO SELLER (check one box only):
      ☐(a) Seller has provided the purchaser with all available records and reports pertaining to lead-based paint and/or lead-based paint hazards in the Property (list documents):_____
      _____ .
      ☐(b) Seller has no reports or records pertaining to lead-based paint and/or lead-based paint hazards in the Property.

C. **BUYER'S RIGHTS** (check one box only):
   ☐1. Buyer waives the opportunity to conduct a risk assessment or inspection of the Property for the presence of lead-based paint or lead-based paint hazards.
   ☐2. Within ten days after the effective date of this contract, Buyer may have the Property inspected by inspectors selected by Buyer. If lead-based paint or lead-based paint hazards are present, Buyer may terminate this contract by giving Seller written notice within 14 days after the effective date of this contract, and the earnest money will be refunded to Buyer.

D. **BUYER'S ACKNOWLEDGMENT** (check applicable boxes):
   ☐1. Buyer has received copies of all information listed above.
   ☐2. Buyer has received the pamphlet *Protect Your Family from Lead in Your Home*.

E. **BROKERS' ACKNOWLEDGMENT:** Brokers have informed Seller of Seller's obligations under 42 U.S.C. 4852d to: (a) provide Buyer with the federally approved pamphlet on lead poisoning prevention; (b) complete this addendum; (c) disclose any known lead-based paint and/or lead-based paint hazards in the Property; (d) deliver all records and reports to Buyer pertaining to lead-based paint and/or lead-based paint hazards in the Property; (e) provide Buyer a period of up to 10 days to have the Property inspected; and (f) retain a completed copy of this addendum for at least 3 years following the sale. Brokers are aware of their responsibility to ensure compliance.

F. **CERTIFICATION OF ACCURACY:** The following persons have reviewed the information above and certify, to the best of their knowledge, that the information they have provided is true and accurate.

_____ _____   _____ _____
Buyer   Date   Seller   Date

_____ _____   _____ _____
Buyer   Date   Seller   Date

_____ _____   _____ _____
Other Broker   Date   Listing Broker   Date

Form OP-L   **01A**

Reprinted by permission from Texas Real Estate Commission.

- Sellers, lessors, and real estate agents share responsibility for ensuring compliance.

- Retain proof of compliance for THREE YEARS.

NOTE THAT THE RULE DOES NOT REQUIRE TESTING, REMOVAL, OR ABATEMENT OF LEAD-BASED PAINT; NOR DOES IT INVALIDATE LEASING AND SALES CONTRACTS.

The statute targets housing built prior to 1978 and specifically does not cover the following:

- housing built after 1977.

- zero bedroom units, such as efficiencies, lofts, and dormitories.

- leases for less than 100 days, such as vacation houses or short-term rentals.

- houses exclusively for the elderly (unless there are children living there).

- housing for the handicapped (unless there are children living there).

- rental houses that have been inspected by a certified inspector and found to be free of lead-based paint.

- houses being sold because of foreclosure.

- renewals of existing leases in which the landlord has previously disclosed all required lead-based paint information.

AGENT RESPONSIBILITIES

There are specific requirements for real estate agents under the final rule. The agents must ensure that:

- sellers and landlords are aware of their obligations.

- sellers and landlords disclose the proper information to buyers and tenants.

- sellers give buyers the 10-day opportunity to conduct an inspection (or other mutually agreed upon period).

- agents should see that a lease includes proper disclosure language and proper signatures.

- the agent must comply with the law if seller or landlord fail to do so.

INTERESTING NOTE! A housing group calling itself the National Multi-Housing Council is dedicating a portion of its legislative agenda to fight new proposals concerning lead-based paint, apparently contending that little, if any, good has come from the laws already on the books. The organization noted that the problem of childhood lead poisoning was well on its way out long before the disclosures were mandated in 1996. According to the Centers for Disease Control and Prevention, the presence of elevated lead levels in the general population decreased 94 percent between 1988 and 1994. The incidence of lead poisoning has dropped even more dramatically, with just 0.4 percent of young children reported as having lead poisoning.

What caused the lead poisoning to drop? The organization notes that the decline in blood levels through the 1990s was the result of the elimination of lead from most gasoline products and lead solder from food and beverage cans and water supply pipes, and limits on the emission of lead from industrial facilities. The organization notes, "Regulations on housing providers embody a costly and cumbersome regulatory approach that increases the cost of and threatens the supply of affordable housing and has little impact on the overall incidence of childhood lead poisoning" (*Real Estate intelligence Report,* Spring 2000).

Chlorofluorocarbon (CFC) Emissions

Chlorofluorocarbons are ozone-depleting. They allegedly contribute to the "global warming effect."

A 1995 phase-out of the manufacturing and marketing of CFC-based products, such as freon, has been called for by the federal government. Since July 1, 1992, there has been a ban on purposefully venting chlorofluorocarbons (CFCs) during the servicing, maintenance, repair, or removal of heating, ventilation, and air conditioning (HVAC) equipment and systems as a requirement of the Clean Air Act. Enforcement comes under the jurisdiction of the Environmental Protection Agency (EPA).

The EPA has been leaning toward certification of general HVAC technicians, including air conditioning and refrigeration technicians, servicers, and maintainers. The Clean Air Act requires the certification of car air conditioning technicians.

Electromagnetic Fields (EMFs)

Electromagnetic fields are created by the flow of electric current through wires. They occur in the wiring of household appliances and in high tension/high voltage wires.

Although many believe that there is a health risk in electromagnetic fields, there is no conclusive evidence to support this belief.

In 1996, the National Research Council of the National Academy of Science published a report stating that electromagnetic fields generated by power lines and household appliances cannot pose a threat to human health. After reviewing more than 500 studies, the scientists found no link between electromagnetic fields and diseases such as cancer. Courts are also researching the same conclusion. One court has held the diminished value of a plaintiff's land resulting from public concerns about a nearby electromagnetic generation is not the kind of directed substantial injury allowed in inverse condemnation cases. The court pointed out that there was no physical invasion of, or interference with, the plaintiff's land, analogizing the problem to the plane overflight cases. *San Diego Gas & Electric Co. v. Covalt*, 55 Cal. Rptr.2d 724 (Cal. 1996); *Borenkind v. Consolidated Edison Corporation*, 626 N.Y.S.2d 414 (App. Div. 1995).

The Comprehensive Environmental Response, Compensation and Liability Act (CERCLA)

CERCLA was originally enacted by congress in 1980 in response to the environmental and public health hazards imposed by improper disposition of hazardous waste. Congress intended CERCLA to effect the prompt abatement of the health and environmental risks from leaking abandoned hazardous waste dumps and other releases of toxic substances. The statute created a "super fund" to be utilized by the Federal Environmental Protection Agency and state and local governments to clean up certain waste sites that have been designated by the EPA, commonly referred to as "superfund" sites. One of the critical areas of the statute is its creation of liability for literally all parties in the chain of title for disposition of that waste, including the truck driver and any owner in the chain of title, regardless of their knowledge of the hazardous waste deposit.

This has created an entire new industry of environmental assessments, which must be performed prior to acquiring title to real estate. The statute applies primarily to raw land, although there are a number of situations in commercial real estate in which there have been discharges as a result of use of property by chemical plants, lead smelting plants, and other heavy industries. We now impose a standard of due diligence on purchasers, and presumably real estate brokers, to know that environmental assessments are required for any tract of land that may have a history of discharged deposits of hazardous substances. This is typically done by doing a 50-year title search of the site to see who the prior owners were and then a Phase I Environmental Assessment by an environmentalist. If necessary, a Phase II or even Phase III Environmental Assessment will have to be performed before the new purchaser can be considered to be an "innocent purchaser" and protected from enforcement under the Act.

Even in residential real estate, there may be equal impositions of due diligence if the buyer is concerned about radon, asbestos, or other potentially toxic substance. Note that TREC now provides a specific addendum for environmental assessments (TREC Form 28-0, see Figure 11-3). Recall that when a TREC-promulgated form addendum is specifically applicable to a given transaction, it is required for use. A prudent licensee should be sure to identify the potential for environmental hazards and confirm the existence or absence of it in the Seller's Disclosure Notice form.

ENVIRONMENTAL ASSESSMENT, THREATENED OR
ENDANGERED SPECIES, AND WETLANDS ADDENDUM

10-25-93

ENVIRONMENTAL ASSESSMENT, THREATENED OR ENDANGERED SPECIES, AND WETLANDS ADDENDUM

PROMULGATED BY THE TEXAS REAL ESTATE COMMISSION (TREC)

ADDENDUM TO EARNEST MONEY CONTRACT BETWEEN THE UNDERSIGNED PARTIES CONCERNING THE PROPERTY AT _____
(Address)

☐ A. ENVIRONMENTAL ASSESSMENT: Buyer, at Buyer's expense, may obtain an Environmental Assessment Report prepared by an environmental specialist.

☐ B. THREATENED OR ENDANGERED SPECIES: Buyer, at Buyer's expense, may obtain a report from a natural resources professional to determine if there are any threatened or endangered species or their habitats as defined by the Texas Parks and wildlife Department or the U.S. Fish and Wildlife Service.

☐ C. WETLANDS: Buyer, at Buyer's expense, may obtain a report from an environmental specialist to determine if there are wetlands, as defined by federal or state law or regulation.

Within _____ days after the Effective Date of the contract, Buyer may terminate the contract by furnishing Seller a copy of any report noted above that adversely affects the use of the Property and the Earnest Money shall be refunded to Buyer. If Buyer does not furnish Seller a copy of the unacceptable report within the prescribed time and give Seller notice that Buyer has terminated the contract, Buyer shall be deemed to have accepted the Property.

_____   _____
Buyer   Seller

_____   _____
Buyer   Seller

The form of this addendum has been approved by the Texas Real Estate Commission for use only with similarly approved or promulgated forms of contracts. No representation is made as to the legal validity or adequacy of any provision in any specific transactions. It is not suitable for complex transactions. (10-93) TREC No. 28-0.

01A   TREC No. 28-0

12

FEDERAL LEGISLATION AFFECTING REAL ESTATE BROKERS—PART II

PURPOSE

After carefully reading Chapter 12, the student will be able to:

- Discuss the ADA.

- Apply the Fair Housing Act and Texas Fair Housing Law to the practice of real estate.

- Avoid antitrust problems.

- Define: *familial status, handicap, steering, Internal Revenue Code Form 1099, block busting, tester.*

- Explain the Condominium and Cooperative Abuse Relief Act, price fixing, boycotting, and tying claims.

Key Words to look for in this chapter:
1. Americans With Disabilities Act
2. Fair Housing
3. Protected Classes
4. Handicapped
5. Familial Status
6. Steering
7. Blockbusting
8. Agent's Duties
9. Testers
10. Texas Fair Housing Law
11. Condominium and Cooperative Abuse Relief Act
12. Antitrust Laws
13. Price Fixing
14. Fee Splitting
15. Boycotting
16. Tying Claims

THE INTERNAL REVENUE CODE

In the late 1980s, reporting requirements were imposed upon a person responsible for closing real estate transactions. For years, the IRS required a form 1099 to provide that income information be turned into the Internal Revenue Service on the sale of property by the transferor depending on the person responsible for closing the real estate transaction. Changes to the Code in 1997 now limit that requirement somewhat, but the burden falls on the real estate broker to file this information with the Internal Revenue Service if the title company or attorney in charge of the closing does not do so.

AMERICANS WITH DISABILITIES ACT

The Americans with Disabilities Act (ADA) was enacted on July 26, 1992. Generally stated, it provides access requirements and prohibits discrimination against people with disabilities in public accommodations, state and local government, transportation, telecommunications, and employment. Anyone that has had a physical or mental handicap, or that is "perceived" as having such that interferes with a "major life activity," is covered by the Act.

The primary focus for real estate licensees is Title III, which broadly expands the concept of "disability" and imposes regulations on existing buildings. The Act specifically affects the real estate brokerage industry in that real estate licensees need to determine whether the product the licensee is selling, managing, or leasing is in compliance with the Act. A licensee should always be cautioned, however, that the statute is very detailed, and there are a number of gray areas in the statute that still lack clear interpretation. Title III applies to both the owner and the operator for public accommodations and commercial facilities.

The Americans with Disabilities Act relates to real estate practitioners in many ways. A real estate broker/salesperson is not, as such, qualified to advise a principal about compliance or requirements. However, a real estate agent should make clients, particularly commercial property clients, aware of the ADA without giving them legal advice.

The ADA will affect areas of real estate specialization. It would appear that agents of those covered by the Act take on their principals' responsibilities, although the principals cannot escape their responsibilities. Principals cannot escape their responsibility by transferring the job of compliance to someone else. Property managers and other agents who are in a decision-making position about ADA provisions are bound by its regulations.

Appraisers, in their appraisal report regarding statements of underlying assumptions and limiting conditions, need to disclose that the appraiser has made no determination of property compliance with ADA. Even this may not protect the appraiser for failing to identify and estimate the affect on value of obvious barriers to the handicapped for his principal. Real estate counselors and advisors will need a working knowledge of the Act. Compliance, or the ability to comply, with the ADA will affect the value, use, and financing of real property.

Many real estate professionals will also come under ADA employment requirements. Some may have to meet employment guidelines because no decision has been made as to whether real estate salespeople come under the Act's definition of employees. Therefore, real estate companies with a combination of fifteen or more agents and/or other employees might be responsible for meeting ADA employment requirements. Real estate agencies with fifteen or more employees (nonindependent contractors/agents) and/or real estate brokers acting as the agent of a person with fifteen or more employees in a particular business area will come under the provisions of the Act. And ADA requirements affect real estate agents' places of service and business. Their offices are facilities of public accommodation and commercial establishments. The agent, therefore, will need to be familiar with the Act.

Real estate agencies may qualify for some tax relief in meeting ADA qualifications. There is a tax deduction of up to $15,000 per year for expenses incurred in removal of barriers. There is also a tax credit available to some small businesses.

So far we have few court precedents to help us with interpretation of the Americans with Disabilities Act. Problems in compliance will occur. Examples: If a water fountain is placed low enough for someone in a wheel chair to use, what happens to the tall person who has difficulty in bending? Lowering a fire extinguisher for easier access to the person in the wheelchair also gives easier access to small children. Something that is "child proof" will also be inaccessible to someone with limited use of his or her hands.

There can be little doubt that the Americans with Disabilities Act will be one of the most important and far-reaching acts of legislation in our time. Millions of people who have been denied the right to work and live their lives to the fullest will now have that right. Millions of dollars will be spent to comply with this Act and give those people that right, as our constitution gives each of us the equal right to "life, liberty, and the pursuit of happiness."

CAVEAT: Become familiar with the ADA and consult or recommend consulting with qualified experts and professionals for understanding and interpreting the law and for help in compliance with the law. Make "a good faith effort" to comply with ADA and keep an accurate record of these efforts for future reference.

Scope of Title III

The antidiscrimination and the removal of barrier requirements of the ADA applies to "places of public accommodations," and the accessibility requirements of the ADA with respect to new construction and alterations applied to public accommodations and "commercial facilities."

"Places of public accommodations" encompasses 12 categories of retail and service businesses, including places of lodging; food and drink establishments; places of exhibitionary entertainment; places of public gathering; sales and rental establishments; services establishments such as law firms, accounting firms, and banks; public transportation stations; places of public display or collection; places of recreation; educational facilities; social service center establishments; and exercise clubs. It is presumed that this definition includes brokerage offices, even if they are located in private homes.

"Commercial facility" is defined as a facility: (1) whose operations affect commerce; (2) that is intended for nonresidential use; and (3) that is not a facility expressly exempted from coverage under the Fair Housing Act of 1968.

The ADA contains a broad prohibition affecting the public accommodations and discriminating against those with disabilities by denying them the full and equal enjoyment of goods, services, facilities, privileges, advantages, and the accommodations of any place of public accommodation. Facilities need to be usable by those with disabilities.

New Construction

All new construction that became available for occupancy after January 23, 1993 must meet new structural requirements for disability access. The Act deals only with construction that becomes available for "first occupancy." Therefore, the Department of Justice regulations state that the projects for which a completed building permit application was certified as received by the appropriate government entity before January 26, 1992 will fall outside the Act. If a building permit was issued after January 26, 1992 but has a certificate of occupancy before January 26, 1993, it falls outside the Act's requirements. The new construction requirements apply to all commercial facilities.

Special barrier removal requirements came into effect on January 26, 1992 and apply only to facilities that are "places of public accommodations" as defined under the Act. The Act requires removal of architectural and communication barriers that are structural in nature, where such removal is readily achievable (easily accomplishable and able to be carried out without much difficulty or expense). Barrier removal would include installing ramps and curb cuts in sidewalks and entrances, repositioning shelving, rearranging tables and chairs, repositioning telephones, adding raised markings on elevator control buttons, installing flashing alarm lights, widening doors, eliminating turnstiles, providing for alternate paths of travel, and so on.

Alterations

All commercial facilities must also be accessible to the maximum extent feasible whenever alterations are being performed on the facility. Alteration is defined as any change that affects the feasibility of a facility. If the alterations are made to a lobby or work area of the public accommodation, an accessible path of travel to the altered area and to the bathrooms, telephones, and drinking fountains serving that area, must be made accessible to the extent that the added accessibility costs are not disproportionate to the overall cost of the original alteration. Disproportionate cost is defined for the purposes of the Act as cost that exceeds 20 percent of the original alteration. The cost of alteration means all costs and renovating in particular proportion to the facility in a three-year period.

Other Modifications

The Act requires modifications to procedures so that the disabled individuals are not excluded from regular programs. Places of public accommodations must make reasonable modifications to the policies and procedures in order to accommodate individuals with disabilities and not create restrictions that tend to screen out individuals with disabilities, such as requiring a person to produce a drivers' license or not allowing more than one person in a clothes changing area when a disabled person needs the assistance of another.

The Act also requires auxiliary aids and services to ensure effective communication with individuals with hearing, vision, or speech impairments. These requirements would include interpreters, listening headsets, television closed caption decoders, telecommunication devices for the deaf, video tech displays, Braille materials, and large-print materials.

Defenses and Exclusions

There are several defenses and exclusions available under the Act, but most are extremely narrow in scope. They include:

- **Threat to Health or Safety**

  Refusing to serve a disabled person or offer equipment, goods, and services if such individual poses a direct threat to the health or safety of others (amusement park rides, rafting exhibitions, or difficult swimming maneuvers).

- **Private Clubs**

  Private clubs are excluded under Section 307 of the Act. A private club is defined in the ADA as being in accordance with Title II of the 1964 Civil Rights Act.

- **Religious Organizations**

  Religious organizations are also exempt even if it is a church that operates a day care center, nursing home, or private school.

- **Not Readily Achievable**

  Barrier removal is not required of the public accommodations if it is not readily achievable. "Readily achievable" means easily accomplishable and able to be carried out without much difficulty or expense.

■ **Structural Impracticality**

Structural impracticality is a defense if the circumstances are such that incorporating excessive disability features into the structure would destroy the structural integrity of the facility.

■ **Technical Infeasability**

Technical infeasibility is something that has little likelihood of being accomplished because of existing structural conditions that would require removing or altering a load-bearing member, which is a structural frame.

■ **Residential Structures**

Residential structures are normally not included in the Act unless they accommodate the public, and then would fall under the public accommodation portion of the statute. Similarly, owner-occupied boarding houses or bed and breakfast establishments are also not covered by the Act if they have five rooms or less.

■ **Asbestos Removal**

Asbestos removal projects do not trigger the "alterations" requirements under the Act.

■ **Historic Structures**

Qualified historic structures need not comply with the requirements of the Act if compliance would "threaten or destroy the historic significance of the building or facility."

In general, the ADA imposes the plans and building compliance obligations on the building owner, rather than the tenant or manager. It may not exclude the agent from liability if he or she is negligent in securing the owner's compliance or fails to inform the owner of the building's noncompliance. Many landlords' leases put all compliance expenses required by federal, state, or local law to be borne by the tenant. In that case, it is presumed that the landlord could pass the cost on to the tenant.

The Department of Justice has suggested different formulas or standards for allocation of cost between landlords and tenants but received comments criticizing arbitrary standards. However, the Department has indicated that the time remaining on the lease should not be a factor in the allocation of responsibility, but that the term of the lease is irrelevant in determining what is readily achievable for the tenant. It may be helpful to address the issue in the "compliance with laws" provision of the leases, particularly in situations where the building's occupancy is such that only one or two tenants may be responsible for complying with the ADA, while other tenant's may be exempt.

Another issue is foreclosure. In the event a lender is going to foreclose on an office building, the office building may not be a structure required to be in compliance with the ADA prior to foreclosure. After foreclosure, however, when the building becomes part of the lender's portfolio, it may become a place of public accommodations, and the cost of barrier removal will fall on the lender because of the building's change in use or ownership. It may be a wise move for lenders to do an ADA audit of the building, similar to a toxic waste or environmental site assessment, prior to foreclosure.

Enforcement

Both the Department of Justice and private individuals may maintain a cause of action to enforce Title III against commercial building owners. The Department may seek monetary damages or injunctive relief, but private individuals are entitled only to seek injunctive relief under the statute. Apparently a tort claim may create a cause of action for monetary damages.

DEPARTMENT OF JUSTICE ENFORCEMENT

In order to enforce the provisions of ADA, the Department of Justice must enforce the provisions of Title III by establishing a pattern of practice of discrimination, failure to comply, or by establishing "that any person, or a group of persons, has been denied any of the rights granted by Title III, and that such denial raises an issue of general public importance."

The civil penalties imposed are $50,000 for the first violation and $100,000 for each subsequent violation. The Attorney General may also seek monetary damages on behalf of aggrieved individuals. Any individual who believes that he or she has been subjected to discrimination prohibited by the ADA can request the Department of Justice to investigate.

PRIVATE CAUSE OF ACTION

Under 36.501, an individual has a right to bring a suit for injunctive relief if that individual has reasonable grounds for believing that he or she is about to be or has been subjected to discrimination. The private suit can be brought in court without pursuing the administrative remedies, and the individual may even be entitled to a court appointed attorney "if the court deems such appointment to be just under the circumstances."

ADA: Texas Regulations

Similar to Texas's adoption of fair housing legislation under the Texas Fair Housing Act, the Texas Department of Licensing and Regulation has adopted regulations of the administration and enforcement of the Architectural Barriers Act. The **Architectural Barriers Act** requires that all buildings qualifying as "public accommodations" and buildings funded by government funds or leased to government agencies must comply with the accessibility requirements of that Act.

The Act requires those owners, architects, and engineers to submit construction plans and specifications in order to confirm compliance with the technical accessibility standards. The 1993 amendments to the Act made it applicable to virtually all commercial buildings or facilities with a cost of $50,000.00 or more that are constructed or substantially renovated, modified, or altered on or after September 1, 1993. These buildings must be registered with the Department of Licensing and Regulation; and the construction documents must be submitted for compliance review prior to the start of the work.

The new regulations went into effect on June 1, 1994 and are found under Volume 16 of the Texas Administrative Code.

FAIR HOUSING

The federal legislation has been liberally applied to virtually all areas of discrimination—race, color, creed, national origin, alienage, sex, marital status, age, familial status, and handicapped status. The theories supporting these federal laws are applied differently though, depending on the source of the law and enforcement of the applicable statute. Let's review these theories in greater detail.

Constitutional Impact on Ownership of Real Property

The most fundamental rights in real property are obtained in the U.S. Constitution. These rights are so firmly established and so broadly affect real estate that they deserve discussion at the outset. The Declaration of Independence declared that all men are created equal and set the stage for the attitude of the government, which we enjoy in the United States. It was with this forethought that our founders wrote the United States Constitution, which instilled in all citizens, certain inalienable rights of which they can never be deprived. As far as real property ownership is concerned, the most significant of these rights are stated in the Fifth, Thirteenth, and Fourteenth Amendments to the Constitution.

The Fifth Amendment clearly states that no person shall be deprived of life, liberty, or property without due process of law. It was from this fundamental statement that we developed the inherent right that nobody can have their property taken from them without court proceedings. This concept has been expanded over the last 25 years or so to include the prohibition of certain types of discrimination, creating certain "protected classes" of people who may not be discriminated against.

To date, the types of discrimination that have been deemed suspect by the United States Supreme Court have included discrimination on the basis of race, color, religion, national origin, or alienage. It is logical in that citizens of the United States cannot alter their race, color, national origin, or alienage and are entitled to practice the religion of their choice. Therefore, the courts have established very strict constitutional prohibitions to eliminate these types of discrimination for any citizen in the United States. It should be emphasized that there is no constitutional prohibition of discrimination on the basis of sex, age, handicap, or marital status.

One of the most significant areas of litigation has been based on racial discrimination. This applies to all federal activity through the Fifth Amendment, and to state and individual actions through enforcement of interpretation of the Thirteenth and Fourteenth Amendments of the U.S. Constitution.

The Thirteenth Amendment to the United States Constitution prohibits slavery and involuntary servitude. This amendment formed the basis for the most significant landmark case on discrimination, *Jones v. Alfred H. Mayer Company*. That case basically held that any form of discrimination, even by individuals, creates a "badge of slavery," which in turn results in the violation of the Thirteenth Amendment. The Supreme Court stated that in enforcing the Civil Rights Act of 1866, Congress is empowered under the Thirteenth Amendment to secure to all citizens the right to buy whatever a "white man" can buy and the right to live wherever a "white man" can live. The Court further stated, "If Congress cannot say that being a free man means at least this much, then the Thirteenth Amendment was a promise the Nation cannot keep." This case effectively prohibits discrimination of all types and is applicable to real estate transactions.

The Fourteenth Amendment prohibits any state (as distinguished from the federal government) from depriving a person of life, liberty, or property without due process of law, and prohibits any state from denying any person within its jurisdiction the equal protection of the laws. The significant case in interpreting the Fourteenth Amendment as it applies to the states was *Shelley v. Kraemer*, 344 U.S. 1 (1948). In this Supreme Court case, some white property owners were attempting to enforce a deed restriction, which required that all property owners must be Caucasian. The state courts granted the relief sought. The Supreme Court, however, reversed the case. It stated that the action of state courts in imposing penalties deprived parties of other substantive rights without providing adequate notice. The opportunity to defend has long been regarded as a denial of due process of law as guaranteed by the Fourteenth Amendment. The Court stated that equality and the enjoyment of property rights was regarded by the framers of the Fourteenth Amendment as an essential precondition to realization of other basic civil rights and liberties, which the Fourteenth Amendment was intended to guarantee. Therefore, it was concluded that the equal protection clause of the Fourteenth Amendment should prohibit the judicial enforcement by state courts of restrictive covenants based on race or color.

Fair Housing Laws

This is becoming a more difficult concept to discuss. The original Fair Housing statutes, which were meant to provide access to housing for all Americans, is now taking on a different focus to some federal agencies. They are using the Fair Housing statutes as a sword rather than a shield; to punish rather than protect. In addition, society has changed since the laws were initially passed in 1968.

In addition to the constitutional issues, there are two major federal laws that prohibit discrimination in housing. The first is the Civil Rights Act of 1866. It states that "All citizens of the United States shall have the same right in every State and Territory, as is enjoyed by the white citizens thereof to inherit, purchase, lease, sell, hold, and convey real and personal property." In 1968, the Supreme Court affirmed that the 1866 Act prohibits all racial discrimination, private as well as public, in the sale of real property. The second major federal law is the Fair Housing Law, officially known as Title VIII of the Civil Rights Act of 1968, as amended. This law makes it illegal to discriminate on the basis of race, color, religion, sex, national origin, physical disability, or familial status in connection with the sale or rental of housing and any vacant land offered for residential construction or use.

New amendments to the Civil Rights Act of 1968 became effective on March 12, 1989. They expanded the Civil Rights Act of 1968 to provide for housing for the handicapped as well as people with children under the age of 18. The Civil Rights Act now provides protection for any form of discrimination based on race, color, religion, national origin, sex, familial status, or handicapped status. These are referred to as **"protected classes."** As set out in one case, discussed later, familial status and handicapped status are not as easy to identify as the other protected classes. The new law's application is becoming very broad and needs to be discussed in more detail.

"HANDICAPPED"

The law defines "handicapped" as:

- having a physical or mental impairment that substantially limits one or more major life activities.
- having a record of having such an impairment.
- being regarded as having such an impairment.

The Act apparently includes recovered mental patients as well as those who are presently suffering from a mental handicap.

The full extent of how the discrimination against handicapped will affect us is really not known.

It is surely going to change our attitude about certain restrictions. It is assumed, for instance, that a blind person could live with a guide dog in a housing project that prohibits pets. The handicapped are also allowed to make reasonable modifications to existing units, as long as it is at the handicapped's expense. The handicapped renter must also restore the unit to its original use upon termination of occupancy. The law also makes it unlawful for a landlord or owner to refuse to make reasonable accommodations, rules, policies, practices, or services when it is necessary to afford a handicapped person an equal opportunity to use and enjoy the dwelling. In addition, all new multifamily dwellings with four or more units must be constructed to allow access and use by handicapped persons. If the building has no elevators, only first floor units are covered by this provision. Doors and hallways in the buildings must be wide enough to accommodate wheelchairs. Light switches and other controls must be in convenient locations. Most rooms and spaces must be on an accessible route, and special accommodations such as grab bars in the bathrooms must be provided.

There are some exceptions under the handicapped person provision. The term "handicapped," for instance, does not include current illegal use of or addiction to a controlled substance. Nor does handicapped status include any person whose tenancy imposes a direct threat to the health, safety, and property of others. However, there are no guidelines as to how a licensee, apartment manager, or homeowner's association can determine either of these two exceptions. Since there are no clear guidelines, all licensees are advised to treat all people they perceive to have a mental or physical handicap as members of a protected class of individuals, which may not under any circumstances be discriminated against.

FAMILIAL STATUS

Familial status is defined as one or more individuals (who have not obtained the age of 18 years) being domiciled with a parent or another person having legal custody of such individual or individuals or the designee of such parent or other person having such custody, with the written permission of such parent or other person. These protections also apply to any person who is pregnant or is in the process of securing legal custody of any individual who has not obtained the age of 18 years.

The most significant effect of this amendment is that all homeowner association property, apartment projects, and condominiums now must have facilities adapted for children and cannot discriminate against anyone on the basis of familial status when leasing, selling, or renting property.

There are specific exemptions to this portion of the Act also. A building can qualify for an exemption if: (1) it provides housing under the state or federal program that the Secretary of Housing and Urban Development determines is specifically designed and operated to assist elderly persons; (2) it provides housing intended for, and is generally occupied only by, persons 62 years of age or older; or (3) it provides housing generally intended and operated for at least one person 55 years of age or older per unit and meets certain regulations that will be adopted by the Secretary of Housing and Urban Development.

The penalties for violation of the Act are severe. The first violation of the Act results in a fine of not more than $50,000, and for subsequent violations, a fine of not more than $100,000. The fines are in addition to other civil damages, potential injunctions, reasonable attorney's fees, and costs.

Amendments to the Fair Housing Law have a significant impact for all licensees attempting to sell, list, lease, or rent real estate. It is unlawful to refuse to sell or rent or to refuse to negotiate the sale or rental of any property based on familial status or handicapped status. Any printing and advertising cannot make any reference to preference based on handicapped or familial status. As stated previously, the landlord cannot deny the right of a handicapped tenant to make any changes in the physical structure of the building provided that the tenant agrees to reinstate the building back to its original form when he or she leaves.

It is safe to say that there are a lot of fact situations and circumstances that will occur that have not been specifically addressed by the statute. It is critically important that licensees recognize these two new prohibitions against discrimination and deem them just as serious violations of an individual's civil rights as are violations of the more traditional theories of race, color, religion, national origin, and sex.

Specifically, what do these two federal statutes prohibit, and what do they allow? The 1968 Fair Housing Law provides protection against the following acts if they discriminate against one or more of the protected classes:

- Refusing to sell or rent to, deal or negotiate with any person.
- Discriminating in the terms or conditions for buying or renting housing.
- Discriminating by advertising that housing is available only to persons of a certain race, color, religion, sex, or national origin, those who are not handicapped, or adults only.
- Denying that housing is available for inspection, sale, or rent when it really is available.
- Denying or making different terms or conditions for home loans by commercial lenders.
- Denying to anyone the use of or participation in any real estate services, such as brokers' organizations, multiple listing services, or other facilities related to the selling or renting of housing.
- Steering or blockbusting.

STEERING

Steering is the practice of directing or channeling home seekers to or from particular neighborhoods based on race, color, religion, sex, national origin, nonhandicapped, or adult-only housing. Steering includes efforts to exclude minority members from one area of a city as well as to direct them to minority or changing areas. Examples include showing only certain neighborhoods, slanting property descriptions, and downgrading neighborhoods. Steering is often subtle, sometimes no more than a word, phrase, or facial expression.

Nonetheless, steering accounts for the bulk of the complaints filed against real estate licensees under the Fair Housing Act.

BLOCKBUSTING

Blockbusting is the illegal practice of inducing panic selling in a neighborhood for financial gain. Blockbusting typically starts when one person induces another to sell his or her property cheaply by stating that an impending change in the racial or religious composition of the neighborhood will cause property values to fall, school quality to decline, and crime to increase. The first home thus acquired is sold (at a mark-up) to a minority member. This event is used to reinforce fears that the neighborhood is indeed changing. The process quickly snowballs as residents panic and sell at progressively lower prices. The homes are then resold at higher prices to incoming residents.

Note that blockbusting is not limited to fears over people moving into a neighborhood. In a Virginia case, a real estate firm attempted to gain listings in a certain neighborhood by playing upon residents' fears regarding an upcoming expressway project.

Are there different rules for buyer's brokers?

Fair Housing; Brokers; Duty to Disclose Diversity

In *Hannah v. Sibcy Cline Realtors*, 769 N.E.2d 876 (Ohio Ct. App. 2001), the Court was asked to determine whether a real estate agent or a broker has the fiduciary duty to: (1) inform a client whether a neighborhood or community is ethnically diverse; or (2) direct the client to sources to provide ethnic diversity information. The Hannahs had three school-age sons and were considering moving their family from Virginia to Cincinnati, Ohio. They contacted Sibcy Cline, a real estate brokerage company, explaining that they wanted a five-bedroom house in move-in condition and further specified that the house be located in an excellent school district in an ethnically diverse neighborhood. The broker sent the Hannahs a relocation packet that contained a guidebook, a map, and general brochures. While looking at prospective homes, the Hannahs constantly asked the broker if the areas in which the houses were located were ethnically diverse. The broker told them that she could not give them that information. She did, however, imply that a neighborhood was diverse by stating that it "fit the Hannahs' criteria." The Hannahs asked where they could get information concerning ethnic diversity in schools and communities and asked what organization existed that the Hannahs could contact regarding ethnic diversity neighborhoods. The Hannahs never received the requested information from the broker. The Hannahs contacted six schools using the telephone numbers supplied by the guidebooks received from the broker, and asked the person she contacted at school whether or not the school is racially diverse, stating that they did not want their child to be the only African-American in his class, and also contacted a children's advocacy group in local N.A.A.C.P. and the Urban

League, but did not receive any information about ethnic diversity. The Hannahs ultimately signed a contract in Milford. Mrs. Hannah contacted the principal at the school, who told her the school was ethnically diverse. The Hannahs moved into the neighborhood, they were "uncomfortable," and one of their sons was the only African-American child in the fourth grade. All three of their sons were called derogatory names and were taunted and hit both at school and on the bus on a regular basis.

The broker had confirmed that she told the Hannahs that she was precluded from disclosing racial diversity information concerning neighborhoods. She further stated that she directed Mrs. Hannah to the schools for information and provided the Hannahs with a copy of the Cincinnati Magazine School Guide, which contained diversity statistics regarding schools with the relocation packet she sent them.

The trial court ruled that the Hannahs had failed to demonstrate that there was a duty for a real estate agent to inform the client whether a neighborhood was ethnically diverse or to direct the client to resources concerning this information. The Hannahs appealed. The appeals court noted that a real estate agent was normally instructed not to discuss the racial composition or diversity of an area. The reason for this cautious attitude is that such comments could be misconstrued so as to result in claims that an agent had violated the Fair Housing Act. The Court noted that:

"Nowhere have we found that an agent or broker has the fiduciary duty to disclose such information. In fact, our reading has convinced us that, in order to avoid claims of unlawful steering in violation of the Fair Housing Act, it would not be in the best interests of an agent or broker to do so."

The Court further noted that:

"Imposing a duty on real estate agents or brokers to give information about the ethnic makeup of a neighborhood, even for benign purposes such as those here, would prove detrimental to the goal of fair housing."

In its conclusion, the Court noted that it was a court of law and its ability is limited to correcting legal wrongs, not social wrongs.

Liability for Sponsoring Brokers

In *Holley v. Meyer,* 386 F.3d 1248 (2004) (9th Cir. 10/26/04), the case originated in a claim by a biracial couple and a builder that a real estate agent working for Triad Realty committed violations of the Federal Fair Housing Act in refusing to submit the buyers' offer to the builder for racially discriminatory reasons. Triad was owned by Meyer, who was also the designated supervising broker (known in California speak as the "designated officer") for the agency.

In *Meyer v. Holley,* 537 U.S. 280 (2003), the Supreme Court reversed and vacated a prior Ninth Circuit decision in this case and held, contrary to the Ninth

Circuit's view, that liability would not lie against the owner/broker for the agent's actions on the basis that the duty to obey laws relating to racial discrimination under the FHA is nondelegable. The Supreme Court also found that Meyer could not be held liable as the designated officer/broker of Triad based solely on his duty to control the agent. The Supreme Court remanded, however, for further discussion of issues of California law relating to vicarious liability and other liability theories. The Ninth Circuit here serves up a whole passel of such additional theories and remands for further proceedings at the district court level to evaluate the facts relating to such theories.

With a little innovative thinking on rehearing, the Ninth Circuit panel first determined that the plaintiffs preserved the claim that Meyer was liable under traditional state law vicarious liability theories even though they had pressed their original appeal based upon HUD regulations.

First, the Court recognized liability might lie on the basis of negligent supervision. Certainly, if Meyer in fact had a duty to supervise and was not supervising while he was pursuing other business and leaving the office unsupervised by a properly licensed broker, this would appear to be a viable claim.

Another theory of liability posed by the court is the notion that Meyer would be liable for the acts of Triad's employees because he was the owner of Triad. Although Triad was a corporation, which would preclude individual liability, the Court suggests that California law would recognize certain factors in this case that would support "piercing the corporate veil" to justify disregarding the employer's corporate status and impose liability directly on the corporate owner.

Here, the Court states, the allegations in the complaint suggested that Meyer had "wide ranging control" of Triad as its owner, president and designated officer/supervising broker. The Court further notes that Meyer did not always punctiliously observe corporate niceties. For instance, Meyer paid Triad's taxes pursuant to his own tax ID number instead of under Triad's. Further, the corporation was thinly capitalized. That was enough for the Court to remand for a determination on the issue of "piercing the corporate veil" and sticking Meyer with liability for all sales associate acts in violation of the Fair Housing Act.

The Supreme Court is apparently telling us that corporate liability will be upheld; however, if a corporate officer, director, shareholder, or supervisor is complicit in any misconduct, there will be vicarious liability for that supervisor as well as for the corporation. It will not, however, hold innocent officers, directors, and shareholders personally liable for misconduct of an employee.

Housing Covered by the 1968 Fair Housing Law

The 1968 Fair Housing Law applies to the following types of housing:

- Single-family houses owned by private individuals when (1) a real estate broker or other person in the business of selling or renting dwellings is used and/or (2) discriminatory advertising is used;

- Single-family houses not owned by private individuals.
- Single-family houses owned by a private individual who owns more than three such houses or who, in any two-year period, sells more than one in which the individual was not the most recent resident.
- Multifamily dwellings of five or more units.
- Multifamily dwellings containing four or fewer units, if the owner does not reside in one of the units.

Acts Not Prohibited by the 1968 Fair Housing Law

Not covered by the 1968 Fair Housing Law are the sale or rental of single-family houses owned by a private individual who owns three or fewer such single-family houses if (1) a broker is not used, (2) discriminatory advertising is not used, and (3) no more than one house in which the owner was not the most recent resident is sold during any two-year period. Not covered by the 1968 Act are rentals of rooms or units in owner-occupied multidwellings for two to four families, if discriminatory advertising is not used. The Act also does not cover the sale, rental, or occupancy of dwellings that a religious organization owns or operates for other than a commercial purpose to persons of the same religion, if membership in that religion is not restricted on account of race, color, or national origin. It also does not cover the rental or occupancy of lodgings that a private club owns or operates for its members for other than a commercial purpose. Housing for the elderly may also allow discrimination in not permitting children or young adult occupants in the development or building, provided that the housing is primarily intended for the elderly, has minimum age requirements (55 or 62), and meets certain HUD guidelines.

Note, however, that the previously listed acts not prohibited by the 1968 Fair Housing Law are prohibited by the 1866 Civil Rights Act when discrimination based on race occurs in connection with such acts.

Fair Housing Enforcement

There are three ways that adherence to the 1968 Act can be enforced by someone who feels discriminated against. The first is to file a written complaint with the Department of Housing and Urban Development in Washington, D.C. The second is to file court action directly in a U.S. district court or state or local court. The third is to file a complaint with the U.S. Attorney General. If a complaint is filed with HUD, HUD may investigate to see if the law has been broken; may attempt to resolve the problem by conference, conciliation, or persuasion; may refer the matter to a state or local fair housing authority; or may recommend that the complaint be filed in court. A person seeking enforcement of the 1866 Act must file a suit in a federal court.

No matter which route is taken, the burden of proving illegal discrimination under the 1968 Act is the responsibility of the person filing the complaint. If successful, the following remedies are available: (1) an injunction to stop the sale or rental of the property to someone else, thus making it available to the complainant; (2) money for actual damages caused by the discrimination; (3) punitive damages; and (4) court costs. There are also criminal penalties for those who coerce, intimidate, threaten, or interfere with a person's buying, renting, or selling of housing.

Agent's Duties

A real estate agent's duties are to uphold the 1968 Fair Housing Law and the 1866 Civil Rights Act. If a property owner asks an agent to discriminate, the agent must refuse to accept the listing and the same applies to make a similar request. An agent is in violation of fair housing laws by giving a minority buyer or seller less than favorable treatment or by ignoring minorities or referring them to an agent of the same minority. Violation also occurs when an agent fails to use best efforts or does not submit an offer because of race, color, religion, sex, national origin, physical handicap, or occupancy by children. A broker is required to display the Fair Housing Emblem.

It needs to be emphasized that the duties of a property owner in fair housing cases do not pass to the real estate agent. If the agent engages in conduct that violates the Fair Housing Act, the owner is also liable, even when the agent acts outside the scope of authority and against the owner's explicit instructions. *Walker v. Crigler*, 976 F.2d 900 (4th Cir. 1992). The agent's negligence or intentional acts create liability for the owner!

Testers

From time to time fair housing testers may approach a licensee. These are individuals or organizations that respond to advertising and visit real estate offices to test for compliance with fair housing laws and ADA compliance. The tester does not announce himself or herself as such or ask if the office follows fair housing practices. Rather, the tester plays the role of a person or a couple looking for housing to buy or rent and observes whether fair housing laws are being followed. If not followed, the tester lodges a complaint with the appropriate fair housing agency.

Texas Fair Housing Law

In 1989, Texas passed the Texas Fair Housing Act, which, in most respects, parallels the Federal Fair Housing Law of 1968. The statute creates a Commission on Human Rights, which is authorized to receive, investigate, and seek to conciliate any active complaints violating the Texas Fair Housing Act. The Commission must investigate discriminatory housing practices if the complaints filed are: (1) in writing, (2) under oath, and (3) in the form prescribed by the Commission, not later than one year after the discriminatory housing practice has occurred or terminated, whichever is later. On the filing of a complaint, the Commission shall give the aggrieved person notice that the complaint has been received, and notify the respondent of the alleged discriminatory housing practice. The respondent may then file an answer, which must also be: (1) in writing, (2) under oath, and (3) in the form prescribed by the Commission. The Commission is then required to investigate the complaint and encourage conciliation, if possible. If the Commission concludes that prompt judicial action is necessary, it shall file an investigative report to the Attorney General, who shall file an action on behalf of the aggrieved person in district court and seek relief for which the alleged discriminatory housing practice has occurred.

The Texas statute may be enforced by a private person, who may also file a civil action in district court not later than the second year after the occurrence or the termination of an alleged discriminatory housing practice, or the breach of a conciliation agreement entered into under the Texas Fair Housing Act, whichever occurs last, or to obtain relief to the breach of discriminatory housing practice. If the court finds that the discriminatory practice has occurred, or is about to occur, the court may award to the plaintiff actual and punitive damages, reasonable attorney's fees and court costs, and any permanent or temporary injunction.

The Texas Fair Housing Act also provides a fair housing fund for the sole purpose of administering the Act.

The Texas Fair Housing Act has particular significance because it has been certified by HUD as being substantially equivalent to the Federal Fair Housing Act; therefore, Texans can elect to have the complaint decided before a state district court instead of federal district court.

You should note that the Texas Real Estate License Act prohibits discrimination (see Section 1101.652(b)(32)) as do the rules of the Texas Real Estate Commission (note Section 531.19). The TREC rules are very specific.

> "No real estate licensee shall inquire about, respond to, or facilitate inquiries about, or make a disclosure which indicates or is intended to indicate any preference, limitation or discrimination based on the following: race, color, religion, sex, national origin, ancestors, famial status, or handicap of an owner, previous or current occupant, potential purchaser, lessor, or potential lessee of real property. For the purpose of this section, handicap includes a person who had, may have had, has, or may have AIDS, HIV-related illnesses, or HIV infection as defined by the Centers for Disease Control of the United States Public Health Service."

It should also be noted that in addition to federal and state laws, a city might have its own fair housing law.

Fair Housing Cases

We all know the basics. Court cases, however, often confuse the issue. Statutes are not always well written, which produces unanticipated results. The issue may be further complicated for two other reasons: (1) the original statutes were passed 40 years ago in a very different societal environment (they may be antiquated); and (2) the concepts of "handicap" and "familial status" do not have clear definitions.

SPECIAL SALES EFFORTS

Special efforts to attract buyers, however, apparently do not fall within the prohibition. In *South-Suburban Housing Center v. Greater South-Suburban Board of Realtors*, 935 F.2d 868 (7th Cir. 1991), a broker agreed to make special efforts to attract white buyers in a predominately black neighborhood. The Seventh Circuit held that this was no violation of the Fair Housing Act because the race-conscious market merely provided additional information to white home buyers concerning the property they might not ordinarily know about or consider, and involved no lessening of efforts to attract black home buyers.

STEERING

Steering, discussed previously, is the practice of directing prospective home buyers interested in equivalent properties to different areas according to their race, color, religion, national origin, sex, handicap, or familial status. The conduct also applies to rental situations. The nature of the conduct of real estate agents makes them more likely defendants than almost any other party to a real estate transaction. There is a practice called "benign steering" that involves the intentional steering or restricting of housing for the express purpose of fostering integration rather than discrimination. A conflict was noted in the case of *Starrett City Associates v. United States*, 488 U.S. 946, 109 S. Ct. 376 (1988). The Second Circuit noted that the quotas promote the Fair Housing Act Immigration Policy, but they contravene the antidiscrimination policy. The result is to promote "immigration maintenance," which are plans implemented to prevent "tipping." Tipping is the result when a neighborhood population reaches a certain level of minority concentration, causing the majority to abandon the neighborhood.

DISCRIMINATION BASED ON FAMILIAL STATUS

The Act prohibits discrimination on the basis of familial status, defined as a pregnant woman, a minor being domiciled with a parent, a person having legal custody of the minor, or the designee of such parent or legal custodian. In *Gorski v. Troy*, 929 F.2d 1173 (7th Cir. 1991), the Court upheld a foster parent's right as a designee of a child's legal custodian, even though the parent and child had not yet achieved familial status. This type of discrimination would include a policy of renting one-bedroom apartments to only single persons, as it indicates an intent to discriminate against people with children. *U.S. v. Badgett*, 976 F.2d 1176 (8th Cir. 1992). A policy against unrelated persons living together may not be prohibited. One case has held that this was a discrimination based on conduct, not familial status. *Dane County v. Norman*, 497 N.W.2d 714 (Wis. 1993).

In *Soules v. United States Department of Housing and Urban Development*, 967 F.2d 817 (2nd Cir. 1992), a REALTOR® who listed, managed, and rented properties listed one-half of a two-family dwelling in Buffalo, New York. An elderly couple with poor eyesight occupied the other part of the dwelling. The owner of the property made an effort to tell the REALTOR® to find a lessee who could live harmoniously with the elderly couple.

When a mother inquired about available housing, the REALTOR® responded with the question "How old is your child?" The agent was trying to determine whether a child would be noisy and not live harmoniously with the elderly neighbor. The plaintiff (Soules) was apparently "unpleasant" and she "challenged" the REALTOR® on the phone and had a "very bad attitude" in response to the questioning by the REALTOR®. The plaintiff then arranged for testers to test the REALTOR®, and at least one tester was shown the property even though the tester had children. The Court noted that the Fair Housing Act Amendments of 1988 were "not intended to place a straightjacket on landlords or unnecessarily to chill their speech," and that the administrative law judge found legitimate, nondiscriminatory reasons for not renting the Byrd apartment to Soules, partially because of Soules's negative and combative attitude. The Court further found that there are situations in which it is legitimate to inquire about the number of individuals interested in occupying an apartment and their ages. Local zoning regulations or local health laws may constitute valid reasons. If there are conditions of the neighborhood known to be either ideally suited to or inherently dangerous to occupants of a family with children, an inquiry about the ages of the family members may be permitted. The Court noted that standing alone, an inquiry into whether a prospective tenant has a child does not constitute a Fair Housing Act violation.

What does a real estate agent do if the premises are inherently unsafe for children? There are fact situations that exist where a house may have a pool with no guard rail, stairs, or lofts that may create an unusual danger for smaller children. This creates insurance problems and may create a high potential for lawsuits. This was addressed in *United States v. Grishman*, 818 F. Supp. 21 (D. Me. 1993), where the Court held that the owner of the house violated the familial status provisions of the Fair Housing Act when he refused to rent the house to a family with young children because the home had a deck ten feet above the ground. The Court held that the concerns of safety for children were a concern for parents not that of a landlord. Given the high potential for liability of the landlords, one wonders whether the same result would have been achieved had it been a personal injury suit by a tenant.

HANDICAPPED STATUS

The 1988 amendments make it unlawful to discriminate on the basis of the sale or rental of a dwelling to: (1) any buyer or renter based on the handicap of the renter or buyer; (2) a person who lives with or intends to live with the handicapped renter or buyer; or (3) any person associated with the handicapped renter or buyer. There is also now a significant authority that an AIDS patient is handicapped, and refusal to issue a special use permit for AIDS patients violates the Fair Housing Act. *Baxter v. City of Bellville*, 720 F. Supp. 720 (S.D. ILL. 1989). Drug rehabilitation and mental handicaps have also been addressed.

In *United States v. Southern Management Corporation*, 955 F.2d 914, the Court considered the issue of whether a person in the reentry phase of a drug rehabilitation program was "handicapped." The Court noted that the terms "familial status" and "handicapped" have meaning less concrete than race, color, religion, sex, or national origin, and require further definition. Citing the *School Board of Nassau County v. Arline*, 480 U.S. 273 (1987), the Court noted that the inability to obtain an apartment is on a par with the inability to obtain a job and therefore creates an impairment. The Court compared the existing situation to refuse to rent housing to a similar situation under a drug rehabilitation program under the Rehabilitation Act, in which Congress has specifically referred to mere participation in a drug rehabilitation program (coupled with nonuse) as an adequate basis for inclusion in the definition of handicapped. The Court held that the Fair Housing Act does per se exclude from its coverage every person who would be considered a drug addict. It held that Congress intended to recognize that addiction is a disease a person may recover from through rehabilitation and that an individual who makes the effort to recover should not be subject to housing discrimination based on society's accumulated fears and prejudices associated with drug addiction. Therefore, while drug addicts are apparently exempt from the protection of the Fair Housing Act, recovering drug addicts are not.

In *City of Edmonds v. Oxford House, Inc.*, 1995 W.L. 283468 (1995), recovering alcoholics and drug addicts sought an injunction to prohibit Edmonds from enforcing zoning and building ordinances to deny two houses for recovering alcoholics and drug addicts from operating within the city's single-family residence zoning district. The City of Edmonds had an ordinance that provided for a single-family residential zoning provision, which defines "family" as one or more persons occupying a single-dwelling unit, provided that unless all members are related by blood, marriage, or adoption, no such family shall contain over five persons.

In this case, the United States Supreme Court resolved a conflict between the Ninth and Eleventh Circuits on the definition of family and exemptions provided under the Fair Housing Act Section 3607(b)(1).

The Court held that land use restrictions can designate districts in which only compatible uses are allowed and incompatible uses are excluded, to prevent problems caused by the "pig in the parlor instead of the barnyard situation." Maximum occupancy restrictions, on the other hand, cap the number of occupants per dwelling, typically in relation to the available floor space and the number and type of rooms. These restrictions ordinarily apply uniformly to all residents of all dwelling units. Their purpose is to protect health and safety by preventing dwelling overcrowding. The Court noted that Congress added Section 3607(b)(1) exemption for maximum occupancy restrictions at the same time it expanded the Fair Housing Act to include any amount of discrimination based on familial status, so that landlords cannot be forced to allow large families to crowd in a small housing unit.

The Court also noted that the effect of the capping wouldn't apply to siblings, parents, and grandparents that would exceed the five-person limitation. Therefore, the focus of this statute was on regulatory use, not capping. There was a vigorous dissent by Justices Thomas, Scalia, and Kennedy, who reasoned that the ordinances limiting "a group of five or fewer persons who are not related" was plain on its face, should be considered controlling under the FHA exemption, and would have upheld the district court's prohibition of the Oxford Housing Project.

In *Oxford House-C v. City of St. Louis*, 843 F. Supp. 1556 (E.D. Mo. 1994), the court held that recovering alcoholics and addicts are persons with handicaps within the meaning of 42 U.S.C.A. 3602(h) and 3604 and granted a permanent injunction enjoining the city from enforcing its zoning codes to prohibit the Oxford House development of two houses for recovering alcoholics.

The mentally retarded are also protected. In *United States v. Scott*, 788 F. Supp. 1555, the Court struck down an attempt to block the sale of a home that was going to be used for handicapped individuals. There was an allegation by the plaintiffs that the occupancy of the homes by the handicapped individual would cause depreciation in property value. The more disturbing case, however, is *Roe v. Sugar River Mills Associates*, 820 F. Supp. 636 (E. New Hampshire 1993). In this case, a tenant filed an action against the federally subsidized housing complex alleging discrimination in violation of the Fair Housing Amendments Act of 1988. The tenant was engaged in erratic behavior and threatening and harassing conduct toward other tenants. The plaintiff's conduct led to his conviction for disorderly conduct in violation of the New Hampshire statute. The landlord filed eviction proceedings. The tenant alleged that his "outburst" was the product of his mental handicap and alleged that under the Fair Housing Act, the landlord had a duty to make reasonable accommodations to afford the tenant an equal opportunity to use and enjoy the dwelling, arguing that only if he constitutes a threat to the safety of others after defendants have made a reasonable effort to accommodate his handicap may the defendant refuse to offer him continued housing. The court found that the tenant was "handicapped" under the definition of the statute, and the landlord had to reasonably accommodate the individual to minimize the risk he poses to others in the apartment project before the landlord could lawfully evict him.

In *Deep East Texas Regional Mental Health and Mental Retardation Services v. Kinnear*, 877 S.W.2d 550 (Tex. App.-Beaumont 1994), a neighboring property owner brought action for injunctive relief to prevent construction in a subdivision of a proposed community home for mentally handicapped individuals, alleging that such a home was not a "single-family residence" as required by the restrictive covenant. The court held that the term "single-family residence" in a restrictive covenant referred to architectural character of structure, not its use, and that a neighboring property owner could be sued for violation of the Fair Housing Act based on an attempt to enforce restrictive covenants to prevent mentally handicapped individuals from residing in the neighborhood.

In *Martin v. Constance*, 843 F. Supp. 1321 (E.D. Mo. 1994), developmentally disabled adults living in a state-owned and-operated group home brought action to enjoin enforcement of a restrictive covenant that would bar continued operation of the home. The neighborhood, Compton Heights, was a designated historic neighborhood and was subject to a restrictive covenant recorded in 1893. The covenant provided that "each of said lots in such building shall never be used or occupied for any purpose except for that of a private residence exclusively, nor shall any part or portion thereof ever be used or occupied except solely as a residence. . . ." When the state began looking into purchasing a certain dwelling in Compton Heights to be used as a group home for six mentally retarded/developmentally handicapped adult males and two adult supervisors, the residents sought to enforce the restrictive covenants as prohibiting the intended use. The state responded by alleging fair housing violations. The Court held that the group home would be more closely akin to a family residence than a business or boarding house with transient occupants and held in favor of the plaintiff upholding the violation of 42 U.S.C.A. 3604(f) by under both the "discriminatory intent" and the "discriminatory effect" criterias.

In *Gittleman v. Woodhaven Condominium Association, Inc.*, 972 F Supp. 894 (D.N.J. 1997), a condominium association refused to grant an exclusive parking space to a handicapped unit owner because the Master Deed stated that parking spaces were to be nonexclusive common elements owned by all unit owners as tenants in common. As such, the condominium association claimed it was forbidden from taking any action that would diminish the proportionate undivided interest in the common elements held by each unit owner, and asserted that the only way to grant a particular parking space was by a two-thirds affirmative vote of unit owners. Such a vote was taken, but the handicapped unit owner did not receive the requisite number of votes. The unit owner then filed suit for relief under the Fair Housing Amendments Act, which makes it unlawful to discriminate against any person in the provision of services or facilities on his or her dwelling because of that person's handicap. Under the Fair Housing Amendments Act, "discriminate" includes refusal to make reasonable accommodations in rules, policies, or services when they may be necessary to afford a person equal opportunity use and enjoyment of a dwelling.

The U.S. District Court agreed that the parking spaces were nonexclusive and that two-thirds approval from the rest of the unit owners was required, yet maintained that the association was not powerless, and in fact was required by the Fair Housing Amendments Act to grant an exclusive parking space. The court held that the Master Deed and By-laws of the condominium gave power to the association to regulate use of the common elements. The court then stated that any provisions of the Master Deed that violate the Fair Housing Amendments Act are unlawful and cannot be enforced, and that the association, as manager of the common elements, had an affirmative duty to ensure that the common elements were managed so as to comply with federal housing law. Accordingly, the court held that the association was bound to regulate use of the common elements so as to comply with the Fair Housing Amendments Act and to avoid enforcing provisions of the Master Deed that have a discriminatory effect. Since application of the provision at issue would violate the Fair Housing Amendments Act, the court refused to grant the association's motion for summary judgment. The court also cited case law and legislative history of the Fair Housing Amendments Act prohibiting discrimination based on the enforcement of private agreements, such as a Master Deed.

In *Jankowski Lee & Associates v. Cisneros*, 91 F.3d (7th Cir. 1996), the tenant had multiple sclerosis and requested the manager of an apartment complex to provide either an assigned space or a sufficient number of handicapped spaces. The apartment manager denied the request.

After the tenant filed a complaint with HUD, the number of handicapped spaces at each building was increased from two to four. Nevertheless, the Administrative Law Judge (ALJ) determined there was a violation of FHA and required granting the tenant his own parking space and assessed a penalty against the building manager, the corporation that owned the building, and the managing partner (petitioners) who sought review of the decision for two reasons: (1) petitioners were not aware of the extent to which the tenant's condition limited his mobility; and (2) they did not violate the law because they granted the tenant's request by increasing the number of handicapped parking spaces.

The Seventh Circuit upheld the decision of ALJ. If a landlord is skeptical of a tenant's alleged disability, it is incumbent upon the landlord to request documentation. The tenant's complaint with HUD was merely a request for a reasonable accommodation. It was a question of fact and ALJ found that the two additional handicapped spaces were not a reasonable accommodation. The court also decided that the tenant's agents and employees might hold the owners of the real estate vicariously liable for discriminatory acts.

FAMILY STATUS AND NATIONAL ORIGIN

In *Maki v. Laakko*, 88 F.3d 361 (6th Cir. 1996), the Maki family brought suit against the landlords, the Laakko family, alleging discrimination based on family status and national origin. The Makis were living in an apartment on a month-to-month basis. After several months passed, the landlord proposed a rent increase of $100 more per month. Both sides hired lawyers and all communication ceased except between the lawyers. When the tenant refused the rent increase, the landlord sent a letter terminating the tenancy. The trial court granted a summary judgment for the landlord.

The court stated that to create a prima facie in a case of housing discrimination, the plaintiff must show: (1) that he or she was a member of a protected class, (2) that the plaintiff applied for and was qualified to rent or purchase certain property or housing, (3) that the plaintiff was rejected, and (4) that the house or rental property remained available. The court noted that the testimony was uncontroverted that the landlord established that he was willing to keep the tenants, as long as they were going to pay the rent increase. The tenants were given two chances to retain the apartment, but refused the offer of a one-year lease. The tenant alleged that the rent increase constituted impermissible discrimination on the basis of family status, alleging that the landlord decided on a rent increase because the tenants had children. The tenants argued that the Fair Housing Act makes it illegal for landlords to charge additional rent on the basis of the number of persons occupying the dwellings if the "persons" are children. The tenant's lawyer (a law professor) argued explicitly that the status of children would be unprotected if the landlord can charge the same rent for two adults and one child as for three adults, because then there will have been an increase "because of" the child, even though there would have been exactly the same increase "because of" a third party. The court noted that this argument was one of first impression "because it is a claim with such breathtaking audacity that no one ever dared raise it before."

The essence of nondiscrimination is to treat persons the same, despite the alleged discriminatory condition. The court held that a rental pricing system that charges additional rent for additional occupants is a rental policy that is neutral with respect to family status. The court further noted that the landlord merely attempts to raise the rent in that apartment, which is wholly within the landlord's rights, and that the dispute was far from costless. The court stated "As a result of the current creative and artful, (though meritless) lawsuit instituted by a law professor, the Laakko's have been forced to incur at least $36,000 in legal fees. . . . Events such as this tend to bring disrepute both to a legal profession and laws originally passed to address serious social ills."

OCCUPANCY RESTRICTIONS

In *Pfaff v. U.S. Dept. of Housing and Urban Development*, 99 F.3d 739 (9th Cir. 1996), the Ninth Circuit refusal to apply HUD "compelling business justification test" to landlords' occupancy restrictions takes HUD to task. Landlords had a very small two-bedroom house for rent. One of the bedrooms was 10×10. There was a "den" consisting of an alcove opening into the living room. There was a "very little yard," no basement, and an "undersized garage." The house had 1,200 total square feet. The landlords instructed their rental agents to restrict rentals in this house to no more than four persons. They had other rental houses, which they rented to larger groups, including families with children and nontraditional family groups. They concluded that this house, however, would suffer economic deterioration if occupied by more than four residents.

The agent nevertheless showed the house to a family of five, with three young children. When the landlords told the agent that the four-occupant limit was firm, the real estate agent argued with the landlords that their policy violated the Fair Housing Act. The landlords fired the agent and the tenants had to look elsewhere. Tenants claimed that they suffered considerable inconvenience in identifying substitute housing that this experience led to the breakup of their marriage and that they felt "demeaned" by the imposition of the occupancy limits upon them.

Ultimately, a HUD hearing officer found that the Fair Housing Act imposed liability on landlords for occupancy limits regardless of whether the landlords intentionally discriminated against families with children. The impact, not the intent, matters, although the Fair Housing Act does permit the landlord to rebut the prima facie case of discrimination by showing business justification for its policy. The officer then assessed the landlords with $20,000 in damages for emotional distress, $8,000 civil penalty, and $4,200 in compensatory damages; issued an injunction; and (presumably) also socked the landlords for attorneys' fees.

The Ninth Circuit panel upheld the hearing officer's ruling that HUD had established a prima facie case of discrimination. Intent to discriminate is unnecessary, he ruled, and the Court affirmed, but then reversed the decision. After the Court ruled that intent was not an issue, then this case, and any case in which there is an occupancy limit imposed, will satisfy the prima facie test. HUD is in the position where it can pick and choose.

HUD earlier issued an interpretation of the Fair Housing Act that provided that the act did not embody Congressional intent that "an owner . . . would be unable in any way to restrict the number of occupants . . . in a dwelling . . . in appropriate circumstances, owners . . . may develop and implement reasonably occupancy requirements [although] the Department will carefully examine any such non-governmental restriction to determine whether it operates unreasonably to limit or exclude families with children." The court held that this expressed policy (not itself a rule) was so inconsistent as to mislead landlords into activity that HUD would conclude was worthy of civil sanction and significant damage awards, as in this case.

PROCEDURE

In *Kelly v. U.S. Department of Housing and Urban Development*, 97 F.3d 118 (6th Cir. 1996), the plaintiff, a single mother of twin five-year-old daughters, called the telephone number on a "For Rent" sign outside an apartment owned by defendants. After describing her family situation, the plaintiff was informed that the defendants only allowed "one child per bedroom," which implied that the two-bedroom apartment she had asked about would not be available to her. After a month and a half, she rented another apartment, which was not as convenient, increasing her commute to work and creating other transportation and childcare problems. She filed her complaint with HUD alleging housing discrimination on May 17, 1990.

HUD appointed an investigator to investigate the claim and also to act as conciliator between the parties. According to the Sixth Circuit, this investigator had shown distinct bias against the defendants in the past but still was selected to be a "conciliator" here. The investigator completed his investigation in October 2, 1990, after which time he made no further contact with the Kellys. HUD did not issue its Charge of Discrimination until March 2, 1992, two years after the incident took place.

After a hearing in May 1992, the ALJ (Administrative Law Judge) found the defendants liable under 42 U.S.C. 3604 and awarded $10,430.76 in damages.

The Sixth Circuit Court apparently decided to make an object lesson here. On appeal from the HUD decision, the Sixth Circuit reduced the damages claim significantly. It operated on the assumption that HUD, pursuant to its statutory mandate, normally should bring an action on a housing discrimination complaint within one year from completion of its investigation. Thus, it prorated the damage award to reflect the shorter period of emotional distress damages and actual damages attributable to a more appropriate one-year period, rather than the two years that actually occurred.

One sentence of the Sixth Court's language is enough to convey the court's attitude: "This is a case of an administrative agency run amok."

The court also required that HUD pay $20,000 of the defendant's attorney's fees. Although the court acknowledged that the defendants lost on the principal issue of discrimination in the case, the court nevertheless concluded that defendants prevailed on a significant issue relating to HUD's propriety and therefore are entitled to compensation. A stinging dissent by Judge Ryan characterizes the majority opinion as "an unedifying exercise in unrestrained judicial power." Judge Ryan points out in particular that the Equal Access to Justice Act limits attorneys fees to $75 per hour in most cases and requires a careful accounting. The Sixth Circuit panel here required no such accounting but just handed the lump sum $20,000 award to the defendants.

Judge Ryan also criticizes the characterization of the defendants as "prevailing parties" just because they won a few skirmishes that Judge Ryan views as minor in light of the overall conclusion that discrimination occurred.

In *United States of America v. Branella*, 972 F. Supp. 294 (D.N.J. 1997), the owners offered their one-bedroom condominium unit for rent. When a pregnant woman applied as a tenant, one of the owners told her that occupant restrictions of the condominium association might preclude occupancy by two people, the woman and her child.

The next day, the woman called the condominium project's rental office and learned there were no occupancy restrictions applicable to the unit in question. The woman called the Department of Housing and Urban Development, which filed a complaint alleging discriminatory housing practices on the basis of familial status in violation of the Fair Housing Act. A prima facie showing under the Act requires a plaintiff to show either intentional disparate treatment or disparate impact, which does not require proof of discriminatory intent. The landlord moved for summary judgement.

In denying the landlord's motion, the district court pointed out that the prohibition of discrimination on the basis of familial status is part of the Fair Housing Act, out of an expressed concern for single-parent, young, and poor families. Therefore, the Act extends to pregnant women.

The Act further makes it illegal to represent to a prospective tenant, because of familial status, that a dwelling is unavailable for rent when it is in fact available.

BLOCKBUSTING

New York State Association REALTORS®, Inc. v. Shaffer, 27 F.3d 834 (2nd Cir. 1994), was an interesting case involving an association of real estate brokers who brought an action challenging the constitutionality of state regulations aimed at combating blockbusting. There were regulations passed under New York statute that banned solicitation of residential property owners by owners in designated geographic areas, ostensibly as a means of combating the evil known as "blockbusting." The Court, reflecting on the definition of blockbusting, noted that it was "a practice whereby real estate agents artificially stimulate sales of residential property by making representations to homeowners regarding the migration of a particular racial, ethnic, religious, or social group into the neighborhood. In its most systematic and crudest form, blockbusting entails the 'churning' of a local real estate market, a practice in which real estate brokers engage in frenzied solicitation practices that prey upon the racial and ethnic fears of a person residing in transitional neighborhoods as a means for increasing the volume of residential real estate transactions."

In 1969, the New York legislature outlawed the practice of blockbusting, creating an enforcement provision for a "cease and desist" order whereby homeowners residing in blockbusting-prone communities could notify the state in writing that they did not want to be solicited by brokers seeking to sell or lease their property. Eight years later, the Appellant Division in New York upheld the suspension of a REALTOR®'s license for violating a nonsolicitation order covering designated areas in Queens County. The court held that the speech restricted by the New York regulation was properly classified as "commercial free speech" (a business has the right to talk) and therefore was too restrictively written and did not serve the public interest.

The REALTORS® alleged that the nonsolicitation regulation violated commercial free speech because it neither directly advanced the state's substantial interests in promoting stable communities, nor did it provide the state with a reasonable tailored means for eliminating the evil. The court noted that the REALTOR®'s solicitations were straightforward inquiries as to whether the homeowner might be interested in listing a property for sale. The court held that the regulation's exemption of real estate advertisements and newspapers of general circulation fail to offer REALTORS® the type of cost-effective alternative that might arguably bring the regulation within the requirements of federal law. The Court noted that its opinion was a very narrow one, but it is interesting to note that the anti-blockbusting legislation can, in itself, be a restriction on free speech.

DISCUSSION QUESTION

■ When does the limitation on an agent's "commercial free speech" become too restrictive?

Zero Tolerance

In *Rucker v. U.S.,* 122 S. Ct. 1450 (2002), the basic issue in this case overruled the interpretation in an earlier case, *Tucker v. Oakland Housing Authority,* 237 F.3d 1113(9th Cir. 2001), which held that the statute should be interpreted to expose tenants to eviction only if they had personal knowledge of or involvement in drug trafficking.

The Court concluded that the "zero tolerance" policy goes beyond that and authorizes housing authorities, pursuant to mandated language in the authority leases, to terminate the tenant's occupancy whenever any criminal activity that threatens the health, safety, or peaceful enjoyment by tenants in a public housing project, or, more specifically, drug-related criminal activity on or off the premises by the tenant, any member of the tenant's household, or any guest or other person under the tenant's control.

Tenants had argued that the law requires that the tenant know, or have reason to know, of the offending activity in order to be liable for termination of the lease. The Housing Authority had argued that there is no such requirement. "Zero tolerance" means that, innocent though the tenant may be, if those around tenant are involved in drugs, the tenant must leave. The case, clearly designed to put some "bite" into the decision for the Court, involved a disabled tenant whose caretaker and associates of the caretaker were found to be in possession of cocaine on the premises; grandparents whose grandchildren were caught smoking marijuana in the housing project parking lot; and a mother whose resident daughter was caught with cocaine three blocks away from the project.

Much of the unanimous opinion deals with the phrase "under the tenant's control," which modifies only "other person" and does not modify the terms "member of the tenant's household" or "any guest." If household members or guests are involved in drug crimes, whether or not they are under tenant's control, the tenant is liable to get ousted.

The Court differentiates the statutes in question here from the drug crime civil forfeiture statutes under which the government can confiscate property used in a drug crime or acquired with its proceeds. That statute has an "innocent owner" provision that is not involved in the housing statute here.

The Court then supplied the rationale for the Congressional judgment that it had defined (quoting from the Federal Register):

> "[T]here is an obvious reason why Congress would have permitted local public housing authorities to conduct no-fault evictions: Regardless of knowledge, a tenant who cannot control drug crime, or other criminal activities by a household member which threaten health or safety of other residents, is a threat to other residents and the project."

Although the Ninth Circuit en banc panel had found that a narrower interpretation of the statute was necessary to avoid Constitutional invalidity, the Supreme Court concluded that the above rationale was completely supportable and safely within the Constitutional discretion of the Congress.

Some other Constitutional authority had held that government cannot deprive parties of property interests without any relationship to their own wrongdoing. The Court here distinguished that authority on the grounds that it dealt with acts of government as sovereign. Here the government is doing nothing more than contracting for housing. The Court does not deny that the tenants had an existing property right in that housing, but that property right, as indicated, is conditional under the lease. The tenants are assured of Due Process in the determination of whether the conditions on that right had been violated, since the Court assumes there will have to be an eviction procedure involving a court hearing.

SEX OFFENDER?

Fair housing always stirs additional questions and concerns about what constitutes a "protective class." Although those items appear to be well defined under both federal and state laws, there is a recent constitutional question as to whether or not it violates the Constitution to limit the ability of sex offenders to acquire title to real estate in certain locations. At least one court has made it very clear that sex offenders are not protected classes, nor do such limitations limit the right of a sex offender to travel interstate.

In *Doe v. Miller*, 405 F. 3d 700 (8th Cir. 2005), the court represents that this is a case of first impression in U.S. courts.

In 2002, in an effort to protect children in Iowa from the risk that convicted sex offenders may reoffend in locations close to their residences, the Iowa General Assembly passed, and the Governor of Iowa signed, a bill that prohibits a person convicted of certain sex offenses involving minors from residing within 2000 feet of a school or a registered child care facility. The district court declared the statute unconstitutional on several grounds and enjoined the Attorney General of Iowa and the county attorneys in Iowa from enforcing the prohibition.

On appeal, the Eighth Circuit Court of Appeals panel reversed. The court ruled unanimously that the residency restriction is not unconstitutional on its face.

The statute defines "sex offender" to include only persons found guilty of sexual crimes involving minors. The statute was promptly challenged in a class action brought by persons affected by the statute for themselves, other similarly situated, and other convicted sex offenders who might plan to move to Iowa. In reaching its decision that the statute was unconstitutional, the trial court reviewed maps and heard testimony from a county attorney, and found that the restricted areas in many cities encompass the majority of the available housing in the city, thus leaving only limited areas within city limits available for sex offenders to establish a residence. In smaller towns, a single school or child care facility can cause all of the incorporated areas of the town to be off limits to sex offenders. The court found that unincorporated areas, small towns with no school or child care facility, and rural areas remained unrestricted, but that available housing in these areas is "not necessarily readily available."

The appellate court, reversing the district court, stated, more or less, that the fact that a person could find few places to reside in Iowa didn't mean that a person could not travel there:

> "The Iowa statute imposes no obstacle to a sex offender's entry into Iowa, and it does not erect an "actual barrier to interstate movement.". . . There is "free ingress and regress to and from" Iowa for sex offenders, and the statute thus does not "directly impair the exercise of the right to free interstate movement." Nor does the Iowa statute violate principles of equality by treating nonresidents who visit Iowa any differently than current residents, or by discriminating against citizens of other States who wish to establish residence in Iowa. We think that to recognize a fundamental right to interstate travel in a situation that does not involve any of these circumstances would extend the doctrine beyond the Supreme Court's pronouncements in this area. That the statute may deter some out-of-state residents from traveling to Iowa because the prospects for a convenient and affordable residence are less promising than elsewhere does not implicate a fundamental right recognized by the Court's right to travel jurisprudence."

> "The Iowa residency restriction does not prevent a sex offender from entering or leaving any part of the State, including areas within 2000 feet of a school or child care facility, and it does not erect any actual barrier to intrastate movement. . . . John Does also urge that we recognize a fundamental right 'to live where you want.' This ambitious articulation

of a proposed unenumerated right calls to mind the Supreme Court's caution that we should proceed with restraint in the area of substantive due process, because '[b]y extending constitutional protection to an asserted right or liberty interest, we, to a great extent, place the matter outside the arena of public debate and legislative action.' "

Although the court acknowledged that there was some evidence that the statute would present a severe restriction on living accommodations for some individuals, the court concluded that the state's only burden was to show that this restriction was rationally consistent with the civil purpose of the enactment. The court cited evidence in the record that convicted sex offenders generally are not fully deterred by punishment and cannot be cured. Consequently, it was rational for the state to protect its children by separating them as a class from places where children congregated.

Two dissenting judges concluded that the statute swept too broadly, and imposed a "banishment" result on persons who did not present the high level of threat to children that the statute was designed to address:

> "There is no doubt a class of offenders that is at risk to re-offend and for whom such a restriction is reasonable. However, the restriction also applies to John Doe II, who pleaded guilty to third degree sexual abuse for having consensual sex with a fifteen-year-old girl when he was twenty years old. The restriction applies to John Doe VII, who was convicted of statutory rape under Kansas law. His actions which gave rise to this conviction would not have been criminal in Iowa. The restriction applies also to John Doe XIV, who pleaded guilty to a serious misdemeanor charge in 1995 after he exposed himself at a party at which a thirteen-year-old girl was present. John Doe XIV was nineteen at the time of his offense. The actions of these and other plaintiffs are serious, and, at least in most cases, illegal in this state. However, the severity of residency restriction, the fact that it is applied to all offenders identically, and the fact that it will be enforced for the rest of the offenders' lives, makes the residency restriction excessive.

Things are just never as simple as they might seem. A young, stupid act, seemingly innocent, could brand somebody a sex offender for the rest of his or her life.

CONDOMINIUM AND COOPERATIVE ABUSE RELIEF ACT

This statute applies to all condominium and cooperative projects created by conversions, where the real estate has five or more residential units in each structure, and the units or interests were sold or leased by a direct or indirect use of any means of instruments or transportation or communication of interstate commerce or the mail. The statute prohibits abuses by developers for long-term, self-dealing contracts for management services or control of the project. It applies to the developer as well as any affiliate of the developer.

There was apparently a common abuse in some states for developers to convert existing projects into condominiums, control the project through a series of self-dealing contracts that enrich the developer to the detriment of the consumer. When marketing large residential condominium projects, which are conversions, brokers should investigate the statute in detail to eliminate the potential for federal enforcement and resulting liability to the broker under negligence or conspiracy theories.

ANTITRUST LAWS AFFECTING REAL ESTATE BROKERS

Antitrust laws are designed primarily to aid the consumer. They rest on the premise that unrestrained competitive forces will yield the best allocation of our economic resources, the lowest prices, and the highest quality and the greatest in material progress. *Marin County Board of Realtors, Inc. v. Palsson*, 16 C.3d 920 (Cal. 1976). There are five primary areas of concern for real estate brokers that make the brokerage business and industry peculiarly susceptible to antitrust litigation: (1) price fixing; (2) boycotting; (3) mergers or takeover; (4) tying arrangements; and (5) possibilities of class action status for plaintiffs.

Antitrust law has been a difficult topic to deal with in real estate brokerage issues because in many ways, the antitrust theories don't seem to apply to real estate. The area of antitrust law is a highly complex area involving legal issues of moral, political, and socio-economic areas of concern. In many ways, it is philosophical with ivory tower, large corporation–type issues involving market share studies, "facial invalidities," and broad-based theories of anticompetitive versus procompetitive activities. In the real estate business, this is contrasted with a large number of real estate licensees nationwide, many of whom have had a nominal level of education. Real estate licensees tend to be aggressive, gregarious, and outgoing types. They are highly competitive rather than anticompetitive, and have, for decades, been dealing in the business as wholly regulated within the boundaries of a single state. In most areas of business, we consider this type of activity to be wholly intrastate and not susceptible to federal government intervention. Federal government jurisdiction under the federal antitrust laws, however, has been considered twice by the U.S. Supreme Court in *McLain v. Real Estate Board of New Orleans, Inc.*, 44 U.S. 232 (1980). The Court determined that real estate broker's conduct can invoke antitrust jurisdiction law enforcement by demonstrating a "substantial effect on interstate commerce" generated by brokerage activity.

Substantial effect "with interstate commerce in real estate transactions involved" the fact that: (1) the activities of a real estate brokerage company are within the flow of interstate commerce and have an effect upon that commerce; (2) the services of brokers were employed in connection with a purchase or sale of real estate by persons moving into and out of the area; (3) real estate brokers assist their clients with securing financing and insurance involved in the purchase of real estate in the area, which financing and insurance are paid from sources outside the state; and (4) real estate brokers engaged in an unlawful restraint of interstate trade and commerce in the offering or sale of real estate brokering services.

In *The United States v. Foley*, 598 F.2d 1323 (4th Cir. 1979), the Foley court also identified other aspects of interstate commerce: (1) that the brokers capitalize on their highly trained second nature of the real estate market; (2) they participate in national relocation services; (3) there is an extensive use of interstate channels of communication; (4) they engage in extensive advertising in out of state media; and (5) financing is available from out-of-state lending institutions and a substantial number of loans guaranteed by federal agencies. In short, what was once thought of as a wholly intrastate regulated business now engages in so many facets of interstate commerce that the federal government clearly has jurisdiction to enforce antitrust legislation.

Price Fixing

The first U.S. Supreme Court case dealing with price fixing involving real estate was *United States v. National Association of Real Estate Boards*, 339 U.S. 45 (1950), in which the U.S. Supreme Court held that price fixing for real estate commissions is per se an unreasonable restraint of trade and violated the Sherman Antitrust Act. There is both civil and criminal liability under the Sherman Act. One could be acquitted of the criminal offense but still be convicted under the civil offense.

"Per Se" Illegality

Certain agreements or practices are so plainly anticompetitive and so often lacking in any redeeming virtue that they are conclusively presumed to be illegal without further examination. A court need not inquire whether its restraints actually possess the power to inflict public injury, nor will the court accept an argument if the restraint and the circumstances are justified by any procompetitive purpose or effect. In the National Association of Real Estate Board case, the U.S. Supreme Court stated that:

> "Price-fixing is a per se and unreasonable restraint of trade. It is not for the courts to determine whether in particular settings price-fixing serves an honorable or worthy end. An agreement, shown either by adherence to a price schedule or by proof of consensual action fixing the uniform or minimal price is itself illegal under the Sherman Act, no matter what end it was designated to serve."

Note, however, that a real estate brokerage can set prices inside its own firm, just as it sets its own policy for running the business. It is the agreement or conspiracy of one broker fixing prices with a competitor that creates a violation of the antitrust laws.

In *Freeman v. San Diego Association of Realtors*, 322 F. 3d 1133 (9th Cir. 2003), real estate agents who were subscribers to a countywide listing service (known as Sandicor) sued the Sandicor and local associations who founded Sandicor and were shareholders in it. The suit alleged claims under the Sherman

Act for price fixing and conspiracy to monopolize market for support services. The allegedly fixed prices were the prices charged to individual realtors by the service for monthly service charges.

Prior to 1992, twelve Multiple Listing Services (MLSs) had been operated in San Diego County, California, by different real estate trade associations serving subscribers in different parts of the county. As in other parts of the United States, the MLS lets real estate agents share information about available properties through a computerized database. In addition to providing database access to subscribers, the MLS operators also provided support services to members, though the nature and price of the support services varied between the associations.

The eleven MLS operators who were also local Associations of Realtors decided to combine databases to form a single MLS, thereby reducing costs of operating the database. Sandicor was the entity created by the associations to run the database, and the associations became Sandicor's shareholders and appointed its directors. Notwithstanding this centralization of service, the associations decided to continue to provide local support services for the MLS independently. The associations' costs for providing support services "varied widely," with the largest association (San Diego Association of Realtors) spending $10 per month (per user) and the smallest association spending close to $50. To accommodate the smaller associations, Sandicor was created under a centralized model whereby the associations signed up subscribers and collected MLS fees on Sandicor's behalf, but Sandicor decided on a uniform fee that all agents had to pay. The MLS fees were delivered to Sandicor, but Sandicor then paid a fee for support services back to the associations. Under the service agreements between Sandicor and the associations, the associations were prohibited from discounting the MLS fee in any way.

Under the original agreement, the support fee was set by the associations at $25 per month, meaning that SDAR (which spent $10 per subscriber for support) received more than its cost per subscriber and the smaller associations had to be subsidized for their losses in providing support services.

These facts formed the basis of plaintiff's claim that Sandicor's MLS fee was inflated because the support fees paid by Sandicor to the associations was "fixed at a supracompetitive level." Plaintiffs alleged that by fixing support fees in the service agreements between Sandicor and the associations, defendants violated section 1 of the federal Sherman Act, which bars "[e]very contract . . . or conspiracy in restraint of trade or commerce among the several States." 15 U.S.C. 1.

Plaintiffs also claimed that defendants violated Section 2 of the Sherman Act by conspiring to monopolize the market for support services. This claim was based on Sandicor's denial of plaintiff Freeman's request to operate a support service center for Sandicor's customers.

Plaintiffs filed a class action in federal court seeking an injunction and damages in excess of $10 million, naming as defendants Sandicor, the associations, the California Association of Realtors, and assorted officers and directors. The district court refused to certify the class. Following summary judgment motions by both sides, the district court rejected defendants' claim that their conduct had no substantial effect on interstate commerce but sustained their claim to immunity under Section 1 because they were a single entity under *Copperweld Corp. v. Independence Tube Corp.*, 467 U.S.752 (1984). Both sides appealed.

The Ninth Circuit found price fixing, but not conspiracy. Starting with interstate commerce, the Court readily found a "substantial effect" from the MLS activities by noting that Sandicor's MLS handled over $23 billion in home sales over a four-year period, with approximately $10 billion in interstate home mortgage financing.

Dispensing with each of the offered defenses, the Court held that the associations engaged in price fixing and the plaintiffs had standing to sue. "The associations purposely fixed the support fee they charged to Sandicor at a supracompetitive level. Sandicor passed on some portion of that inflated support fee to agents, who paid higher prices for MLS as a result. This is precisely the type of injury the antitrust laws are designed to prevent."

Regarding Sandicor's claim to immunity as a single entity, the Court examined the potential and actual competitive nature of the associations in providing support services and found that they were not a single entity.

In the end, the Court made it clear that joint ventures among competitors are not all bad and that combining MLS databases can be legal. However, deciding to fix support fees is not.

It doesn't appear to matter whether the defendants made out a case that the price fixing in this case was good for the economy—it is price fixing and that is per se a bad thing.

The United States v. Foley, 598 F.2d 1323 (4th Cir. 1979)

It was one of the worst times in real estate. Property wasn't moving; getting financing was next to impossible; business expenses were sky-rocketing. Such was the real estate climate on September 5, 1974, when the newly elected President of the local Real Estate Board, John Foley, hosted a dinner at the country club for nine of his REALTOR® friends and associates.

After dinner, Foley rose from his seat. After making some remarks about real estate that his business was going down the tubes, Foley announced that his firm was raising its commission rate by one percent. He sat down, and a discussion followed about rate changes. Each of the defendants present was a real estate licensee competing in the residential sales business. Each was a member of the Board and its listing service. Within months, each of the defendants implemented the new commission rate.

The six corporate and three individual defendants were convicted in the United States District Court for conspiracy to fix real estate commissions in violation of the Sherman Act. They appealed.

The Court of Appeals held that there was a sufficient relationship to interstate commerce to support convictions under the Sherman Antitrust Act. The court held that as a "matter of practical necessity," "real estate transactions were part of interstate business." Given as examples were mortgage brokerage, federally guaranteed loans, and long distant telephone calls. The Court also ruled that there was evidence of a conspiracy and that each defendant participated in it.

The defendants appealed their felony convictions for conspiracy to fix real estate commissions. The convictions were affirmed by the Supreme Court, which found that there was proof that the defendants acted with knowledge that their conduct would affect prices.

DISCUSSION QUESTIONS

- What should Mr. Foley have done during the meeting at the country club?

- What should the others have done when Mr. Foley made his speech?

- What is a reasonable procedure to use when a competitor starts asking you about prices?

- List the ways that you could illustrate that real estate broker's commissions are negotiated and competitive.

Fee Splitting

Another issue concerning price fixing is the splitting of fees between discount brokers and full fee brokers. Some years ago the Greater Minneapolis Area Board of Realtors adopted a cooperative sale listing form, a real estate commission fee splitting arrangement, that would pay the selling broker the amount regularly charged by the selling broker for sales of that type. *Penne v. Greater Minneapolis Area Board of Realtors*, 604 F.2d 1143 (8th Cir. 1979). In other words, the discount broker could get no more than half of his or her regular discount brokerage fee and would not be able to split the full fee with the listing broker. This was termed a "punitive fee split" by the court. The Court found that a number of brokers conspired to fix and maintain brokerage fees by the use of three devices: (1) imposing punitive divisions of commissions on cooperative sales; (2) black-listing brokers who charged a lower rate; and (3) making deprecatory statements concerning the discount brokers.

Another point on price fixing is that it is legal to verify what other brokers are charging. These are "inquiries" and can be procompetitive inquiries to determine what the rest of the market is charging. The important concern, however, is that another party can overhear a seemingly innocent inquiry or perceived by the person responding to the question as a pressure tactic or effort to seek a price fixing conspiracy between the two brokers. It is not what one has said necessarily, but how the other parties may perceive it, that may create the conspiracy. The better rule is to never, never, never discuss prices with other licensees outside your office.

Boycotting

The real estate brokerage community has developed a multiple listing service that, in essence, serves as a trade exchange for the purchaser in the sale of real estate. *United States v. Realty Multi-List, Inc.*, 629 F.2d 1351 (5th Cir. 1980). The central function of MLS® is to provide a multiple listing service for its members from the agreements that form the basis for this service. If the listing is taken as an MLS® listing, MLS® members obligate themselves to attempt to obtain from sellers exclusive (whether exclusive right to sell or exclusive agency) rather than open listings of real estate, and to pool their exclusive listings through the MLS®. MLS is the central processing and distributing point for its members' listings. It compiles the listings it receives into a members' listing book, online database, or other database accessible by its members, which includes listing data submitted by its members as well as photographs of the property. With the age of electronics, listings are upgraded almost daily using the information provided by the Multiple Listing Service®. Member brokers are able to cooperate in bringing together buyers and sellers much more efficiently. Technology is making it possible to expand ideas and information in larger market areas. The brokers then determine by their own agreement how the commission from the sale will be divided.

Unlike price fixing, boycotting is subject to the "rule of reason." Under the rule of reason, the practice may tend to reduce competition but nevertheless operate to make the market more efficient aiding the reduction of prices and a better allocation of resources, *Realty Multi-List*, supra. MLS® is generally considered to have procompetitive effects as homeowners do not possess the necessary experience to effectively present to the public information on real estate offered for sale, and it helps the broker stay more knowledgeable in gaining better access to a wider selection of properties within a shorter period of time. *Grillo v. Board of Realtors*, 219 A.2d 635 (1966). There are anti-competitive effects to MLS®

primarily dealing with denial of access to the system. It is important to note that certain types of exclusion that do not have a bearing on the cost or effectiveness of the system are generally held to be non-competitive. For instance, arbitrating membership fees, *United States v. Realty Multi-List, Inc.*, supra, exclusion of part-time brokers, *Marin County Board of Realtors, Inc. v. Palsson*, 16 C.3d 920 (Cal. Sup. Ct. 1976), or reputation in the community, *Collins v. Main Land Board of Realtors*, 304 A.2d 493 (Penn. Sup. Ct. 1973).

It has been held that access to MLS® can be protected through the federal copyright laws as the restricted access to MLS® protects the listing agent's rights to agreed commission upon sale and the privacy and property of the residential real estate seller against unwanted visitors. *Supermarket of Homes, Inc. v. San Fernando Board of Realtors*, 786 F.2d 1400 (9th Cir. 1986).

Tying Claims

A tying claim requires that a consumer be tied to a particular product. For instance, if a consumer is required to use a broker because of previous conduct, it is anticompetitive behavior. If brokers agree to perform their services for no charge on the condition that you are required to use them at some future date for another transaction, regardless of the quality of their services, they have "tied" themselves into the transaction. The tying arrangements can be analyzed under either the per se rule or the rule of reason but are generally analyzed under the rule of reason. The general criteria for tying arrangements are: (1) that there are two separate products, a "tying" product and a "tied" product; (2) that those products are in fact "tied" together—that is, the buyer was forced to buy the tied product to get the tying product; (3) that the seller possesses a sufficient economic power and the tying product to coerce buyer acceptance of the tied product; and (4) the involvement of a "non-insubstantial" amount of interstate commerce in the market of the tied product.

Tying has surfaced in two separate issues. In *King City Realty, Inc. v. Sun Pace Corporation*, 633 P.2d 784 (Ore. 1981), a listing contract provided that the defendant would purchase seven lots but included a "list-back" under which the defendant agreed to list exclusively with the plaintiff realty company for resale of all of the lots purchased by the defendant under the agreement after construction of houses on such lot. In *Thompson v. Metropolitan Multi-List, Inc.*, 934 F.2d 1566 (11th Cir. 1991), the Court held that tying the multiple listing service to a real estate board membership may also constitute an unfair competition and therefore an antitrust violation.

13

FEDERAL LEGISLATION AFFECTING REAL ESTATE BROKERS—PART III

PURPOSE

After carefully reading Chapter 13, the student will be able to:

■ Explain federal asset forfeiture and RICO.

■ Discuss the Flood Disaster Protection Act and federal flood insurance.

■ Apply copyright restrictions to real estate practice.

Key Words to look for in this chapter:
1. Crime Control Act of 1954
2. Racketeer Influenced and Corrupt Organization Act
3. The Flood Disaster Protection Act of 1973
4. Flood Insurance Program
5. Copyright Act

FEDERAL ASSET FORFEITURE

The rise in drug-related crimes has mandated increased law enforcement, and Congress has enacted two statutes that provide for forfeiture of real property under both civil and criminal provisions, the comprehensive Crime Control Act of 1954 and the Racketeer Influenced and Corrupt Organization Act (RICO). Both statutes gave the government the power to seize and take control of real estate, including the management thereof, without notice to anyone. A real estate licensee, while working with listings as well as management contracts, needs to be aware that these statutes are effective and what to do to avoid enforcement of these statutes against properties with which the licensee is involved. A licensee may be convicted of money laundering if the agent is willfully blind to the facts of existing illegal conduct. In a recent case, an agent was convicted of money laundering when the agent was willfully blind to cash payments made at a closing that were not reflected on the HUD-1 closing statement. *U.S. v. Campbell*, 977 F.2d 854 (4th Cir. 1992). This adds additional concern to violations of RESPA discussed in Chapter 10. The scope of this discussion will dwell solely on the Act and RICO as it applies to real property.

Civil Forfeiture

If real property is used, or intended to be used, in any manner or part to commit or facilitate the commission of a violation of the Act, the real property is subject to forfeiture. However, the language is extremely broad and all real property as well as any specific right, title, or interest in the real property is subject to forfeiture. An interest in real property includes the joint tenancy interest of a spouse, a judgment lien, or mortgagee's interest as well as tenancy in common interests, and fee simple title. The Act has also been applied to residential property for small violations (the sale of 12.8 grams of cocaine). Recent cases have given some comfort that at least due process is required prior to assets being seized, but the threat is so great that any effort to avoid violation is a wise move. See generally *United States v. James Daniel Good Real Property*, 114 S. Ct. 492 (1993); *U.S. v. 92 Buena Vista Avenue*, 113 S. Ct. 1126 (1993).

Property Seized

Regardless of the scope of the illegal activity, the entire tract that is owned may be subject to forfeiture. The entire tract may be subject to forfeiture even if the illegal activity occurred only on a small portion of the land. The value of the property subject to the severity of the violation is irrelevant. In addition, an owner, lender, or lessor of property may forfeit its interest upon proof that the property is negligently entrusted to a tenant, borrower, or occupant who uses the property to commit illegal acts; this puts a high duty of care on a real estate broker who may be managing a property but without doing all that the managing agent could do to prevent unlawful use of the premises. The Act also provides for forfeiture for real property acquired for exchange for an illegal substance or as proceeds of an illegal drug transaction and also applies to real property that is purchased with proceeds that are traceable to an illegal transaction.

STANDARDS FOR FORFEITURE

Three standards exist for determining whether property is subject to forfeiture: the substantial connection test, the minimal connection test, and the probable cause standard. The substantial connection test requires the government to prove, by preponderance of the evidence, that a substantial connection existed between the property and the criminal activity. The minimal connection test is easier for the government to meet, as it requires that the use of the property in any manner in connection with an illegal drug transaction is sufficient to justify the forfeiture. Only the Ninth Circuit has adopted a probable cause standard. Under this standard, the government must present evidence that shows more than mere suspicion, but less than prima facia proof that the property was used to facilitate an illegal transaction.

Forfeiture Under Racketeer Influenced and Corrupt Organization Act (RICO)

RICO was originally intended to require divestiture of legitimate businesses that organized crime control. The courts have construed it to reach any person who is convicted of investing in, acquiring control of, or conducting an enterprise with money derived from a pattern of racketeering activity. The "enterprise" reaches virtually everybody and every type of business. To establish a "pattern" of racketeering activity, the government must show at least two years of racketeering activity that occurred within ten years of each other. The forfeiture provision applies to any interests in property that a RICO defendant may possess. The entity itself may be legitimate business, but if it is operated "directly or indirectly" as a criminal enterprise, then all its assets may be subject to forfeiture.

Standards for Forfeiture

Under RICO, the standard to determine whether property is subject to forfeiture is whether the property is part of a criminal enterprise. In addition, the government employs a relation back doctrine under the Act. Once the government proves that the property was used to further an illegal drug transaction or that the property was purchased with funds from an illegal transaction, then the government is deemed to have title to the property interest from the date of the illegal transaction. This doctrine serves to cut off the mortgagee, owner, or lessor who acquired the lien or ownership interest after the date of the illegal transaction. Similar to the Act, RICO has a relation back doctrine that relates back to the date of the criminal activity.

DEFENSES TO FORFEITURE

Under the RICO, a statutory defense is provided for any owner in the subject property who establishes that the illegal activity occurred without the knowledge or consent of the owner. The word "owner" includes virtually anyone who owns an interest in the property, including the owner and lien interests.

The innocent owner defense can prevail if the owner shows: (1) that it "was uninvolved in and unaware of the wrongful activity;" and (2) that it "had done all that reasonably could be expected to prevent prescribed use of the property." The owner is not innocent if the owner simply chose to ignore the use of the property; the owner must prove that he or she lacked actual knowledge of the misconduct. The owner, then, or the lessor, or the owner's agent, or lender should take steps to investigate the borrower or lessee and the property in order to meet his or her first opponent in the ownership defense. The second criterion for the ownership defense is that the defendant must show that he or she did all that reasonably could be expected to prevent the illegal use of the property. Therefore, owners and lessees should establish procedures for the investigation of borrowers and lessees and follow them faithfully in order to prevent illegal use of the property, if possible, and to establish a record that would enable them to claim the innocent owner defense.

RICO provides that an owner's interest in real property will not be forfeited to the government if the owner is a transferee of the property from the criminal defendant and if the owner establishes that he or she is a bona fide purchaser for value of such property who, at the time of the purchase, was reasonably without cause to believe that the property was subject to forfeiture under RICO. Therefore, it is suggested that owners, owner's agents, lenders and lessors, and managing agents should take similar steps to investigate tenants.

Forfeiture Procedures

Under the Act and the Federal Rules of Civil Procedure, the U.S. Attorney's office may bring an action for forfeiture by filing a claim for Certain Admiralty and Maritime Claims. To pursue the forfeiture, the U.S. Attorney's Office brings an action for the forfeiture by filing a complaint in the United States District Court. If the court finds probable cause to support an action against the identified property, the court will issue an order authorizing a warrant for the arrest (seizure). The government must also provide public notice of the action and arrest in a newspaper for general circulation in the district. Assumingly, the only way one could note that this proceeding had taken place is by reviewing the public notices provided by the U.S. Attorney's Office in the paper of general circulation. Rule C(6) requires that the claim must be filed within ten days after the marshal serves the warrant for the arrest of the property or within the time specified in the public notice. If the claim is not filed in a timely manner, the interest in the property may be lost.

Under RICO, the government commences a criminal procedure by filing an order for forfeiture with the Federal District Court in which the defendant was convicted of a RICO violation. After the entry of the order, the government will publish a notice of its intent to dispose of the property. The claimant must petition the court for a hearing to judicate the validity of the government's alleged interest in the property within 30 days of the final publication notice or its receipt of actual notice, whichever is earlier. Failure to petition in a timely manner may result in loss of all interest in the property.

In *United States v. Ursery*, 116 S. Ct. 2135 (1996), the U.S. Supreme Court held that civil forfeiture is not "punishment" for purposes of the Double Jeopardy Clause. The defendant cultivated marijuana in a wooded area near his house. He had no ownership interest in the area in which he cultivated the marijuana. Acting on the reasonable belief that the defendant did own the cultivated area, however, police, after finding marijuana at that location, searched the house. In the house they found marijuana seeds, stems, stalks, and a growlight. Based upon this evidence, the government was able to sustain its burden of proof that the house was used for the distribution of marijuana.

After the defendant had been convicted and sentenced for manufacturing marijuana, the government seized the house in a forfeiture proceeding. There was no evidence that the proceeds of sale of contraband had been used to acquire the property. The contention was that the presence of the stems, seeds, and growlight, plus the conviction for cultivation, established that the house had been used for criminal activity.

The defendant argued that the forfeiture proceeding constituted double jeopardy in that he was being punished twice for the same crime. The court of appeals agreed.

The U.S. Supreme Court reversed. Civil forfeitures do not invoke the Double Jeopardy Clause. A majority opinion (6-3) noted that civil forfeiture has enjoyed a long period of acceptance from our nation's judiciary. Consequently, civil forfeiture should not be viewed as "punishment," and successive impositions of a criminal sanction and civil forfeiture do not amount to double jeopardy.

It is important to note that the government can seize your client's property on reasonable suspicion, and your client may lose income from that property while trying to establish himself or herself as an "innocent owner." Property managers: Attention!

In *Bennis v. Michigan*, 116 S. Ct. 994 (1996), the Detroit police arrested John Bennis after observing that he engaged in a sexual act with a prostitute in an automobile while it was parked on a Detroit city street. Bennis was convicted of gross indecency. The car in question was an eleven-year-old Pontiac sedan recently purchased by John and Tina Bennis for $600. The William County Circuit Court declared the car a public nuisance and ordered the car's abatement, recognizing: (1) the couple's ownership of "another automobile" so they would not be left without transportation; and (2) the Court's authority to order the payment of one-half of the sales proceeds after deduction of cost to "the innocent co-title holder," but declined to order a division of the sales proceeds because of the age and value of the car.

The Michigan Court of Appeals reversed, but was in turn reversed by the State Supreme Court, which concluded that the Michigan statute's failure to provide an innocent owner defense was without federal constitutional consequence.

The U.S. Supreme Court agreed to hear the case to determine whether Michigan's abatement scheme deprived Mrs. Bennis of her interest in the forfeited car without due process (in violation of the Fourteenth Amendment) or whether the State has taken her interest in the car for public use without compensation (in violation of the Fifth Amendment as incorporated by the Fourteenth Amendment).

The petitioner claimed that she was denied due process and notice of an opportunity to protest the abatement of her car; the petitioner claimed that she was entitled to contest the abatement by showing that she did not know her husband would use it to violate Michigan's indecency law, the "innocent owner" defense.

The Supreme Court held that a long and unbroken line of cases holds that an owner's interest in property may be forfeited by reason of the use to which the property is put, even though the owner did not know that it was to be put to such use. The Court based its opinion on a 75-year history of U.S. Supreme Court decisions on forfeiture laws holding that the acts of the possessors bind the interest of the owner whether that owner is innocent or guilty. In *Van Oster v. Kansas*, 272 U.S. 465 (1926), the court referenced that the car used for the illegal transportation of intoxicating liquor allowed the forfeiture of property entrusted by the interest-owner as not being a violation of the due process clause in the Fifth Amendment. The court cited similar cases in maritime law. In *Calero-Toledo v. Pearson Yacht Leasing Co.*, 416 U.S. 663 (1974), the court concluded that cases authorizing actions of this kind are "too firmly fixed in the punitive and remedial jurisprudence of the country to be now displaced." The court acknowledged that the State sought to deter illegal activity that contributes to neighborhood deterioration and unsafe streets. The Bennis automobile, it was conceded, facilitated and was used in criminal activity.

One may wonder if this case has any precedent-setting application as it pertains to real estate. Probably not. Several prior decisions have taken the position that real estate is not used to transport contraband and can be used in the engagement of illegal activity without the landlord's or investor's knowledge, particularly in light of the value and complexity of seizing real estate without due process. The law does not require landlords nor investors in real estate to be police officers or enforcers of the law. Seizures of real estate do not necessarily constitute seizure of an item, which facilitated the conduct of a criminal act. Note *U.S. v. James Daniel Good Real Property*, 114 S. Ct. 493 (1993), wherein the court noted that real property is not subject to being hidden or put beyond the jurisdiction of the court, and that the importance of private interests at risk overrides the government's need for real property. A similar holding is found in *U.S. v. A Parcel of Land Known as 92 Buena Vista Avenue*, 113 S. Ct. 1126 (1993).

In *Lot 39, Section C, Northern Hills Subdivision, Grayson County, Texas v. State of Texas*, 85 S.W.3d 429 (Tex. App.-Eastland 2002, pet. den), Helm was convicted of running a methamphetamine lab out of his house. The State brought an action for forfeiture of the house under Article 59 of the Code of Criminal Procedure. Helm claimed that his homestead exemption protected the property from forfeiture.

The constitutional and statutory provisions relating to homestead both provide that a homestead is exempt from seizure for the claims of creditors. Although the issue in this case appears to be one of first impression in Texas, there are a few published opinions from Texas courts that indicate a homestead was forfeited pursuant to Chapter 59 because of drug-related activity. None of these cases, however, dealt with the homestead exemption. Nonetheless, there is another Texas case in which the Court addressed the homestead exemption and held that it did not protect a homestead from public nuisance laws. *1018-3rd St. v. State*, 331 S.W.2d 450 (Tex. Civ. App.-Amarillo 1959, no writ). In *1018-3rd St.*, the Court upheld the closing and padlocking of a house for a period of one year upon the finding that the house, which was the defendant's homestead, had been used in violation of the Texas liquor laws.

The issue has been addressed in other states with similar homestead exemptions, and the outcomes are varied. Courts in Florida, Illinois, Iowa, Kansas, and Oklahoma have held that homesteads are protected from seizures and forfeitures based upon the occurrence of criminal offenses. Courts in Arizona, Colorado, and Washington have held that their respective homestead exemption applies to protect homesteads from forced sales arising from the owner's debts but does not apply to protect homesteads from forfeitures brought about by the owner's use of the property to conduct criminal activity.

The court found the reasonings of the courts in Arizona, Colorado, and Washington to be persuasive. Helm's reliance on the cases from Florida, Illinois, Iowa, and Kansas was misplaced because the homestead provisions in those states contain broader exemption language than the Texas provisions and are, therefore, distinguishable. In Florida, homesteads are exempt from forced sale under process of any court. In Illinois, homesteads are exempt from attachment or judgment for the payment of debts or other purposes. In Iowa, homesteads are exempt from judicial sale unless there is a special statutory declaration to the contrary. In Kansas, homesteads are exempt from forced sale under any process of law. In none of those states is the homestead exemption limited to seizures based upon the owner's debts. The court did note, however, that the homestead exemption in Oklahoma is limited to seizures based upon the owner's debts and that the homestead provision is not distinguishable from ours. However, it disagreed with the Oklahoma court's holding in which the Court disregarded the limiting language of the homestead provision and held that the homestead exemption was not limited to forced sales for the payment of debts.

Although conscious that the homestead exemption is to be construed liberally and that forfeiture statutes are to be strictly construed in a manner favorable to the person whose property is being seized, the Court did not believe the homestead exemption should be construed to protect Helm's homestead from foreclosure in this case. The Texas constitutional and statutory provisions pertaining to the homestead exemption specifically indicate that homesteads may not be seized or subjected to forced sales for the payment of the owner's debts or the claims of creditors. The forfeiture of real property based upon the owner's use of that property to conduct criminal activity, such as the manufacture or delivery of methamphetamine, is not forfeiture for the payment of the owner's debts or the claims of creditors.

The Court in *1018-3rd St.* recognized that the Texas homestead exemption was created as a direct result of the loss to creditors of numerous homestead farms during the depression. The Court stated that the purpose of the homestead exemption was to preserve the integrity of the family and to provide the debtor with a home and a means to support his family.

Neither in this history, nor in any reliable Texas case book authority, do we find even a suggestion that our forebearers conceived of a homestead exemption for the purposes of erecting a barrier behind which criminals might ply their trades while thumbing their noses at law enforcement officers diligently and sincerely seeking to enforce prohibitions that residents of the areas had expressed a desire for at the ballot box.

CONCLUSION

From a real estate licensee's standpoint, there are a few guidelines for determining how one protects oneself as an agent for an innocent owner, innocent lender, or innocent landlord.

- Substantiate sources of income of the tenant or prospective purchaser.

- Note whether a proposed tenant or purchaser has a large income and little experience, education, or skills.

- Obtain a chain of title search from a title company and investigate any unusual conveyances, particularly property held for a short period of time.

- Inquire about the source of any down payments or deposits or large prepayments of rent.

- Note cash payments for real property and the source of that cash.

- When possible tour the premises periodically to determine whether the property is operated as a "front" for criminal activity.

- When possible, interview employees of the premises. Note: discuss business with the employees of the premises.

- Obtain financial statements from all prospective tenants and, if possible, purchasers.

- Investigate three years' prior tax returns.

An agent can also be held liable for being willfully blind to the fact that purchase money was derived from illegal activities. In one recent case, the defendant's client purchased real property in his parents' name with money derived from allegedly illegal activity by paying a $60,000 payment not reflected in the HUD-1 Settlement Statement. The Court held that the real estate agent possessed knowledge that the transaction was designed to conceal illegal proceeds, and therefore, had liability. *U.S. v. Campbell*, 977 F.2d 854 (4th Cir. 1992).

THE FLOOD DISASTER PROTECTION ACT OF 1973

Introduction

Congress originally enacted a flood insurance program in 1968 to (1) authorize a flood insurance program by means of which flood insurance can be made available in a nationwide basis through the cooperative efforts of the federal government and the private insurance industry; (2) provide flexibility in the program so that such flood insurance may be based on workable methods of pooling risks, minimizing costs, and distributing burdens equally among those who will be protected by flood insurance and the general public; (3) encourage state and local governments to make appropriate land use adjustments to constrict the development of land that is exposed to flood damage and minimize flood damage cost; (4) guide the development of proposed future construction, where practicable, away from locations that are threatened by flood hazards; (5) encourage lending and credit institutions, as a matter of national policy, to assist in furthering the objectives of the flood insurance program; (6) assure that any federal assistance provided under the program will be related closely to all flood-related programs and activities of the federal government; and (7) authorize continuing studies of flood hazards in order to provide for a constant reappraisal of the flood insurance program and its effect on land use requirements.

The Act was amended in 1969 to provide similar protection against damage resulting from mud slides caused by accumulations of water on or under the ground and amended further in 1973 to provide for protection against damage and loss resulting from the erosion and undermining of shore lines by waves or currents in lakes or other bodies of water exceeding anticipated cyclical levels. The 1973 amendments substantially increased the limits of coverage authorized under the national flood insurance program and provided by the expeditious identification of and the dissemination of information concerning flood-prone areas. They required states or local communities, as a result of future federal financial assistance, to participate in the flood insurance program and to adopt adequate flood plain ordinances to effect enforcement provisions to reduce or avoid future flood losses. The amendments also required the purchase of flood insurance by property owners who are being assisted by federal programs or by federally supervised, regulated, or insured agencies or institutes in the acquisition or improvement of land or facilities to be located in areas identified as having special flood hazards.

Flood Insurance Program

As originally enacted, the Secretary of Housing and Urban Development was authorized to establish and carry out a national flood insurance program. This enabled the purchase of insurance against loss resulting from physical damage to or loss of real property arising from any flood occurring in the United States.

276

The Secretary was specifically authorized to arrange for appropriate financial participation and risk sharing in the program by insurance companies and other insurers, as well as appropriate participation other than on a risk-sharing basis. The program was later amended to provide for a Director of the Federal Emergency Management Agency to replace the Secretary of Housing and Urban Development. All functions vested in the Secretary of Housing and Urban Development were transferred to the Director under the reorganization plan of 1978.

SCOPE OF PROGRAM

As currently enacted, the Director is required to make flood insurance available to cover residential properties that are designed for occupancy from one to four families, church properties, and business properties that are owned or leased and operated by small business concerns. If the Director determines that it would be feasible to extend the flood insurance program to cover other properties, he or she may make the flood insurance available to cover other residential properties, other business properties, agricultural properties, properties occupied by private or nonprofit organizations and properties owned by state and local governments and agencies thereof. The Director can make the flood insurance available only in those states or areas that evidence a positive interest in securing flood insurance coverage under the flood insurance program. They have to give satisfactory assurance to the Director that adequate land use and control methods have been adopted for the state or area, which are consistent with comprehensive criteria for land management and use developed under Section 4102 of the statute.

The statute is self-enforcing. No federal officer or agency can approve any financial assistance for acquisition or construction purposes for use in any area that has been identified by the Director as an area having special flood hazards, and in which the civil flood insurance has been made available under this chapter, unless the building has an adequate amount of insurance coverage protecting against floods. The Act also applies to extensions and renewals of loans.

The statute was intended primarily to encourage wise land use management in order to prevent future economic loss resulting from flooding. Oddly enough, the statute only provides for federal enforcement. It does not provide for any action by an individual because the loan was made in violation of the statute or the lender did not require the purchase of flood insurance in compliance with the Act.

IDENTIFICATION OF FLOOD-PRONE AREAS

To establish the flood-prone areas, the Director is authorized by the statute to consult with, receive information from, and enter into any agreements or other arrangement with the Secretaries of the Army, the Interior, Agriculture, and Commerce, the Tennessee Valley Authority, and the heads of other federal departments or agencies. The statute also allows the Director to enter into any contracts with any persons or private firms in order to: (1) identify and publish information with respect to all flood plain areas, including coastal areas located in the United States, which have special flood hazards; and (2) establish flood risk zones in all such areas and make estimates with respect to the rates of probable flood caused loss for the various flood risk zones for each of these areas. This resulted in a massive identification and mapping of flood hazard areas and flood risk zones throughout the United States that assist the Director in determining the special flood hazard areas.

The criteria changes from time to time, but the statute generally encourages restrictions on development of land that is exposed to flood damage. It guides the development of proposed construction away from locations that are threatened by flood hazards and improves the long-range land use management and use of flood-prone areas. Once the flood-prone areas are determined, the Act requires the Director to publish the proposed areas in the Federal Register for comment by direct notification of the Chief Executive Officer of the Community, and in the primary local newspaper. Any owner or lessee of real property who believes his or her property rights will be adversely affected by the proposed determinations may appeal to the local government. The owner or lessee is entitled to challenge whether the designation of such special flood hazards is scientifically or technically incorrect. The claimant can be reimbursed to the extent of fees expended if he or she wins the appeal pursuant to a form established by the statutes. The protest must be made in a timely manner and supported by scientific or technical evidence.

CONCLUSION

Clearly, from a real estate broker's perspective, a broker's ability to list and effectively market property can be greatly affected by the designation of the property as in a special flood hazard area or flood-prone area. As stated previously in this section, such designation (or lack thereof) will affect financing, the purchaser's ability to get building permits, and, in the final analysis, just the common law duty of knowing whether an area is subject to special flood hazards because there has been a common knowledge in the community that the area is prone to flooding. This falls in areas of whether the broker "should have known" of such defect or flood-prone nature of the property, and whether such representation or misrepresentation results in fraud, misrepresentation, or deception in a federal or state statute.

COPYRIGHT ACT

The Copyright Act of 1976 enables authors and other talented creators to exercise exclusive control over their creations and the economic awards they generate. The Act provides for both civil and criminal relief.

At first glance, one would think that real estate brokers would have little reason to concern themselves with copyright laws unless they were authors or publishers. The value of the copyright to protecting the MLS® interest, however, was the primary conflict in *Supermarket of Homes v. San Fernando Valley Board of Realtors*, 786 F.2d 1400 (9th Cir. 1986), wherein the Board of Realtors compiled the traditional multiple listing book containing descriptions of various properties for sale in their region. The Association limited access to the compilation by restricting the use of the book only to licensed brokers and limiting the use of the listing book by showing it to customers only in the broker's presence. There was a total prohibition against the broker selling or distributing copies. A real estate broker in Supermarket of Homes chose to copy and sell certain pages to various customers. The Court upheld the copyright protection.

The basic thrust of this decision is to make real estate brokers cautious in dealing with multiple listing information. This information can contain private and confidential details such as: when a property will be vacated, loan information, names and telephone numbers, working and sleeping habits, etc. The misuse of the information can result in both civil and criminal liability.

EMPLOYMENT

PURPOSE

After carefully reading Chapter 14, the student will be able to:

- List and explain the various types of listing agreements.

- Discuss the changes technology is making in the real estate market.

- Define: *a ready, willing, and able buyer*; *procuring cause*; and *personal assistant*.

- Apply a knowledge of employee versus independent contractor status to a broker-salesperson relationship.

- Identify Wage and Hour Laws and Workman's Compensation Laws.

Key Words to look for in this chapter:
1. Listing Agreement
2. Exclusive Authority to Purchase
3. Multiple Listing Service®
4. Broker Compensation
5. The Broker's and Appraiser's Lien on Commercial Real Estate Act
6. Procuring Cause
7. Employees versus Independent Contractors

Employment issues are multifaceted as they affect the real estate licensee. There are a number of federal laws and state laws concerning wage and hour compensation, income taxation, and issues of "employee" versus "independent contractor" relationships. The primary concern of most licensees, however, is getting a job, doing it well, and getting paid. In most circumstances this is effected through employment contracts and listing agreements.

LISTING AGREEMENT

A real estate listing is an employment contract between a property owner and a listing real estate broker. Through the listing the property owner appoints the broker as the owner's agent for the specific purpose of finding a buyer or tenant who is willing to meet the conditions set forth in the listing. It does not authorize the broker to sell or convey title to the property or to sign contracts. The Texas Real Estate Commission takes the position that a real estate licensee is obligated to advise a property owner as to the licensee's opinion of the market value of the property when negotiating a listing. See T.A.C., Section 535.16(d).

Although people licensed as real estate salespersons perform listing and sales functions, they are actually extensions of the broker as subagents. A seller may conduct all aspects of a listing and sale through a salesperson licensee, but it is the broker sponsoring the salesperson with whom the seller has the listing contract and who is legally liable for its proper execution. If you plan to be a salesperson for a broker, be aware of what is legally and ethically required of a broker because you are the broker's eyes, ears, hands, and mouth. If your interest is in listing your property with a broker, know that it is the broker with whom you have the listing contract even though your day-to-day contact is with the sales associates.

Sales associates are the licensed salespersons or brokers who work for a broker. When a property owner signs a listing, all the essential elements of a valid contract must be present. The owner and broker must be legally capable of contracting, there must be mutual assent and consideration, and the agreement must be for a lawful purpose. Texas requires that a listing be in writing and signed to be valid and enforceable for a broker to pursue a commission from the seller or buyer in a court of law.

Figure 14-1 is a TAR® Form 1101 **Residential Exclusive Right to Sell Listing** agreement. Other listing contracts may be longer and more complex and vary in detail from one contract to the next. Beginning at [1] are the names of the parties. A prudent licensee needs to confirm the correct identity of the owners and secure both signatures if the owners are married (you may need to ask). The name of the broker must also be specifically designated in order to maintain suit for real estate commission. The legal description of the property is to be filled in at [2] along with the seller's disclosure as to whether the property is subject to mandatory membership in a homeowners' association. [3] shows the items of personal property that will not be included with the real estate. Both items [2] and [3] are important because the information is required in the contract for sale. At [4] is the listing price. Note that the property can also sell for any other price the seller may accept, and the commission is still due. At [5] you must fill in the term of the listing. Recall that §1101.652(b)(12) of the Texas Real Estate License Act requires that the listing agreements have a definite termination date or the licensee is subject to license suspension or revocation. You may recall one case, which held that this omission makes the employment agreement void, *Perl v. Patrizi*, discussed earlier. In residential real estate, five to six months is a

TEXAS ASSOCIATION OF REALTORS®

RESIDENTIAL REAL ESTATE LISTING AGREEMENT
EXCLUSIVE RIGHT TO SELL

USE OF THIS FORM BY PERSONS WHO ARE NOT MEMBERS OF THE TEXAS ASSOCIATION OF REALTORS® IS NOT AUTHORIZED.
©Texas Association of REALTORS®, Inc. 2003

1. **PARTIES:** The parties to this agreement (this Listing) are:

Seller: _____

Address: _____
City, State, Zip: _____
Phone:_____ Fax: _____
E-Mail: _____

Broker: _____
Address: _____
City, State, Zip: _____
Phone:_____ Fax: _____
E-Mail: _____

Seller appoints Broker as Seller's sole and exclusive real estate agent and grants to Broker the exclusive right to sell the Property.

2. **PROPERTY:** "Property" means the land, improvements, and accessories described below, except for any described exclusions.

A. Land: Lot_____, Block_____, _____
_____ Addition, City of_____,
in _____ County, Texas known as _____
_____ (address/zip code),
or as described on attached exhibit. (If Property is a condominium, attach Condominium Addendum.)

B. Improvements: The house, garage and all other fixtures and improvements attached to the above-described real property, including without limitation, the following permanently installed and built-in items, if any: all equipment and appliances, valances, screens, shutters, awnings, wall-to-wall carpeting, mirrors, ceiling fans, attic fans, mail boxes, television antennas and satellite dish system and equipment, heating and air-conditioning units, security and fire detection equipment, wiring, plumbing and lighting fixtures, chandeliers, water softener system, kitchen equipment, garage door openers, cleaning equipment, shrubbery, landscaping, outdoor cooking equipment, and all other property owned by Seller and attached to the above-described real property.

C. Accessories: The following described related accessories, if any: window air conditioning units, stove, fireplace screens, curtains and rods, blinds, window shades, draperies and rods, controls for satellite dish system, controls for garage door openers, entry gate controls, door keys, mailbox keys, above-ground pool, swimming pool equipment and maintenance accessories, and artificial fireplace logs.

D. Exclusions: The following improvements and accessories will be retained by Seller and excluded: _____
_____.

E. Owners' Association: The property ❑ is ❑ is not subject to mandatory membership in an owners' association.

FIG 14-1   *(continued)*

Residential Listing concerning _____

3. LISTING PRICE: Seller instructs Broker to market the Property at the following price: $_____ (Listing Price). Seller agrees to sell the Property for the Listing Price or any other price acceptable to Seller. Seller will pay all typical closing costs charged to sellers of residential real estate in Texas (seller's typical closing costs are those set forth in the residential contract forms promulgated by the Texas Real Estate Commission).

4. TERM:

   A. This Listing begins on _____ and ends at 11:59 p.m. on _____.

   B. If Seller enters into a binding written contract to sell the Property before the date this Listing begins and the contract is binding on the date this Listing begins, this Listing will not commence and will be void.

5. BROKER'S FEE:

   A. <u>Fee</u>: When earned and payable, Seller will pay Broker a fee of:

   ❑ (1) _____% of the sales price.

   ❑ (2) _____.

   B. <u>Earned</u>: Broker's fee is earned when any one of the following occurs during this Listing:
      (1) Seller sells, exchanges, options, agrees to sell, agrees to exchange, or agrees to option the Property to anyone at any price on any terms;
      (2) Broker individually or in cooperation with another broker procures a buyer ready, willing, and able to buy the Property at the Listing Price or at any other price acceptable to Seller; or
      (3) Seller breaches this Listing.

   C. <u>Payable</u>: Once earned, Broker's fee is payable either during this Listing or after it ends at the earlier of:
      (1) the closing and funding of any sale or exchange of all or part of the Property;
      (2) Seller's refusal to sell the Property after Broker's Fee has been earned;
      (3) Seller's breach of this Listing; or
      (4) at such time as otherwise set forth in this Listing.

      Broker's fee is <u>not</u> payable if a sale of the Property does not close or fund as a result of: (i) Seller's failure, without fault of Seller, to deliver to a buyer a deed or a title policy as required by the contract to sell; (ii) loss of ownership due to foreclosure or other legal proceeding; or (iii) Seller's failure to restore the Property, as a result of a casualty loss, to its previous condition by the closing date set forth in a contract for the sale of the Property.

   D. <u>Other Fees</u>:

      (1) <u>Breach by Buyer Under a Contract</u>: If Seller collects earnest money, the sales price, or damages by suit, compromise, settlement, or otherwise from a buyer who breaches a contract for the sale of the Property entered into during this Listing, Seller will pay Broker, after deducting attorney's fees and collection expenses, an amount equal to the lesser of one-half of the amount collected after deductions or the amount of the Broker's Fee stated in Paragraph 5A. Any amount paid under this Paragraph 5D(1) is in addition to any amount that Broker may be entitled to receive for subsequently selling the Property.

      (2) <u>Service Providers</u>: If Broker refers Seller or a prospective buyer to a service provider (for example, mover, cable company, telecommunications provider, utility, or contractor) Broker may receive a fee from the service provider for the referral. Any referral fee Broker receives under this Paragraph 5D(2) is in addition to any other compensation Broker may receive under this Listing.

(TAR-1101) 10-16-03   Initialed for Identification by Broker/Associate _____ and Seller _____, _____   Page 2 of 8

FIG 14-1   *(continued)*

Residential Listing concerning _____

    (3) <u>Transaction Fees or Reimbursable Expenses</u>: _____
_____
_____ .

E. <u>Protection Period</u>:

    (1) "Protection period" means that time starting the day after this Listing ends and continuing for _____ days. "Sell" means any transfer of any interest in the Property whether by oral or written agreement or option.

    (2) Not later than 10 days after this Listing ends, Broker may send Seller written notice specifying the names of persons whose attention was called to the Property during this Listing. If Seller agrees to sell the Property during the protection period to a person named in the notice or to a relative of a person named in the notice, Seller will pay Broker, upon the closing of the sale, the amount Broker would have been entitled to receive if this Listing were still in effect.

    (3) This Paragraph 5E survives termination of this Listing. This Paragraph 5E will not apply if:
        (a) Seller agrees to sell the Property during the protection period;
        (b) the Property is exclusively listed with another broker who is a member of the Texas Association of REALTORS® at the time the sale is negotiated; and
        (c) Seller is obligated to pay the other broker a fee for the sale.

F. <u>County</u>: All amounts payable to Broker are to be paid in cash in _____
_____ County, Texas.

G. <u>Escrow Authorization</u>: Seller authorizes, and Broker may so instruct, any escrow or closing agent authorized to close a transaction for the purchase or acquisition of the Property to collect and disburse to Broker all amounts payable to Broker under this Listing.

6. LISTING SERVICES:

❏ A. Broker will file this Listing with one or more Multiple Listing Services (MLS) by the earlier of the time required by MLS rules or 5 days after the date this Listing begins. Seller authorizes Broker to submit information about this Listing and the sale of the Property to the MLS.

    <u>Notice</u>: MLS rules require Broker to accurately and timely submit all information the MLS requires for participation including sold data. Subscribers to the MLS may use the information for market evaluation or appraisal purposes. Subscribers are other brokers and other real estate professionals such as appraisers and may include the appraisal district. Any information filed with the MLS becomes the property of the MLS for all purposes. **Submission of information to MLS ensures that persons who use and benefit from the MLS also contribute information.**

❏ B. Broker will not file this Listing with a Multiple Listing Service (MLS) or any other listing service.

7. ACCESS TO THE PROPERTY:

A. <u>Authorizing Access</u>: Authorizing access to the Property means giving permission to another person to enter the Property, disclosing to the other person any security codes necessary to enter the Property, and lending a key to the other person to enter the Property, directly or through a keybox. To facilitate the showing and sale of the Property, Seller instructs Broker to:
    (1) access the Property at reasonable times
    (2) authorize other brokers, their associates, inspectors, appraisers, and contractors to access the Property at reasonable times; and
    (3) duplicate keys to facilitate convenient and efficient showings of the Property.

B. <u>Scheduling Companies</u>: Broker may engage the following companies to schedule appointments and to authorize others to access the Property: _____ .

(TAR-1101) 10-16-03   Initialed for Identification by Broker/Associate _____ and Seller _____, _____   Page 3 of 8

FIG 14-1   *(continued)*

Residential Listing concerning _____

   C. <u>Keybox:</u> **A keybox is a locked container placed on the Property that holds a key to the Property. A keybox makes it more convenient for brokers, their associates, inspectors, appraisers, and contractors to show, inspect, or repair the Property. The keybox is opened by a special combination, key, or programmed device so that authorized persons may enter the Property, even in Seller's absence. Using a keybox will probably increase the number of showings, but involves risks (for example, unauthorized entry, theft, property damage, or personal injury). Neither the Association of REALTORS® nor MLS requires the use of a keybox.**

     (1) Broker ❏ is ❏ is not   authorized to place a keybox on the Property.

     (2) If a tenant occupies the Property at any time during this Listing, Seller will furnish Broker a written statement (for example, TAR No. 1411), signed by all tenants, authorizing the use of a keybox or Broker may remove the keybox from the Property.

   D. <u>Liability and Indemnification:</u> When authorizing access to the Property, Broker, other brokers, their associates, any keybox provider, or any scheduling company are not responsible for personal injury or property loss to Seller or any other person. Seller assumes all risk of any loss, damage, or injury. **Except for a loss caused by Broker, Seller will indemnify and hold Broker harmless from any claim for personal injury, property damage, or other loss.**

8. COOPERATION WITH OTHER BROKERS: Broker will allow other brokers to show the Property to prospective buyers. Broker will offer to pay the other broker a fee as described below if the other broker procures a buyer that purchases the Property.

   A. <u>MLS Participants:</u> If the other broker is a participant in the MLS in which this Listing is filed, Broker will offer to pay the other broker:
     (1) if the other broker represents the buyer: _____% of the sales price or $_____; and
     (2) if the other broker is a subagent: _____% of the sales price or $_____.

   B. <u>Non-MLS Brokers:</u> If the other broker is not a participant in the MLS in which this Listing is filed, Broker will offer to pay the other broker:
     (1) if the other broker represents the buyer: _____% of the sales price or $_____; and
     (2) if the other broker is a subagent: _____% of the sales price or $_____.

9. INTERMEDIARY: *(Check A or B only.)*

❏ A. <u>Intermediary Status:</u> Broker may show the Property to interested prospective buyers who Broker represents. If a prospective buyer who Broker represents offers to buy the Property, Seller authorizes Broker to act as an intermediary and Broker will notify Seller that Broker will service the parties in accordance with one of the following alternatives.

     (1) If a prospective buyer who Broker represents is serviced by an associate other than the associate servicing Seller under this Listing, Broker may notify Seller that Broker will: (a) appoint the associate then servicing Seller to communicate with, carry out instructions of, and provide opinions and advice during negotiations to Seller; and (b) appoint the associate then servicing the prospective buyer to the prospective buyer for the same purpose.

     (2) If a prospective buyer who Broker represents is serviced by the same associate who is servicing Seller, Broker may notify Seller that Broker will: (a) appoint another associate to communicate with, carry out instructions of, and provide opinions and advice during negotiations to the prospective buyer; and (b) appoint the associate servicing the Seller under this Listing to the Seller for the same purpose.

     (3) Broker may notify Seller that Broker will make no appointments as described under this Paragraph 9A and, in such an event, the associate servicing the parties will act solely as Broker's intermediary representative, who may facilitate the transaction but will not render opinions or advice during negotiations to either party.

(TAR-1101) 10-16-03   Initialed for Identification by Broker/Associate _____ and Seller _____, _____   Page 4 of 8

FIG 14-1 *(continued)*

Residential Listing concerning _____

☐ B. <u>No Intermediary Status</u>: Seller agrees that Broker will not show the Property to prospective buyers who Broker represents.

Notice: **If Broker acts as an intermediary under Paragraph 9A, Broker and Broker's associates:**
- **may not disclose to the prospective buyer that Seller will accept a price less than the asking price unless otherwise instructed in a separate writing by Seller;**
- **may not disclose to Seller that the prospective buyer will pay a price greater than the price submitted in a written offer to Seller unless otherwise instructed in a separate writing by the prospective buyer;**
- **may not disclose any confidential information or any information Seller or the prospective buyer specifically instructs Broker in writing not to disclose unless otherwise instructed in a separate writing by the respective party or required to disclose the information by the Real Estate License Act or a court order or if the information materially relates to the condition of the property;**
- **may not treat a party to the transaction dishonestly; and**
- **may not violate the Real Estate License Act.**

10. **CONFIDENTIAL INFORMATION:** During this Listing or after it ends, Broker may not knowingly disclose information obtained in confidence from Seller except as authorized by Seller or required by law. Broker may not disclose to Seller any confidential information regarding any other person Broker represents or previously represented except as required by law.

11. **BROKER'S AUTHORITY:**

A. Broker will use reasonable efforts and act diligently to market the Property for sale, procure a buyer, and negotiate the sale of the Property.

B. In addition to other authority granted by this Listing, Broker may:
   (1) advertise the Property by means and methods as Broker determines, including but not limited to creating and placing advertisements with interior and exterior photographic and audio-visual images of the Property and related information in any media and the Internet;
   (2) place a "For Sale" sign on the Property and remove all other signs offering the Property for sale or lease;
   (3) furnish comparative marketing and sales information about other properties to prospective buyers;
   (4) disseminate information about the Property to other brokers and to prospective buyers, including applicable disclosures or notices that Seller is required to make under law or a contract;
   (5) obtain information from any holder of a note secured by a lien on the Property;
   (6) accept and deposit earnest money in trust in accordance with a contract for the sale of the Property;
   (7) disclose the sales price and terms of sale to other brokers, appraisers, or other real estate professionals;
   (8) in response to inquiries from prospective buyers and other brokers, disclose whether the Seller is considering more than one offer, provided that Broker will not disclose the terms of any competing offer unless specifically instructed by Seller;
   (9) advertise, during or after this Listing ends, that Broker "sold" the Property; and
   (10) place information about this Listing, the Property, and a transaction for the Property on an electronic transaction platform (typically an Internet-based system where professionals related to the transaction such as title companies, lenders, and others may receive, view, and input information).

C. Broker is not authorized to execute any document in the name of or on behalf of Seller concerning the Property.

(TAR-1101) 10-16-03   Initialed for Identification by Broker/Associate _____ and Seller _____, _____   Page 5 of 8

Residential Listing concerning _____

12. SELLER'S REPRESENTATIONS: Except as provided by Paragraph 15, Seller represents that:
   A. Seller has fee simple title to and peaceable possession of the Property and all its improvements and fixtures, unless rented, and the legal capacity to convey the Property;
   B. Seller is not bound by a listing agreement with another broker for the sale, exchange, or lease of the Property that is or will be in effect during this Listing;
   C. any pool or spa and any required enclosures, fences, gates, and latches comply with all applicable laws and ordinances;
   D. no person or entity has any right to purchase, lease, or acquire the Property by an option, right of refusal, or other agreement;
   E. there are no delinquencies or defaults under any deed of trust, mortgage, or other encumbrance on the Property;
   F. the Property is not subject to the jurisdiction of any court;
   G. all information relating to the Property Seller provides to Broker is true and correct to the best of Seller's knowledge; and
   H. the name of any employer, relocation company, or other entity that provides benefits to Seller when selling the Property is: _____.

13. SELLER'S ADDITIONAL PROMISES: Seller agrees to:
   A. cooperate with Broker to facilitate the showing, marketing, and sale of the Property;
   B. not rent or lease the Property during this Listing without Broker's prior written approval;
   C. not negotiate with any prospective buyer who may contact Seller directly, but refer all prospective buyers to Broker;
   D. not enter into a listing agreement with another broker for the sale, exchange, or lease of the Property to become effective during this Listing;
   E. maintain any pool and all required enclosures in compliance with all applicable laws and ordinances;
   F. provide Broker with copies of any leases or rental agreements pertaining to the Property and advise Broker of tenants moving in or out of the Property;
   G. complete any disclosures or notices required by law or a contract to sell the Property; and
   H. amend any applicable notices and disclosures if any material change occurs during this Listing.

14. LIMITATION OF LIABILITY:

   A. If the Property is or becomes vacant during this Listing, Seller must notify Seller's casualty insurance company and request a "vacancy clause" to cover the Property. Broker is not responsible for the security of the Property nor for inspecting the Property on any periodic basis.

   B. **Broker is not responsible or liable in any manner for personal injury to any person or for loss or damage to any person's real or personal property resulting from any act or omission not caused by Broker's negligence, including but not limited to injuries or damages caused by:**
      (1) other brokers, their associates, inspectors, appraisers, and contractors who are authorized to access the Property;
      (2) acts of third parties (for example, vandalism or theft);
      (3) freezing water pipes;
      (4) a dangerous condition on the Property; or
      (5) the Property's non-compliance with any law or ordinance.

   C. **Seller agrees to protect, defend, indemnify, and hold Broker harmless from any damage, costs, attorney's fees, and expenses that:**
      (1) are caused by Seller, negligently or otherwise;
      (2) arise from Seller's failure to disclose any material or relevant information about the Property; or
      (3) are caused by Seller giving incorrect information to any person.

FIG 14-1 *(continued)*

Residential Listing concerning _____

15. SPECIAL PROVISIONS:

16. **DEFAULT:** If Seller breaches this Listing, Seller is in default and will be liable to Broker for the amount of the Broker's fee specified in Paragraph 5A and any other fees Broker is entitled to receive under this Listing. If a sales price is not determinable in the event of an exchange or breach of this Listing, the Listing Price will be the sales price for purposes of computing Broker's fee. If Broker breaches this Listing, Broker is in default and Seller may exercise any remedy at law.

17. **MEDIATION:** The parties agree to negotiate in good faith in an effort to resolve any dispute related to this Listing that may arise between the parties. If the dispute cannot be resolved by negotiation, the dispute will be submitted to mediation. The parties to the dispute will choose a mutually acceptable mediator and will share the cost of mediation equally.

18. **ATTORNEY'S FEES:** If Seller or Broker is a prevailing party in any legal proceeding brought as a result of a dispute under this Listing or any transaction related to or contemplated by this Listing, such party will be entitled to recover from the non-prevailing party all costs of such proceeding and reasonable attorney's fees.

19. **ADDENDA AND OTHER DOCUMENTS:** Addenda that are part of this Listing and other documents that Seller may need to provide are:
   - [X] A. Information About Brokerage Services;
   - ☐ B. Seller Disclosure Notice (§5.008, Texas Property Code);
   - ☐ C. Seller's Disclosure of Information on Lead-Based Paint and Lead-Based Paint Hazards (required if Property was built before 1978);
   - ☐ D. MUD, Water District, or Statutory Tax District Disclosure Notice (Chapter 49, Texas Water Code);
   - ☐ E. Request for Information from an Owners' Association;
   - ☐ F. Request for Mortgage Information;
   - ☐ G. Information about On-Site Sewer Facility;
   - ☐ H. Information about Special Flood Hazard Areas;
   - ☐ I. Condominium Addendum to Listing;
   - ☐ J. Keybox Authorization by Tenant;
   - ☐ K. Seller's Authorization to Release and Advertise Certain Information; and
   - ☐ L. _____
     _____ .

20. AGREEMENT OF PARTIES:

   A. <u>Entire Agreement</u>: This Listing is the entire agreement of the parties and may not be changed except by written agreement.

   B. <u>Assignability</u>: Neither party may assign this Listing without the written consent of the other party.

(TAR-1101) 10-16-03   Initialed for Identification by Broker/Associate _____ and Seller _____, _____   Page 7 of 8

FIG 14-1 *(continued)*

Residential Listing concerning _____

    C. <u>Binding Effect</u>: Seller's obligation to pay Broker an earned fee is binding upon Seller and Seller's heirs, administrators, executors, successors, and permitted assignees.

    D. <u>Joint and Several</u>: All Sellers executing this Listing are jointly and severally liable for the performance of all its terms.

    E. <u>Governing Law</u>: Texas law governs the interpretation, validity, performance, and enforcement of this Listing.

    F. <u>Severability</u>: If a court finds any clause in this Listing invalid or unenforceable, the remainder of this Listing will not be affected and all other provisions of this Listing will remain valid and enforceable.

    G. <u>Notices</u>: Notices between the parties must be in writing and are effective when sent to the receiving party's address, fax, or e-mail address specified in Paragraph 1.

21. ADDITIONAL NOTICES:

    A. Broker's fees or the sharing of fees between brokers are not fixed, controlled, recommended, suggested, or maintained by the Association of REALTORS®, MLS, or any listing service.

    B. Fair housing laws require the Property to be shown and made available to all persons without regard to race, color, religion, national origin, sex, disability, or familial status. Local ordinances may provide for additional protected classes (for example, creed, status as a student, marital status, sexual orientation, or age).

    C. Seller may review the information Broker submits to an MLS or other listing service.

    D. Broker advises Seller to remove or secure jewelry, prescription drugs, and other valuables.

    E. Statutes or ordinances may regulate certain items on the Property (for example, swimming pools and septic systems). Non-compliance with the statutes or ordinances may delay a transaction and may result in fines, penalties, and liability to Seller.

    F. If the Property was built before 1978, Federal law requires the Seller to: (1) provide the buyer with the federally approved pamphlet on lead poisoning prevention; (2) disclose the presence of any known lead-based paint or lead-based paint hazards in the Property; (3) deliver all records and reports to the buyer related to such paint or hazards; and (4) provide the buyer a period up to 10 days to have the Property inspected for such paint or hazards.

    G. Broker cannot give legal advice. READ THIS LISTING CAREFULLY. If you do not understand the effect of this Listing, consult an attorney BEFORE signing.

_____ _____   _____ _____
Broker's Printed Name   License No.   Seller   Date

By:_____   _____ _____
    Broker's Associate's Signature   Date   Seller   Date

popular compromise. In commercial transactions, the term is often for a year or longer. Paragraph 6 at [6] authorizes or prohibits the use of the multiple listing service, if any, where this listing information will be filed.

Paragraph 5 designates the fee that will be paid to the broker. Note that the broker's fee is specified to be earned when the broker procures (1) a buyer who enters into a contract; or (2) a buyer who is willing, ready, and able to buy on the listing price or upon the sale to anyone on any price at any terms. While this provision is highly protective of the broker, it is important to note that a broker spends a lot of time, money, and effort in procuring the ready, willing, and able buyer. If that buyer is produced and the seller chooses not to perform, the seller is breaching the listing contract. The broker has earned a commission at that time.

Usually the commission is expressed as a percentage of the sale or exchange price. A stated dollar amount could be used if the owner and broker agreed. The amount of the fee is always negotiable between the owner and the broker. An owner who feels the fee is too high can list with someone who charges less or sell the property himself or herself. A broker knows that if the fee is too low, it will not be worthwhile spending time and effort finding a buyer. The typical commission fee in Texas is 5 to 7 percent of the selling price for houses, condominiums, and small apartment buildings, and 6 to 10 percent on farms, ranches, and vacant land. On multimillion-dollar properties, commissions usually drop to the 1 to 4 percent range.

Brokerage commissions are not set by a state regulatory agency or by local real estate associations. Any effort by brokers to set commission rates among themselves is a violation of federal and state antitrust laws. The penalty can be as much as triple damages and criminal liability.

The broker also has obligations. Note that Paragraph 6 may require the broker to put the property in the multiple listing service and make reasonable efforts to act diligently to sell the property (Paragraph 11.A). Note also that there are numerous notices to the owner under Paragraph 9 concerning the broker's authorization for agency relationships and the handling of conflicts of interest in the event an intermediary relationship is authorized. The owner and the broker both sign the agreement at [9].

Note that Paragraph 9 at [7] specifies the agency relationship the owner agrees to authorize the broker to participate in. This can become a complex area of negotiation between the broker and the owner. If the owner wants to limit the broker's activities (i.e., require that all other brokers be subagents), this may severely limit the property's exposure to the marketplace (buyer's brokers may choose not to show it).

Exclusive Right to Sell Listing

The listing illustrated in Figure 14-1 is called an Exclusive Right to Sell or Exclusive Authorization to Sell Listing. Its distinguishing characteristic is that no matter who sells the property during the listing period, the listing broker is entitled to a commission. This is the most widely used type of listing in Texas. Once signed by the owner and accepted by the broker, the primary advantage to the broker is that the money and effort the broker expends on advertising and showing the property will be to the broker's benefit. The advantage to the owner is that the broker will usually put more effort into selling a property if the broker holds an exclusive right to sell than if the broker has an exclusive agency or an open listing.

Exclusive Agency Listing

The exclusive agency listing is similar to the listing shown in Figure 14-1, except that the owner may sell the property himself during the listing period and not owe a commission to the broker. The broker, however, is the only broker who can act as an agent during the listing period; hence the term "exclusive agency." For an owner, this type of listing may seem like the best of two worlds: the owner has a broker looking for a buyer, but if the owner finds a buyer first, the owner can save a commission fee. However, the broker is less enthusiastic because the owner can undermine the broker's efforts too easily. Consequently, the broker may not expend as much effort on advertising and showing the property as with an exclusive right to sell.

Open Listing

Open listings carry no exclusive rights. An owner can give an open listing to any number of brokers at the same time, and the owner can still find a buyer and avoid a commission. This gives the owner the greatest freedom of any listing form, but there is little incentive for the broker to expend time and money showing the property as the broker has little control over who will be compensated if the property is sold. The broker's only protection is that if the broker does find a buyer at the listing price and terms, the broker is entitled to a commission. This reluctance to develop sales effort usually means that few, if any, offers will be received and the result may be no sale or a sale below market price. Yet if a broker does find a buyer, the commission earned may be the same as with an exclusive right to sell.

Net Listing

A net listing is created when an owner states the price he or she wants for his or her property and then agrees to pay the broker anything above that price as the commission. It can be written in the form of an exclusive right to sell, an exclusive agency, or an open listing. If a homeowner asks for a "net $60,000" and the broker sells the home for $75,000, the commission would be $15,000. By using the net listing method, many owners feel that they are forcing the broker to look to the buyer for the commission by marking up the price of the property. In reality, though, would a buyer pay $75,000 for a home that is worth $60,000? Because of widespread misunderstanding regarding net listings, some states prohibit them outright (Texas does not), and most brokers strenuously avoid them even when requested by property owners.

The Texas Real Estate Commission has taken the position that brokers should take net listings only when the principal insists upon a net listing and when the principal appears to be familiar with current market values of real property. The use of a net listing places an upper limit on the principal's expectancy and places the broker's interest above his or her principal's interest with reference to obtaining the best possible price. A net listing should be qualified to assure the principal of not less than his or her desired price and to limit the broker to a specified maximum commission. See Section 535.16(c).

There is no law that says a broker must accept a listing; a broker is free to accept only those listings for which the broker can perform a valuable service and earn an honest profit.

Exclusive Authority to Purchase

Previous portions of this chapter have presumed the general rule that the real estate broker represents the seller. Historically, it has been the seller who has hired brokers to assist in marketing and selling property. There are circumstances, however, in which buyers may want to employ a broker's services to help them to locate property, or to assist them in negotiating the acquisition of a specified property. In such cases, the broker's primary responsibility is to the purchaser rather than to the seller. In this circumstance, the purchaser can reveal confidential information to the broker and rely on the broker's expertise and competence. This may be particularly helpful in situations where a real estate transaction is complex, the purchaser is unfamiliar with the area, or there are peculiar concerns unique to certain regions of the country (flood-prone areas in Houston, radon in Maine, soil conditions in California) about which a buyer wants to be advised adequately before buying real estate in that area. In some cases, a purchaser simply feels he or she needs expert advice in purchasing real estate.

In these situations, the principal needs to know the scope of employment of the broker (i.e., locating the property, advising as to values, financing alternatives). The broker needs to be assured that he or she is protected and that the buyer does not "go around" the broker and cut the broker out of a fee once earned and payable. Figure 14-2 shows the TAR® Buyer/Tenant Representation Agreement—Residential contract. Note at [1] the parties are named. The real difference in this contract, versus the Listing Agreement, occurs at [2], designating

FIG 14-2   BUYER/TENANT REPRESENTATION AGREEMENT—RESIDENTIAL

TEXAS ASSOCIATION OF REALTORS®
RESIDENTIAL BUYER/TENANT REPRESENTATION AGREEMENT
USE OF THIS FORM BY PERSONS WHO ARE NOT MEMBERS OF THE TEXAS ASSOCIATION OF REALTORS® IS NOT AUTHORIZED.
©Texas Association of REALTORS®, Inc. 2006

1. **PARTIES:** The parties to this agreement are:

   Client: _____
   _____
       Address: _____
       City, State, Zip: _____
       Phone:_____ Fax: _____
       E-Mail: _____

   Broker: _____
       Address: _____
       City, State, Zip: _____
       Phone:_____ Fax: _____
       E-Mail: _____

2. **APPOINTMENT:** Client grants to Broker the exclusive right to act as Client's real estate agent for the purpose of acquiring property in the market area.

3. **DEFINITIONS:**
   A. *"Acquire"* means to purchase or lease.
   B. *"Closing"* in a sale transaction means the date legal title to a property is conveyed to a purchaser of property under a contract to buy. *"Closing"* in a lease transaction means the date a landlord and tenant enter into a binding lease of a property.
   C. *"Market area"* means that area in the State of Texas within the perimeter boundaries of the following areas:_____
   _____
   _____
   _____.
   D. *"Property"* means any interest in real estate including but not limited to properties listed in a multiple listing service or other listing services, properties for sale by owners, and properties for sale by builders.

4. **TERM:** This agreement commences on _____ and ends at 11:59 p.m. on _____.

5. **BROKER'S OBLIGATIONS:** Broker will: (a) use Broker's best efforts to assist Client in acquiring property in the market area; (b) assist Client in negotiating the acquisition of property in the market area; and (c) comply with other provisions of this agreement.

6. **CLIENT'S OBLIGATIONS:** Client will: (a) work exclusively through Broker in acquiring property in the market area and negotiate the acquisition of property in the market area only through Broker; (b) inform other brokers, salespersons, sellers, and landlords with whom Client may have contact that Broker exclusively represents Client for the purpose of acquiring property in the market area and refer all such persons to Broker; and (c) comply with other provisions of this agreement.

7. **REPRESENTATIONS:**
   A. Each person signing this agreement represents that the person has the legal capacity and authority to bind the respective party to this agreement.
   B. Client represents that Client is not now a party to another buyer or tenant representation agreement with another broker for the acquisition of property in the market area.

(TAR-1501) 4-14-06   Initialed for Identification by: Broker/Associate _____, and Client _____, _____   Page 1 of 4

FIG 14-2 *(continued)*

Buyer/Tenant Representation Agreement between _____

   C. Client represents that all information relating to Client's ability to acquire property in the market area Client gives to Broker is true and correct.

   D. Name any employer, relocation company, or other entity that will provide benefits to Client when acquiring property in the market area: _____.

8. INTERMEDIARY: *(Check A or B only.)*

❏ A. <u>Intermediary Status</u>: Client desires to see Broker's listings. If Client wishes to acquire one of Broker's listings, Client authorizes Broker to act as an intermediary and Broker will notify Client that Broker will service the parties in accordance with one of the following alternatives.

    (1) If the owner of the property is serviced by an associate other than the associate servicing Client under this agreement, Broker may notify Client that Broker will: (a) appoint the associate then servicing the owner to communicate with, carry out instructions of, and provide opinions and advice during negotiations to the owner; and (b) appoint the associate then servicing Client to the Client for the same purpose.

    (2) If the owner of the property is serviced by the same associate who is servicing Client, Broker may notify Client that Broker will: (a) appoint another associate to communicate with, carry out instructions of, and provide opinions and advice during negotiations to Client; and (b) appoint the associate servicing the owner under the listing to the owner for the same purpose.

    (3) Broker may notify Client that Broker will make no appointments as described under this Paragraph 8A and, in such an event, the associate servicing the parties will act solely as Broker's intermediary representative, who may facilitate the transaction but will not render opinions or advice during negotiations to either party.

❏ B. <u>No Intermediary Status</u>: Client does not wish to be shown or acquire any of Broker's listings.

Notice: **If Broker acts as an intermediary under Paragraph 8A, Broker and Broker's associates:**
- **may not disclose to Client that the seller or landlord will accept a price less than the asking price unless otherwise instructed in a separate writing by the seller or landlord;**
- **may not disclose to the seller or landlord that Client will pay a price greater than the price submitted in a written offer to the seller or landlord unless otherwise instructed in a separate writing by Client;**
- **may not disclose any confidential information or any information a seller or landlord or Client specifically instructs Broker in writing not to disclose unless otherwise instructed in a separate writing by the respective party or required to disclose the information by the Real Estate License Act or a court order or if the information materially relates to the condition of the property;**
- **shall treat all parties to the transaction honestly; and**
- **shall comply with the Real Estate License Act.**

9. COMPETING CLIENTS: Client acknowledges that Broker may represent other prospective buyers or tenants who may seek to acquire properties that may be of interest to Client. Client agrees that Broker may, during the term of this agreement and after it ends, represent such other prospects, show the other prospects the same properties that Broker shows to Client, and act as a real estate broker for such other prospects in negotiating the acquisition of properties that Client may seek to acquire.

10. CONFIDENTIAL INFORMATION:

   A. During the term of this agreement or after its termination, Broker may not knowingly disclose information obtained in confidence from Client except as authorized by Client or required by law. Broker may not disclose to Client any information obtained in confidence regarding any other person Broker represents or may have represented except as required by law.

   B. Unless otherwise agreed or required by law, a seller or the seller's agent is not obliged to keep the existence of an offer or its terms confidential. If a listing agent receives multiple offers, the listing agent is obliged to treat the competing buyers fairly.

(TAR-1501) 4-14-06   Initialed for Identification by: Broker/Associate _____, and Client _____, _____   Page 2 of 4

FIG 14-2   *(continued)*

Buyer/Tenant Representation Agreement between _____

11. BROKER'S FEES:

A. <u>Commission</u>: The parties agree that Broker will receive a commission calculated as follows: (1) ____% of the gross sales price if Client agrees to purchase property in the market area; and (2) if Client agrees to lease property in the market a fee equal to *(check only one box)*: ❑ _____% of one month's rent or ❑ ____% of all rents to be paid over the term of the lease.

B. <u>Source of Commission Payment</u>: Broker will seek to obtain payment of the commission specified in Paragraph 11A first from the seller, landlord, or their agents. If such persons refuse or fail to pay Broker the amount specified, Client will pay Broker the amount specified less any amounts Broker receives from such persons.

C. <u>Earned and Payable</u>: A person is not obligated to pay Broker a commission until such time as Broker's commission is *earned and payable*. Broker's commission is *earned* when: (1) Client enters into a contract to buy or lease property in the market area; or (2) Client breaches this agreement. Broker's commission is *payable*, either during the term of this agreement or after it ends, upon the earlier of: (1) the closing of the transaction to acquire the property; (2) Client's breach of a contract to buy or lease a property in the market area; or (3) Client's breach of this agreement. If Client acquires more than one property under this agreement, Broker's commissions for each property acquired are earned as each property is acquired and are payable at the closing of each acquisition.

D. <u>Additional Compensation</u>: If a seller, landlord, or their agents offer compensation in excess of the amount stated in Paragraph 11A (including but not limited to marketing incentives or bonuses to cooperating brokers) Broker may retain the additional compensation in addition to the specified commission. Client is not obligated to pay any such additional compensation to Broker.

E. <u>Acquisition of Broker's Listing</u>: Notwithstanding any provision to the contrary, if Client acquires a property listed by Broker, Broker will be paid in accordance with the terms of Broker's listing agreement with the owner and Client will have no obligation to pay Broker.

F. In addition to the commission specified under Paragraph 11A, Broker is entitled to the following fees.
   (1) <u>Construction</u>: If Client uses Broker's services to procure or negotiate the construction of improvements to property that Client owns or may acquire, Client ensures that Broker will receive from Client or the contractor(s) at the time the construction is substantially complete a fee equal to:
   _____ .
   (2) <u>Service Providers</u>: If Broker refers Client or any party to a transaction contemplated by this agreement to a service provider (for example, mover, cable company, telecommunications provider, utility, or contractor) Broker may receive a fee from the service provider for the referral.
   (3) <u>Other</u>: _____
   _____
   _____ .

G. <u>Protection Period</u>: "Protection period" means that time starting the day after this agreement ends and continuing for _____ days. Not later than 10 days after this agreement ends, Broker may send Client written notice identifying the properties called to Client's attention during this agreement. If Client or a relative of Client agrees to acquire a property identified in the notice during the protection period, Client will pay Broker, upon closing, the amount Broker would have been entitled to receive if this agreement were still in effect. This Paragraph 11G survives termination of this agreement. This Paragraph 11G will not apply if Client is, during the protection period, bound under a representation agreement with another broker who is a member of the Texas Association of REALTORS® at the time the acquisition is negotiated and the other broker is paid a fee for negotiating the transaction.

H. <u>Escrow Authorization</u>: Client authorizes, and Broker may so instruct, any escrow or closing agent authorized to close a transaction for the acquisition of property contemplated by this agreement to collect and disburse to Broker all amounts payable to Broker.

I. <u>County</u>: Amounts payable to Broker are to be paid in cash in _____ County, Texas.

(TAR-1501) 4-14-06   Initialed for Identification by: Broker/Associate _____, and Client _____, _____   Page 3 of 4

FIG 14-2   *(continued)*

Buyer/Tenant Representation Agreement between _____

12. **MEDIATION**: The parties agree to negotiate in good faith in an effort to resolve any dispute that may arise related to this agreement or any transaction related to or contemplated by this agreement. If the dispute cannot be resolved by negotiation, the parties will submit the dispute to mediation before resorting to arbitration or litigation and will equally share the costs of a mutually acceptable mediator.

13. **DEFAULT**: If either party fails to comply with this agreement or makes a false representation in this agreement, the non-complying party is in default. If Client is in default, Client will be liable for the amount of compensation that Broker would have received under this agreement if Client was not in default. If Broker is in default, Client may exercise any remedy at law.

14. **ATTORNEY'S FEES**: If Client or Broker is a prevailing party in any legal proceeding brought as a result of a dispute under this agreement or any transaction related to this agreement, such party will be entitled to recover from the non-prevailing party all costs of such proceeding and reasonable attorney's fees.

15. **LIMITATION OF LIABILITY**: Neither Broker nor any other broker, or their associates, is responsible or liable for Client's personal injuries or for any loss or damage to Client's property that is not caused by Broker. Client will hold broker, any other broker, and their associates, harmless from any such injuries or losses. Client will indemnify Broker against any claims for injury or damage that Client may cause to others or their property.

16. **ADDENDA**: Addenda and other related documents which are part of this agreement are:
    ☑ Information About Brokerage Services   ☐ Protect Your Family from Lead in Your Home
    ☐ Protecting Your Home from Mold   ☐ Information about Special Flood Hazard Areas
    ☐ Information Concerning Property Insurance   ☐ For Your Protection: Get a Home Inspection
    ☐ General Information and Notice to a Buyer   ☐ _____

17. **SPECIAL PROVISIONS**:

18. **ADDITIONAL NOTICES**:

    A. **Broker's fees and the sharing of fees between brokers are not fixed, controlled, recommended, suggested, or maintained by the Association of REALTORS® or any listing service.**

    B. **Broker's services are provided without regard to race, color, religion, national origin, sex, disability or familial status.**

    C. **Broker is not a property inspector, surveyor, engineer, environmental assessor, or compliance inspector. Client should seek experts to render such services in any acquisition.**

    D. **If Client purchases property, Client should have an abstract covering the property examined by an attorney of Client's selection, or Client should be furnished with or obtain a title policy.**

    E. **Buyer may purchase a residential service contract. Buyer should review such service contract for the scope of coverage, exclusions, and limitations. The purchase of a residential service contract is optional. There are several residential service companies operating in Texas.**

    F. **Broker cannot give legal advice. This is a legally binding agreement. READ IT CAREFULLY. If you do not understand the effect of this agreement, consult your attorney BEFORE signing.**

_____	_____	_____	_____
Broker's Printed Name	License No.	Client	Date
By:_____		_____	_____
Broker's Associate's Signature	Date	Client	Date
(TAR-1501) 4-14-06			Page 4 of 4

the property to be acquired in general terms, so that the broker has guidance as to what type of property to be looking for. Compensation is different also. Most buyer's brokers would anticipate being able to access commission splits through the traditional MLS® system. If, however, a seller or listing broker refuses to split a commission, there must be an alternative for compensation at [4] for that buyer's broker. Note at [5], there is an expiration date for the term of the agreement, at [3] a requirement by the owner to refer inquiries to the broker, and at [6] a signature provision for both the buyer's broker and the purchaser.

The types of buyer/lessee representation are similar to the types of seller/lessor representation:

- the buyers/lessees could choose to represent themselves (like a "for sale by owner");

- similar to an open listing, the buyers/lessees may choose to work with several buyer/lessee agents promising compensation only if they purchase/lease with the representation and guidance of one of those agents, but retaining the right to purchase on their own and pay no commission;

- purchasers might give exclusive agency to a particular licensee promising only agent compensation, but retaining the right to buy themselves and pay no fee; or

- the purchasers/lessees might grant an exclusive right to represent with a promise of compensation to their agent no matter how a property was purchased/leased.

Buyers/lessees have several choices when it comes to compensation:

- the purchaser can choose to pay an hourly rate.

- the buyers/lessees can pay a retainer fee to their representative.

- the purchasers/renters can agree to pay a commission to their agent.

- the purchaser can require that their agent seek compensation from the sellers/lessors or their representative.

- the buyers/lessees can require that their agent seek compensation from the sellers/lessors before coming to the buyers/lessees for that compensation.

MULTIPLE LISTING SERVICE®

A **Multiple Listing Service** (MLS®), an offering of local NAR® Associations, enables a broker with a listing to make a blanket offering of cooperation, and/or compensation to brokers who are members of that same local association's MLS®, thus broadening the market exposure for a given property. Property information is available across the U.S. for local members. Member brokers are normally authorized to show each other's properties to their prospects. If a sale results, the commission may be divided between the broker who found the buyer and the broker who obtained the listing. The commission is shared at the discretion of the listing broker, but is normally agreed to by the property's owner. The division can be different between seller agent and subagent or between seller agent and buyer agent as disclosed. The commission division is part of the MLS® listing information.

Market Exposure

A property listed with a broker who is a member of a multiple listing market area receives the advantage of greater sales exposure and consumer information, which means a better price and a quicker sale. For the buyers, it means learning what is for sale at many offices without having to visit each individually and receiving buyer services to help with their decision to purchase. For a broker or salesperson with a prospect but not a suitable property listed in that office, the opportunity to make a sale is not lost because the prospect can be shown the listings of other brokers.

To give a property the widest possible market exposure and to maintain fairness among its members, most multiple listing organizations obligate each member broker to provide information to the organization on each new listing within three to seven days after the listing is taken if the listing is to be placed in MLS®. To facilitate the exchange of information, multiple listing organizations have developed customized listing forms. These forms are a combination of an exclusive right to sell or exclusive agency listing agreements (with authority to place the listing into MLS®) and a data sheet on the property. The data sheet information, which contains physical and financial characteristics of the property and one or more photographs of the property are placed in an online computer data base and/or published in a multiple listing book that is distributed to MLS® members. Then, if Broker B has a prospect interested in a property listed by Broker A, Broker B arranges to show the property. If Broker B's prospect makes an offer on the property, Broker B contacts Broker A and Broker A calls on the seller with the offer.

MLS® permits brokers to offer the splitting of fees with buyer's brokers. The MLS® profile sheets provide the listing broker the opportunity to make an offer to compensate the buyer's brokers through a feature of MLS®. Profile sheets allow the buyer's broker, who is a member of MLS®, to access all the benefits of MLS® but to reject any offer of subagency. In effect, the buyer's broker can access the commission split but maintain his or her fiduciary duty to the purchaser, rather than to the seller of the property.

MLS® organizations have been taken to court for being open only to members of local real estate associations. The role that multiple listing services play directly or indirectly in commission splitting is also being tested in the courts. Another idea that has been tested in courts is that an MLS® be open to anyone who wants to list a property, broker or owner. It is generally held, though, that owners lacking real estate sophistication would place inaccurate information in the MLS® and this would do considerable harm to MLS® members, who must rely on that information when describing and showing properties. It is also important to note that the sharing of MLS® information to nonmembers violates federal copyright laws.

MLS® information is copyrighted, and there are stringent regulations for the proper use of the materials it contains. This is an area where many new problems will arise. How much of the MLS® information should be made available to the buyer's broker? Will there have to be two books and two computer access codes, one for seller and one for buyer agent? What about a company that offers both types of agency?

DISCUSSION QUESTION

- What information should not be given to MLS® that might be on listing forms because of buyer agents?

Computerized MLS®

In addition to publishing MLS® books or in place of them online databases containing MLS® data, multiple listing services store their listing information in computers. Associations make other computer programs available to their members (i.e., amortization tables, buyer and seller closing statements, rent versus buy, etc.). Title companies, lenders, and taxing authorities also make information electronically available to agents. Salespeople with a laptop computer or terminal capable to interface with the MLS® computer can access up-to-the-minute information for any property in that computer and, if they have access to a printer, produce a hard copy. Agents can also download information into a handheld computer from the database and carry it with them. This is a popular system with salespeople who are constantly in the field showing property.

Computers can also show purchasers how a property would look with a different color scheme, updated bath or kitchen, without a non-loadbearing wall, with their furniture in place, and so on. They can provide a map of the area showing nearby shopping, schools, and other things of interest to the purchaser. Listing presentations are available on diskette. More and more MLS® information is being made available to the public through the Internet.

The Texas Real Estate Center has also joined cyberspace at:

http://recenter.tamu.edu.

Its categories are News, Information, Publications, Data, and Cybersites.

You will find TREC at:

http://www.trec.state.tx.us.

The Consumer site of the National Association of REALTORS® is available at:

http://www.realtor.com, and the member site is available at www.realtor.org.

Electronic Marketing

A prospective buyer can now take a visual tour through a neighborhood without leaving the broker's office via video or the Web. Using computerized access to MLS® files, the salesperson can show a prospect a color picture of each property for sale along with pictures of the street and neighborhood plus nearby schools and shopping facilities.

Most MLS® systems allow up to eight photographs to be loaded into each property listing so that the buyer can see several pictures of the property prior to a personal inspection. There are also "virtual tours" or "visual tours" available on most MLS® data systems. It is up to the listing broker whether these additional marketing tools will be utilized. Both the multiple photographs and the virtual tour system are very effective marketing devices.

The Web now dominates the market for both practitioners and individual buyers and sellers. Not only can an individual seller post on many Internet services (alternative sources are available for buyers and buyer's brokers), but the MLS® is also on the Internet in all locations. In addition, most real estate offices have their own Web sites (both buyer's and seller's brokers) and a few real estate companies have been developed to market solely to the Internet customer and client. Some of these companies offer fewer services, and, as a result, offer lower fees, or rebates, to their principals. Those that are full-service companies sometimes take the position that they are providing their services more efficiently and with fewer personnel hours, so they can charge lower fees.

Free enterprise and competition is a wonderful thing!! In just a few short years the Web and the Internet have made a huge impact on the way real estate agents handle their business.

BROKER COMPENSATION

There are a number of issues that come into play in determining a broker's right to a commission: (1) whether the licensee meets all the requirements of the Texas Real Estate License Act and its appurtenant regulations and requirements; (2) whether the broker performed the duties required under the agency agreement and the Law of Agency; (3) whether the broker procured an agreement on all essential terms of the bargain; and (4) whether the broker was a procuring cause of the transaction.

A broker may be able to collect a commission even if no contract is signed in two situations. The first is when the broker produces a prospect who is agreeable to the terms of the lessor/seller but the lessor/seller changes his or her mind or refuses to enter into the agreement or contract, or when the broker has produced a lessee/buyer who is ready, able, and willing to accept the principal's terms. The broker has earned a commission, as a principal cannot take advantage of his or her obstruction of the contract process; *Duckworth v. Field,* 516 F.2d 952 (*5th* Cir., 1975). When the parties have reached an agreement to sell or lease, the broker's job is done.

A second situation arises when the lessee or buyer may be at fault, or when the parties have a good faith disagreement as to the enforcement of the agreement. But in both circumstances, the broker has performed and is not at fault, and the broker is entitled to the commission. See *Davidson v. Suber,* 553 S.W.2d 430 (Tex. Civ. App.-Austin, 1977); *Cotton v. Deasey,* 766 S.W.2d 874 (Tex. App.-Dallas, 1989); *Stiles v. DeAngelo,* 706 S.W.2d 175 (Tex. App., 1986). But see *Nugent v. Scharff,* 476 S.W.2d 414 (Tex. Civ. App., 1971).

Texas Real Estate License Act

Real estate broker license laws are regulatory in nature and are designed to protect the public from dishonest or incompetent brokers and include penalties for violation of their provisions, *Henry S. Miller v. Treo Enterprises,* 585 S.W.2d 674 (Tex., 1979). Contracts held in violation of license laws are generally held to be illegal and nonenforceable, *Terry v. Allied Bancshares,* 760 S.W.2d 45 (Tex. App.-Ft. Worth, 1988); *Shehab v. Xanadu, Inc.,* 698 S.W.2d 491 (Tex. Civ. App., 1985). It is only required that the licensee be licensed at the time the brokerage function is to be performed, not when the commission is payable, so deferred commissions are still payable even if the broker has retired and may not be licensed anymore; note *Collins v. Best,* 840 S.W.2d 788 (Tex. App.-Ft. Worth, 1992, writ denied).

Strict compliance with the Texas Real Estate License Act is a prerequisite to a suit for a commission, *H.E.Y. Trust v. Popcorn Express Co., Inc.,* 35 S.W.3d 55 (Tex. App.-Houston [14th Dist.], 2001). The Texas Real Estate License Act requires the following in order to recover a commission:

1. The person bringing the acts of the commission must be a duly licensed real estate broker or salesperson at the time the services are commenced (all exceptions are strictly construed, *Shehab v. Xanadu, Inc., ante.*);

2. The agreement for the payment of commission must be in writing;

3. The broker must advise the purchaser in writing that the purchaser should have the abstract of title covering the real estate that is the subject of the contract examined by an attorney, or obtain a policy of title insurance (presumably this would not apply to a lease transaction); and

4. The broker must produce the ready, willing, and able buyer or lessee.

These rules do not apply to suits for commissions between licensees to share compensation, or to a cause of action among brokers for interference with a business relationship (tortious interference). *Occupations Code, Section 1101.806.*

Only the broker can sue for a commission, as all salespersons earn their commission through the sponsoring broker, *Cissne v. Robertson,* 782 S.W.2d 912 (Tex. App.-Dallas, 1990, writ den.). Although not a Texas case, this is at least one case that says the broker may assign his or her cause of action.

In *Ritchie v. Weston, Inc.,* 757 N.E.2d 835 (Ohio App. 8 Dist. 2001), Ritchie, a real estate agent (but not a licensed broker), was an employee of the firm of Grubb & Ellis in 1987, who represented Weston, an owner of a commercial building in an industrial park. While working with Grubb & Ellis, Ritchie was able to procure a commercial tenant, AUS, for Weston's building.

Weston and Grubb & Ellis agreed that Grubb & Ellis would receive a commission based upon a fixed percentage of the lease amount. The lease provided for an original four-year term, two three-year renewals (going through 1996), and one five-year renewal (beginning in 1997) at a rate to have been determined by the parties.

In 1995, Ritchie left Grubb & Ellis to work for a different firm. The separation agreement between Ritchie and Grubb & Ellis stated that Ritchie would be entitled to commissions that arose from transactions in which he was originally involved as a salesperson, including lease renewals. In 1996, Ritchie represented AUS in connection with AUS's desire to purchase Weston's building. Ritchie notified Weston of his representation of AUS. The purchase discussions were not productive and thereafter Ritchie represented AUS in negotiating the 1997 five-year renewal. At this point, Weston objected to Ritchie's involvement and Ritchie withdrew from the negotiations.

AUS went on to renew the lease and Ritchie requested his percentage of the lease as a fee owed from his prior agreement with Grubb & Ellis. Weston refused to pay the commission. Grubb & Ellis, which did a substantial amount of business with Weston, did not wish to pursue the commission claim. But, as it was obligated by contract to give the commissions to Ritchie, it assigned the commission claim to Ritchie, and Ritchie filed suit.

The Common Pleas Court entered judgment for Ritchie. Weston appealed.

The Appeals Court agreed with Weston that an unlicensed broker would not be entitled to commission. The question for the Appeals Court, however, was whether Ritchie could step into the shoes of Grubb & Ellis and therefore could bring a claim for the commission owed. The Court held that the accrual date in this case was the date upon which the commission arose (i.e., when Grubb & Ellis earned the commission in 1987). As assignee to those rights under the separation agreement, Ritchie stands in the shoes of the assignor (Grubb & Ellis) and succeeded to all the rights and remedies, including the right to bring the cause of action against Grubb & Ellis for commission owed.

Corporate and business entities fall under the same rules. A corporation will require two licenses, one for the corporation and one for the designated broker, which the statute requires be named as a part of the corporation's license, *Henry S. Miller v. Treo Enterprises, supra.* See also *Coastal Plains Development Corp. v. Micrea, Inc.,* 572 S.W.2d 285 (Tex. 1978).

A limited liability company must also designate one of its managers to act on its behalf. *Occupations Code §1101.355.*

Partnerships are not required to be licensed if they are acting through a partner who is a licensed broker. *Occupations Code §1101.005(9). Arthur P. Gayle Realtors v. Belisle,* 694 S.W.2d 195 (Tex. App.-Dallas, 1985); *Kaufhold v. Curtis and Ewing,* 557 S.W.2d 334 (Tex. App.-Houston [1st Dist] 1977).

A broker can split fees from brokers licensed in other states provided the out-of-state broker does not conduct any negotiations for which the commission or other compensation is paid in this state. *Occupations Code §1101.651(a)(2).*

The Requirement That the Commission Agreement Be in Writing

The Texas Real Estate License Act requires an employment agreement to be in writing in order to be enforceable. Amendments to the employment agreement, often made to accommodate the client, can be costly. In *Friendswood Development Company v. McDade & Company,* 911 S.W.2d 541 (Tex. 1996), a real estate broker representing a lessee (American Bureau of Shipping) entered into a "standard exclusive brokerage contract" that provided McDade was the sole broker and had the exclusive right to obtain a lease or purchase of premises on the buyer's behalf. The buyer informed McDade of its ongoing discussions with Friendswood and other Exxon affiliates, but Friendswood had no space available to rent at the time. McDade inserted an exception to the "standard brokerage contract" to create a broad exclusion for Friendswood from the contract, thus permitting ABS to contract with either McDade or Friendswood for office space. Thereafter, ABS accepted a Friendswood proposal for an interim lease for one year, in property that Friendswood didn't own, pending Friendswood space becoming available later in the year. When McDade discovered that Friendswood had leased space to ABS, which it didn't own, he filed a suit against ABS alleging a breach of the brokerage contract and against Friendswood for tortiously interfering with the brokerage contract.

The Texas Supreme Court held that the contract was clear on its face, contained no latent or patent ambiguities, and that Friendswood, in any capacity, was exempt and excluded from the terms of the brokerage contract. Moral: Any changes or exclusions to employment agreements written by the broker should be carefully made, as they will be construed against the drafter.

In *Texas Builders, et al. v. Keller,* 928 S.W.2d 479 (Tex. 1996), the Texas Supreme Court again held that a real estate licensee cannot recover for a breach of contract if there is no written agreement that satisfies the Texas Real Estate License Act. The court stuck to the traditional theory that "the writing must furnish, either within itself or by reference to some other existing document, the means or data by which the real estate at issue may be identified." The sufficiency of the description is the same that is necessary to satisfy the Statutes of Frauds (to identify the property with reasonable certainty).

In addressing the fraud claim the court held that even if Texas Builders committed fraud, Keller couldn't circumvent the requirements of the Texas Real Estate License Act by claiming the lost commission as damages for fraud.

This creates an interesting question as a buyer's broker. It is often impossible to determine the identity of the property to be purchased at the time the Buyer's Representation Agreement is signed. How, then, can a buyer's broker maintain an action for commission? There is at least some authority from a lower court that, under these circumstances, the legal description is not necessary. (See *LA & N Interest, Inc. v. Fish*, 864 S.W. 2d 745 (Tex. App. Houston [14th Dist.], 1993, no writ.) The only other alternative would be to insert the legal description at a later date, when the property is identified. That may be a good idea.

In *Trammell Crow Company No. 60, et al. v. William Jefferson Harkinson*, 944 S.W. 2d. 631 (Tex. 1997), a tenant authorized the broker to act as its exclusive representative in locating rental space. The broker found suitable space in Dallas. The owners told the broker that they would pay $4\frac{1}{2}\%$ cash commission to the broker and sent the broker a commission agreement, which the broker redrafted and sent back to the owners to execute. The owners never signed it.

The tenant ultimately negotiated with the owners, going around their tenant representative agreement, apparently assuming they would get cheaper rent.

The owners paid their in-house broker a commission but refused to pay the tenant's broker a commission, alleging that there was no agreement in writing, and therefore no right to a commission. The court noted that the exclusive representation agreement did not specify a commission to be payable by the buyer but only indicated that the commission would be paid by the seller. Therefore, it was not a commission agreement.

With no agreement in writing, the broker lost his right to pursue the commission. The broker also alleged tortious interference by the broker who did receive the commission, alleging that he interfered with the rights of the broker who represented the buyer. The court held that the broker could not sue for tortious interference if it was merely a claim for a commission, and specifically disapproved the prior Texas case of *LA & N Interests v. Fish supra*, to the extent that it permitted a claim for tortious interference.

There was a well-reasoned dissent, relying on contract principles of tortious interference and violations of Section 15(a)(6)(N) [now 1101.652(b)(22)] of the Real Estate License Act by the broker who did receive the commission. The clear import of the case, however, is that if one is to be a buyer's broker: (1) one needs to get a commission agreement in writing and signed by the person who is supposed to pay the commission, or (2) be sure an alternative commission is to be paid by the buyer in the event the seller refuses to pay a commission. Unfortunately, in many circumstances the buyer is not going to support the buyer's broker who pursues his commission if the buyer thinks he is going to get a cheaper deal without the commission. It is a tough lesson to learn.

Contractual Provisions

The right to a commission must arise out of some kind of contract, *Frady v. May,* 23 S.W.3d 558 (Tex. App.-Ft. Worth, 2000); *Callaway v. Overholt, ante.* There is no cause of action in Texas for *quantum meruit, Vandever v. Goethre,* 678 S.W. 2d 630 (Tex. App.-Houston [14th Dist.], 1984, ref. n.r.e.), nor are suits under the doctrine of partial performance. *Boyert v. Tauber,* 834 S.W.2d 60 (Tex. 1992).

The Texas Association of REALTORS® publishes listing agreements for both the sale and the leasing of real estate. TAR puts forth a significant effort in making sure these forms are updated, current, and in compliance with the Real Estate Commission's Rules and Regulations. While some brokers think the forms are too complicated, the forms are a good format for customizing your own agreement. Assuming that most brokers will use an Exclusive Right to Sell or Exclusive Right to Lease form, the broker is entitled to be paid upon procuring a ready, willing, and able buyer. One exception, however, is the "if, as and when" clause, wherein a broker can agree that no commission will be paid until the transaction is finally consummated, *Callaway v. Overholt,* 796 S.W.2d 826 (Tex. App., 1990), *Frady v. May, supra.* This clause still does not shield a lessor from liability to pay a commission if failure to finalize the transaction is the lessor's fault. Under Texas law, lease is considered a sale within the contemplation of the state's licensing statute. Note *Moser Company v. Awalt Industrial Properties, Inc.,* 584 S.W.2d 902 (Tex. Civ. App.-Amarillo, 1979). The difficulty of leasing commissions is that they can be paid over a long period of time and represent personal obligations and are not covenants running with the land unless lien rights are preserved in the listing agreement and the listing agreement is of record so that purchasers will be on notice of the obligation to pay the commission out of the proceeds of the collective rentals.

PERFORMANCE OF PURCHASER/LESSEE UNDER THE CONTRACT

The brokers suing a lessor for payment of a commission must generally show that they produced a ready, willing, and able buyer with the financial ability to perform. However, when the seller or lessor enters into a binding written contract with a lessee or buyer produced in good faith by the broker, the most general view is that the lessor accepts the tenant as a person ready, willing, and able to perform under the lease the broker has performed, so long as the lessor has had a reasonable opportunity to investigate the ability of the lessee to perform and there is no fraudulent misrepresentation on the part of the broker, *Sticht v. Shull,* 543 So.2d 395 (Fla. 1989). NOTE: If one party refuses to execute the lease (spouse, partner), some case laws indicate that the commission is still payable, *Caneer v. Martin*, 238 S.W.2d 828 (Tex. Civ. App., 1951); *Cotton v. Willingham*, 232 S.W. 572 (Tex. Civ. App., 1921). This rule doesn't apply if the broker knows that a noncontracting party will refuse to agree, *Peters v. Coleman*, 263 S.W.2d 639 (Tex. Civ. App., 1953).

REQUIREMENTS OF BROKERAGE AGREEMENTS

The Texas Supreme Court has held that real estate brokerage agreements fall under the statute of frauds and are required to be in writing in order to pursue an action for a commission, *Givins v. Doughtery*, 671 S.W.2d 877 (Tex. 1984). In general terms, a listing agreement is normally considered to be use specific enough when:

1. It is in writing and signed by the person to be charged with a commission.

2. It promises the debt of commission will be paid or refers to a written commission schedule.

3. It specifies the name of the broker to whom the commission is to be paid.

4. It must either by itself, or by reference to some other existing writing, identify with reasonable certainty, the premises to be leased, *Knight v. Hicks*, 505 S.W.2d 638 (Tex. Civ. App.-Amarillo, 1974).

The agreement must also comply with all the rules and regulations of the Texas Real Estate Commission, including a definite termination date, *Occupations Code §1101.652(b)(12)*. Failure to do so may make the contract unenforceable, *Perl v. Patrizi*, 20 S.W.3d 76 (Tex. App.-Texarkana, 2000), but see *Northborough Corporate*, LLP v. Cushman and Wakefield of Texas, Inc., 162 S.W.3d 816 (Tex.App.-Houston [14th Dist.], 2005, no writ) that seems to say that the listing agreement is still enforceable without a termination date.

MODIFICATIONS

The same theory applies to modifications. In *American Garment Properties, Inc. vs. CB Richard Ellis-El Paso, L.L.C.*, 155 S.W.3d 431 (Tex. App.-El Paso, 2004) (discussed in Chapter 1), a real estate brokerage firm brought action against a seller of a building for alleged failure to pay the full amount of the real estate commission. The obligation to pay the commission was contained in both the agency agreement and the purchase agreement. The agency agreement specified that the owner would pay the real estate broker 6% commission on the purchase price if the procuring agent represented the purchaser. The agency agreement contained a clause providing that the agreement could only be modified in writing, and signed by the parties. The owner refused to pay the full commission at the closing, alleging that the broker had verbally agreed to lower the commission in order to make the sale.

The broker filed a summary judgment motion which was granted on the basis of the statute of frauds: an agreement that is in writing cannot be orally modified. There is an exception, and that is when the modification does not materially affect the obligations of the underlying agreement. The court held that an oral modification asserted in this case (changing the commission amount) was "material", and violated the statute of frauds.

EFFECT OF BREACH OF FIDUCIARY DUTY

Brokers are viewed as fiduciaries and have a duty to put the interests of the principal above that of their own. As a general rule, if the broker violates this fiduciary duty, he or she is not entitled to a commission, *Perl v. Patrizi, supra., NRC, Inc. v. Huddleston,* 886 S.W.2d 526 (Tex. App.-Austin, 1994); *Roquemore v. Ford Motor Company,* 290 F. Supp. 130, affirmed 400 F.2d 255. This includes a failure to disclose, a breach of the duty of loyalty. *Southern Cross Industries, Inc. v. Martin ,* 604 S.W. 2nd 290 (Tex. App. San Antonio 1980, ref. n.r.e.). The same is true if the agent acts as dual agent and does not adequately disclose his or her conflict of interest to both parties. *Porizky v. United Fidelity Life Insurance Company* 178 S.W.2d 157 (Tex. App. Dallas 1943, writ ref'd); *Porter v. Striegler,* 533 S.W.2d 478 (Tex. Civ. App.-Eastland, 1976).

The Broker's and Appraiser's Lien on Commercial Real Estate Act

The Texas Legislature has also enabled commercial real estate brokers and appraisers to put liens on real estate for commissions due. This applies to most commercial real estate transactions, but it specifically does not apply to:

1. a transaction involving a claim for a commission of less than $2,500.00.

2. a transaction involving a claim for a commission of $5,000.00 or less if the commercial real estate:

    (a) is the principal place of business of the record title owner.

    (b) is occupied by more than one and fewer than five tenants.

    (c) is improved with 7,500 square feet or less of total gross building area.

The statute defines "commercial real estate" as:

    (a) all real estate except real estate improved with one to four residential units.

    (b) a single-family residential unit including a condominium or townhouse.

    (c) real estate that includes the person's homestead.

    (d) real estate that is not improved with a structure and is (i) zoned for single family residential use, or (ii) restricted for single-family use under restrictive covenants that will remain in effect for at least the next two years.

    (e) real estate that (i) is primarily used for farming and ranching purposes, (ii) will continue to be used primarily for farming and ranching purposes, and (iii) is located more than three miles from the corporate boundaries of any municipality.

In general terms, the lien statute applies to only commercial real estate, not residential or agricultural real estate. See Property Code §62.002.

A critical issue, and one of extensive litigation, is when the commission is earned. The statute provides that a commission is earned on the *earlier* of the date that: (i) the date defined under the Commission Agreement; or (ii) the person obligated to pay the commission enters into a purchase contract or lease during the period prescribed by the commission agreement. In commercial lease transactions, the statute provides that when a broker has earned a commission under a commission agreement relating to a lease transaction, and the commission agreement provides that the broker may receive an additional commission when the lease is modified to expand the lease space or renewed, the additional commission is earned: (i) when the broker performs all the defined services related in the commission agreement, or (ii) when the broker first earned a commission under the commission agreement if the commission agreement does not specifically require the broker to perform additional services (it relates back to the original commission payment date). The commission is apparently earned when the initial services are performed, but it is not payable until the later date when the lease is renewed or extended. See Property Code §62.004.

FILING THE LIEN

The broker has a lien on the commercial real estate interest of a seller, or lessor, if the broker has earned the commission and the notice of lien is filed and recorded in the county clerk's office in the county in which the commercial real estate is located. The lien is available only to the broker named in the commission agreement (not to an employee or independent contractor of the broker) and must be disclosed in the commission agreement. **So a commercial broker, wanting to pursue the lien claim, must make sure the lien right is clearly stated in the commission agreement.**

The broker's lien cannot be waived in a sales transaction. It will be waived automatically if the commission is earned in a lease transaction and the commission agreement is included as a provision in the lease agreement. QUERY: If the lien right is not contained in the employment agreement, isn't it effectively waived?

THE LIEN DOCUMENT

The Notice of Lien must be signed by the broker or by a person authorized to sign on behalf of the broker and must contain the following:

1. a sworn statement of the nature and amount of the claim, including:

    (a) the commission amount or the formula used to determine the commission.

    (b) the type of commission at issue, including a deferred commission.

    (c) the month and year in which the commission was earned.

2. the name of the broker and real estate license number of the broker.

3. the names reflected on the broker's records of any person who the broker believes is obligated to pay the commission under the Commission Agreement.

4. the name reflected in the broker's records of any person the broker believes to be the owner of the commercial real estate interest on which the lien is claimed.

5. a description legally sufficient for identification of the commercial real estate interest sought to be charged with the lien.

6. the name of any cooperating broker or principal in the transaction with whom the broker intends to share the commission and the dollar or percentage amount to be shared.

7. a copy of the commission agreement in which the lien is based.

After the broker files the lien, the broker must mail a copy of the notice of lien by certified mail, return receipt requested, or registered mail to the owner of record of the commercial real estate on which the lien is claimed, or the owner's authorized agent, and the perspective buyer or tenant, and any escrow agent named in the contract for the sale or lease of the commercial real estate interest in which the lien is claimed. The notice is deemed sent when deposited into the United States mail, postage prepaid, and addressed to the persons entitled to receive the notice.

LIEN PRIORITY

A recorded lien, mortgage, or other encumbrance on commercial real estate, including a recorded lien securing a revolving credit and future advances for a loan recorded before the date the broker's lien is recorded, has priority over the broker's lien. Basically, the "barber shop rule" (first in time, first in right) still applies. There are two exceptions: (1) A purchase money mortgage lien executed by the buyer of the commercial real estate has priority over the broker's lien, as does (2) a mechanic's lien that is recorded after a broker's lien but relates back to the date before the broker's lien is recorded (similar to other mechanic's liens priorities). If requested, the broker must execute and acknowledge a subordination agreement of the above-referenced liens before a notary public not later than the seventh day after the date the broker receives the subordination agreement.

The broker's lien is extinguished if the property is zoned single-family use or restricted for single-family use within 360 days after the broker's commission is payable and those zoning ordinances or restrictive covenants are in effect until at least the second anniversary of the date the commission is payable.

TIME FOR FILING THE LIEN

If representing the seller, the lien must be filed after the commission is earned and before the conveyance of the commercial real estate interest. If representing the buyer, the lien must be filed after the buyer acquires legal title to the commercial real estate interest and before the buyer conveys that commercial real estate interest. If it is a lease transaction, the broker must record the notice of lien after the commission is earned and the *earlier* of: (i) the 91st day after the date the event in which the commission becomes payable, or (ii) the date the person obligated to pay the commission records a subsequent conveyance of that person's commercial real estate after executing the lease agreement.

If the notice of lien is not filed within the time required, the lien is **void**.

SUIT TO FORECLOSE THE LIEN

The broker can bring a suit to foreclose lien in any district court in the county in which the commercial real estate is located, which suit must be filed on or before the second anniversary of the date the notice of lien is recorded. If it is a deferred commission, the suit must be filed before the second anniversary date on which the commission is payable or the tenth anniversary of the date the lien is recorded, or the tenth anniversary date the broker records a subsequent notice of the lien as a renewal of the broker's right to the lien, whichever date is later.

As an alternative, the broker claiming the lien must bring suit to foreclose the lien not later than the thirtieth day after the date the broker receives a written demand to bring a suit to foreclose the lien. If the suit to foreclose the lien is not brought within the above-referenced time periods, the lien is **void**. QUERY: Can the landowner demand that the broker sue within 30 days or the lien is void?

RELEASE OF LIEN

A broker's lien is discharged only by:

1. a court order discharging the lien.

2. paying the broker the commission named in the Commission Agreement.

3. establishing an escrow account in which an escrow agent can deposit amounts sufficient to satisfy the lien, plus 15 percent of that amount.

The escrow account will be maintained by the escrow agent until the matter is resolved, the lien is no longer enforceable, or the funds are interpleading into the district court in the county in which the commercial real estate is located.

BROKER LIABILITY

The new statute also gives the court the right to discharge the broker's lien if the broker fails to timely comply with any of the provisions of the statute. It additionally awards the owner or tenant damages (actual damage, including attorney's fees and court costs) and can award a civil penalty in an amount not to exceed three times the amount of the commission claimed. This is not much help against an insolvent broker, however.

Nothing in the statute prevents a person from filing a complaint with the Texas Real Estate Commission nor prevents the Texas Real Estate Commission's investigation or disciplinary proceedings.

This is a complicated statute. While potentially protecting the broker's interest, it does create liability if the terms of the statute are not strictly adhered to.

PROCURING CAUSE

A broker who possesses an open listing or an exclusive agency listing is entitled to a commission if he or she can prove that the resulting sale was primarily due to his or her efforts. That is, the broker has to have been the procuring cause, the one whose efforts originated procurement of the sale. Suppose that a broker shows an open-listed property to a prospect and, during the listing period or an extension, that prospect goes directly to the owner and concludes a deal. Even though the owner negotiates his or her own transaction and prepares his or her own sales contract, the broker is entitled to a full commission for finding the buyer. This would also be true if the owner and the buyer used a subterfuge or strawman to purchase the property to avoid paying a commission. Texas law protects the broker who has in good faith produced a buyer at the request of an owner.

When an open listing is given to two or more brokers, the first one who produces a buyer is entitled to the commission. For example, Broker 1 shows a property to Prospect P but no sale is made. Later P goes to Broker 2 and makes an offer, which is accepted by the owner. Although two brokers have attempted to sell the property, only one has succeeded, and that one is entitled to the commission. The fact that Broker 1 receives nothing, even though he or she may have expended considerable effort, is an important reason why brokers dislike open listings.

Terminating the Listing Contract

This topic is basically the same as termination of agency (Chapter 7). The usual situation in a listing contract is that the broker finds a buyer acceptable to the owner. Thus, in most listing contracts the agency terminates because the objective of the contract has been completed. In the bulk of the listings for which a buyer is not found, the agency is terminated because the listing period expires.

Even when a listing calls for mutual consideration and has a specific termination date, it is still possible to revoke the agency aspect of the listing before the termination date. However, liability for breach of contract still remains, and money damages may result. An owner who has listed his or her property may tell the broker not to bring any more offers, but the owner still remains liable to the broker for payment for the effort expended by the broker up to that time. Depending on how far advanced the broker's work is at that point, the amount could be as much as a full commission.

MUTUAL AGREEMENT

A listing can be terminated by mutual agreement of both the owner and broker without money damage. Because listings are the stock in trade of the brokerage business, brokers do not like to lose listings; but sometimes this is the only logical alternative since the time and effort in setting and collecting damages can be very expensive. Suppose, however, that a broker has an exclusive right-to-sell listing and suspects that the owner wants to cancel because he or she has found a buyer and wants to avoid paying a commission. The broker can stop showing the property, but the owner is still obligated to pay a commission if the property is sold before the listing period expires. Whatever the broker and seller decide, it is best to put the agreement into writing and sign it.

With regard to open listings, once the property is sold by anyone, broker or owner, all listing agreements pertaining to the property are automatically terminated. The objective has been completed, and there is no further need for the agency to exist. Similarly, with an exclusive agency listing, if the owner sells the property himself or herself, the agency with the exclusive broker is terminated.

ABANDONMENT, AND SIMILAR INSTANCES

Improper performance or abandonment can also terminate agency by the agent. Thus, if a broker acts counter to his or her principal's best financial interests, the agency is terminated. No commission is payable. The broker may be subject to a lawsuit for any damages suffered by the principal. If a broker takes a listing and then does nothing to promote it, the owner can assume that the broker abandoned it and has grounds for revocation. The owner should keep written documentation in the event the matter ever goes to court.

Remember, an agency is automatically terminated by the death of either the principal or the agent, or if either is judged legally incompetent by virtue of insanity, and might also be terminated if the owner becomes bankrupt.

Perceived Value

Before leaving the topic of listings, it will be valuable to spend a moment on the perceived value of real estate sales services. Several studies have been conducted that show home sellers feel the fee charged by brokers is too high in relation to time spent selling the property. Those in the real estate business know that the amount of time and effort to market a property is extensive and that often it is all for nothing if the property does not sell. However, the public does not see this and believes that very little effort is involved, especially if the home sells at market value in two or three weeks after being shown only a handful of times.

Ironically, a market value sale within a month and without the inconvenience of dozens of showings is what the seller is actually seeking. The broker's efforts to make the transaction as easy as possible often makes it look simple. Once it is achieved, however, the seller may think that the fee seems too expensive for the time involved. This leads some sellers to think in terms of selling their property themselves, perhaps with the aid of a self-help brokerage service.

Self-help brokerage services have seen a dramatic increase with companies such as Seller's Choice and other niche marketers. Some of the companies rebate their fees back to the principals (perfectly legal under the Texas Real Estate License Act), acknowledging that they are not offering a full range of services and therefore aren't going to charge a full commission. One should remember that this creates a competitive marketplace, fewer antitrust issues, and a unique opportunity for marketing "outside the box."

What stops more people from do-it-yourself selling is that they need a broker to evaluate the property, describe current market and financing conditions, estimate the most probable selling price, write the sales contract, and handle the closing. To a considerable degree, a real estate licensee's success will come from providing the services homeowners feel they need, listing property at or near market, emphasizing the value of services rendered, and operating in a professional manner to bring about a smooth and speedy sale.

EMPLOYEES VERSUS INDEPENDENT CONTRACTORS

When a real estate broker hires sales personnel to represent his or her brokerage company in seeking listings and negotiating real estate transactions, something that is far too often overlooked is whether that sales agent should be classified as an independent contractor or as an employee. There has been a long history of legislation and federal agency opinions as to how salespeople should be treated for tax unemployment purposes. Do the federal or state statutes apply? The answer makes a significant difference as to whether the employer is subject to the myriad of federal and state statutes, and whether the employee is entitled to the protection afforded in those statutes. Factors can include:

- respondent superior liability.
- employment discrimination laws.
- wage and hour laws.
- statutory employee benefits laws.
- collective bargaining laws.
- the WARREN Act (advance notification of mass layoffs).
- the Polygraph Protection Act.
- intellectual property ownership, rights, and duties.
- Texas unemployment compensation.
- workman's compensation act liability and shield.

Real estate licensees have always fallen under the category of "suspect," as being on the border between employee and independent contractor. (See

"Employees and Independent Contractors" by Richard R. Carlson, Advanced Real Estate Law Course, The State Bar of Texas 1994, page 6.) In addition, there are simple practical aspects relating to overhead and operations of a broker's office. A summary of "Employers" covered by federal laws, prepared by Laura Ayoub Keith, is included at the end of this chapter.

The broker normally assumes that the sales agent will be an independent contractor. There are a number of advantages, from the broker's point of view, favoring independent contract status of the sales personnel. These advantages generally include a smaller amount of paperwork and fewer records to maintain. No office hours are required to be kept. The sales personnel are more motivated to sell if they work on a commission basis only. There also are tax savings to the firm because there are no social security and unemployment taxes to be paid by the firm. The system tends to promote more professionalism and advantages for more experienced sales agents. The independent contractor status basically provides for a more professional, harder working, motivated sales agent because there is no limit to potential income, and there are fewer controls on the individual's time and effort.

If classified as an employee, the individual salesperson may not be as well motivated since the basic check amount is the same every month regardless of whether any results are achieved. Furthermore, the employing broker's overhead remains relatively constant but quite high. Accounting and bookkeeping become more expensive because of the larger amount of paperwork and office records required; and there are added costs of social security taxes and unemployment benefits, as well as other requirements by the federal government that apply to employees generally.

THE IRS RULES

In 1976, the Internal Revenue Service set forth guidelines as to how it would look at a broker-salesperson relationship to determine whether or not a sales agent would be classified as an independent contractor or as an employee. Revenue Ruling 76-136 sets out the guidelines to determine when the sales personnel are not employees (see following). These guidelines were based on the facts set forth in a landmark case, *Dimmitt Rickhoff-Bayer Real Estate Co. v. Finnegan*, 179 F.2d 882 (8th Cir. 1950).

- The sales personnel should be compensated solely by commission on their sales of real estate, and the companies cannot give them advances against their commissions. However, the company can make facilities and offices available to salespeople and can furnish them with the necessary forms and stationery.

- The broker may furnish a manual for policies and procedures, but it may be advisory only, and the sales personnel cannot be required to follow the policies and procedures as criteria for their own employment.

- The sales personnel should not be required to work a set number of hours.

- The salesperson should pay his or her own expenses, such as his or her own license fees, transportation expenses, association memberships, business entertainment expenses, and the like.

- There should not be mandatory sales meetings or requirements to participate in any training programs.

- Salespersons should not be allowed to participate in any group insurance or retirement programs of the broker companies.

Although all of these factors are important, no one single factor is controlling; nor are these factors exclusive. The relationship is to be ascertained by an overall view of the entire situation. The result in each case must be governed by the special facts and circumstances surrounding each fact situation. *Illinois Tri-Seal Products, Inc. v. United States*, 353 F.2d 216 (U.S. Ct. Claims 1965).

Revenue Ruling 76-137 sets out the guidelines for real estate salespeople as employees with the company. This ruling, along with Revenue Ruling 76-136, distinguishes very clearly between employee status and independent contractor status. Generally, the distinction is based on the scope of control the broker has over the sales personnel, as well as on how the sales personnel consider themselves in the broker-salesperson relationship. Basically, the guidelines are the opposite of Revenue Ruling 76-136 and are generally set out as follows (for designation of employee status):

- If they [the salespeople] are sponsored and the registration fees are paid for by the broker.

- If the broker makes available office furniture, stenographic help, and telephone services, as well as stationery and business cards.

- If there are company rules and policies that must govern how transactions are negotiated, and if there is an attempt to control the salesperson's actions on a day-to-day basis.

- If the company has the right to discharge salespersons for any violation of instructions, or if it sets up quotas and minimum sales requirements for the sales agents.

- If the sales agents generally consider themselves as part of a team, all of whom are governed by the same rules and regulations, rather than having individualistic rules between the independent contractor and the broker.

- If the brokerage company's plan for dividing commissions between salespeople depends on rotation of outside referrals and required time in the office by certain agents.

- If there is a guaranteed minimum monthly compensation.

The IRS regulations (for Ruling 76-137) do not preclude having monthly sales agents' meetings, but the requirement of mandatory attendance may make a difference in the eyes of the Internal Revenue Service as to whether the sales-person is classified as an independent contractor or as an employee. Educational facilities or review classes for sales agents who make frequent errors may still be offered by the broker as long as attendance is not required for the independent contractor. It is a good idea if the broker also reminds these sales agents (independent contractors) of their obligations to pay quarterly income taxes, to file their Schedule C of the federal income tax form along with Form 1040, and to pay the self-employment tax. It should be emphasized that no single criterion (and all of the criteria of the revenue rulings are not discussed here) is controlling, but very great care should be taken to generate the proper emphasis on the independent contractor status if the broker wishes to maintain this type of broker-salesperson relationship.

This issue has been greatly simplified for the services of real estate agents. The **Tax Equity and Fiscal Responsibility Act** of 1982 provides a "safe harbor" to eliminate the vast majority of conflicts that have existed for real estate agents. The new federal law is an addition to the Internal Revenue Code and provides that a qualified real estate agent shall not be treated as an employee nor shall the person for whom such services are performed be treated as an employer. The key of compliance with the statute revolves around the definition of "qualified real estate agents." It includes any individual who is a salesperson if: (1) such individual is a licensed real estate agent; (2) substantially all the remuneration is directly related to sales rather than to the number of hours worked; and (3) the services are performed pursuant to a written contract between such individual and the person for whom the services are performed and such contract provides that the individual will not be treated as an employee with respect to such services for federal tax purposes. This has also been held to apply to real estate appraisal services as well, Internal Revenue Code, 3508.

This presumably exempts real estate licensees from other "employer-employee" issues such as coverage for health insurance, optional profit sharing, and/or pension plans, the Texas Unemployment Compensation Act, the Federal Unemployment Tax Act, the Texas Commission of Human Rights Act, and the Equal Employment Opportunity Act. It must be emphasized, however, that merely because the employer-employee relationship may not exist under the Internal Revenue Code because of the safe harbor or other interpretations of the Internal Revenue Code, there is no legal confirmation that the independent contractor relationship exempts real estate agents from the application of other employment-based statutes. This remains a gray area with very little guidance from agency interpretations or from the court.

THE FEDERAL COMMON LAW APPROACH

The U.S. Supreme Court has provided a common law approach for the employee/independent contractor status: (1) the hiring party's right to control the manner and means by which the product is accomplished; (2) the skill required;

(3) the source and instrumentalities and tools; (4) the location of the work; (5) the duration of the relationship between the parties; (6) whether the hiring party has the right to assign additional projects to the hired party; (7) the extent of the hired party's discretion over when and how long to work; (8) the method of payment; (9) the hired party's role in hiring and paying assistants; (10) whether the party is part of a regular business of the hiring party; (11) whether the hiring party is in business; (12) the provision of employee benefits; and (13) the tax treatment of the hired party. *Nationwide Mutual Insurance Company v. Darden*, 112 S. Ct. 1344 (1992); *A Community for Creative non-Violence v. Reid*, 109 S. Ct. 2166 (1989).

The Fifth Circuit Court of Appeals listed the following factors: (1) the hiring party's control over the details of the work; (2) the worker's opportunity for profit and loss; (3) the worker's investment in his or her business; (4) the permanence of the relationship; and (5) the skill required of the worker. *Hickey v. Arkla*, 699 F.2d 748 (5th Cir. 1983). Texas has a similar guideline established under Texas law. *Thompson v. Traveler's Indemnity Company of Rhode Island*, 789 S.W.2d 227 (Tex. 1990).

PERSONAL ASSISTANTS

One of the factors in determining the employer/independent contractor status is the ability of the independent contractor to hire personal assistants. *EEOC v. Zippo*, 713 F.2d 32 (3rd Cir. 1983). There has been a growing use of personal assistants in the real estate business, particularly in the large metropolitan market. Many real estate brokers who have large inventories of listings and demanding clients have discovered that the use of a personal assistant makes them much more efficient in scheduling and maintaining records. There is no requirement that personal assistants be licensed, but in every case the personal assistant, licensed or unlicensed, is under a very tight scope of control exercised by the agent with whom he or she is working. One might presume that if the personal assistant is licensed, independent contractor status might be maintained so long as the parties complied with the provisions of the Internal Revenue Code. A nonlicensed personal assistant, however, is a much more difficult situation to deal with. In almost every case, one would think that the employer-employee relationship would be mandated.

In every case, the policy directives of the sponsoring broker must be established and the assistance of a qualified attorney familiar with employment matters be consulted.

WAGE AND HOUR LAW

The primary federal legislation that covers wages and hours of work is the Fair Labor Standards Act, 29 U.S.C.A. 201 et seq. The legislation applies to all nonexempt employees and have minimum wage and overtime requirements.

Since real estate licensees in most circumstances are not considered to be employees by federal law, they do not fall under the coverage of the Fair Labor Standards Act. In the event a licensee becomes recategorized as an employee at any time during the working relationship, presumably the Fair Labor Standards Act and the Texas Minimum Wage Act would apply. How a salesperson would be recategorized can depend on a number of factors. If salespeople are stationed to the fixed site, such as a model home or development, the Department of Labor may not regard them as "outside salespeople," even if the model home or development is not the employer's property. See Labor Law Reporter [CSH]: Wages-Hours/Administrative Rulings, Paragraphs 3818 and 3819 (August 1961–November 1966).

WORKMAN'S COMPENSATION ISSUES

There have been a number of changes in Workman's Compensation Law in Texas. The Texas Unemployment Compensation Act defines "employment" as "a service, including a service in interfaced commerce, performed by an individual for wages or under an express or implied contract for hire, unless it is shown to the satisfaction of the commission that the individual's performance of the service has been and will continue to be free from control or direction under the contract and in fact." Texas Labor Code 201.041. There is a constant concern as to whether a real estate broker should carry workman's compensation coverage on his or her salespeople. A recent amendment to the Workman's Compensation Laws allows that an employer may elect workman's compensation coverage but is not required to if the employee is a licensed real estate salesperson or broker and compensated solely by commissions, Tex. Rev. Civ. Stat. Art. 8308-3.06.

DISCUSSION QUESTIONS

■ Some brokers want control over their agents because of liability issues. What other laws could this involve?

■ Why would the IRS be so concerned about the independent contractor issue?

GENERAL SUMMARY OF EMPLOYERS COVERED BY FEDERAL LAWS THAT WOULD HAVE POTENTIAL APPLICATION TO REAL ESTATE AGENTS AS EMPLOYERS

Federal Law	Who Is Covered
Title VII of the Civil Rights Act of 1964	All employers with 15 or more employees engaged in interstate commerce
Civil Rights Act of 1866	All employers regardless of size
Civil Rights Act of 1991	All employers with 15 or more employees engaged in interstate commerce
Uniform Guidelines on Employee Selection Procedures	All employers covered by Title VII and Executive Order 11246
Age Discrimination in Employment Act	All employers with 20 or more employees engaged in interstate commerce
Americans With Disabilities Act	All employers with 25 or more employees engaged in interstate commerce; as of July 26, 1994, the Americans With Disabilities Act covers all employers with 15 or more employees engaged in interstate commerce
Rehabilitation Act of 1973	Government contractors and subcontractors with contracts/subcontracts in excess of $2,500
Veterans' Reemployment Rights Statute	All employers, including private employers, the United States, and state governments
Vietnam Era Veterans' Readjustment Assistance Act	Government contractors with contracts/subcontracts in excess of $10,000
Executive Order 11246	Government contractors with contracts of subcontracts in excess of $10,000
Fair Labor Standards Act	All employers regardless of size engaged in interstate commerce
Employee Retirement Income Security Act	All employers regardless of size engaged in interstate commerce, excluding churches and federal, state, and local government employers
Equal Pay Act	All employers regardless of size engaged in interstate commerce

Federal Law	Who Is Covered
Fair Credit Reporting Act	All consumer credit reporting agencies as well as users of information obtained from such agencies
Federal Insurance Contributions Act	All employers with one or more employees
Federal Unemployment Tax Act	All employers who employ at least one individual for some portion of the days in each 20 days during the current or preceding calendar year, each day being in a different calendar week
Consumer Credit Protection Act	All employers regardless of size
Family and Medical Leave Act	All employers with 50 or more employees; covers employees who have completed at least 1,250 hours of service with the employer during the previous 12-month period; effective date: August 5, 1993
Consolidated Omnibus Budget Reconciliation Act	All employers with 20 or more employees that have a group health plan, as well as state or local governments that receive funds under the Public Health Service Act
Immigration Reform and Control Act of 1986	All private employers; private employers with three or more employees only are covered by the Act's citizenship discrimination provisions
Occupational Safety and Health Act	All employers engaged in interstate commerce; employers with 10 or fewer employees and federal and state governments are exempt from certain of the Act's requirements
National Labor Relations Act	Generally covers all employers engaged in interstate commerce (note: the National Labor Relations Board, which enforces the Act, in determining whether it will assert jurisdiction over a business, generally considers the employer's volume of business); the dollar volumes considered by the NLRB range from $50,000 for nonretail enterprises to up to $500,000 or more for retail enterprises

AGENCY RISK CONTROL

PURPOSE

After carefully reading Chapter 15, the student will be able to:

- Identify ways we handle risk.

- Tell how risk can be avoided or transferred.

- Apply ways to disclose in real estate practice.

- Discuss the advantages and disadvantages of alternative dispute resolution.

Key Words to look for in this chapter:
1. Avoidance
2. Transfer
3. Control
4. Policies
5. Arbitration and Mediation
6. NAR® Code of Ethics—Broker Disputes
7. NAR®—Seller and Buyer Disputes

How do we handle risk? We can avoid or transfer it, or retain and control it. These are the choices when faced with the risks of agency. Some choices are complex and require competent advice. A lot of risk management, however, involves good common sense.

AVOIDANCE

We can avoid risk by separating ourselves from agency and leaving the real estate business. We can attempt to change the way we have been looking at real estate practitioners and limit our agency role. If it is possible, we can remove the cloak of agency and declare licensees to be "facilitators," or something similar, supposedly working with no fiduciary duty to anyone. This was discussed in earlier chapters. The more efficient question is the ability to bring buyers and sellers together without choosing sides.

TRANSFER

There are several ways that we can transfer, or at least share, risk. We can transfer some of the risk by obtaining **Errors and Omissions** insurance (E and O insurance). But this is not enough. It is the bandage on this wound, but it will not protect from the wounds to come. We can transfer and share our risks with other experts and professionals. People with whom you daily share the agency risk or on whom you can shift the risks are property inspectors, consultants, title companies, home warranty companies, lenders, environmental experts, accountants, attorneys, sellers, and other brokers. Seek their advice and use their expertise. Let them do their jobs so that you can be better at yours. You should be cautious, however, you can multiply your risk if you recommend one of these to a client. Let your client choose from an available list of experts and consultants. Make good use of the Seller's Disclosure Statement.

CONTROL

We can also reduce risk through control. We control agency risk by thinking lawsuit. Education, research, excellent documentation, recordkeeping, disclosure, and explanation can help reduce and control risk. We must be careful of what we do and say. We must understand that what we do and say can hurt us. Every broker's office should have a written company policy on agency.

We are in an increasingly litigious society. To ward off litigation, be continually aware of the possibility of a lawsuit. Take the necessary precautions. Remember that no one is above or outside of the law.

Arm yourself with research and education. Know what problems and disasters can await you. Use your problem-solving skills. Be well informed and up-to-date on legal matters and current real estate practice.

Watch what you say and how you say it. "Sticks and stones may break [your] bones," but words will really hurt you. Every day well-meaning salespeople who are agents of the seller cross the line of agency in their dealings with the public. Your conduct in words, deeds, and/or actions can create implied agency relationships in spite of the titles you attach to yourself or the contracts you have signed.

Due to the protective nature and the needs to establish rapport, many sales-people's conduct will lead buyers or sellers to believe that they are represented when they are not. We label them customers, disclose that they are customers, and treat them as clients. As we have seen in this text, the courts understand the scope of our fiduciary duties to clients and customers; and they punish practitioners who do not.

Be careful when talking to buyers, sellers, other agents, lenders, inspectors, and anyone in the real estate process. Avoid using possessive pronouns in reference to customers such as "my buyers." Don't share anything told you in confidence by your principal. For example, you know that the seller is anxious to sell; if you divulge this to another agent, that agent may someday be the agent of a buyer interested in the property. Just running an ad that says that the owner will consider all offers might weaken a seller's negotiation powers.

Don't give the customer opinions, advice, or help them with what wording to put into a contract. Your candor can result in liability. Even if you are convinced that a property is overpriced and have the facts to back up your opinion, do not tell the buyers your opinion or show them your information if you are the agent of the seller.

Avoid conveying confidential information to the wrong parties. Even if you think that you know the answers, avoid answering customer's questions such as: "How much will it take?" "Would they consider an offer of _____?" or "Will they pay the points?" unless the client has given you permission to do so in writing. Do not advise the customer on negotiations nor negotiate on their behalf. However, be sure that you divulge all pertinent information on the customer to the client.

Do not practice law. Make only statements of fact and business detail changes to contracts and then only at the direction of the principal. Do not offer advice to the customer.

DISCUSSION QUESTION

■ What other scenarios can you think of where real estate agents can "stick their foot in their mouths"?

There is evidence that buyers and sellers do not understand agency relationships. It would seem obvious then that brokers and salespeople are not effectively explaining the fiduciary relationships and duties. Be sure customers and clients understand your position and your loyalties.

Disclose, disclose, disclose, and then disclose again any known defects required to be disclosed by law and those things that would be prudent for you to disclose. Do it now—it might be too late next time. Remind the customer throughout the real estate process whom you represent. Explaining the responsibilities helps to eliminate confusion. Disclosure is good business practice.

Undisclosed agency is the cause of many agency suits. The timing of disclosure can be essential. State laws differ on when the disclosure should take place. Disclosure should take place before the third party can convey by word or deed pertinent, material information that could hurt the broker's position with the principal. In Texas, disclosure must take place at first contact with a party.

Have a paper trail. Document your contacts with all prospects, including their needs and questions and your responses and reactions. Record the contacts, document them (time, date, and circumstances), save them, and file them. Take and keep notes on your conversations and meetings. What questions were asked and what were your responses? What actions were taken and why? Do this during or immediately after the meetings or conversations take place while your memory is fresh. Write, send, and file copies of letters that reinforce and corroborate your notes.

Be sure to use Seller's Disclosure Forms and agency disclosure forms. File copies of waivers, disclosures, and comments made about the disclosures. Send important papers by messenger service or certified mail to have proof of delivery.

Date, keep, and file everything, even notes you made on a paper napkin at lunch. Ask for, and file, written permission for any action done for a principal that might seem contradictory to your fiduciary relationship. For example, the sellers are so desperate that they request you convey their urgency to the buyer; document the request. Update your records after each contact.

DISCUSSION QUESTION

■ What varied and interesting things would you expect to find in an agent's well-documented files?

POLICIES

The best way to establish guidelines, establish methods of practice, supervise practice, and handle agency problems is to have a published, written office policy on the company policies and positions on agency. These policies will not only outline your practice, they will illustrate your knowledge of and compliance with the law. They will serve as examples of your professionalism.

The policies should be clear, precise, detailed, and easily understood. The policies should be universal and all-encompassing. Exceptions should be expressly and duly noted.

Be sure that everyone in the office has received a copy of and has read and understands these policies. Be sure that this is documented in the company files. This policy manual and documentation will help protect both the broker and the salesperson.

Rethink and revamp sales meetings. The information presented in a sales meeting should depend on the company's agency policy. What is discussed in an all-seller or all-buyer agency might not be appropriate if the company has both buyer and seller agents.

DISCUSSION QUESTION

- What comments could be inappropriate or dangerous in a sales meeting where agents representing both seller and buyers are present?

Most important, know and follow the rules and regulations. However, if you have a conflict, consider alternatives to the courtroom. Lawsuits are expensive and time consuming for all parties.

ARBITRATION AND MEDIATION

It is the policy of the state of Texas to encourage peaceful resolution of disputes through alternative dispute resolution procedures. This encouragement is set out in both the TAR® listing agreement forms and also in the TREC-promulgated contract forms. You may recall that Texas promulgated its mediation addendum, shown in Figure 5-2.

There are generally two theories to alternative dispute resolution: arbitration and mediation.

Mediation, particularly from a consumer standpoint, is considered the "win-win" situation. It is often characterized as a nonadversarial process that focuses on the mutual goals of the disputing parties and actively involves them in the process of resolving their differences. In theory, mediated settlements are generally acceptable to all of the parties, who can enter into a binding agreement as a result of their agreed settlement in the mediation. This can lead to long-term goodwill between the parties.

There are disadvantages, however. The biggest disadvantage to mediation is that parties often feel like they must "win" when there is a dispute. The purpose of mediation is to reach compromise, and in doing so both parties usually give up something in a good faith attempt to reach a final resolution.

Arbitration reaches a binding resolution and is not appealable when a final resolution is reached. The only way an arbitration award can be appealed to district court is if the arbitrator was arbitrary, capricious, or had a conflict of interest. Courts generally tend to uphold the arbitration process rather than find fault with it.

Arbitration provides the consumer with a decision. The arbitrator in almost every case is well-trained, experienced in the subject matter, and has highly trained technical skills through a professional arbitration association such as the American Arbitration Association.

Expense

The strongest argument in favor of alternate dispute resolution is the lowered expense, whether it be mediation, arbitration, mini-trial, and so on, in that it saves the cost of "scorched earth" discovery and the pitfalls of a highly technical presentation necessary to pursue a full-blown jury trial. In addition, alternative dispute resolutions can usually be achieved in a very short period of time (a few days) rather than the lengthy delays that one may encounter during a court proceeding. In some Texas counties it takes two to four years to get to trial.

While this is true in concept, the consumer does experience significant expense in preparing for the mediation or arbitration (which in any event is not cheap). In arbitration, you can at least confirm that there will be a result. In mediation, you cannot confirm the result. You may go to the expense of the mediation, and reach an impasse. The consumer discovers that he or she will have a full-blown expense of trial ahead after incurring the expense of the mediation, which reached no result. In effect, the client may pay twice in mediation, which is a cost increase, not a cost savings. In addition, participants still have to prepare expert reports, testimony, and the mediator's fee.

Procedure

The procedure in arbitration is very similar to trial. The rules of evidence aren't quite as technical, so the parties are in a more relaxed atmosphere and the purpose of the arbitration is to let the story be heard without the interference of technical trial procedures. After all sides present their evidence and facts, the arbitrator simply makes a decision within the following few days.

In mediation, the procedure is quite different and depends entirely on the mediator. In most cases, the mediator will put the parties together in one room to discuss the various facts involved in the mediation so that both parties can hear each other's side of the story. The mediator often promotes discussion between the parties and assists them in seeing the other's point of view. If a resolution is not reached quickly, the mediator usually breaks the parties into separate rooms, referred to as "break out" sessions, where the mediator can talk in confidence to the respective parties and discuss the various merits or weaknesses of the various parties' point of view and suggests compromises, which may bring the dispute to a resolution.

In both procedures, the information is deemed confidential, will not be disclosed to other parties, and is not open to the public.

NAR® CODE OF ETHICS—BROKER DISPUTES

Under the Code of Ethics and Arbitration Manual of the National Association of REALTORS®, all brokers (REALTORS®) agree to submit to arbitration by the association facilities all disputes with other members. Every member who is a principal broker of a real estate firm has the right to invoke the Association's arbitration facilities in any dispute arising out of a real estate business with a REALTOR® who is a principal broker in another real estate firm. The Code also provides for a client of a REALTOR® to invoke their arbitration facilities and their business dispute with a REALTOR® arising out of an agency relationship provided the client agrees to be bound by the arbitration.

The Association reserves the right to decline the arbitration because of the amount involved or the legal complexity of the controversy. While the Association of REALTORS® has experienced broad success in the binding arbitration for REALTORS®, consumers have rarely used this procedure. The agreed binding arbitration accesses the state arbitration statute, which effectively eliminates the litigation in all but the rarer circumstances.

NAR®—SELLER AND BUYER DISPUTES

To facilitate the dispute resolution system between home sellers and homebuyers, the National Association of REALTORS® has published a dispute resolution system handbook for mediation as "a constructive alternative to litigation" which provides guidelines for members, boards, and associations. The program is designed to provide sellers, buyers, brokers, and other parties in a real estate transaction an efficient, affordable method that settles disputes out of court. NAR chose to encourage mediation rather than arbitration, defining mediation as "a non-adversarial process that focuses on the mutual goals of the disputing parties and actively involves them in the process of resolving their differences," which "would contribute more to long-term goodwill between brokers and their clients and customers than would arbitration" and claims the following benefits:

- faster than litigation.

- less expensive than litigation.

- discourages litigation of frivolous claims.

- parties do not forfeit their legal rights to arbitrate or litigate the dispute if mediation is unsuccessful.

- parties actively participate in the process to control the outcome.

- process contributes to long-term goodwill between agents and their clients and customers.

- provides a service which agents and sales agents can offer to their clients and customers.

- improves the image of NAR®, boards/associations, and members because they have taken initiative to find and provide alternatives to litigation.

- potential for lowering cost of the E & O insurance by lowering the number of claims that must be settled or litigated by the insurance company.

SUGGESTIONS FOR SAFE BROKERAGE

Keep good notes on every transaction. Follow every conversation with a short letter. Keep a diary in your transaction folder, noting phone calls, subjects discussed, and persons with whom you have discussed them.

Encourage buyers to hire inspectors. If they refuse, note it and have the buyer sign off on the refusal.

Ask the purchaser questions. Listen. Find out every fact ascertainable that may make a difference to a prudent purchaser in making the decision to purchase. Don't assume that the buyer knows anything.

Disclose. When in doubt as to any information that may cause liability for any party, disclose it in writing. Confirm the receipt or have the written document initialed.

Don't fail to disclose. Important facts which are omitted create liability for you and the seller. Help your seller understand that your liability may well be the seller's liability later.

Study. Knowledge is your best defense as well as your best confidence builder. Attend seminars often.

Trust your instincts. In all transactions, money will never compensate you for a reputation of mistrust, dishonesty, or working with undesirable people. Some people, put simply, can't be trusted to be honest. Stay away from them.

Do your homework on every deal. No deal is easy, and they are all different. Hard work breeds quality knowledge and experience. Some people get 10 years' experience; some get one year of experience ten times. True professionals never stop learning.

Be honest. You can only lose your reputation once.

Communicate. Tell the whole truth. Do not hide facts.

Use the TREC-promulgated forms. Study them and know to which transactions they apply.

Do not write in legal provisions. Filling in due-on-transfer information and contingencies may be practicing law without a license. If a principal "directs" you to fill in a provision, keep back-up proof of his or her "direction." If the provision turns against the principal later in the transaction, he or she will forget his or her "directions." It is safer to have principals write in their own provisions, in their own handwriting.

Don't handle anyone else's money, if possible. It is all work and no reward. Let the bonded escrow agent (title company) hold the earnest money or other escrow deposits.

TABLE OF CASES

C

S

T

U

REAL ESTATE LICENSE ACT
CROSS REFERENCE TABLE BETWEEN
V.T.C.S. ARTICLES 6573a, 6573a.1 AND TITLE 7,
OCCUPATIONS CODE, CHAPTER 1101*

VTCS, Art. 6573a	Occupations Code	VTCS, Art. 6573a	Occupations Code
§1(a)	§1101.001	§2(6)	§1101.002(3)
§1(b)	§1101.351	§3	§1101.005
§1(c)	§1101.803	§3(1)	§1101.005(1)
§1(d)	§1101.651	§3(2)	§1101.005(2)
§1(e)	§1101.651	§3(3)	§1101.005(3)
§2(1)	§1101.002(5)	§3(4)	§1101.005(4)
§2(2)	§1101.002(1)	§3(5)	§1101.005(5)
§2(2)(A)	§1101.002(1)(A)(i)	§3(6)	§1101.005(6)
§2(2)(B)	§1101.002(1)(A)(ii)	§3(7)	§1101.005(7)
§2(2)(C)	§1101.002(1)(A)(iii)	§3(8)	§1101.005(10)(A)
§2(2)(D)	§1101.002(1)(A)(iv)	§3(9)	§1101.005(8)
§2(2)(E)	§1101.002(1)(A)(v)	§3(10)	§1101.005(10)(B)
§2(2)(F)	§1101.002(1)(A)(vi)	§3(11)	§1101.005(10)(C)
§2(2)(G)	§1101.002(1)(A)(vii)	§3(12)	§1101.005(9)
§2(2)(H)	§1101.002(1)(A)(viii)	§4	§1101.004; .501
§2(2)(I)	§1101.002(1)(A)(ix)	§5(a)	§1101.051;.054;. 055;.056;.151
§2(2)(J)	§1101.002(1)(A)(x)	§5(b)(1)	§1101.053;.103
§2(3)	§1101.002(1)(B)	§5(b)(2)	§1101.053
§2(4)	§1101.002(7)		

*Some provisions of Article 6573a are not included in Occupations Code Chapter 1101 and may be found in other Government Code provisions or general law. The Texas Legislative Council's Revisor's Report on TITLES 6, 7, 8, 12, 14, and 15 Occupations Code contains further information regarding the omissions.

VTCS, Art. 6573a	Occupations Code	VTCS, Art. 6573a	Occupations Code
§5(c)	§1101.051;.052	§7(a)(8)	§1101.003(a)(4)
§5(d)	§1101.057	§7(a)(9)	§1101.003(a)(8)
§5(e)	§1101.057	§7(a)(10)	§1101.003(a)(1)
§5(f)	§1101.057	§7(a)(11)	§1101.003(a)(2)
§5(g)	§1101.058	§7(b)	§1101.003(c)
§5(h)	§1101.151;.751	§7(c)	§1101.362;.402
§5(i)	§1101.101;.105	§7(d)	§1101.356
§5(j)	§1101.151	§7(e)	§1101.358;.454
§5(m)	§1101.154	§7(f)	§1101.301;.302
§5(n)	§1101.006	§7(g)	§1101.356;.357
§5(p)	§1101.206	§7(h)	§1101.358
§5(q)	§1101.202	§7(i)	§1101.404
§5(r)	§1101.201	§7(j)	§1101.003
§5(s)	§1101.102	§7(k)	§1101.403
§5(t)	§1101.101;.151	§7A(a)	§1101.452;.455
§5(u)	§1101.106	§7A(b)	§1101.359
§5(v)	§1101.106	§7A(c)	§1101.367
§5(w)	§1101.106	§7A(d)	§1101.152
§5(x)	§1101.104	§7A(f)	§1101.456
§5(y)	§1101.206	§7A(g)	§1101.457
§5(z)	§1101.156	§8(a)	§1101.601;.602;.609
§6(a)	§1101.352(a);.366;.367	§8(b)	§1101.603
§6(b)	§1101.354	§8(c)	§1101.603;.604
§6(c)	§1101.453	§8(d)	§1101.605
§6(d)	§1101.502	§8(e)	§1101.606
§6A	§1101.353	§8(f)	§1101.606;.607
§7(a)	§1101.003;.401;.405	§8(g)	§1101.611
§7(a)(1)	§1101.003(a)(3)	§8(h)	§1101.608;.609;.610
§7(a)(2)	§1101.003(a)(5)	§8(i)	§1101.655
§7(a)(3)	§1101.003(a)(9)	§8(j)	§1101.604
§7(a)(4)	§1101.003(a)(7)	§8(k)	§1101.608
§7(a)(5)	§1101.003(a)(10)	§8(l)	§1101.612
§7(a)(6)	§1101.003(a)(11)	§8(m)	§1101.614
§7(a)(7)	§1101.003(a)(6)	§8(n)	§1101.610

VTCS, Art. 6573a	Occupations Code
§8(o)	§1101.613
§8(p)	§1101.610
§8(q)	§1101.615
§9(a)	§1101.363;.503;.554
§9(b)	§1101.501
§9(c)	§1101.451;.504
§9(d)	§1101.451;.454;.504
§9(e)	§1101.452
§9A(a)	§1101.501
§9A(b)	§1101.151(a)(3)
§9A(c)	§1101.653
§9A(d)	§1101.151
§10(a)	§1101.364;.505
§10(b)	§1101.364;.505
§10(c)	§1101.365
§11	§1101.152;.154;.603
§11A(a)	§1101.153
§11A(b)	§1101.153
§12(a)	§1101.552
§12(b)	§1101.552
§12(c)	§1101.553
§12(d)	§1101.553
§12(e)	§1101.506;.507
§13	§1101.367
§13A	§1101.366
§14(a)	§1101.651
§14(b)	§1101.357;.360;.552
§14(c)	§1101.360;.361
§15(a)	§1101.0055;.204;.652
§15(a)(1)	§1101.652(a)(1)
§15(a)(2)	§1101.652(a)(2)
§15(a)(3)	§1101.652(a)(3)
§15(a)(4)	§1101.652(a)(4)
§15(a)(5)	§1101.652(a)(9)

VTCS, Art. 6573a	Occupations Code
§15(a)(6)(A)	§1101.652(b)(3); .652(b)(4)
§15(a)(6)(B)	§1101.652(b)(5)
§15(a)(6)(C)	§1101.652(b)(6)
§15(a)(6)(D)	§1101.652(b)(7); (8)
§15(a)(6)(E)	§1101.652(b)(9); (10)
§15(a)(6)(F)	§1101.652(b)(11)
§15(a)(6)(G)	§1101.652(b)(12)
§15(a)(6)(H)	§1101.652(b)(13)
§15(a)(6)(I)	§1101.652(b)(14); (15)
§15(a)(6)(J)	§1101.652(b)(16)
§15(a)(6)(K)	§1101.652(b)(17)
§15(a)(6)(L)	§1101.652(b)(18)
§15(a)(6)(M)	§1101.652(b)(21)
§15(a)(6)(N)	§1101.652(b)(22)
§15(a)(6)(O)	§1101.652(b)(19)
§15(a)(6)(P)	§1101.652(b)(23)
§15(a)(6)(Q)	§1101.652(b)(24)
§15(a)(6)(R)	§1101.652(b)(25)
§15(a)(6)(S)	§1101.652(b)(26); (27)
§15(a)(6)(T)	§1101.652(b)(28)
§15(a)(6)(U)	§1101.652(b)(29)
§15(a)(6)(V)	§1101.652(b)(2)
§15(a)(6)(W)	§1101.652(b)(1)
§15(a)(6)(X)	§1101.652(b)(9); (33)
§15(a)(6)(Y)	§1101.652(b)(30)
§15(a)(6)(Z)	§1101.652(b)(31)
§15(a)(6)(AA)	§1101.652(b)(32)
§15(a)(7)	§1101.652(a)(5)
§15(a)(8)	§1101.652(a)(6)
§15(a)(9)	§1101.652(a)(7)
§15(b)	§1101.801
§15(c)	§1101.802
§15(d)	§1101.204

VTCS, Art. 6573a	Occupations Code	VTCS, Art. 6573a	Occupations Code
§15(e)	§1101.157	§18	§1101.658
§15B(a)	§1101.204	§18A	§1101.155
§15B(b)	§1101.656	§18B(a)	§1101.202
§15B(c)	§1101.656	§18B(b)	§1101.203
§15B(d)	§1101.656	§18B(c)	§1101.203
§15B(e)	§1101.204	§19(a)	§1101.758
§15C(a)	§1101.558	§19(b)	§1101.754
§15C(b)	§1101.558	§19(c)	§1101.752
§15C(c)	§1101.557	§19(d)	§1101.752; .753
§15C(d)	§1101.558	§19A(a)	§1101.701
§15C(e)	§1101.558	§19A(b)	§1101.702
§15C(f)	§1101.558	§19A(c)	§1101.702
§15C(g)	§1101.558	§19A(d)	§1101.703
§15C(h)	§1101.559	§19A(e)	§1101.703
§15C(i)	§1101.559	§19A(f)	§1101.704
§15C(j)	§1101.651	§19A(g)	§1101.704
§15C(k)	§1101.560; .651	§19A(h)	§1101.705
§15C(l)	§1101.561	§19A(i)	§1101.706
§15C(m)(1)	§1101.558	§19A(j)	§1101.707
§15C(m)(2)	§1101.551; .559	§19A(k)	§1101.707
§15C(m)(3)	§1101.002(4)	§19A(l)	§1101.707; .708
§15C(m)(4)	§1101.551	§19A(m)	§1101.707
§15C(m)(5)	§1101.002(8)	§19A(n)	§1101.709
§15D	§1101.804	§19A(o)	§1101.603
§15E	§1101.556	§20(a)	§1101.806
§15F	§1101.805	§20(b)	§1101.806
§16(a)	§1101.654	§20(c)	§1101.555; .806
§16(b)	§1101.654	§20(d)	§1101.806
§16(c)	§1101.254	§24(a)	§1101.002(6)
§16(d)	§1101.252	§24(b)	§1101.351
§16(e)	§1101.155; .652(8)	§24(d)	§1101.553
§17(a)	§1101.657	§24(f)	§1101.757
§17(b)	§1101.157	Art. 6573a.1	§1101.756

INDEX

A bold page number indicates that the term is defined on that page. An f following the page number indicates a form. Definitions for key terms are indicated by Def. Cases are in a separate Table of Cases.